'I CAME TO THE CONFIDENCE WORKSHOP,' ALLY BEGAN SLOWLY, NOTICING THAT SUSIE WAS WATCHING HER AS CLOSELY AS THE OTHERS, 'BECAUSE FOR EIGHTEEN YEARS I'VE BEEN A HAPPY HOUSEWIFE...

'I've loved making a home and being there for my family. I've got a charming husband and two lovely daughters. In lots of ways I'm very lucky. But lately I've realized something else. That my husband is selfish as well as charming and quite a lot of the time he forgets I exist, and my two lovely daughters don't really need me any more.' She paused, thinking it through as she said it, almost forgetting where she was. 'And I've just decided that I'm going to do something about it.' She gazed round, astounded that today had actually made a difference. She was feeling more confident by the moment. 'I've decided I'm going to get a job.'

'Good for you!' Barbara's voice rang with warmth and encouragement. 'I'm so glad you came today.'

And looking at her friendly face Ally knew that she meant it. Then she realized everyone was clapping, because they knew, as she did, that she'd just taken the first step towards changing her life for the better.

MAEVE HARAN

SCENES FROM THE SEX WAR

A SIGNET BOOK

SIGNET

Published by the Penguin Group
27 Wrights Lane, London W8 5TZ
Viking Penguin Inc., 375 Hudson Street, New York, New York 10014, USA
Penguin Books Australia Ltd, Ringwood, Victoria, Australia
Penguin Books Canada Ltd, 10 Alcorn Avenue, Toronto, Ontario, Canada M4V 3B2
Penguin Books (NZ) Ltd, 182–190 Wairau Road, Auckland 10, New Zealand

Penguin Books Ltd, Registered Offices: Harmondsworth, Middlesex, England

First published by Michael Joseph 1993
Published in Signet 1994
1 3 5 7 9 10 8 6 4 2

The quotation on page 120 from 'The Love Song of J. Alfred Prufrock',
Collected Poems 1909–1962 by T. S. Eliot, is reproduced by kind permission of
Faber and Faber Ltd

Printed in England by Clays Ltd, St Ives plc

For my mother, who would
have loved all the fun

Chapter 1

Lying back on their big double bed, Allegra Boyd watched her husband Matt remove his socks with one hand, the other still firmly holding on to the sports' section, and drop them to the carpet where they would remain as if rendered magically invisible by some male chauvinist genie until she or Mrs O'Shock, their Irish cleaning lady, picked them up.

Still engrossed in the description of Spurs' magical defence tactics, he took off his boxer shorts and reached for the cotton pyjama top next to him on the bed. He insisted on buying these in an identical design but a dozen different colours, then proceeded to wear only the top half so that his balls peeped out engagingly, provoking howls of derision from his two teenage daughters and a knowing look from Mrs O'Shock as she worked her way through the ironing.

Watching him climb into bed, Ally felt a wave of tenderness and wondered what his female viewers would make of the sight of Britain's top chat-show host minus his pyjama bottoms. Love it, no doubt. His secretary had once told her that Matt's postbag would have brought a blush to the face of Linda Lovelace. Ally shook her head as she picked up the offending clothes, knowing she should have told him to do it himself. Thank God her best friend Susie wasn't here to witness the scene. Susie was always accusing her of being a doormat.

As she chucked them into the dirty clothes' basket Matt looked up from his paper and smiled. 'Coming to bed soon?' he enquired, patting her side of the bed lasciviously.

Ally grinned. Turning forty suited him, only adding to

the roguish charm that made him come over so well on television. That and the disreputable twinkle in his blue eyes. Matt Boyd was definitely not a New Man. He was, in fact, as unreconstructed as they come. And the audience loved it. The audience, of course, didn't have to live with him.

'Just coming.' She leaned down and kissed him before slipping next door to take off her clothes.

Once in the bathroom Ally pulled her bra down to her waist, swiftly yanked it round so that the hooks were in the front and undid it. This was the method her mother had taught her at thirteen, and for some reason she was still doing it at thirty-eight. Normally she didn't notice this minor peculiarity but tonight, because she was standing in front of the bathroom mirror, she did.

Why had her mother not taught her to undo it from behind, seductively, like a pouting Marilyn Monroe? Not that it mattered, since for months now she'd been undressing in here. Looking in the mirror she wondered why. Her body was still firm, except for the small bulges at the base of the hips and a slight thickening of the waist. Her shoulder-length hair was as glossy and brown as it had ever been with only a little help from L'Oreal. In teenage days she'd ironed it to get it straight, but now she was glad it fell in gentle waves, hiding the crows' feet that were sneaking round her eyes. Matt always said her eyes were her best feature, a clear greeny-blue. And she didn't begrudge those lines. They came from laughter, not disappointment. And her pale skin, she noticed, was dotted with freckles by the early sunshine they'd been having this year. All the same, she felt embarrassed at exposing herself. Maybe it was the thought of all those glamorous young women who flocked to TV as though it were the auditions for Miss World. But there was something else. A slight distance had grown up between her and Matt lately, and Matt had been moody and irritable for reasons she didn't really understand.

But not tonight. Maybe tonight they could get back some of the old tenderness. Remembering Matt's inviting look, she quickly brushed her teeth and ran a comb through her hair. She sprayed a little perfume behind her ears and swiftly breathed into her hand. Minty fresh. Smiling to herself, she strode back into the bedroom.

She'd probably been out of the room no more than a minute or two. In bed Matt still clutched his paper firmly. But as she bent down to kiss him she saw that his eyes were closed and that he was fast asleep.

Gently she took the paper out of his hands and brushed her lips against his, feeling the reassuring scratch of his moustache against her chin, the moustache Matt refused to shave off because he liked its swashbuckling air despite the taunts of Medallion Man from the make-up ladies.

As she reached for her nightdress she felt, to her slight shame, not the ache of unfulfilled desire but a disconcerting sense of relief. Now she could read her book.

Three times a week for more than ten years, Matt Boyd had proved he was the chat-show king. Younger, hipper rivals had come and gone, but Matt had stayed the course. Viewers liked the way he actually listened to his guests, yet cut the pompous down to size with his withering one-liners. He always seemed to know exactly what people at home wanted to know and dared to ask it. And somehow he got away with it. Most important of all, the stars felt safe in his hands. And their agents liked the size of his audience figures.

A lot of people thought they knew Matt very well. Ally, his wife, Stephen Cartwright, his programme controller, and Bernie Long, the show's executive producer. But there was one thing about him they didn't know.

Matt Boyd was getting bored.

Matt glanced round the studio while the sound man miked him up. He loathed the new set. All lilac and fuchsia with a giant neon sign announcing *The Matt Boyd Show*. This, Matt shuddered, must be what gay night looked like at Heaven disco.

As he joked with a trainee on camera four, Matt scanned the running order for tonight's show. The usual format. First the nonentity, Andy Green, a streaked-haired 'actor' in a second-rate soap opera given to posing bare-chested with a cucumber down his trousers. The chance of him saying anything even faintly interesting was remote. Next the middle-ranking celeb, Linzi Watson, a rock journalist with a sharp tongue and a penchant for toy-boys, marginally more lively than Green. If she was sober.

Finally The Star, or what passed for a star in an age where every celebrity in town did the round of breakfast television, daytime television and evening chat-shows until the audience knew more about them than their own mother. And cared less. Tonight it was Jon Leighton, the latest of the Hollywood movie brats. Only twenty-two and he could command three million dollars a film despite his reputation for moodiness and for taking himself very seriously indeed.

The sound man was ready for some level. Matt smiled wolfishly.

'Producer, producer, through the wall.' He waved his script and spoke clearly and distinctly into the microphone for the benefit of everyone hidden from sight in the control room, 'Who is the dullest guest of all?'

In the control room the PA giggled nervously and looked behind her to the glass-fronted gallery where stars were occasionally kept before they appeared on the show. Andy Green was there, but fortunately he'd missed the remark, absorbed in admiring a picture of himself in *Coffee Break*.

4

'What the fuck's the matter with Matt?' snapped Bernie Long, the executive producer.

'Search me,' shrugged the PA, trying not to laugh. She liked Matt. He treated her like a human being. Bernie Long, on the other hand, saw the PA as a cross between a double bed and an automatic coffee-making machine.

Belinda Wyeth, the producer of the day, pushed back her long dark hair angrily. 'Well, he'd better pull himself together. We're on air in two minutes.'

Belinda closed her eyes and swore under her breath. She was new to the show and determined to prove she was better than the two male producers who took it in turns to produce a show a week. But frankly she was getting fed up with Matt bloody Boyd.

For weeks now he'd been getting increasingly difficult. Short-tempered, rude about the guests. On occasions rude *to* the guests. If it was up to Belinda she'd dump him and find someone else.

'One minute to on air,' reminded the PA and began her countdown. 'And cue grams.' The familiar *Matt Boyd Show* theme tune started up.

For the next fifteen minutes Belinda watched with mounting irritation as Matt coasted through the first two interviews. When Andy Green, the soap star, unburdened himself on the trials and tribulations of being mega-famous, Matt barely suppressed a yawn.

'Jesus Christ!' Belinda rolled her eyes and turned to Bernie. 'Why on earth do you keep him on?'

The PA glared at her sourly. At that moment the floor manager led Jon Leighton through the control room and out towards the floor, introducing him to Belinda and Bernie on the way. Leighton barely looked in their direction. At the door he stopped and leaned on the wall.

5

'Oh, my God,' whispered Belinda, unable to believe her bad luck. 'He's pissed.'

Hearing the music from Jon Leighton's latest film, Matt stood up. 'And now please welcome my final guest.' He looked round expectantly, just in time to see Leighton stumble across the floor and collapse elegantly on the sofa.

Belinda's stomach lurched and her palms began to sweat. It had been she who'd insisted on having Jon Leighton and Matt who'd argued against him, saying he was dull and self-important. God, why hadn't she checked on him when he'd arrived? Then she could at least have found a substitute or given Matt some warning. Belinda hid her face in her hands in horror. They had twelve more minutes of prime-time television still to get through. Trying to keep her head she ran through the options. They could fade to black and put up a slide. Presentation would have some cartoons standing by. But that would be a humiliating defeat. She willed herself to watch the screen in front of her.

Without missing a beat Matt had taken in what was happening. 'Oh, dear.' He turned to the audience, smiling broadly and clearly enjoying every minute. 'Does anyone have any Alka Seltzer?'

The storm of applause and laughter seemed to last for ever. Very tentatively, Belinda opened her fingers and looked through.

It would be all right. Matt wasn't thrown. He was going to play it for laughs. Slowly, hoping no one had noticed, she sat up straight and began to relax.

'You asked why we keep Matt on.' Belinda could feel Bernie Long's sardonic gaze boring deep into her back. 'Well, now you know. Because Matt Boyd's the best there is.'

By the time the closing credits rolled the entire crew

gave Matt a standing ovation as Leighton's embarrassed PR man helped him out of the studio. Belinda guessed he wouldn't be coming up to hospitality.

Normally she would have followed the others on to the floor to congratulate Matt too, but instead she stayed for a moment in the dark of the empty control room pretending to gather up her things.

The door swung open and Matt stood there. 'Seen Bernie?'

Belinda glanced up, embarrassed at how much she'd underestimated him. 'I think he went in to congratulate you.'

Matt smiled and opened the door again.

'Matt . . .' Belinda's voice trailed off uncertainly.

He turned round, surprised by her sudden lack of confidence. Belinda terrified everyone on the programme with her razor sharp mind and her short skirts, which confusingly seemed to indicate not so much sexual availability as a reminder of what was strictly off-limits. 'A post-feminist' Bernie had once called her, meaning to insult her. But Belinda had laughed.

'I just wanted to apologize.' She looked away, shuffling her script. 'About Jon Leighton, I mean. I should have found out and warned you.'

'I enjoyed it.' Matt grinned disarmingly and she realized that he meant it. 'He was more interesting than when he's sober.'

Belinda met his eyes, feeling the strength of his powerful charm for the first time.

'Anyway' – there was a hint of embarrassment in Matt's tone too – 'I'm the one who should be apologizing. I've been hell lately.'

'Yes.' She finally smiled back. 'You've been an absolute pain in the arse.'

Matt shrugged, suddenly serious. 'I know.' He hesitated for a moment, as though deciding whether to go on. 'The trouble is I'm bored to death. I've been doing this show for ten years. At least tonight was some kind of challenge.' He stopped, aware that he hadn't admitted any of this to himself, so why was he telling her?

Suddenly he noticed how close she was and the disturbing brashness of her perfume. He stepped back fractionally.

'If that's the way you feel about the show' – the challenge in her dark eyes was almost male in its directness but with a hint of provocation that was anything but masculine – 'Then why don't you do something about it?'

Ally arrived outside Janey and Jess's school fifteen minutes early to be sure of getting a parking space where they'd see her. She hadn't told them she'd be picking them up, but it was such a beautiful day that she'd decided to surprise them with a picnic. She'd spent hours making tiny cucumber sandwiches, and baking Janey's favourite double chocolate cupcakes. She'd laughed at herself as she packed a proper white tablecloth and teacups and saucers. Perfect picnics were one of Ally's passions. She was always a sucker for those features in magazines where they showed you how to knock up salmon mousse for four by the side of a waterfall. Even the certain knowledge that the food had been coated with varnish to make it more photogenic didn't puncture her fantasy.

She pressed the button to roll back the roof and imagined their faces when they came out. They hadn't had a real picnic for years. As the first few schoolgirls filtered out of Hill Hall School in their brown and white check summer dresses, Ally suddenly felt self-conscious. What if they didn't want to go?

It was a great pity she couldn't resign herself to being a Lady Who Lunched like the other celebrity wives. But it looked like hell to Ally, getting dressed up to the nines and going to wonderful restaurants to eat three lettuce leaves and drink nothing but Perrier because you had to stay slim and beautiful for your husband. Last time she'd been she'd yearned for a T-shirt saying 'MINERAL WATER KILLS'.

Ally knew the way she was feeling at the moment was probably her own fault. She'd never really learned to let go of Janey and Jess. The trouble about being a mother was that there were plenty of handbooks telling you how to care for small children, but none about how to let go of big ones. You knew they had to take risks, break away, forget about you. But no one told you how painful it was when they did, what a gap it left in your life. The admen had a name for women like her: empty nesters. For a moment she envied Matt his all-absorbing career. She could hardly remember her own now. Funny to think that she'd been a TV presenter too, in her own small way, reading the news for MidWest TV. And she'd been good at it.

But the babies had arrived and she'd given up the job. When Jess was two she'd been offered it back. She'd been tempted, too, but then along came Matt's big chance and they'd moved south and after that he'd been too famous and successful for working to be worth her while. And she hadn't regretted it. She'd loved bringing up her children and being there for them, the solid rock at the centre of her family.

But today, for the first time, Ally felt a little rush of fear. Matt had been strange and distant lately apart from that one night he'd wanted to make love. In some deep unfaced part of herself she knew he was drifting away from her. And soon the children would be gone.

9

'Hey, Mum!' Jess's shout cut across her thoughts and she looked up smiling. 'What are you doing here?'

'I made a picnic.' Ally pointed to the basket next to her on the seat. 'I thought perhaps we could go and find somewhere nice to have it.'

'But I told you this morning.' Jess shrugged off her backpack and put it in the back of the car, the faintest tone of impatience in her voice. 'I'm going round to Alice's to listen to her new Take That tape.' A flash of guilt spread across Jess's face like a cloud crossing the sun. 'Shall I tell her I can't come?'

'No, of course not.' Ally fiddled with the wing mirror to mask her disappointment. 'Where's Janey?'

'It's Wednesday. Drama night. She won't be out till six.'

Ally laughed and stretched out her hand to her daughter. 'I'd forgotten. How dumb of me.'

'You know your trouble, Mum.' Jess leaned down from the great wisdom of her fifteen years. 'You don't have enough to do.' Not noticing the pain in Ally's eyes she waved frantically at her friend Alice. 'Why don't you get a job like all the other mothers?'

Chapter 2

Ally looked at the alarm clock in surprise. Janey and Jess were due at school in less than an hour and it was Matt's turn to drop them off. She jumped out of bed and stumbled through the pitch darkness to pull the curtains. They'd just had the bedroom done up by an interior designer who'd made curtains so thick and impenetrable that no trickle of light could sneak in and they kept oversleeping. On top of that Matt complained that there was so much chintz everywhere he felt like he was sleeping in a flower-bed.

Ally knocked on Janey's door, noticing with annoyance that she'd left her jeans drying on the banisters for the tenth time.

'Janey!' she shouted at the sleeping figure still completely under the duvet. 'It's eight o'clock. And how many times have I told you not to leave your jeans on the banisters?'

A sleepy head emerged from the covers, bright blue eyes gazing out at her from under a brown mane, so like Matt that it always took Ally by surprise.

'Where am I supposed to dry them then,' Janey asked, pulling off her Stop Chopping the Rainforest nightshirt, 'now that your poncy decorator's covered up the radiators with trellis?'

'Why not try the tumble dryer?' Ally suggested, knowing there was bound to be a flaw in her parental logic.

'Mum,' Janey replied slowly and patiently as if talking to a Romanian tourist, 'everyone knows you can't put 501s in the tumble dryer. They're preshrunk.'

Ally abandoned the unequal fight of arguing with a seventeen-year-old, especially your own.

11

Sun streamed into the large kitchen, one of the few rooms untarted-up by the decorator. There was actually a cushion that didn't match the curtains, God forbid. Ally gazed around, appreciating its amiable shabbiness and decided to ban all further colour swatches and paint charts from the house. The room felt like home.

Before they'd lived here Fairlawns, with its Victorian turrets, its gables and its warren of rooms, had once been a club. The genteel private sort where aged gents popped in for a snifter and a game of billiards while pretending to take the peke for a constitutional. When they'd moved in Matt had insisted they keep the billiard table in the hall and very occasionally an old boy in a Panama hat with a billiard cue under his arm still wandered in and asked for a G. and T.

Ally switched on the kettle and shouted upstairs again to Matt and the girls. She got out cereal bowls and laid the table. Opening the dishwasher she found it full of dirty crockery. No one had bothered to turn it on last night. Typical.

Ally felt irritation swell up in her and reached out to put on a soothing dose of Radio Four. Instead ear-splitting rock music shredded her eardrums and made her spill her coffee down her dressing gown.

She took a deep breath. Family life.

'Hello, Mum.' Ally swung round to find her younger daughter, Jess, dressed and ready, smiling at her from behind the money section of the *Daily Mail*. 'I didn't know you were a heavy metal fan.' Jess was a devoted student of the financial pages. Since the age of nine she'd worked out that with each Young Saver account you opened they gave you a present. Within a year she'd opened nine and acquired a free Snoopy pencil case, two ceramic piggy banks, an Action Savers T-shirt and a lifetime subscription to *Junior Computer World*. If Ally ever got short of cash she knew who to turn to, and from time to time Matt threatened to fire his accountant and take on Jess instead.

'Do you want toast?' Ally asked her, one eye on the clock.

'Aren't there any croissants?'

'No, there are not,' Ally said firmly. How on earth had they given birth to a child that expected croissants on a weekday? Matt's mother would be appalled. The Boyds prided themselves on their working-class roots. 'They're for treats.'

'Pity,' said Matt appearing, miraculously fully dressed. 'I wouldn't mind one myself.'

Ally patted the slight thickening of his waist. 'Definitely not for you. The camera adds ten pounds, remember.'

'Thank you, darling.' He grabbed her from behind, his hands diving inside her dressing gown, heading straight for the midriff bulge. 'Just as well you're not on TV then.'

Ally pushed his hands away laughing.

'Why can't you two behave like adults?' inquired Jess, without looking up from the Moneywatch analysis of the year's best unit trusts.

'Absolutely,' echoed Janey who had just come in, looking seventeen going on twenty-five, despite the fact that she was wearing school uniform. Janey had the capacity for subtle alteration – a hemline raised an inch, cuffs rolled to elbow length, collars standing up – which made even Hill Hall's dowdy uniform look like something off the catwalk. If Matt was right and the get-up was designed to protect their morals it had failed dismally in Janey's case.

Janey's sense of chic was not, Ally reflected gazing down at her now coffee-stained dressing gown, a quality she'd inherited from her mother.

Ally smiled, remembering how even at three Janey had had style. Left alone in front of the television to watch *Blue Peter* on how to make pixie hats from crêpe paper, Janey had taken a shortcut and snipped the corners off their best Heal's cushions instead. And when Ally lost her temper Janey had explained coolly that *her* hats looked so much better than the ones on the telly.

'Come on, eat up your breakfast like a good girl,' teased Matt, grabbing the *Daily Mail* from Jess before she had time to protest and turning to the TV preview page. To his irritation a large picture of Danny Wilde, Big City TV's young talk-show host, smiled cheekily back at him. *The Matt Boyd Show* rated a mere three lines.

Matt closed the paper. It was ridiculous to mind. The press liked a new face. Danny Wilde wasn't a serious rival. He appealed only to the young and trendy. Matt's audience was five times as big.

Jess, her toast finished, her school bag ready at her side, flicked the remote control and the television on the worktop buzzed into life. Matt looked up as the face of the Prime Minister filled the screen. Disgusted, Jess flicked again and Danny Wilde appeared, trailing his show that night.

'Hey, great! He's got King Rap on.' Jess began to jiggle to the insistent beat as Matt tried to grab the remote control. Jess held it tantalizingly out of his reach. 'Dad,' she asked innocently, 'why don't you have interesting people like King Rap on your show?'

Matt paused for a moment, searching for an answer. Finally he leaned over and grabbed the remote control, giving him the satisfaction of zapping Danny Wilde into the ether. He realized as he did so that he had no idea who King Rap was.

'Come on, you lot. Move it.' Ally thought for a moment

about whether to ask Matt what time he'd be home. She liked to cook something so they could sit and talk about the day. Yet every time she asked she felt like a nagging wife. She said it anyway.

'What time will you be back tonight, love?'

Matt considered briefly. 'There's drinks after the show and I may need to talk to Bernie about next week. I'm not really sure.'

Matt heard the evasiveness in his own voice and felt a flash of guilt. 'What time will you be back?' was one of the eternal unresolved questions between men and women, conferring power on the person being asked and taking it from the asker. Maybe it was a sense of this that made him sometimes feel like the occupant of a parking space being asked if he is about to leave. Resentful for no good reason.

'Tell you what.' He acknowledged the bloody-mindedness of wanting to stay in the parking space. 'Why don't you come to hospitality and have a drink after the show?'

Ally felt a wave of panic at the thought of the clever, smart young people who worked on Matt's programme. She'd been to these occasions before and always ended up feeling like somebody's mother. Fifteen years ago she might have been able to hold her own, but years of school runs and PTA meetings had softened her brain. What on earth would she talk to them about? Her answer came a fraction too quickly.

'I can't. It's Jess's piano lesson.'

'Oh, Mum.' Jess shook her head despairingly. 'Don't be daft. I'll get the bus. You go and have fun with the glamorous TV types.'

With a flash of insight Ally realized Jess didn't *want* to be picked up. The truth was even Jess didn't need her any more.

Ally paused for a moment, torn. She shouldn't be so

pathetic about meeting TV people. Then the thought of seeing Bernie Long, Matt's producer right back to the days when they'd both worked at MidWest TV, made up her mind for her. Bernie Long was crass, unpleasant and patronizing. Once she'd overheard the nickname he'd given her: semi-detached suburban Mrs Boyd.

'Maybe next week,' she heard herself saying, trying to avoid Jess's eye.

As they piled into Matt's car and Ally stood in the garden waving them goodbye, she realized what a picture of boring wifedom she must present with no make-up, still in her slippers. Her mother had always said it was feckless to be in your dressing gown after eight thirty.

Ally glanced down at her watch. Eight forty-five.

Matt rolled down his window and blew her a kiss. 'Come. You'll enjoy it.'

She watched the car disappear down the drive. It was a beautiful morning. Already the sky was a bright, optimistic blue, with only a few fluffy clouds high up. It never ceased to amaze her that their Surrey village was only twenty-five miles from London and yet as green and quiet as the country. But unlike the real country all their neighbours were rich and invisible behind high hedges. It wasn't the sort of area where you leaned over the garden wall for a cup of sugar. People round here had Filipinos to make sure they didn't run out.

Suddenly Ally pulled her dressing gown tighter around her. To hell with her mother and with snobby TV people, too. She turned round and walked towards the house, feeling the sun warming her back, and came to a decision. Matt had made a gesture and she'd been ridiculous to refuse it. She would go to Century tonight and give him a surprise.

'Here'll be fine, Dad.' Matt grinned at Janey's anxiety to

be dropped well out of sight of the school gates. Janey loathed it when people mentioned who her father was. The one time he'd been asked to do a school prize-giving she'd pretended to have flu.

Matt turned to kiss her as she opened the door, eager to get out before anyone saw them. Looking at her tall, almost womanly body as she eased herself out of the car Matt felt a shock. She wasn't his little girl any more. Yet it hardly seemed a moment since he'd nervously smoked a cigarette outside the maternity ward, vowing to kick the habit for ever if everything was all right. And it had been all right. He could still picture the exact moment when the midwife had put Janey, bawling and bonny, into his outstretched arms. He'd felt a powerful desire to dance a jig, but had been too scared of dropping the fragile body swaddled so tight that only a scrap of her tiny face was visible.

And, to Ally's great amusement, as soon as she was old enough Matt had proceeded to treat Janey as a mate, a tomboy, sharing with her his passions for chess and football. It was still a joke in the Boyd household that from the age of ten Janey could name every player who'd made it to the Cup Final since 1951.

The truth was that Matt adored women. He thought them wonderful and mysterious. He could still remember hanging round the school playground listening to the girls singing 'In and Out the Dusty Bluebells' and skipping their intricate steps as the boys played British Bulldog and beat each other up.

And he'd made damn sure that his girls felt just as good as any boys. The motto he'd brought them up on was, 'Girls can do *anything*!'

He pressed the button to roll down the window and leaned out.

'Bye, gorgeous,' he shouted, to Janey's excruciating embarrassment. 'And remember. Girls can do –'

'Anything!' muttered Janey, already walking off. Why was Dad always saying it? Of course girls could do anything. Who would ever have thought anything different?

Matt turned to Jess, sitting beside him. 'Aren't you getting out here, too?'

Jess shook her head. Unlike Janey she rather enjoyed her father's celebrity status.

'It's OK, Dad. You can drop *me* at the front gate.'

Outside the gates of Hill Hall School, Volvo estates and Range Rovers were three deep. Most of the parents dropping off their children were used to moving in circles of power and influence and knew far better than to stand and stare. But all the same a number of heads turned subtly in their direction to watch Matt Boyd open the door for his younger daughter. And one or two mothers, who wouldn't have ever admitted it, felt a stab of envy as he folded Jess in his arms in an extravagant bearhug of affection.

Jock Wilson, one of the security guards on duty, caught sight of Matt's car approaching the ramp into Century Television's underground car park and pressed the button to raise the barrier. He waved as the car drew into its usual bay. Unlike some of the other stars he could name, Matt was as friendly off camera as he was on. And Jock was amazed by his capacity to remember your name and whether your wife's lumbago was any better this week. Some people said it was just a technique he'd developed for the show, but Jock chose not to believe them.

'Morning, Jock. Beautiful day.'

'God's own.' The man smiled, feeling fortunate that he could at least see a sliver of it from his box. 'Pity you'll be shut away in the studio.'

'Not yet. A two-hour meeting first on the sixteenth floor.'

Matt smiled back at the man and headed for the lift, stopping for a moment to charm Bryony, otherwise known as the Rottweiler, the terrifying receptionist who sat behind a vast grey desk littered with telephones and guarded the entrance to the inner sanctum of Century Television. Matt sometimes wondered if Bryony had indeed been employed simply to keep everyone out of the building rather than the more predictable course of letting some of them in. At least she was democratic. When the King of Norway had arrived, after much delicate negotiation by the news department, to appear on the lunchtime bulletin, legend had it Bryony had leaned forward and shouted, ''Ere, you! Where did you say you were king of?'

Matt arrived in the board room high above Millbank a few minutes before the weekly ideas meeting was due to start. He helped himself to a cup of coffee and stood staring down at the sun on the river hundreds of feet below. Century Television had the best position in London, on a bend in the Thames with stunning views of Lambeth Bridge and the Houses of Parliament. In five minutes you could walk to the Tate Gallery. Matt sometimes sloped off at lunchtime and lost himself in the Turners.

But today he didn't even notice the beauty spread out below him shimmering in an early summer heatwave. He was too preoccupied with wondering what the hell he should do. This boredom and restlessness of his was building to dangerous proportions.

He didn't need Bernie Long to tell him – though he knew Bernie would relish doing so – that if he wasn't careful he might wreck his own career. Already he knew his irritation was beginning to show on camera, and that was unforgivable.

'Hello, Matt old son.' Matt swung round at the familiar

19

growly East End tones. 'I'm glad I've caught you on your tod.'

'It's all right, Bernie, you don't have to say it.'

'Say what?' asked Bernie calmly, taking off his battered leather jacket and draping it round a chair. Underneath he wore a sweatshirt and tracksuit – deeply misleading, since Bernie liked to claim he was one of the least fit people in London. The only exercise he ever took was the raising of the wrist. And, as both of them knew, he did that rather too often.

'That you're pissed off with me.'

The corner of Bernie's mouth lifted a millimetre. 'Not as pissed off as when we got Tom Jones on MidWest and you kept calling him Engelbert Humperdinck.'

'That was fifteen years ago,' objected Matt. 'Anyway it was April Fools' Day.' He grinned at the memory. He'd almost been fired over that, until Bernie persuaded the directors it had all been a joke.

'We've come a long way since then.' Bernie put his hand on Matt's shoulder. It was true, they had. Further than either of them could have dreamed. A year later they'd put together a chat-show format with Matt as front man and Bernie as producer, and Century Television, eager for something new, had taken a punt on it. To everyone's astonishment it had gone to the top of the ratings, making Matt Boyd one of the most famous names in television. And fourteen years on he was still there.

Matt looked Bernie in the eye. 'And now you think I'm ballsing it up.'

Bernie glanced at the river for a moment. 'You're not respecting the audience, Matt. Don't think they won't notice.' He looked back at Matt, his pitted criss-crossed skin reminding Matt of a war-battered old rhinoceros. Matt had rarely seen him so serious. 'You're breaking the rules, mate. It's a contract. They enjoy it because you enjoy it. You're selling them short.'

Behind them a door opened and Bernie's secretary, Marie, appeared brandishing her shorthand book to take notes for the meeting. The rest of the team trickled in. The keen ones, usually new and eager to prove themselves, came in first, clutching enough newspaper clippings to start a cuttings service. Last, wearing dark glasses as though she'd had a hard night, and holding a large glass of mineral water, was Belinda.

Despite the weather she was wearing what looked like a man's suit but underneath was a white silk camisole, one of its shoestring straps clearly visible, the kind of garment made more for the bedroom than the board room. Matt decided she must take pleasure in confusing signals.

Bernie called the meeting to order. He hoped to Christ Matt wasn't going to be difficult. Matt was the only presenter he knew who bothered to come to the ideas meetings in the first place. Most star names insisted they wanted more control over the material but weren't prepared to leave their mock-Tudor mansions to put in the effort. They soon learned it was easier to take the glory and let other people do the real work. But Matt had always been different.

Bernie banged his coffee cup on his saucer for silence.

'Right, you lot, let's get down to it. Who's got any brilliant inspirations for the next few shows?'

Matt waited, knowing he could guess with almost a hundred per cent accuracy the dull and predictable names that would come up, each of them only prepared to appear on the show if they had a book, film or show to plug or were so past it that they were of no interest anyway.

He gazed out of the window trying to make up his mind. He and Bernie had been together for so long, he didn't want to shaft him. Then, without glancing in her direction, he knew that Belinda's eyes were on him and that she was remembering their conversation of the other night. He looked round. Slowly she smiled as though she were reading his thoughts.

Matt decided it was time he acted. 'Bernie, before we get down to specifics,' Matt kept his voice casual. He didn't want to get Bernie's back up at this stage. 'Could we talk a bit about the show in general?'

Bernie raised his eyes from the ruled pad he always used for meetings and put down his favourite propelling pencil. He'd been expecting something like this. 'Certainly, Matt. Feel free.'

'The problem with the show,' Matt continued, 'is that it's becoming the bland leading the bland. Leighton coming on drunk the other night was the most exciting thing that's happened in months.' Matt met his old friend's gaze. 'We need to take more risks, do some dangerous interviews, go nearer the edge. If we don't the audience will fall asleep.' He smiled his famous provocative smile. 'Or I will.'

'So who agrees with Matt?' Bernie asked.

The members of the team glanced at each other nervously, sensing the dangers of jumping without thinking through the consequences.

Belinda thought about it for a second. She knew Bernie would never forgive her if she spoke out. The kind of democratic discussions Bernie favoured were over whether the coffee should be fresh or instant. And even then he got his way in the end.

But before she could speak someone else got in first. 'I'm with Matt.' It was Helen, the PA.

Matt smiled, knowing what it would have cost her to speak out. She was a shy girl and one who could easily be replaced. It must have taken a lot of courage.

22

Belinda waited, annoyed at being upstaged. Finally she spoke. 'So am I. It's time we shook the show up.'

Almost imperceptibly, Matt winked. To her surprise Belinda felt herself basking in his approval.

Matt turned to his old friend. 'Come on, Bernie, what do you think?'

'What I think' – Bernie's small eyes twinkled dangerously – 'is that we've got a bloody successful show and we should stick with it. Now, let's get back to the ideas meeting, shall we?'

Matt stood up and for a moment Bernie thought he was going to walk out. Instead he walked slowly over to the table at the side of the room and poured himself a cup of coffee. Picking up a plate of biscuits he offered them round the room. 'Anyone for a ginger nut?'

There was a stifled giggle from the other end of the table and everyone smiled with relief, the tension defused. Except Bernie. He knew Matt well enough to know that this wasn't the end, only the beginning. And as he watched Matt catch Belinda's eye and hold it for a moment he wondered if they were in it together.

Ally stood under the powerful stream of freezing water and threw back her head. The water was so cold that at first it had taken her breath away but now she abandoned herself to its masochistic charms. This was the first house they'd lived in where the shower had any power. Matt, always a bath man, had been converted to showers overnight on an American trip. Now he showered twice a day, sometimes, if she wasn't in too-efficient and housewifely a mood, pulling Ally in with him.

Stepping out from under it, Ally reached for a huge fluffy towel and wrapped herself in it luxuriously. She sometimes thought that if they lost everything tomorrow the bath towels should be the last thing to go. Her mother, out of a puritan sense of utility rather than lack of cash, had believed that bath towels ought to go on for ever. She had washed them until they were thin and stiff – fabric softener not yet being even a twinkle in Lever Brothers' eye – and bound up the fraying edges with ribbon. In those days the bath sheet was seen as a foreign indulgence. British towels came in two sizes: too small or much too small.

Ally wrapped herself in five feet of warm brushed cotton and went into the bedroom. It was strewn with clothes. If she was going to hold her own among the terrifying young trendies on Matt's show she must be confident. And whether she liked it or not confidence depended at least in part on looking good.

The trouble was she'd tried on almost everything in her wardrobe and found that though she had clothes for dressing up to the nines or for slopping round in the house, the stunning but understated number to wow Matt's production team with her sophistication and subtlety was sadly lacking.

Delving in her cupboard, she pulled out a tunic with technicolour swirls which the sales assistant had convinced her was the spit of Versace at a quarter of the price. She slipped it on with its matching leggings and gazed at herself in the mirror. It was certainly noticeable.

Downstairs she heard the front door click. Jess must have come for her piano music. Janey was electing to stay on at school for A-level study most days and wouldn't be home till six. Good. Jess could advise her.

A few minutes later the bedroom door opened and Jess peered round clutching a peanut butter and jam sandwich.

'Hiya, Mum.' She considered her mother's outfit for a moment. 'Going to a fancy dress?'

Ally resisted the desire to wring Jess's neck and shoved

her towards the wardrobe. Jess, almost totally disinterested in her own clothes, had a knack with other people's.

'All right, Ms Fashion Editor, *you* choose.'

Jess put down her sandwich and rifled among the hangers for a few minutes, finally pulling out two outfits.

'What image does Modom wish to create tonight?' she inquired. 'More Madonna or Simone Signoret?'

'Somewhere between the two, perhaps?' Ally asked hopefully.

Jess handed her a dark green suit she'd bought for a cousin's wedding. Ally put it on.

'Drabsville,' pronounced Jess, screwing up her face and reaching for her other choice, a black crêpe-de-Chine shift dress.

Ally looked at it with surprise then remembered she'd never worn it because the hem stopped three inches above the knee.

'Go on. Let's at least see you in it.'

Ally peeled off the green suit and slipped into the shift. As Jess stood behind her to zip it up she realized with surprise that Jess had grown again. Her daughter was a good inch taller than she was already.

The dress done up, Ally glanced at herself in the mirror and was taken aback at how young and smart she looked. 'OK.' She grinned at Jess. 'I'll wear it.'

'Great decision.' Jess folded her mother into a big hug of congratulations making the hem ride up another two inches. Ally began to have second thoughts. The dress would look terrific on Janey or Jess but surely on her it was mutton dressed as lamb? 'No,' she retracted. 'I can't wear it. They'll laugh at me.'

'Oh, Mum!' Ally could hear the exasperation in her daughter's voice. 'You're such a wimp! It looks terrific.'

Ally took the dress off and reached for the suit. She'd supposed that by nearly forty she wouldn't care what people thought. But life didn't seem to work like that. Not for her, anyway.

Jess shrugged and took her sandwich off to start on her homework.

Ally opened her knicker drawer and pulled out an olive green pair of tights but somehow they exaggerated the dowdiness. She took them off and hunted for a sheer pair with bows at the heels. Sitting on the bed she pulled them on carefully, looking at her legs in the mirror. Were they too tarty?

Suddenly she closed her eyes. Jess was right. She was pathetic. Who gave a stuff what tights she wore? In her anger with herself she put her finger through the fragile mesh and tore them. She slumped on the bed, close to tears. Once she'd been bouncy and self-confident. Now the smallest decision seemed to incapacitate her. How the hell was she going to find something to do with the rest of her life if she couldn't even decide which pair of tights to wear?

Ten minutes later Janey almost tripped over her mother in the hall as she got back from school. Ally was getting her coat and couldn't resist deadheading the huge bunch of lilies on the hall table as she passed.

'Hiya, Mum. Where are you off to?'

'To the studios to whisk Dad off for a surprise dinner.'

'You'll be late back then?' The disinterest in Janey's voice didn't fool Ally for a moment. She hugged Janey, reading her mind. 'Too late for you to borrow the car. How do I look?'

Janey put her head on one side. 'Very suitable.'

Ally sighed.

It was still a beautiful day and Ally felt her spirits lift as she puttered her way slowly along leafy lanes towards the A3. She realized she was beginning to feel a crazy, girlish excitement at the prospect of turning up unexpect-

26

edly and taking Matt off to dinner. A bit more spontaneity in their marriage was exactly what they needed. Matt was so much in demand these days you had to book him up months in advance.

An hour later she drew up outside the studios just as a salesman with a bulging briefcase jumped into his car and pulled out of a parking space.

Ally drove neatly into it, picked up her bag from the back seat and hummed as she walked up the steps to Century's impressive grey marble entrance. Tonight could be a new beginning, a way of her getting more involved in Matt's work. It had been stupid of her to avoid coming here just because the people could be intimidating.

She smiled as she walked across the foyer, expecting to see Bryony on the reception desk. But it wasn't Bryony. It was a new but equally stern-looking young woman she'd never seen before. Matt always suspected Century's receptionists of being trained by the SAS.

'Can I help you?' she asked.

'I've come for the drinks after *The Matt Boyd Show*.'

The girl checked her list. 'What did you say your name was?'

'Boyd. I'm Matt Boyd's wife. But I won't be on your list.'

The girl consulted her piece of paper again. 'I'm afraid you're not on the list.'

'No, I said I wouldn't be. It's a surprise.'

The receptionist stared at her suspiciously and asked her to sit down on one of the deep grey sofas grouped round a large television screen in the reception area. She then swivelled round and talked to someone on the phone in a soft voice so that Ally couldn't hear.

This wasn't turning out to be such a great idea after all.

'I'm sorry, Mrs Boyd,' the girl called out, 'but there doesn't seem to be anyone in the office. I expect they're in the studio.'

'Couldn't I go there then?'

The girl looked as though Ally had asked to do a tango on *News at Ten*. 'It's a live show. No one but the guests are allowed during a live show.'

For almost half an hour Ally sat watching Matt's show on the TV screen wishing she was the type who could make scenes. Her best friend Susie wouldn't be sitting here. Susie would have banged her fist and demanded someone sort things out. Unfortunately she wasn't Susie. She checked her watch for the tenth time. She might as well be at home.

'Allegra, how lovely to see you.' Ally spun round to find Stephen Cartwright, Century's Director of Programmes, standing behind her. 'Have you come to watch Matt?'

Ally breathed a sigh of relief. 'Stephen, hello. Yes. I decided to give Matt a surprise and drag him out to dinner.' She looked at the suddenly attentive receptionist with satisfaction. 'But this young lady can't rustle anyone up from the show.'

'For God's sake, Melanie, why didn't you just send Mrs Boyd to hospitality?'

'She's not on the list.'

'Send her straight up, for God's sake. Don't bother with a pass.' He walked her to the lifts himself. 'I'm so sorry, Allegra. Melanie isn't exactly Einstein.' He smiled apologetically. 'But then if she was she wouldn't be on our reception desk. Have fun.'

Ally stepped out of the lift and stopped for a moment, wondering which direction to go. On her left she could hear a television and she followed the sound into a large open-plan room with a bar at one end. This was where the cast, crew and guests plus assorted freeloaders came after the show. A white-coated barman was putting out crisps in small dishes.

Two young women glanced up as she came in. The taller of them wore pale yellow shorts with thick black tights underneath and a black polo-neck sweater. Her hair was short and spiky. In one ear she wore an earring shaped like the female gender symbol you learned in biology. The other girl wore a white T-shirt with the word 'SPUNK' emblazoned across it. The everyday uniform of television folk.

The room began to fill, and Ally guessed the show must have just finished. She helped herself to a drink. She had a feeling she was going to need it. From every side telly conversations lapped around her, incomprehensible in their jargon.

'Hello, Allegra,' Ally whipped round to find Bernie Long next to her, his smile as welcoming as battery acid. 'I didn't know you were coming tonight.'

Ally smiled back. She wasn't going to let Bernie get to her. After all these years she ought to be used to him.

'It's a surprise.'

'How very nice.' He looked as though he found something very funny. 'How's the family?'

Ally was tempted to say, 'Fine. Janey's into Ecstasy and Jess is on the game.' But Bernie probably wasn't listening anyway. She began to regret coming. This wasn't her world. The room was packed and it was incredibly hot with no sign of Matt anywhere. Maybe he wasn't coming, after all? She excused herself and slipped quietly to the ladies'. Leaning against the door of one of the cubicles she felt the cooling air from the ventilation system and it made her feel better. In a moment she'd go back in.

Outside she could hear the two girls in the outrageous

outfits bitching as they backcombed and gelled in front of the mirror.

'Are they, do you think?' one asked the other.

'Are they what?'

'You should know, you're the world's living expert on bonking the boss.'

'Oh, that.'

'Yes, *that*.'

Office gossip, Ally reflected. It was as much a part of the working world as the coffee machine or the weekly pay cheque. The eternal speculation about who was doing what to whom. It was one of the things she rather missed.

'No, I don't think so. Or anyway not yet.'

Ally flushed the loo noisily and opened the door. She nodded to the two girls and they nodded back, wondering who she was.

Telling herself not to be a coward, Ally straightened her hair and strode back towards the hum of voices. The first person she saw when she went into the noisy, crowded room was Matt, deep in conversation with a famous actor. It always took her aback to see Matt in his working mode. He was so much the hub, the centre. Next to him a small queue of people lined up hoping to catch his eye. Aspiring stars, a PR agent, a young researcher with an old lady on her arm who looked like her granny, their eyes bright at the prospect of meeting Matt Boyd and finding out if his charm was as powerful off camera as it was on. She watched him for a moment, easy and laughing, his physical presence so strong that she knew they wouldn't be disappointed.

And then he saw her. Instantly he came over, smiling with pleasure. 'Ally, love, you didn't say you were coming!' He put his arm round her and kissed her. 'What happened to Jess's piano lesson?'

'She got the bus.'

'So what made you change your mind?' He stopped a waiter and got her another glass of wine. 'I thought you found us TV types trivial and self-obsessed.'

'I do.' She squeezed his hand affectionately. 'That's why I've booked dinner so I can take you away from their influence.'

'Oh, God, love, why didn't you say this morning?' His voice sounded genuinely disappointed. 'I've promised to go to Joe Allen's. Everyone is. A rare outbreak of team spirit. Why don't you come too? It'll be fun.'

Ally's heart sank. 'OK. Sure. I'd love to.'

'Great. I'll tell Bernie's secretary. She's organizing it.'

Ally sipped her wine. It wasn't quite what she'd planned, but still. She'd wanted to get more involved with his work and this was his work.

On the other side of the room he stopped to talk to a startling looking girl with long dark hair who seemed to be wearing a man's suit. She was tall and chic and radiated the kind of effortless confidence that had always eluded Ally. Even from this far away Ally could see that she was standing unnecessarily close to him and that she kept touching his arm. Then she smiled up at him with an expression of such intimacy it was as though they were alone. Ally felt a warning flash of fear.

She turned to Bernie Long, who had squeezed in to help himself to another drink. 'Bernie' – Ally leaned over to him – 'who's the dark girl talking to Matt?'

Bernie looked from Ally to the girl and back. 'That's Belinda, the new producer. It's her birthday we're going out to celebrate tonight.' He raised his glass and chinked it against Ally's. 'Didn't Matt mention it?'

Ally stared across at them, puzzled. And then she remembered the conversation she'd overheard in the ladies' and she knew at once who it had been about.

And she didn't feel like going out to dinner any more.

31

Chapter 3

'Hiya, Ma.' Janey, lying on the sofa in front of the television, stretched her arms up towards her mother, surprised. 'You're home early.'

Ally, touched by the unaccustomed warmth in her elder daughter's welcome, bent down and kissed her, then sat down next to her on the fat chintzy cushions. Janey was going through an independent phase. Ally knew this was quite right and proper and a natural part of growing up, but since it had involved refusing all physical contact and treating even simple requests of where she was going as unbearable intrusions into her personal liberty it had been somewhat wearing.

As Janey snuggled up to her Ally noticed with exasperation that she had her army surplus boots on the new upholstery. It was a habit she'd inherited from her father, though at least he took his shoes off first.

'Feet off,' she commanded, swatting Janey's leg.

'Oh, Mum,' Janey complained, 'this is supposed to be a home, not a museum.'

Ally grinned at the outrageousness of the suggestion. Despite the inroads made by the interior designer, which Ally had now decided to put a stop to, Fairlawns was anything but a museum. Even in the sitting room there were piles of belongings which Ally endlessly tried to return to their rightful places. Matt's shoes, Janey's huge earrings which she took off because they pinched, only to accuse Jess of stealing them, discarded sweaters covered in white hair from Sox, their Old English sheepdog, all competed to make the place homely in the extreme.

In principle Sox was not allowed to get on the sofa, but

since she was the only failed graduate of Miss Watson's Dog Training Academy she did. After the maximum number of lessons and virtually no progress Miss Watson had begged them not to bring her any more because she was a bad influence. Ally sympathized with Sox. Her own school reports had said much the same thing.

Ally noticed the worn patches on the Turkish rugs. She much preferred them old and faded to bright and new against the golden wood of the polished boards. Sox hated the rugs because she kept skidding on them and knocking things over till Ally discovered magic non-slip tape to fix on the underside. Ally smiled, catching sight of Sox's bowl of water which Jess insisted on leaving in every room during the hot weather. Yesterday Matt had stood in it and then chased Jess round the room threatening to pour it down her neck unless she put it back in the kitchen where it belonged. Occasionally Ally couldn't help wishing the whole place looked a bit more *Homes & Gardens*, then remembered that if it did no one would relax in it.

'Where's Jess?' she asked, realizing there was no evidence of her younger daughter.

'Upstairs on the dreaded computer. Don't you think it's unhealthy for a fifteen-year-old to waste her life on computer games?'

'Knowing Jess she'll be marketing her own soon.'

'You always liked her better than me.' Janey's tone was jokey, but Ally could hear the traces of sibling rivalry. Sometimes it didn't seem that long ago that a jealous two-and-a-half-year-old had been so outraged at getting a baby sister that she'd fed Jess potting compost.

'Janey, you're my big girl, my firstborn. You'll always be special.'

In a weak moment Janey allowed herself to be cuddled. 'I don't suppose,' she said winningly, 'that since you're

33

back so early you'd let your firstborn borrow the car for an hour?'

'Go on.' She held out the car keys. 'As long as you promise to drive at forty. And no further than Guildford.'

Janey jumped up, all signs of rivalry miraculously evaporating. 'Thanks, Ma. See you later. Have fun.'

Ally stood up to watch her go. It was quite late but still amazingly light. Suddenly she felt like a walk round the garden.

It was cool and smelt of wallflowers and night-scented stock. She'd never liked wallflowers, finding their reds and oranges too garish next to the subtler pinks and purples of cottage flowers. But recently she'd come to see their quiet charms. She sat for a moment under the lilac tree and breathed deeply. Above her the birds were starting up on their dusk chorus. In the lilac tree she could hear a blackbird. Or was it a thrush? On an impulse she stood on the bench and picked an armful of lilac and walked back towards the house with it.

'Mum, you can't bring that inside.' Jess had abandoned her computer and was standing barefoot in the hall. 'It's bad luck!'

'Jessy, shame on you! You've been listening to your granny again.' Ally's mother Elizabeth was the world's leading authority on bad luck. No shoes on the table, it meant there'd be a death in the family. No peacock feathers or you'd get the evil eye. Don't turn your jumper round if you've been wearing it the wrong way, God knows why. Never wear red and white, it was a reminder of blood. Don't buy pearls for other people, they've got to choose their own. To Elizabeth the world was full of hazardous choices.

Jess watched balefully as Ally arranged the fat, fragrant blooms and buried her face in them, drinking in their scent.

'I'm not superstitious,' pointed out Ally.

'I know,' conceded Jess, 'but it's so out of character. You're pessimistic, anxiety-ridden and a born worrier. Why aren't you superstitious too?'

'Maybe the Good Lord thought I had enough on my plate.' Ally remembered how Matt had once told her she was the kind of person who saw a cloud behind every silver lining.

'Well, I hope you know what you're doing.'

'I do.'

When she turned from straightening up the last bloom and adding a few trailing strands of ivy, Jess had gone. In a moment she'd hear the beep of her computer again. It was supposed to be only boys who locked themselves away in their rooms for hours chained to their keyboards, but Jess hated the suggestion there was *anything* boys could do that girls couldn't do better. At least that's one good thing we've taught her, thought Ally, heading back into the sitting room and settling on the sofa. Idly she flicked through a magazine then looked for the remote control for the television. As usual someone had lost it so she got up and switched it on herself. When she turned round Jess was standing by the sofa with a glass of wine in her hand.

'For you.' She put it down on a coffee table. 'So. Why are you back so soon?'

'Dad had already promised to go out to dinner with the team. It's Belinda's birthday.'

'Who's Belinda?'

'Their new producer. Huge brown eyes. Ambition to match.' Ally tried to think of some faults and brightened. 'Big bum, though.'

'How revolting. Men like big bums. Why didn't you go too?'

'I was going to.' Ally avoided her daughter's hawklike

gaze. 'But you know what they're like. All they ever talk about is television.'

'So no romantic dinner for two?'

'Nope.'

'Oh, Mum.'

Ally picked up the glass of wine and forced herself to smile at Jess's tone. She didn't want her children to feel sorry for her. That would be too much.

'You know what?' Jess sat down next to her and put her arm round her mother protectively. 'I love Dad to pieces but there's one thing you're going to have to face about him.'

'What's that?'

'He's turning into a selfish shit and you know it.'

Ally choked on her wine. She knew she should tell Jess off for such an outrageous accusation. Instead she threw back her head and laughed.

'You'll have to do something about it, Mum.'

'I'll drink to that.' Ally held out her hand and took her daughter's in hers. It was almost a relief to stop making allowances for Matt and admit to herself how much she'd started resenting him. 'Any ideas where I should start?'

The first thing Ally noticed when she woke up the next morning was that Matt's clothes were piled neatly on the chair, a fact stunning enough in itself to merit a story in a gossip column. She wondered what time it had been when he'd got back. She'd gone to sleep at midnight and there'd been no sign of him.

Ally's friend Susie had once calculated that three a.m. was the acid test for infidelity. Until two o'clock it was just possible to find some activity in London with your feet still on the ground. But by three it could only be one thing.

As she looked over at Matt's sleeping face she knew she didn't really believe he'd been up to anything. She might be kidding herself but instinctively she felt that he'd need a whole lot of provocation, and that something would have to be very wrong with their relationship before he risked eighteen years of marriage for a sexy twenty-five-year-old. Matt might be selfish but he'd never been the unfaithful type.

Quietly, so as not to wake him, she crept into the bathroom and poured blue herbal bath foam into the water until it was a deep sapphire, the colour of the sea in fantasies and holiday brochures. It was Saturday and Janey and Jess were sleeping in. Janey, good girl that she usually was, had brought the car back safely at eleven and parked it far more expertly than Ally ever managed in its bay in the double garage.

Ally slipped into the hot bath and shampooed her hair. Then she lay back and let the water swirl round her deliciously. Under here the world outside was muffled and distant. You felt both vulnerable and invulnerable at the same time.

Was Matt really becoming as selfish as Jess said? If he was it was her fault too. She'd let him get away with it. It was built on the bed of her compromises. His fame had made it worse, of course, because there were so many ordinary things she couldn't ask him to do. But if he hadn't been famous would it have been so very different?

Suddenly Ally knew Jess was right. She'd let things drift and she had to do something about it. She had to stop being a doormat and start being an equal. She remembered the way he'd talked to Belinda, the spark of challenge in his eyes. Well, she could be challenging too. She didn't have to be semi-detached and suburban.

She stood up, her hair streaming down behind her, and reached for a towel.

'I *will* do something about it,' she said aloud, her voice muffled by the towel, 'and what's more I'll start today.'

She rubbed her hair roughly, removed the towel and screamed.

Matt was two inches away from the side of the bath holding a bath towel out for her and laughing. To her astonishment she saw that his willy was waving at her engagingly and that on the end of it was a blue stripey sock.

'I'm really sorry about last night, love.' His blue eyes crinkled at the corners in the smile she loved. 'You must have thought I was letting you down, but I really couldn't get out of it.'

At the sight of Matt and his sock Ally was conscious that her certainty and sense of purpose were draining away with the bathwater. She stepped into the towel he was holding and wound her hair in a hand towel which she twisted into a turban on top of her head. This get-up had a certain imperial charm and she started to feel more in control. She would refuse to be sidetracked either by Matt's excuses or his sock-covered member.

'Too right I thought you were selfish.' She swept regally past him. 'I honestly don't see why you *had* to go to Belinda's birthday party instead of having dinner with me.'

'But, Ally' – Matt's voice rang with injustice – 'I didn't even know you were coming. When I asked you to hospitality you looked horrified.'

One of Ally's biological handicaps was her tendency to see other people's points of view. Fortunately this time she caught herself before she made the mistake of admitting it. She had to stick to her guns. That was what men did. Women lost because they tried to be too reasonable.

'Tell you what,' said Matt, smiling appealingly, 'since it's Saturday why don't I cook a romantic dinner tonight instead? We can always send the girls off to a crack party.'

Despite herself Ally giggled. As he came towards her she could tell from the angle of the sock that he was maintaining his position despite the odds.

'Come on, Mrs Boyd.' He began to undo her towel. 'It's Saturday. Why don't we go back to bed for a bit?'

Half an hour later Ally skipped down the steps to the kitchen humming. She took down a small cafetière and began to fill it.

Jess was sitting at the table eating chocolate mousse and drinking diet Coke. She watched her mother closely as she laid a tray with the cafetière and one cup.

'Who's that for?' she asked suspiciously.

'For whoever it is who's in my bed. Sting, perhaps? Or was it Tom Cruise? I forget.'

'Mum, stop humming. It's obscene. You haven't said anything to him yet, have you?'

'What about?' Ally pretended not to understand and busied herself with heating up milk.

'About not taking you out to dinner. About coming back God knows when. About being selfish.'

'He couldn't help it about the dinner. He'd already promised.' Ally avoided her daughter's eye, which was sharp and deadly as an eagle in its uncompromising youth and certainty.

Jess walked over to the fridge for some more diet Coke. As she came close she noticed the red marks on her mother's neck. 'Honestly, Mum, they used to bribe the peasants with bread and circuses. All you needed was a French stick.'

Ally laughed and pulled her dressing gown tighter. 'Anyway, he's cooking supper tonight to say sorry.'

'Dad's cooking?' Jess clutched her forehead in mock amazement. 'Sorry, Mum, I've just remembered a long-standing invitation.'

'Good,' replied Ally. 'Then Dad and I can have our romantic dinner alone.'

Suddenly Sox, sleeping peacefully in her basket in a corner of the kitchen, erupted into a fit of barking.

'Bad Sox!' Jess grabbed her collar to try and stop her scrabbling at the garden door. Outside they could hear an answering bark and the garden door opened to reveal Elizabeth, Ally's mother, dragging her huge standard poodle behind her.

'Granola!' screeched Jess, rushing up to her grandmother and kissing her. 'What are you doing here?'

'Oh, my God,' muttered Ally, suddenly remembering that her mother had talked her into looking after the ghastly animal while she went to London for the day.

'Can't stay,' announced her mother as though someone had just offered her a cup of coffee, which they hadn't. 'Taxi's waiting. Here's his food.' She put two tins of dog food on the kitchen table. 'Back at five.'

'He can't eat all that in one day,' Ally protested.

'Yes, you can, can't you, my sweet?' cooed Elizabeth. 'He's a growing boy.'

The growing boy was beginning to show an unhealthy interest in Sox's nether regions. Sox snapped at him.

'Stop it, Bitzer,' commanded Ally. 'She doesn't like it.'

'Oh, yes she does,' contradicted Elizabeth. And to Ally's shame, Sox now seemed to have wantonly abandoned herself to Bitzer's attentions.

'The trouble with you,' said Jess, stroking Sox behind the ears and gently removing her from Bitzer's scope of operations, 'is that you can't make up your mind what you want.' Jess shot a wicked glance at her mother. 'Rather like your mistress.'

'Bloody hell!' Ally ignored Jess's remark and sat down, watching Elizabeth's retreating back. 'Now we'll have to spend the whole day keeping them apart.'

'Like Romeo and Juliet.'

40

'How on earth did I get myself lumbered with Bitzer? I loathe the wretched animal.'

'Because you're just a girl who can't say no.' Jess examined the labels on the tins of dog food. Gourmet Chunks of Choice Rabbit and Mr Woof's Cordon Bleu Chicken Supreme. 'Look on the bright side. If Dad screws up the supper, at least we'll have something to eat.'

Ally noticed the cooling coffee pot. 'Oh, God. I promised Dad a cup of coffee hours ago.'

'Never mind.' Jess tickled Sox's chin. 'Say six Hail Marys and maybe he'll come and get it himself. Miracles do happen.'

Ally ignored her and put some more coffee in the cafetière. As she spooned it in, to make it thick and strong the way Matt liked it, there was another knock on the garden door.

'Maybe Granny's decided not to go,' suggested Jess hopefully, gently kicking the now sleeping Bitzer.

This time Ally went to the door herself. 'Susie!' Her eyes glowed with unexpected pleasure at finding her best friend on the doorstep, 'Come in. Have a cup of coffee.'

Susie took off her cashmere cardigan and hung it on the back of a chair. She took particular delight in appearing conventional and being anything but. Tall and rangy, with pale skin and fine blonde hair which was pulled back off her face by a black velvet hairband, and given to wearing white lace blouses and pleated skirts, Susie looked like a deb and talked like a navvy.

'Where's Trevor?' Ally got another cup and saucer out and put it in front of Susie. Susie's husband was the ultimate New Man. 'Don't tell me. Battling through Tesco's while you have your nails done?'

Susie laughed. Instead of having to be dragooned into the Saturday shop and coming back, hours later, with pickled eggs and Holsten six-packs but no washing powder, Trevor volunteered.

'Darling Trev.' Susie helped herself to a biscuit. 'He's turned shopping into an art form. Do you know, he's even got a plan of Safeways on the word processor?' She sighed happily. 'Just the thought of that seething humanity at the deli counter makes me feel tired. So I dropped in for a chat. Where's Matt?' She laughed hollowly. 'Gone to Sainsbury's?'

Jess and Ally exchanged glances.

Susie eyed the cafetière with longing. 'Is that coffee going begging?'

'Have it,' advised Jess. 'Mum was about to take it up to Dad but I told her she's pandering to the unjustified male expectation that women should run around after them.'

'Excuse *me*,' Susie apologized, laughing. 'I thought it was a pot of coffee, not a symbol of women's oppression.'

'I'll put the kettle on and make some more.' Ally stood up. Then she turned and looked at Susie intently. 'Do *you* think Matt's selfish, Susie?'

Susie was unfazed by the sudden turn in the conversation.

'Is the Pope a Catholic? Of course he's selfish. All men are. It's in the nature of the beast. All that testosterone. They ought to have "Warning, Hazardous Chemicals" stamped on their underpants.'

'But *why* are they so selfish?'

'Do you want the charitable version or the truth? They'd say it's because they think differently. They don't see tidying up as a priority. They see watching the rugby as a priority and tidying the house as an option if there's time after the game, which there never is. That's the kind version. The unkind version says they know if they leave it long enough we'll do it later. Which, of course, we do.'

Susie sipped Matt's coffee. 'Haven't you heard the old saying: "Women hope men will change when they marry, but they don't. Men hope women won't change, but they do." '

Ally and Jess began to giggle. So neither of them noticed Matt open the door.

'What happened to my coffee?' he inquired. 'I was really looking forward to it. Hello, Susie, I didn't know you were here.' Three heads swivelled round at this textbook example of men at work. Matt smiled his most endearing smile. 'All right, all right. You can stop looking at me like that, all of you.'

'Like what, Matt?' Sparring with Matt was one of the most enjoyable things about coming round to the Boyd household. Trevor was no fun. If she made a crack at him he just asked her if she had PMT.

'Like I'm the commandant in *Tenko* and you're the newest crop of British virgins.'

Susie leaned back in her chair and watched him for a moment. 'Ally was just asking me whether I thought you were very selfish or just averagely selfish.' Ally shook her head but Susie ignored her. 'What do you think?'

Matt grinned. 'I don't think I'm selfish at all.'

'All men think that.' Susie started fishing around in the depths of her vast bag. 'It's one of the characteristics of being male.' Finally she found what she was looking for. A slightly dog-eared brochure. 'This is what you need.' She passed the brochure across to Ally. 'It's a confidence workshop I'm going to next Saturday. Why don't you come along? Take the first step towards sorting Matt out.'

Matt laughed nervously. 'If you were any more confident, Susie, you'd be running the SS.'

Ally glanced doubtfully at the brochure. She didn't much like touchy-feely events where you had to bare

43

your soul before elevenses. 'I don't think it's really me, Susie.' She handed back the brochure.

'Of course some people might say' – Susie sipped her coffee and smiled sweetly at Matt – 'that men only get away with being selfish because women let them.'

Matt smiled back and turned to Ally. 'Where did you say you'd put my cup of coffee?'

'Do you know, Susie?' Ally said, pouring herself the last few drops of the coffee she'd made him. 'Maybe I will come after all.'

As he drove to Century two days later, turning over some thoughts about the programme in his mind, Matt found himself wondering if there was anything in what Susie and Ally had said. Was he really that selfish? He did his bit. A damn sight more than his father ever did. He emptied the dishwasher now and then, he mowed the lawn. OK, he didn't exactly do much in the house but what was Mrs O'Shock for? By the time he drove under the bar at the Century car park he'd resolved to try and be more helpful and felt better immediately. Rather like deciding to go on a diet or making a New Year's resolution, you got the immediate moral glow without any of the actual effort.

To his annoyance someone had parked in his usual space, but Bernie's slot was still empty. It was 10.05. The ideas meeting was due to start at ten o'clock. That would teach Bernie to come in late. He was supposed to set a good example.

Up in *The Matt Boyd Show* offices, Matt put down his briefcase and picked up his mail. On top was a buff envelope which Matt opened without looking at the outside. It was the show's ratings. Usually, secure in his position as the most popular chat-show on television, Matt didn't bother to keep an eye on them, but today he glanced down the columns. The show had lost some viewers, but that wasn't surprising given the wonderful weather they'd been having. People were probably out in the garden mowing the lawn. He cast an eye across at the opposition's ratings to see how they'd survived the heatwave, and had to look again. Big City, their rival TV company, hadn't lost viewers. It had gained them.

It wasn't the weather that had stolen Matt's audience. It was Danny Wilde. He put the sheets of paper in Bernie's in-tray and stood there for a moment, looking out of the window. They were going to have to do something. They had been confident for too long.

'What are you doing up here still?'

Matt whipped round, a shade guiltily, to find Bernie Long standing in the door.

'Just on my way down.' From the scowl on Bernie's raddled face Matt deduced the hangover must be bad today and toyed with the idea of suggesting his granny's patent hangover cure: chewing garlic. But for some reason he didn't think Bernie would appreciate the tip. 'You're late today.'

'Yes,' said Bernie sourly. 'Some bastard parked in my parking space.'

'Tch, tch,' Matt sympathized as he walked out of the door. 'Who'd be inconsiderate enough to do that?'

Stephen Cartwright, Century's Director of Programmes, sat in his corner office and stared out of the window. He had been to some lengths to make the room feel comfortable and plush, like a suite of rooms in one of the smartest and newest hotels, and usually its sense of space, its magnificent views over London, gave him great pleasure.

But today Stephen took none of his usual enjoyment in the subtle lavender carpet or the grey suede sofas. Even the scent of the huge arum lilies he had delivered daily from the New Covent Garden Market in Nine Elms didn't penetrate his consciousness. Stephen had things on his mind: *The Matt Boyd Show* for a start.

When the door opened a fraction and Janet, his secretary, put her head in to ask if he wanted to run through his meetings, Stephen shook his head and she melted away. Janet was one of the best things about the job. A career secretary – something almost unknown in television where every secretarial job had two hundred glamorous applicants, none of them with typing on their mind – Janet had been a secretary for twenty years, was nononsense and middle-aged and worth her weight in gold. She harboured no ambitions to rise up the executive ladder, become a producer or sleep her way to the top. Instead she was superb at what she did. When Stephen travelled she handed him a plastic folder with directions in it and every conceivable question answered. Sometimes Stephen didn't even know where he was going until he got there. Consequently Stephen gave her a large salary and a company car and she became his eyes and ears and lurked in times of stress in the ladies' loo listening to gossip.

And one of the titbits she'd picked up was that things were not going well on Stephen's pet project *Hello*, a new daytime show to be hosted by Century's grande dame and royal pain in the arse, Maggy Mann. For some reason Stephen could never understand, the audience believed Maggy to be a kind, caring individual who had their best interests at heart. Whereas everyone close to Maggy knew her to be a driven neurotic with a highly developed sense of what was best for Maggy Mann and a passionate loathing of the public who loved her. She appeared at the hospitality after shows only for the briefest period in case any member of the public dared to try and engage her in conversation. And yet the audience went on loving her.

46

The phone buzzed on his desk and Janet came on the line. 'It's Bill Ford, Stephen. He says it's urgent.'

Stephen sighed. Bill Ford was the overpriced and, as it was turning out, untalented producer they'd hired to launch *Hello*. What the hell was the problem now?

'Bill.' Stephen's tone was not encouraging. 'What can I do for you?'

'Well, Stephen, we've run into a little difficulty.' Stephen listened to Bill Ford's petulant voice and wondered not for the first time why on earth they'd hired him. He was well known in the light entertainment world and had come highly recommended as the man who could give *Hello* the pizazz a new daytime show needed. But so far he wasn't delivering.

'So, what's the problem?'

'It's this advice slot. We've tested out every bloody agony aunt in London, not to mention a few uncles, and none of them has been halfway right. I'm tearing my hair out here. The only one out of the whole lot who wasn't too syrupy or too preachy was June Reynolds.'

'Look, Bill.' God, the man was a cretin! They'd *been* through all this five times. 'June Reynolds is lovely. Warm, cheerful, likable. But she's Cititele's agony aunt. We were going to find someone new, remember? Not a complete unknown, maybe, but someone who's never been an agony aunt. An actress, maybe, or psychologist, so we can create our own identity.' Stephen spoke very slowly to underline the fact that he didn't want to have to repeat himself again. 'This isn't supposed to be the conventional agony slot. We want to do something bold and adventurous that will get us the headlines.'

'I know, Stephen, I know. But I just haven't found the right person so far.'

Stephen began to get annoyed. 'Well I'm sorry, sunshine, but that's *your* job, not mine. That's why we're paying you two grand a week. If anyone has sleepless nights it's going to be you. You'd better get your address book out, hadn't you? Where have you looked so far?'

'Women's magazines, *Spotlight*, we've phoned every agent in town, local radio stations. All the obvious places.'

'Maybe you should start a little lateral thinking, then. Try looking in the *un*obvious ones. I suppose you could always audition.'

'God, Stephen, do us a favour. When *True Story* advertised they got ten thousand replies and the auditions took months.'

'In that case you'd better come up with another way of finding someone, hadn't you, Bill? Now I must go. Another meeting beckons.'

'Stephen?'

'Yes, Bill?' Really. He had enough to do without being burdened with Bill Ford's trivial problems.

'It's Maggy.'

Stephen sighed and looked at his watch. 'What about Maggy?'

'She thinks her friend Anne Adamson on the *Sunday Examiner* would be absolutely perfect.'

'And what do you think? You're the producer.'

'I'd rather tell my problems to a traffic warden.'

'Then be upfront with Maggy and say thanks but no thanks. She's a pro. She'll be all right. Maggy's like all bullies. If you stand up to her she respects you.'

'OK, Stephen.' Bill sounded anything but convinced. 'I'll tell her.'

Stephen buzzed Janet for a cup of Earl Grey and turned his attention to the next and far more pressing problem on his list. What the hell was he going to do about Matt Boyd?

Chapter 4

Ally woke up, rolled into the middle of the bed, curled herself like a spoon against the warmth of Matt's body and kissed the back of his head. Without Matt appearing to wake, an arm snaked out from under the covers and held her briefly.

At the back of her mind Ally knew there was a reason she had to get up early even though it was Saturday, but couldn't quite recall what it was. Then she remembered. It was the day of the confidence workshop. She put her head back under the covers. Oh, God, why had she ever agreed to go? It wasn't her sort of thing, and anyway what difference could a day make to anything? If Susie hadn't been coming round to pick her up in half an hour she would have cried off. Downstairs she could hear the sound of hoovering. Mrs O'Shock must be here already.

She got out of bed, dressed quickly and went downstairs. She needed breakfast before the ordeal ahead. In the kitchen the sunlight streamed in through the open garden door on to the solid ash table and lit up the arrangement of pink old-fashioned roses Ally had put there yesterday evening. She'd read in an article about Grasse, where some of the most famous perfumes in the world were made, that the perfect moment to pick roses is at dawn when the dew is still on them. Ally had her own theory about this. The perfect moment, she'd decided, was the evening. After the first but before the second glass of wine. Maybe she'd write an article about it. But who'd be interested in what she thought about anything?

As she finished making herself some toast and coffee

49

Mrs O'Shock appeared in the doorway holding one of Matt's socks at arm's length.

'I found it under the sofa, Mrs B.' She placed the offending article on top of the washing machine. 'Tell me, now: does Mr Boyd have any Irish in him?' She began to prod it with a pair of barbecue tongs as though it might either crawl off or spring into red-blooded male life. She flipped the sock into the washing machine and snapped the door shut in case it might escape. 'It's the mothers I blame. The Irish man's relationship with his mother is sacred. He thinks she's the Virgin Mary.' She began to pour in the powder. 'And she thinks he's Christ Almighty.' Ally watched speechless as Mrs O'Shock turned on the machine to wash one sock. 'Are you sure there's no Irish in him, Mrs Boyd?'

Ally laughed and shook her head.

Mrs O'Shock picked up the brochure for the workshop and started flicking through it. 'This is what I need now.'

'What's that, Mrs O'Shock?'

'Confidence. To give me the nerve to tell my husband to get off the settee for five blessed minutes when I'm hoovering under it.'

'No, no, no, Mrs O'Shock,' Ally corrected, putting some more bread in the toaster. 'To tell him to get off the settee and do the blessed hoovering himself.'

'Well, Mrs Boyd, I may be a Catholic but I don't believe in miracles.'

Five minutes before Susie was due Ally ran up the stairs to say goodbye to the girls. Janey was still asleep but Jess was pulling off the Young Savers T-shirt she wore in bed. As soon as she saw her mother she shyly held it in front of her.

Ally tried not to smile. Until a month or two ago Jess had been as flat-chested as a boy, then to her hideous embarrassment she'd had a sudden growing spurt. Janey

50

would have been delighted but Jess was different. Still holding the nightshirt in place she pulled on a huge Sloppy Joe jumper.

Ally kissed her goodbye and closed the door. On the landing she bumped into Matt, still in his dressing gown.

'Where's that wretch Jess? She's pinched my favourite sweater again.'

'In her room. She's got it on. I thought it looked familiar.'

Matt started to open the door.

'Matt?'

'Yes, my about-to-be-liberated love?'

Ally dropped her voice. 'Don't mention the boobs.'

Matt was hurt. 'Do you think I'm completely insensitive?'

'Sorry.'

Matt leaned into the room and caught sight of his sweater adorning his younger daughter. 'Hello, Jessy, what big' – he glanced round at Ally provocatively – 'sweaters you wear. Come on, off with it or I'll stop your pocket money.'

Jess folded her arms protectively. 'I haven't had pocket money since I was eleven.'

'I'll stop your allowance, then.'

'Too bad,' she taunted, 'I've got nearly a grand in the Cheltenham and Gloucester at eleven point two five per cent.'

'Bloody hell!' Matt stopped, impressed. 'Have you really? You couldn't lend me a fiver, could you?'

'Come and get it,' Jess said, running past him down the stairs, waving her sweatered arms provocatively.

'God almighty!' muttered Matt. 'Whatever happened to parental authority?'

'You never had any,' pointed out Ally, grabbing her bag which always seemed to be the opposite end of the

51

house whenever she needed it. 'You were always work-ing.'

Smiling she followed Matt and Jess downstairs to get her coat just as the doorbell rang. It was Susie.

Mrs O'Shock took her into the kitchen where Matt sat at the table with Sox on his knee.

'Well, Sox old girl, what do you think?' Matt eyed Susie warily from behind four stone of solid sheepdog. 'Should I be worried? Is this going to be the last day of peace in my lifetime?'

Sox simpered at him adoringly.

'Look at it this way.' Susie held the door open for Ally and indicated her watch. 'You were lucky to get away with it this long.'

As Ally and Susie arrived at the sunny modern campus of Surrey University and queued to register, Ally wondered what she was doing wasting a precious Saturday on something like this. She and Matt could have gone out to the Italian restaurant in Fairley Green and had their usual spaghetti all'Alfredo and one too many glasses of Chianti. The brochure had promised 'A Day That Could Change Your Life', but surely that was cloud cuckoo land?

She couldn't help glancing round at the thirty or so other people who'd given up their Saturdays to be here. All of them, she noted wryly, were women. Why was it men already had confidence or would go to the stake rather than admit they hadn't?

Some of the group were middle-aged and dowdy, but to her surprise at least half were young and smartly dressed. A couple were clearly Ladies Who Lunched, drop-dead chic in their off-white silks and linens. And one young girl even had a pink and black punk haircut, which stood up like an angry cockatoo, and enough chains and safety pins to start a hardware shop. Surely *she* couldn't be shy and retiring?

52

'Name, please.' They'd got to the front of the queue.

'Susie Mills.' The girl with the clipboard wrote Susie's name on her badge in large convent-girl handwriting then turned to Ally. 'And your name is . . .?'

'Allegra Adams,' cut in Ally before Susie could say Boyd. Susie looked at her in surprise. She hardly ever used her single name. 'I just want to be me today,' Ally whispered, 'not Mrs Famous Person.'

'Come on then, we'd better get a move on or those battleaxes in twinsets and pearls will have scoffed all the digestive biscuits.'

Inside the hall everyone stood around chatting until a brisk dark-haired woman asked them to sit down – not next to a friend – and introduced Barbara Major, empress of assertiveness, who was running the course.

To Ally's astonishment a woman in a batik print smock with her iron grey bun skewered by what appeared to be three knitting needles came forward. Matt would have laughed. She looked more like a pottery teacher than a raving feminist about to subvert their house and home.

'Hello.' Barbara's crisp tone belied the arts and craftiness of her appearance. 'To break the ice I usually get you to do a little exercise at this point. So Jane' – she turned to the dark-haired woman who was clearly her assistant – 'could you give out the papers and pencils?'

'Oh, great,' Susie whispered audibly. 'We're playing consequences.'

Barbara ignored her.

'For starters I want you to choose ten words you think would describe yourself.'

Susie raised her eyes to heaven then picked up her pencil and started writing.

Ally smiled at her and did the same.

'One, *mother*,' she wrote without thinking twice. 'Two, *wife*.' Then she stopped, astonished that she had to think.

'Three, *home-maker*.' But was that any different from wife and mother? Susie was already at number ten when she'd only got three. What was she? What were the words that captured her essence? 'Four, *unconfident*.' That was manifestly true.

And suddenly the time was up. As she looked at her list Ally saw that, harmless though it seemed, this was far more dangerous stuff than consequences. Only four words to describe Allegra Boyd and all of them gentle and domestic? What had happened to that spunky, optimistic girl who'd been chosen out of hundreds to read the news when she was only twenty?

Even though everyone else had finished Ally unfolded her paper and added: 'Five, *angry*.'

And Ally, nice accommodating Ally, who had spent her life trying to keep everyone happy, heading off confrontations, avoiding trouble at all costs, realized it was true. She *was* angry. And just admitting it made her feel a whole lot better.

Barbara was standing again. 'Don't worry, I'm not going to make you read them out.'

Everyone laughed with relief, but Ally was startled to recognize in herself a tiny twinge of disappointment. Clearly the heady atmosphere of group confession was getting to her.

'Now another little exercise I think you'll find quite revealing.' Barbara sat in the middle of the group and smiled. People weren't so dismissive this time, Ally noticed. 'Next I want you to describe the person on your right, again in ten words. Be honest, for all our sakes.'

Ally sat for a moment horrified, but everyone else was surveying her neighbour and scribbling away so she picked up her paper and pencil and scanned the person on her right.

This time the descriptions were read out, and Ally steeled herself when it was her neighbour's turn.

'*Attractive*,' said the woman. '*Tall, chic, confident, nice, married, friendly, warm.*'

Ally listened in amazement.

'The point is,' Barbara said, reading her mind with extraordinary perceptiveness, 'that other people don't see you the way you see yourself. And this is the important bit – you can choose their reality instead of yours.'

Ally felt a lump in her throat and an overwhelming sense of relief that made her want to laugh out loud. If other people saw her as confident, warm and friendly, why shouldn't she *be* confident and warm and friendly?

Barbara moved swiftly on. 'I'd like you each to tell everyone what made you decide to come here today.'

And one by one they admitted their weaknesses. Feeling invisible. Unable to stand up to mothers or mothers-in-law who dominated their lives. Angry with their husbands. Walked over by their kids.

'What about you, Allegra? What made you come today?'

For a moment Ally panicked. What happened if someone found out who she really was? But she knew instinctively that there was a bond between the women here today. They'd come because they wanted to throw away the past and start again.

'I came,' Ally began slowly, noticing that Susie was watching her as closely as the others, 'because for eighteen years I've been a happy housewife, I've loved making a home and being there for my family. I've got a charming husband and two lovely daughters. In lots of ways I'm very lucky. But lately I've realized something else. That my husband is selfish as well as charming and quite a lot of the time he forgets I exist, and my two lovely daughters don't really need me any more.' She paused, thinking it through as she said it, almost forgetting where she was. 'And I've just decided that I'm going to do something

55

about it.' She gazed round, astounded that today had actually made a difference. She was feeling more confident by the moment. 'I've decided I'm going to get a job.'

'Good for you!' Barbara's voice rang with warmth and encouragement. 'I'm so glad you came today.'

And looking at her friendly face Ally knew that she meant it. Then she realized everyone was clapping, because they knew, as she did, that she'd just taken the first step towards changing her life for the better.

'Anyone feel like a quick snifter?' suggested Monica, a hearty gin-and-jaguar matron with a hilariously plummy voice, as they gathered up their belongings after the workshop. 'I spotted a wine bar across the road. Tiddles or Tipples or some such damn fool name. I mean' – she slung on her shoulder bag with all the gay bravado of a mutineering foot soldier – 'why should we rush back to hearth and home and put the bloody dinner on?'

Susie laughed and took her arm. 'My thoughts exactly. To the wine bar!'

'It's OK for you,' pointed out Ally, remembering that she'd had no idea the workshop would go on this long and that she hadn't done anything about supper, 'Trevor will have dinner and sixteen veg on the table when you get home.'

'Come on, Ally,' wheedled Susie, 'you're the heroine of the day, our very own Joan of Arc. The one who's supposed to be changing her life. You can't say no to a glass of Chilean Cabernet 'cos hubby might be put out.'

Ally could feel herself weakening. She didn't want to go home and cook dinner either. She wanted to hang on to the spirit of warm, uplifting camaraderie they'd been sharing.

Suddenly she grinned, raising a fist of female solidarity against the oppressor with pipe and slippers the length

56

and breadth of the country. 'Too right. We can always have fish and chips.'

'That's my girl!' applauded Susie.

Ally put one arm round her and the other round Monica. 'What's more,' she said as they piled into the wine bar, 'he can bloody well go and get them himself!'

As Ally got out of Susie's car at seven forty-five she didn't feel quite so brave. She told herself not to be pathetic. OK, it was a bit late, but why *shouldn't* she have gone out for a drink for a change?

She opened the side door and remembered a saying of her father's after he'd done something he knew her mother would hit the roof about: 'I'd better throw my hat in first,' as if her mother would be lurking behind the door with a rolling pin.

But Matt wasn't behind the door.

What was behind the door was a dozen or so carrier bags from Marks & Spencer in various states of undress. Some of the contents were on the table, some still in the bags and a few had been put away safely in the fridge. Without being asked to, Matt had gone shopping.

She opened the bag nearest to her and took out four lobster tails in garlic mayonnaise, a pack of gravadlax and a mixed seafood platter. She tried not to notice the prices.

Helping herself to a glass of white wine she began to unpack the bags and put everything away before it melted. There was no noise from upstairs so she guessed the girls must be out. From the sitting room next door she could hear the TV blaring and knew exactly where he was. Asleep on the sofa.

Twenty minutes later she laid the lobster tails on a tray with French bread and a crisp green salad. He might not be Trevor, but it was a start.

*

The next morning Ally woke deliciously late and remembered that something momentous had happened yesterday. She had decided to take control of her life. Filled with new purpose she decided to get up before Matt distracted her. As she dressed she wondered for a split second if she'd been transported back twenty years. From downstairs she could have sworn she could hear, very loud, a hit from *Hair*, the musical. Intrigued she went to investigate.

Lying on the sofa in the sitting room, with the stereo up full blast, was Jess, calmly reading a copy of *Cosmopolitan*. Ally recognized the music as 'The Dawning of the Age of Aquarius'. It was so irritating the way the young kept colonizing their parents' music and then, if their parents dared to say 'I remember that', destroying them with one glance of scornful contempt.

'Hello, Mum. How was the encounter group?' She smiled and reached out a hand. 'Suppose a cup of coffee's out of the question?'

'Make it yourself.' Ally threw a cushion at her and ignored the dirty plate on the floor next to her. 'I'm warning you, young lady, there are going to be some changes round here. For a start I've decided to get a job.'

'Wow! Something must have happened yesterday.' Jess jumped up and followed her as she swept from the room. 'Did you roll up your trouser leg and swear to abandon your family for the cause?'

Ally ignored her and went into the kitchen. The first thing that met her eye was a pile of dirty dishes sitting on top of the dishwasher and a frying pan, laughingly sold as non-stick, coated in burnt-on yellow goo which no one had even bothered to leave in the sink to soak.

'It wasn't me, it was Janey,' insisted Jess. 'She had a midnight snack attack and knocked herself up a Microprotein Big Mac at two a.m.'

'And the omelette pan?'

'Well, OK, that was me. I had a go at crêpes Suzette.'

'Crêpes Suzette at two a.m.?'

'I thought you wanted to encourage me to eat proper food.'

'Crêpes Suzette aren't proper food. They're calories with alcohol on top.'

'Yum, yum. No wonder I liked them. What are you doing?'

Ally had found two large pieces of paper and had sat down at the table. 'I'm making a sign to go on the dishwasher.' In large letters she wrote 'IN NOT ON' and Blu-tacked it on the front. Then she began to divide the other page into columns.

'Mother of mine,' Jess said, looking at it suspiciously, 'that wouldn't by any chance be a rota?'

'So there are brains between your headphones, are there? You and your sister are about to start helping with the housework.'

'What about Dad?'

'Him too. He'll be down as soon as he realizes he hasn't been brought a cup of tea.'

'Sorry, Mum.' Jess got up and began to edge towards the door. 'I'm a feminist. We don't believe in housework.'

'Empty that dishwasher!' commanded Ally in tones of uncharacteristic wrath.

'OK, OK.' Jess opened the door and began to stack the clean dishes on the table. 'Mum?'

'Yes?' Ally hardened her heart against the next feeble excuse.

'How many feminists does it take to tell a joke?'

'I don't know. How many feminists does it take to tell a joke?'

'Ten.' Jess put another plate on the pile. 'One to tell

the joke and the other nine to say, "I don't see what's funny about that".'

They were still laughing when Matt, in dressing gown and slippers, put his head round the door. 'Any chance of a cup of tea?' he asked hopefully.

There was a sharp intake of breath from Jess. 'I dunno about that, Dad. What does it say on the rota?'

Ally glared at her sternly.

'Of course you can have a cup of tea, my darling. The kettle's there and the tea's in that tin marked TEA. You just put in a teabag and pour on the water.'

Matt could see when he was beaten. 'What's this?' He pointed to the sheet of paper as he waited for the kettle to boil.

'That's the rota.' Jess picked it up and scanned it.

'What on earth do we need a rota for? We have a cleaning woman three times a week.'

'No, we don't,' corrected Jess. 'We have Mrs O'Shock.'

Ally marvelled for the hundredth time at the incapacity, or possibly unwillingness, of the male brain to grapple with how much work there was in running a home. Men seemed to believe that dirty laundry miraculously transformed itself into clean underpants, that dishwashers somehow emptied themselves and that toilet rolls were in some mysterious way self-replacing.

'Mrs O'Shock comes three times a week. The dishwasher has to be emptied three times a day.'

'Does it really?' Matt lifted the pile of plates Jess had stacked and wandered round searching for a home for them like a blind gundog trying to be helpful and picking up the wrong pheasant.

'Hang on, Mum,' Jess said suspiciously. 'Janey and me are in for the dishwasher once a day while Dad's only down to take the rubbish out every other Tuesday.'

'Yes. Well.' Ally looked embarrassed. 'I thought I'd try and break him in gently. Where is Janey, by the way?'

'Still asleep.'

'Come on, Jessy,' Ally opened the fridge and got out a salmon. 'Slice some carrots, will you? It'll be time for lunch in an hour.'

But Jess was deep in the Sits Vac column of *The Sunday Times*. 'You know you said you wanted a job? Here's a good one for you, Mum. "Dynamic tycoon seeks girl Friday to run his office and organize his life." Oh, wow, hear this! Laura Ashley are looking for a head of PR. You'd be brilliant. Dad always says you should go on *Mastermind* to answer questions on the Laura Ashley catalogue. Why don't you apply?'

Matt looked up from the colour supplement. 'What's this about you getting a job? You've never mentioned it before.'

'I only decided yesterday.' She handed him a bag of new potatoes and a scraper. 'Susie's coming round later to help me do a CV.'

'What sort of job do you want?'

'I've no idea. Something that gets my brain going again and fits in with Janey and Jess.'

'But Ally, love.' Matt stood up and put his arms round her. 'You've already got a job. You look after me.'

Over her shoulder Ally saw Jess pretend to strangle herself and giggled. 'I know I have.' She patted him affectionately. 'And the pay's great. But look at the promotion prospects.'

They were saved from further discussion by the door-bell ringing. From her basket under the table Sox began to bark berserkly.

'Who's that?' asked Matt, conscious of being in his dressing gown.

'My mother. I forgot to tell you she's coming to lunch.'

'Oh, great. I was hoping to watch the rugby this afternoon.'

'She'll watch it with you. She likes a nice thigh.'

Matt disappeared discreetly upstairs to change as Elizabeth's ghastly poodle bounded into the room.

'Granola, hi!' Jess flung herself into her grandmother's arms as Bitzer flung himself on to Sox.

'Get down, you disgusting dog!' Elizabeth gave him a swipe with the business news. It was nice and thick with all the news of failing companies. Bitzer yelped.

'Whatever's that?' The rota Ally had pinned to the noticeboard caught Elizabeth's eagle eye.

'Terrible isn't it, Gran? Mum's forcing us to do the housework.' Jess paused dramatically. 'Even Dad.'

Jess had gauged her grandmother's likely reaction with her usual deadly accuracy.

'Allegra! You're not making Matt share the chores, surely?' She stared at her daughter, scandalized, as Ally tried to do eight jobs at once without any offers of assistance. 'I suppose you're trying to turn him into one of these frightful New Men.'

Ally laughed hollowly.

'You musn't, Allegra. He's a charmer. One of the few men I know who're still fun to be with.'

'Oh, yes, Matt's a Real Man all right. You can tell by the fact he's still in his dressing gown at a quarter to one.' Ally stirred the hollandaise while keeping a watchful eye on the salmon poaching gently in its kettle. 'Helping out a little won't do him any harm.'

'Allegra.' Her mother fixed her with a baleful eye as though the object she wore slung round her neck wasn't an oven cloth but an albatross. 'You're changing.'

'Do you really think so, Mum?' Ally looked at her mother brightly. 'I mean you're not just being polite?'

Fortunately her mother's reply was lost due to the arrival of Matt holding his dirty washing.

'The machine's over there, darling.' Ally pointed in the direction of the utility room.

'I know where the washing machine is, Allegra,' Matt rebuked her with an injured air.

'Then why,' Ally said stirring the sauce with unaccustomed vigour, 'are you putting everything in the tumble drier?'

Elizabeth jumped to his rescue. 'Matt, darling, let me do it.'

'Mother, don't!' Ally said, exasperated. 'It's because of mothers like you that men don't know where the kitchen is.'

'Elizabeth, I didn't see you there,' Matt lied, allowing her to take the washing out of his hands and stuff it into the washing machine. 'How are the new gnashers?' Ally watched her mother melt in the warmth of Matt's interest in her false teeth. 'Giving you any problems?'

Ally raised her eyes to heaven as they settled down for a detailed discussion. Matt was amazing. He could be utterly selfish all morning then charm the socks off her mother because he remembered to ask about her dentures. Men!

'Jess, could you lay the table and give Janey a shout?'

Ally lifted the salmon out of its kettle and tried to manoeuvre it, using two egg slices, on to the flat dish she'd been warming in the Aga.

'Oh, Mum, why don't you let her sleep? She'll only lecture us about inflicting pain on God's dumb creatures.'

'But it's a salmon! They're cold-blooded.'

'Now, Mum' – Jess did a perfect imitation of Janey at her most ecomaniac – 'fish have feelings, too.'

Ally sat down at one end of the huge ash table and

watched as Matt busied himself with opening the wine. Why was it that men assumed some household tasks were masculine yet they wouldn't touch others with a barge pole? She'd once considered writing a thesis on 'Men and Carving' after reading that Victorian men always carved in their own homes, but if they had a mistress she carved for them. Carving, as well as inserting corkscrews into the necks of bottles, clearly had some mysterious sexual connotation.

When they'd finished the salmon Ally served the pudding. Matt turned to his mother-in-law. 'So, Elizabeth, what do you think about this decision of Ally's to go back to work?'

Elizabeth nearly choked on her mouthful of the crème brûlée that Ally had knocked up the day before the assertiveness course. 'Darling, you're not thinking of getting a job? What about Matt and the girls?'

Ally glared at Matt. She'd been meaning to work up to this. 'I'm sure they'll survive.'

'Besides,' Elizabeth said, feeling the Brie to see if it was runny enough for her demanding tastes, 'What on earth could you do?'

Ally remembered how little interest her mother had ever taken in any of her achievements. All her friends' progress had been praised to the sky while Ally's was greeted with a raised eyebrow of boredom.

'Thanks, Muv.' Ally began banging the plates as she gathered them up. 'I knew I could rely on your encouragement.'

Chapter 5

'OK, so let's list your talents.' Susie sat poised with pencil and pad.

Ally's mind became a blank. What *were* her talents? She couldn't think of a single marketable skill. 'I'm not sure I have any.'

'Yes, you do.' Jess glanced up from the agony page of *Cosmo*. 'You make a fab crème brûlée and your hospital corners are beyond compare.'

Ally burst out laughing. 'Well, that's a start. Maybe I should run the catering department in a five-star nursing home.'

'Let's go back to basics. Training?'

'As a journalist. Nineteen years ago.'

'Did you learn shorthand?'

'Yes, but I've forgotten it.'

'You could brush it up. Right. Shorthand. Anything else?'

'Well, there was my stint reading the news at MidWest TV, and when Jess went to school I did a marriage guidance course.'

'Did you now?' Susie was fascinated. 'I didn't know that. Has it helped?'

'Oh, yes, tremendously. Now I know the technical name for everything that's wrong with our marriage.'

Susie giggled. 'Right. I think I've got enough here to do the CV.'

'But you've got hardly any facts.'

'Facts?' Susie stood up. 'What do facts matter? I used to be in PR, remember? Come on, Jess, show me how to work your precious computer.'

When Susie handed Ally a copy of the CV she and Jess had put together an hour later, Ally could hardly believe it. Somehow Susie had taken all her ancient and patchy experience and made Ally sound almost high-powered. Even her time out to look after her children and run a home came across like useful practical training.

'Susie, you're a genius!' She hugged her friend, feeling a sudden wave of excitement. 'I almost sound employable!'

'You *are* almost employable. Remember what Barbara said on the course? You come over much more confident than you think you do. Now, the big question is' – she waved the CV triumphantly – 'which lucky employers are we going to send this to?'

Matt drove towards Century Television and wondered how Ally would get on with her search for a job. They'd talked over what she might do for days. Ally had decided she liked the sound of local arts administration or something to do with museums. His own advice had been that she try and work one or two days for a charity. They were always eager for celebrity input, especially if it was free. But Ally had said she wanted a proper job with a salary, no matter how small.

It had been nearly three weeks since she'd sent off her CVs and as far as he knew she hadn't had any replies. It was a competitive field and he hoped she wasn't going to be in for a disappointment.

Matt pressed the button for the roof to open, letting the brilliant summer sunshine in. He knew there was something deep in him which he hadn't dared admit about all this. He rather liked having Ally at home.

As he joined the stream of traffic on the main road into town he reached into his pocket for his sunglasses. Matt always liked to drive himself, but this was where the traffic jams started and being stuck for half an hour with the occupants of every other car shouting, 'Matt! Matt, it is you, isn't it Matt?' tended to get a bit wearing. On the whole he was lucky with his fans. Mostly they were female and turned up to watch every show, hoping he'd catch their eye or remember their names. He tried to make a point of having a quick chat with them, knowing it would make their day and didn't cost him much. But the adulation, and the odd pair of knickers with a phone number written on them that arrived in the post, was just a source of amusement.

He turned his mind away from his faithful followers to a much more worrying problem: how to prevent Danny Wilde winning even more of their viewers. One thing he'd noticed was that Danny Wilde had endless trailers for his show on Big City Television, yet Matt had hardly any. Maybe he'd ask Stephen Cartwright, Century's Director of Programmes, and his wife to dinner soon. He could lobby him discreetly about giving Matt more exposure. Then there was the small question of what to do about livening up the show and persuading Bernie Long to agree to do it.

After Matt and the children had left Ally sat over her coffee and ringed the jobs in the paper that sounded faintly interesting. It might be worth applying for as many as possible to try and get some interviews just for the practice. Being interviewed for jobs wasn't something she had much experience of.

She sighed briefly, trying to hang on to her optimism. For three weeks now she'd rushed down to meet the post each morning and there'd been nothing. Not even a rejection letter or an acknowledgement. Only you, she told herself, could decide to get a job right in the middle of the biggest recession in fifty years.

Shaking off these defeatist thoughts, she packed the dishwasher and reached for her writing pad to send off a few more applications.

Matt was on his way to see Bernie to try and persuade him to make some changes when he heard a voice hissing at him from the photocopying room round the corner from Bernie's office.

From behind the door Belinda appeared, in a short cream suit, beckoning him in. She was holding a file to her chest and looking round nervously. When Matt was inside she closed the door behind him.

'What are we planning?' Matt found this cloak-and-dagger stuff uncomfortable. 'The October Revolution?'

Belinda relaxed a little. 'It's these bloody open-plan offices. There's no privacy anywhere. Most people use the ladies' loo but I could hardly drag you in there, could I? I've been doing some thinking about your idea of revamping the format. Giving it more edge.' She handed him a piece of paper.

Matt read it briefly. There were some dramatically different ideas about how the show could go and instantly he saw they were impressive, that she'd understood Matt's restlessness and played to his strengths.

'Listen, Matt, I know Bernie Long's your friend and you've been together for years, but he's past it.' Belinda dropped her voice a little. 'He'll never agree to any of this. I think we should bypass him and go straight to Stephen.'

Matt handed her back the paper. 'There are some terrific ideas here. But I'm not prepared to shaft Bernie. I'd rather try and talk him round. I know you think he's crap, but his instincts are the best in the business.'

'OK.' Belinda knew she didn't have any choice. She needed Matt on her side. 'But I think you should start soon. We don't want to lose this head of steam.' She looked down at the sheet of paper in her hand. She had stayed up all night writing it. 'Would you like a photocopy?'

As she leaned over to put the paper in the machine she stopped for a moment and touched his arm. 'We understand each other, Matt. We think the same way. We could make the show the most exciting thing on television.'

Matt's eyes held hers for a moment. She had so much conviction. So much certainty. He wasn't used to women like her who knew what they wanted and demanded it. But he admired her for it.

She was now standing so close that he could almost feel the warmth of her body. When he breathed he could smell the musky waves of her perfume.

'Yes,' he said softly. 'Yes, I know.'

'Good.' Belinda smiled slowly, her wide mouth curving upwards in a sensual arc. 'As long as that's settled.'

She turned away, suddenly brisk and efficient, and opened the door, forgetting her proposal was still in the machine.

'Belinda?' Matt caught her just in time.

'Yes, Matt?'

'Hadn't you better pick up your photocopy?' His eyes were teasing. 'You never know who might read it otherwise.'

Belinda turned, flustered. She was horrified that she had nearly left so secret a document where anyone could find it. Reluctantly she smiled, conscious that Matt had quietly taken back the power in the situation. It wasn't something she was used to.

'I've got an interview!' Ally danced round the kitchen waving the letter at Matt and the girls. 'I've finally got an interview!'

'Great stuff.' Matt reached out to have a look at the letter, smiling. 'What's it for?'

'Publicity officer for English Inheritance.'

Jess crowded over her mother's shoulder. 'Aren't they the people who manage the stately homes and stuff? Wow, Janey, you'll be able to have your eighteenth birthday do in a castle!'

'Hang on a minute.' Ally ruffled Jess's hair affectionately. 'It's only an interview.'

'But when they meet you and find out how lovely and talented you are . . .' Jess gestured expressively.

'And who your husband is,' Janey added cynically.

'. . . you're *bound* to get it!'

'I'm not telling them who my husband is, as a matter of fact,' Ally reproved her. 'I've applied in my single name.'

'Good for you, Mum,' applauded Janey. 'Pulling strings is really naff.'

'Oh, I don't know.' Jess grinned. 'I'm thinking of changing my name by deed poll to Jessica, daughter of Matt, like they do in the Old Testament.'

'You would, too, brown-nose. When's the interview?'

Ally grabbed the letter back from Matt. 'Two weeks on Tuesday at two thirty.'

'That rings a bell.' Matt got out his diary. 'I knew it sounded familiar. That's the day Stephen and Patsy are coming to dinner. Do you want me to try and move them?'

Ally thought about it. 'Don't worry. It'll take my mind off the interview. Anyway it won't last more than an hour. It'll be fine.'

'If you're sure. It is quite important.'

'You never know.' She kissed the top of his head, feeling happier than she had for weeks. 'I might feel like celebrating. I may not get the job but it's a first step, all the same, isn't it?'

★

For the next two weeks, every time Matt came home, Ally was up to her ears in brochures on English Inheritance.

'Do you want me to ask you questions?' Matt teased pouring himself a drink. 'Who was the architect who built Castle Drogo? How many visitors tramp across Land's End? Should the Druids be allowed on Stonehenge?'

'Pass.' Ally stretched out and took his hand. 'Hey, aren't you going to offer me a drink too?'

'Sorry, I thought you needed a clear head. How are you feeling?'

'Torn between trying to mug up every known fact about English Inheritance and keeping my brain free to be spontaneous and ready for dealing with the unexpected.'

'I'm sure you'll be wonderful.' He grinned disreputably. 'And if you don't get the job you'll still have me.'

'Yes.' Ally removed the evening paper from his clutches and sat on his knee. 'But is it enough?'

When she woke up the next morning Ally found Matt standing beside the bed pouring out a cup of morning tea. She opened her eyes wide. 'Have I died and gone to heaven?'

Matt ignored her. 'You better have a proper breakfast this morning. Bacon and eggs. Fried bread. Build you up for the day ahead.'

'Matt, it's nearly August!'

'My mother made us a cooked breakfast three hundred and sixty-five days a year.'

'She would. *And* won the contest for the cleanest dustbins.'

Matt started getting dressed. 'You haven't forgotten about Stephen and Patsy tonight in all the excitement?'

'Of course not. What time are they coming?'

'About seven thirty.'

Ally lay back for a moment, mentally planning the day. She was going to serve a vegetable terrine which was time-consuming to make but looked stunning with three different bands of colour. She could easily knock it off this morning. The pudding was in the freezer, and she'd cooked the lamb in filo pastry yesterday and it would only need to be heated up.

Then there was the interview. She'd need to leave about twelve thirty. She hated being in a last-minute rush. Matt was always telling her she arrived at airports so early she could catch the flight before. Feeling nervous but determined to do her best, she leaped out of bed.

But the morning didn't turn out quite as expected. As soon as Matt and the girls were out of the front door, the side door opened and her mother arrived with advice on how to conduct the interview, from what to wear to insisting that Ally tell them she didn't really need the money so she'd at least be cheap.

By the time Ally finally got rid of her it was eleven o'clock. Trying to keep calm, she assembled the carrots, leeks and spinach for the terrine and started to look for the gelatine. That was when Susie arrived with a good luck card and a bunch of flowers. Being Susie, she tactfully announced she'd only stay five minutes and left an hour later. It was almost time to go.

Telling herself there'd be plenty of time later, Ally went up to change. By the time the taxi arrived to take her to the station she was standing ready in the hall, conservatively – but not too conservatively – suited and grateful that at least she hadn't had time for an attack of nerves.

From Waterloo Station it was only a short tube ride to Savile Row, where English Inheritance had their offices. She killed the last ten minutes walking up and down admiring the dark and atmospheric interiors of the tailors' shops. If you wanted to know Prince Charles's inside leg

72

measurement, you were bound to find it in one of these establishments.

And then it was time to go in.

'So, what's she like?' Patsy Cartwright, Stephen's ultra-direct American wife, looked over the top of her menu. They were at Le Caprice, just round the corner from Ally's interview. She'd come up to do some shopping and prevailed on Stephen to take her to lunch. 'I've only smiled at her at parties but never really chatted.'

'Who?' Stephen was engrossed in the starters.

'Allegra Boyd. Our hostess tonight.'

'Quite charming.' Stephen helped himself to another glass of Perrier. 'Not the bolshy type.'

Patsy grinned. 'Unlike me, you mean?'

'Unlike you,' agreed Stephen, laughing. Patsy hated business occasions, loathed always having to be polite and say the right thing. And most of all she loathed the assumption that because she was at home she had nothing whatever to contribute to any conversation.

'Sounds like a wild evening.'

'Oh, come on. Matt's good company. Half the women in England would happily swap places with you.'

'Yes,' said Patsy, deciding on the monkfish in pastry with a saffron sauce, 'but I'm in the half that wouldn't.'

'You wait. You'll adore him. He has the most extra-ordinary effect on women.'

'A good old-fashioned chauvinist, you mean? I doubt it,' Patsy replied crisply, sipping her glass of chilled Chardonnay. 'I loathe men who have the most extra-ordinary effect on women.'

'That's why you love me.'

'Now, now.' She put down her glass and blew him a kiss. 'Stop fishing.'

★

To Ally's amazement and delight the interview seemed to be going well. The man interviewing her was young and charming and not at all forbidding. They'd chatted about her interest in architecture and conservation (Janey had briefed her on that one) and the kind of ideas she might think of to promote English Inheritance at home and abroad. Ally had resisted the temptation to look at her watch twice, but when she finally did, pretending to search for something in her bag, she realized she had been there for an hour and a half.

Was she imagining it, or did he seem really impressed with her? When he finally stood up and she assumed the interview was over, he took her by surprise by suggesting they drop in on an exhibition English Inheritance was holding at the Royal Academy.

By the time she finally said goodbye it was after four thirty. All the way home she fought back the soaring fantasy that she might actually get the job. As she got off the train, she wished Stephen and Patsy were coming another night after all. There was no way she felt like struggling with a fiddly vegetable terrine. She'd much rather call Susie and meet her for a quick drink. Heading for a phone box she called her up and made the arrangement, then dived into Marks & Spencer and headed for the deli section. There, in all its glory, was a three-coloured vegetable terrine, complete with a pack of orange and yellow nasturtium flowers for a garnish and a pouch of ready-made fresh tomato sauce. St Michael be praised! The patron saint of working women. And, who knows, she might soon be one of them.

As soon as Ally got back she took the crème brûlée out of the freezer and turned on the oven. Then she opened a bottle of white wine and poured herself a glass. She'd already had half a bottle with Susie but what the hell? She was feeling good about herself. As she unpacked the shopping bags she glanced at the kitchen clock. There'd be no time for a bath. On the other hand she'd enjoyed her debriefing session and Susie seemed to think the signs were promising.

She'd just finished unpacking the last bag when she heard Matt open the front door. He put down his brief-case and came through to the kitchen. He kissed her briefly. 'What's that? You don't think they'll be offended, getting shop-bought food?'

'Darling!' Ally sounded scandalized. 'Marks & Spencer doesn't count. Everybody does it.' She felt the anger rising in her and she took a large sip of wine. 'I have been a bit busy today, you know.'

The gist of her remark suddenly hit him. 'Ally. My God! I'm sorry, love. How was it?'

'As a matter of fact' – Ally put up her chin and refilled her glass – 'it went rather well. Now for God's sake do something useful. They'll be here in half an hour.'

'Don't tell me you've forgotten the bloody address!' Stephen barked at Patsy irritably, peering at the map as he pulled the car out of the traffic and on to the grass verge. They were going to be late, dammit.

'*I've* forgotten the address?' Patsy stared at her husband in disbelief. 'He's your colleague, not mine. Why should I have their address?'

'Oh, terrific.' Stephen had left work late, trying to make up time after meeting Patsy for lunch and this was the result. 'And they won't even be in the bloody phone book. Now what are we going to do?'

'I don't know. There's no point shouting at me. I'm not your secretary.'

'No,' agreed Stephen. 'My secretary would have had the bloody address. *She*'s efficient. Anyway, I want to shout at someone.'

'Look, Stephen, you're in a lousy mood because you wanted to watch *Inspector Morse* and you know Matt Boyd wants to lobby you about something. I don't suppose it occurred to you that I might have wanted to stay in tonight too? Now for God's sake there's a phone box. Ring your wretched secretary. If she's so bloody efficient she'll have Matt's address.'

Stephen stopped the car and headed for the phone box.

Thirty seconds later he was back. 'Have you got any ten p's?'

Patsy rolled her eyes and delved in her bag. They were already nearly half an hour late. Five minutes later Stephen got back into the car and turned on the engine.

'So? Did she have it?'

'No.' Stephen grated the gears as he changed up. 'But she suggested I ring Century's security and they had it. They didn't want to give it to me, either. I had to answer all sorts of ludicrous questions first.'

'I'm sure Matt would appreciate that, even if you don't. How far is it?'

'About a mile down this road. I don't suppose you've remembered the wine, have you?'

'Stephen darling, you don't take a bottle of plonk to dinner with a man who earns half a million a year. I've brought a bunch of flowers for Allegra.'

Stephen turned off the road into Matt's driveway, tight-lipped and silent. Patsy really could be a superior bitch when she wanted. It was going to be a great evening.

Chapter 6

The moment Ally opened the front door she knew instinctively that Patsy and Stephen had just quarrelled. There was something about their stiffness, the way they didn't look at each other. When Stephen put his hand on Patsy's elbow to guide her into the house she moved it away fractionally. It reminded Ally of the countless times she and Matt had done the same thing. Once, she remembered, they'd been to a dinner party where every couple round the table had quarrelled on the way.

The reason was nearly always the same. Whether they'd left too late, got lost or forgotten the address it was always somehow the woman's fault. Just like it was in the rest of life. Men, in Ally's experience, had the unerring capacity to blame someone else, usually women.

'Stephen, Patsy. How nice to see you.' Matt ushered them in. 'You know my wife Allegra, of course.'

Ally took their coats and hung them on the hooks in the hall.

'So sorry we're late,' apologized Stephen. 'We –'

'I know.' Ally knew she shouldn't say it but couldn't resist it. 'You had a fight in the car. Did you forget the address?'

Patsy and Stephen shot a glance at each other. 'How did you guess?'

'It happens to us all the time, doesn't it, Matt? We invited one couple to dinner who never made it out of the car park under their flat. She criticized the way he nearly hit a pillar and that was that.'

'At least we made it.' Patsy giggled and put out a hand to Stephen. After a second's pause he took it and kissed it.

'Come on.' Ally gestured towards the sitting room. 'Let's go in and have a drink.'

In the sitting room Ally reached for the bottle of champagne she'd put in a cooling bucket.

'How lovely.' Patsy held out a glass. 'Are we celebrating something?'

'I went for an interview today.'

'And did you get the job?'

'God knows.' Ally laughed and poured into the other three glasses. 'I'm just celebrating daring to try.'

Patsy seemed surprised. 'Well, here's to you, then.'

Ally raised her glass. 'To me. The new confident Allegra. If she lasts.'

Matt glanced at her, puzzled. He didn't know what had got into Ally tonight. She was almost like another person. Flirtatious and daring. It wasn't that he didn't like it. It was just that she didn't seem quite like his wife.

Ally got up and went into the kitchen. Patsy followed her.

'Can I help?' She looked at the terrine laid out beautifully with its orange sauce and yellow nasturtium flowers. 'How amazing! It must have taken hours.'

Ally felt slightly guilty. 'To tell you the truth, I bought the lot in M & S. Even the nasturtiums!'

Patsy burst out laughing. 'How brilliant! I loathe cooking. I'm much more impressed than if you'd slaved for hours over a hot hob.'

They smiled conspiratorially and as she went off to tell Matt and Stephen they were ready to eat, Patsy decided she liked Allegra Boyd a lot more than she'd expected to.

After that the meal went off smoothly and pleasantly. Ally had a long conversation with Stephen for the first time and was surprised to find how human he was. Underneath the tough manager there was even a streak of vulnerability. It was ten o'clock by the time they finished and Ally suggested coffee outside.

Matt wandered off with Stephen to show him the garden while Patsy and Ally sat under a huge bower of jasmine.

'I didn't know Matt was a gardener.'

'He's not.' Ally handed her a brandy. 'He just wants to talk Stephen into giving the show some more trailers.'

'Ah.' Patsy nodded. 'Stephen thought it must be something like that. Funny creatures, men. All these power games. Why don't they come straight out and ask?'

'That'd be admitting weakness.'

'Oh, well. We can't have that, can we?' Patsy stretched and looked up at the stars. 'What an incredible night. So, Mrs Boyd, you've got life sorted out. Beautiful house, lovely kids, famous husband. Life must be a bed of roses.'

Ally laughed. She knew some people would have been shocked at Patsy's manner, but she rather liked it.

'Oh, it is, it is. Except that Matt forgets I exist most of the time and the lovely kids will have gone soon and they think I fuss too much over them. I'm overprotective and underemployed according to Jess. Hence the job interview today.'

'Have you never worked?' Patsy didn't make it sound like a criticism.

'Oh, yes. Funnily enough I started life as a trainee newscaster, the youngest on record. I read the bulletins for MidWest TV. That's how Matt and I met.' She smiled at the thought. 'I was a big noise in the Midlands. People used to ask *me* for my autograph. For a whole year I was more famous than Matt.'

'So you were a TV star!'

'Yes, I even opened supermarkets.'

'What happened?'

'Children, I suppose. After Janey they still wanted me back, which was pretty unheard of, but then I got pregnant with Jess and Matt got his job offer in London. After that he was so successful it seemed silly for me to work. He needed a bolthole from all that pressure and we were it.'

'You didn't think of running a dress shop or getting into interior design like the other wives? You can't move in our street for housewives running a little business. Nothing too strenuous – they've got to get their nails polished, after all. I'm the only genuinely lazy slob left around.'

Ally grinned. She really liked Patsy. 'Oh, yes. I had my little crack at independence. Don't laugh. When Jess went to school I trained to be a marriage guidance counsellor.'

'How fascinating!' Patsy leaned forward confidentially. 'And did you ever practise?'

'For a while. And I loved it. Everyone cries on my shoulder anyway. It's something about my face.'

'Why did you give it up?'

'People kept finding out who my husband was. One client worked it out halfway through telling me about his sex problems. And do you know what he did?'

'I have no idea,' said Patsy, riveted.

'He gave me his copy of *Premature Ejaculation: The Facts* and asked if Matt could autograph it.'

Patsy laughed so much that her eyes started watering. What a wonderful woman Allegra was! She'd had no suspicion of this wicked sense of humour.

Suddenly Ally felt self-conscious at talking about herself so much. She raised her glass to Patsy. 'Enough about me. What about you? What's it like being married to the big boss?'

Patsy stirred her coffee. 'So-so. We're very happy when we're together but I hardly ever see him.' Patsy was surprised at herself for telling Ally this. She wasn't normally the confessional type. But somehow she knew she could trust Ally. 'I must admit I'm not exactly a haven for him. More a thorn in his side. Not much of a company wife. They bore me rigid at Century. They think television's a matter of life and death.'

'Tch, tch,' chided Ally. 'I can see you've got the wrong attitude. It's far more important than that!' She leaned a fraction closer. 'Did you never consider having children?'

A shadow of pain crossed Patsy's face so quickly covered by a smile that Ally wondered if she'd imagined it.

'Do you remember when W. C. Fields was asked how he liked children and he said "fried"? I'm a bit like that.'

'Are you?' Ally said. 'I'm surprised. You seem such a warm, funny person I'd have thought you'd have loved them.'

Patsy was taken aback. No one had challenged her stance before. She gazed down into her drink for a moment. 'Actually,' she said, 'we couldn't have any. We tried everything. Tests, laparoscopy, even IV fertilization. Zilch. And the worst thing is it wasn't Stephen. It was me. They told him his sperm could have swum the Atlantic.' She smiled ironically. 'But not up my cunt.'

The four-letter word seemed out of character, but Ally saw immediately that it was designed to shock as a way of deadening the pain. Without thinking she stretched out her hand and Patsy briefly squeezed it, suddenly aware that Ally was the first person outside her family she'd ever told.

When Matt appeared from behind the yew hedge seconds later it was almost a relief. He seemed pleased. Stephen must have come up with the goods.

He sat down and poured a cup of coffee for himself and Stephen. 'So, love,' he said. 'How did the interview go?'

'Yes, do tell,' encouraged Patsy.

'Well, actually, they seemed rather to like me.'

'Don't sound so surprised!' Patsy shook her head. 'You English girls undersell yourselves. They should have snapped you up on the spot.'

Ally thought of Barbara, her assertiveness teacher. She put up her chin and smiled. 'Maybe they will.'

'Patsy, love' – Stephen pointed to his watch – 'it's time we went.'

They stood up and Matt and Ally saw them to their car and waved as they disappeared down the drive.

'What a revelation Allegra Boyd was.' Patsy pressed the button to recline her seat and snuggled in comfortably. Stephen might have his shortcomings but at least he always drove home. 'What a wonderful woman. She's so warm and witty but spiky and fun, too. Do you know she used to be a TV star and gave it up when she had the babies?' Patsy's voice rang with finely tuned outrage at female oppression. 'I call that a damn shame. I hope she gets this job.'

Stephen, who had been thinking about Matt's request for more trailers, nodded without listening. 'You two seemed very thick. What were you talking about?'

'Oh, girlie things. How we lost our virginity, the size of our husbands' organs.'

Stephen smiled as he turned off the main road. Patsy enjoyed being outrageous.

'Actually,' Patsy continued quietly, 'she even managed to worm it out of me that I'm yearning for a little bundle to be sick on my shoulder and keep me awake at night.'

Stephen reached over and took her hand. 'Did she? I've never heard you tell anyone that.'

'No.' Patsy felt faintly embarrassed at the memory. 'She probably thinks I'm the type that tells everyone on the bus how many abortions I've had.'

'I'm sure she doesn't.' Stephen squeezed her hand in

sympathy. He knew exactly how his brave and spunky wife went about burying what she saw as her tragedy with wisecracks.

'I guess it's because she's so easy to talk to.'

Stephen glanced across at Patsy to see if she had cheered up. 'I know. I ended up telling her about my insomnia.' He slowed down so as not to miss the turn-off. 'Pity they can't find someone like her for *Hello*.' He looked over his shoulder at the traffic approaching from his right. 'Did I tell you that cretin Bill Ford hasn't managed to find an agony aunt yet?'

'Hasn't he?' As she sat in the warm darkness, curled up against the fragrant leather of the seats, an idea occurred to Patsy Cartwright. She had warmed to Matt Boyd more than she'd expected, but like most men he took his wife too much for granted. What he could do with was a bit of a shake-up. And she'd just thought of a perfect way to do it.

Ally skipped down to the front door when she heard the postman as she'd done every day since the interview.

There was a large pile of bills, shrink-wrapped copies of winter-break holiday brochures even though it was August and mailshots telling you you'd been selected from six million people to come and view a timeshare in Majorca. There at the bottom was a smart vellum envelope with a crest stamped on it. Ally picked it up and took it into the kitchen.

Matt was already at the table eating a muffin with honey on it. He looked up. 'Is it about the job?'

Ally nodded, slitting the envelope open with the bread knife. Holding her breath she read the letter, admitting to herself for the first time how much she was hoping to be offered it.

It was short and to the point. Ally had done an excellent

interview but one of the other candidates had more recent experience relevant to the job.

She sat down, fighting back the tears. It had been ludicrous to hope she'd find a job so easily. But she had.

'No good?' Matt asked. He picked up the letter.

Jess abandoned the *Daily Telegraph* financial page and put her arms around her mother.

'It's their loss,' threw in Janey. 'Silly people. I never wanted my party in a castle anyway.'

Ally smiled and pulled herself together, cheered by their sympathy. 'Well, I've always got you, haven't I?'

'Come on, Mum, don't give up.' Jess kissed the top of her mother's head. 'Something else'll come along.'

'Tell you what.' Matt put the letter back in its envelope and stood up. 'Since it's Saturday why don't I take you out to a really nice lunch?'

By the time they got back at the end of the afternoon, warmed by the sun and relaxed by some wonderful Australian wine and delicious food eaten on the secluded terrace of a riverside pub, Ally was feeling more optimistic. She only hoped every employer wouldn't want 'more recent experience'.

Ally was just telling herself that it really was time she did some weeding when she heard the phone ringing.

'Mum,' shouted Jess, who always got to it first even if it had only rung once and sometimes, by some act of teenage ESP, even before it rang, 'it's for you. Patsy Cartwright.'

Ally came inside. 'Patsy, hello.'

'Hi. Thanks for the glorious dinner the other night. And for the tip about the nasturtiums. I'm definitely serving them at our next do.' Patsy laughed. 'Though knowing me that'll be 1995. Say, what happened about the job? Did you get it?'

'No.' Ally tried to pass it off lightly. 'They gave it to someone with more recent experience.'

'And I can guess what at. Creeps! I bet it was a bimbo with a degree in oral sex.'

Ally choked back the laughter. 'Anyway, how are you?'

'Great. I really enjoyed talking to you the other night. As I said to Stephen, for a Brit that girl is pretty good news. She actually talks about her feelings.'

'We're not all stiff upper lips over here, you know.'

'Oh, really? So are you still looking for a job?'

'You bet.'

'OK, I'll keep my eyes open.'

As she put the phone down Patsy gazed at her husband dozing in the garden. This was as good a time to talk to him as any. Even though it almost killed her, she made him a cup of his favourite Earl Grey tea and put it on a tray. She added two Chocolate Bath Oliver biscuits and carried it out into the garden.

Stephen tipped his straw hat from over his face as she approached. 'You look beautiful carrying a tray.'

'Well, don't get used to it, buster. This is a once-only offer.' She sat down in the wicker chair next to his. 'I've been thinking.'

Stephen raised an eyebrow in the direction of the teatray. 'Have you, now? I expect you'll tell me what about in a minute.'

'You said Bill Ford can't find an agony aunt for *Hello*.'

Stephen's face closed up with irritation. 'No, he can't. Why? Have you had one of your inspirations?'

Stephen had learned to respect Patsy's suggestions. She pretended to disparage British television and laugh at its pretensions to be the best in the world, but secretly she watched far more than he did. And she had a brilliant eye. A couple of times she'd spotted a newcomer who'd turned out to be a terrific find for Century. And they'd even managed to get them while they were still cheap.

'As a matter of fact I have.' She handed him a chocolate biscuit. 'Mind it doesn't melt on your white suit, darling. What do you think about Allegra Boyd?'

'What do you mean, what do I think about her? She seems a nice woman, warm, sympathetic. What are you getting at?'

'For *Hello*, I mean,' Patsy said, shaking her head in exasperation.

Stephen turned to look at his wife amazed. 'Patsy, darling, Allegra Boyd's a housewife. She's had no television experience.'

'Oh, yes she has.' Patsy loathed it when Stephen used that tone to her. It was his male-chauvinist-shitbag voice. 'As a matter of fact she started off as a newsreader. She told me after dinner.' Patsy played her trump card. 'And she used to be a marriage guidance counsellor. She'd be perfect!'

Stephen went quiet for a moment. Patsy smiled at her husband patiently. She hadn't listened to him talking through his endless work problems without getting a very thorough understanding of how his mind worked.

'Stephen, just think . . .'

'About what?'

'About all the lovely publicity you'd get if you hired Mrs Matt Boyd to be your agony aunt.'

Stephen thought about it. All the things Patsy had said about Allegra Boyd were true. She was warm and funny without being daunting. And they had wanted someone different. For a moment he wondered what Matt would think of the idea. Well, screw Matt for once. He was being a pain in the arse anyway.

'Do you know, Patsy my darling, you might be right?

I'll call Bill Ford. That should ruin his weekend. He'll have to do some work for once and ring her up.'

'Of course I'm right, sweetheart.' Patsy leaned over and kissed him. 'I'm always right. What on earth would you do without me?'

As she sat toasting pleasantly in a garden chair surrounded by the Sunday papers, Ally heard her mother's car turn into the drive and wished that they hadn't got into the habit of having her round quite so often for Sunday lunch lately. It had been pleasant the first few times, and they'd all had the reassuring impression that they were a real family like you saw in France. But maybe the average French granny was less free with her opinions on the shortcomings of everything from shop-bought mayonnaise to Jess's appalling table manners. Ally was going to have to fix up some Sunday events they couldn't cancel.

'Hello, Mother.' Bitzer barked as her mother got out of the car and handed Ally an armful of runner beans. She'd loathed runner beans since childhood. 'How are you?'

'Terrible. A martyr to my dentures.'

Gratefully, Ally saw Matt appear from the house. He could deal with the denture update.

'I'll just put the beans on. Would you like a drink?'

'G. and T. No ice or lemon.' Ally mixed a strong gin and poured in warm tonic water the way her mother liked it. She sipped it and shuddered. But then her mother's generation always liked their chotapegs powerful, gin and It, dry Martinis so strong you could strip paint with them.

In the hall the phone rang. Matt, who'd come in to get Elizabeth's drink, answered it.

'It's for you, Jess,' he shouted up the stairs. 'Someone called Jeremy. He wants to know if you can go to some disco tonight.'

Jess's head appeared at the top of the banisters. 'Oh, God, yuk. Dad, tell him I'm dead. Bubonic plague. Came on suddenly in the night.'

'Jess,' Ally chided, 'you like Jeremy. He's always ringing you up.'

'Correction, ma. He likes *me*,' Jess shouted back. 'Feminists such as myself do not like boys. We find them gauche, tedious and only interested in one thing. And unfortunately that's Nintendo. Tell him I'll ring him back.' She disappeared towards her bedroom. 'In two weeks.'

'Jess, you're horrible to that boy!' Ally said when Jess finally came down to lunch, which Ally had laid out on the garden table.

'I know,' smirked Jess, pinching a prawn from the salad, 'and do you know? It only makes him keener. He'll ring back in five minutes, you'll see.'

'That's appalling. That sort of manipulation went out with the fifties.'

'No, it didn't.' Elizabeth toasted her granddaughter approvingly. 'I use it all the time. I can still get doors opened just using my eyelashes.' She blinked seductively, looking like Marlene Dietrich in drag.

'You should try using your hand,' Matt advised. 'It's much easier.'

Jess stifled a giggle as the phone went again.

'Go on, Mum. Pleeease. I promise I'll ring him back.'

'No, you won't. You'll talk to him now,' commanded Ally, imagining poor Jeremy's ritual humiliation.

Jess picked up the mobile phone in the hall and brought it outside. 'Oh, hi, Jeremy. I'm afraid a disco's out. I can't stand all that rapping. The cinema?' She winked at her grandmother. 'There's not much on though, is there? All those ghastly films about adolescents discovering sex. I'm afraid I've got to go now. We're in the middle of

88

lunch and my father's very big on table manners. Catch you later.'

Ally shuddered at the cruelty of youth and was glad that sort of thing was firmly behind her.

Jess, skinny as half a rake, had second helpings and was contemplating thirds.

'Jess, you are disgusting.'

'Think of all the starving millions, Mum. Better not to waste it. Is there any more chicken?'

Ally smiled, remembering how she'd said the same thing once about the starving millions to Janey when she wouldn't eat her dinner. Kind-hearted Janey had gone away, put it in an envelope and sent it off to Oxfam.

This time when the phone went Matt tutted in irritation and refused to answer it. 'For God's sake, Jess, this boy's turning into a phone pest!' He passed the mobile phone to her. 'Tell him to ring back when we've finished lunch at least.'

Looking disgracefully superior, Jess picked up the phone. 'Hi, Jeremy, it's Jess. OK, let's make it a cappuccino tomorrow.'

The voice on the other end of the phone sounded puzzled and Jess listened for a moment, confused.

'Actually, it's for you, Mum.' She held the phone towards her mother. 'Someone called Bill Ford from Century Television. He says Stephen Cartwright suggested he ring.'

Ally shot a quizzical look at Matt, who shrugged his shoulders.

What on earth would Century Television want with her?

Chapter 7

'Sorry, could you repeat that?' It struck Ally that it might be Susie on the other end of the phone staging some elaborate joke to liven up their Sunday. 'You want *me* to come and test out as the agony aunt on the *Hello* programme?'

Jess began giggling while Matt looked up from his plate, a look of astonishment in his blue eyes.

'My name's Bill Ford,' explained the voice on the other end of the phone. 'I'm *Hello*'s producer. Stephen Cartwright rang me this morning and asked me to get in touch. Stephen no doubt explained we're looking for someone a bit different, not necessarily a TV professional, to do our advice slot.'

'And Stephen suggested *me*?' Ally was even more incredulous. The call appeared to be genuine. Stephen had given no warning of this bombshell.

'He was very excited about you. He felt we should try you out as soon as possible.'

'Well, I . . .' Ally felt herself at a loss. 'That's very kind of him, but I . . .'

All the reasons why she wouldn't be a good agony aunt flashed through her mind: she had no experience, she was too young, she didn't have enough in common with ordinary people's lives. Surely an agony aunt needed the certainty of a politician and the patience of Mother Theresa?

Across the table she noticed Matt put down his knife and fork, listening intently. Suddenly Ally felt the phone being taken from her hands and Jess was talking.

'Excuse me, but my grandmother's swallowed a chicken

bone and we have to phone the doctor instantly. Could my mother call you back? Thank you so much.'

'That child,' pointed out Elizabeth, 'needs to see a trick cyclist. Outrageous behaviour.'

'Jess,' Ally demanded, trying to get the phone back, 'what on earth are you doing?'

'Mum, you were about to say no. This man Bill Thingy is offering you a chance most people would kill for and you're on the point of saying no thank you, I don't think I will today as though he was trying to sell you insurance.' Jess put the phone down and took her mother's hand. 'Just think about it, Mum. You've been moping ever since you didn't get that job. This could be a hundred times more fun!'

Ally was hit by the logic of what Jess was saying. She did want a job. But dishing out advice on television? She'd probably be terrible. And yet. She'd loved the marriage counselling. She'd felt a real kick whenever she'd sorted a couple out. For a moment she felt an impulse to give it a go, then her old self-doubt began to come trickling back.

'What do you think, Matt?' She looked at her husband, aware that he hadn't spoken. But before he could answer she heard her mother's tinkling laugh, like ice cubes dipped in vinegar Matt had once called it.

'Are they serious?' asked Elizabeth, sipping her wine. 'I mean, I've never heard such a silly idea! You've never been able to sort out your own problems, let alone other people's.'

Ally felt the unfamiliar lick of anger.

'You're right behind me when I need you, aren't you, Muv?' Memories of her mother's constant underestimation of her exploded into irritation. 'You always had such a low opinion of me that if I ever did well I felt I'd let you down.'

Elizabeth gazed at Ally in astonishment, then stood on her dignity. 'Of course it's nothing to do with me. What does Matt think? He's the one who'll be affected.'

As it happened this was the question Matt was already asking himself. He found all three women looking at him.

What *did* he think? It was true that Ally was sympathetic and warm, and that people cried on her shoulder. He was always finding the kitchen full of divorcees and teenagers who couldn't talk to their own parents but stayed till dawn baring their souls over Ally's communal casseroles.

But would she come over on television? And – Matt knew the uncomfortable question had to be faced – did he want her to? Television was *his* world and the family was his haven, his release valve from the pressures of his very public life.

'Do you *want* to be an agony aunt?' he sidestepped neatly.

'Why not? I've always found listening to people fascinating. Maybe I'd enjoy it.'

'What about the TV bit?' Matt realized he shouldn't say what he was about to, but couldn't stop himself. 'It's harder than it looks, you know, persuading people to talk. Not like reading the news for MidWest.'

Ally felt another spurt of anger. Neither of them believed in her. They didn't think she was up to it.

'Well, I think you'd be brilliant! People are always bringing you their problems anyway. This way at least you'd get paid.' Jess put her arm round her mother. 'Come on, Mum, have a crack. You've got nothing to lose. If you're awful they won't use you. You've got to at least have a go. Just think,' she added, like a nanny offering a really special treat, 'you could talk to Dad about work.'

Ally laughed. How well Jess knew her! Oh well, why

not? She'd probably never get the job anyway, and if she didn't try she might spend the rest of her life wondering what would have happened.

'Come on, then.' She grinned at Jess, deliberately not looking at Matt or her mother. 'Pass me the phone.'

'Now listen, Mum. A word of advice before you ring him back.'

'Jess, I'm the one who's supposed to be handing out the advice.'

'I know, but you're no good at being tough. Whatever you do, sound cool. Don't let him think you've been waiting for this call all your life. Play hard to get.'

'Jessy, he isn't asking me out. It's a professional arrangement we're making.' She wished Jess wasn't quite so good at making her feel like a naïve younger sister.

'It's exactly the same, though. The more you want them the less they want you.' She gave Ally the phone and muttered darkly, 'Remember Jeremy.'

It took Ally a moment to work out what Jess was talking about and by then Bill Ford had picked up the phone.

'Hello, Mr Ford. Ally Boyd here. When would you like to do this test?'

'It has to be in the next couple of weeks. Thursday afternoon would suit us.'

Ally visualized her blank diary. 'Sorry, that's out, I'm afraid.'

'Friday, then?'

Friday was as empty as the day is long.

'Sorry, Friday's impossible.'

She made a face at Jess, who was nodding vigorously.

'How about next week?' Ally was amazed at the cool in her voice. 'I can't do Monday or Tuesday but Wednesday's a possibility.'

'Wednesday's the day of our pilot.'

93

'Why don't I test out during that? Wouldn't it be more realistic anyway?' Ally was staggered by her own audacity.

Bill Ford hesitated. She was right. It *would* be more realistic if she tested during the pilot itself. At least then they'd have a chance to see how she got on with Maggy Mann and the other presenters. But it would also leave them with almost no time to find someone else if she was useless. Presumably this was what the tricky bitch was up to. If she hadn't been Stephen's personal suggestion he would have told her to get stuffed. As it was he didn't have a lot of choice. But at least, he consoled himself, if she fell on her face it would be Stephen's responsibility not his. As he said goodbye he realized he rather hoped she would. It would serve Stephen right for interfering.

Ally put down the phone just as Janey, barefoot and sleepy, walked into the garden and held her hand to her eyes against the sudden bright light. Instantly she picked up the unfamiliar strain in the atmosphere.

'What's the matter?' She looked from one face to another. 'Has somebody died?'

'Of course not, dumbo,' Jess giggled. 'Mum's just been asked to audition for a TV programme.'

'Ah.' Janey nodded, immediately understanding. 'That's why everyone's so upset.'

Shamed by Janey's wicked perceptiveness Matt pushed back his chair and jumped up. He pulled Ally to her feet and fastened her in a breathless bearhug. 'And she's going to be bloody brilliant, aren't you, Allegra?'

Jess winked at Janey. 'Another week and he'll be saying it was his idea.'

Finally Ally fought her way out of Matt's embrace, laughing. 'So what do you think about your old Mum being an agony aunt on the telly?'

'Fine.' She reached out her hand to Ally. 'Just as long as you don't start ladling out advice to *me*.'

'I wouldn't dare,' said Ally truthfully.

'So.' Janey picked up a lettuce leaf and nibbled on it. 'Things are going to change around here then.'

'I probably won't get it anyway,' Ally reached out a hand to her daughter. 'I'm sure they'll be trying out loads of people.'

'Come on, Dad,' Jess put her arm round him comfortingly. 'Cheer up. She was bound to throw your slippers in the fire sometime. It's the inexorable march of women's progress.'

'Is that what it is?' Matt ruffled her hair. 'To think that all I was worried about was who was going to make my tea.'

'Mrs O'Shock will. She adores you. She thinks, as male chauvinists go, you're a perfect specimen.'

To Ally's relief, by Monday everyone seemed to have forgotten the whole business. As Matt set out, she waved goodbye from the doorstep, still in her dressing gown, and felt not the usual emptiness but a sense of anticipation. It was another glorious day. She decided to leave the front door open as she went inside, humming to herself, and stopped for a moment as she caught sight of herself in the hall mirror. The jade green velvet of her dressing gown did good things for her skin. Perhaps jade was the colour she should wear for this test?

She laughed, remembering her mother's advice about never wearing a dressing gown after eight thirty. She'd asked her mother about it yesterday, and Elizabeth had revealed it was because people might think you were a tart. Especially if you had make-up on. Her mother really was the most extraordinary woman.

As she picked up the post she stopped for a moment. All the same, it had been so unlike her to snap at her mother as she'd done at lunch yesterday. She never snapped at her mother. But it had been liberating, too. And she realized that already this TV offer, conditional though it was, was having an effect on her. Slowly she smiled. It might be a bit subversive, but she had to admit it was an effect she was enjoying.

'Hello, is that Ally Boyd? It's Bill Ford here. Have you got a moment?'

Ally was halfway through sorting the washing into coloureds, whites and things she wouldn't want Mrs O'Shock within a mile of when the phone had gone.

'Yes, that's fine. Fire away.' Then she remembered she'd better write down what he said. Why was it there was never a paper and pen when you needed it and you ended up scrawling messages in kohl eye pencil on letters from the bank manager?

'The format for the pilot is that we select a reader's letter, then you give the advice partly talking to camera and also chatting with our main presenter, Maggy Mann.'

How original, Ally thought, but didn't say so. She wasn't the producer, he was. And she already sensed a certain veiled resentment. He reminded her faintly of a small boy who had been told to ring his granny when he'd much rather be playing in the garden.

'For the test next week we've chosen a girl suffering from what the shrinks call the Electra syndrome.'

What on earth was that? Ally felt panic rising. Why had she thought she knew enough to advise other people? She'd be exposed as a charlatan. She decided ignorance was the best policy or she'd only end up in trouble.

'What exactly *is* the Electra syndrome?'

'It's what happens when deep-down a girl wants to sleep with her father, and because that's not allowed she screws every married man she can lay her hands on.'

'Oh, fine.' Ally couldn't help smiling at his deadpan tone. 'I've met the type.'

'Perhaps,' Bill Ford said doubtfully, 'you'd better do some research.'

'What time will you need me?'

'Eleven would be fine. We'll send a car.'

'Don't worry, my friend Susie is bringing me.' She paused. 'For moral support. By the way, what shall I wear?'

'Anything you like, sweetheart. Just remember that it's a coffee-time show so leave the sequins at home.' What Ally had in mind was a smart dogtooth check that looked like Chanel but came from Country Casuals. 'The only rules are no blue because it sets off the chromakey.' Ally could tell that, whatever this was, it was serious. 'Oh, and no stripes or checks, they make the camera strobe. Lay off black and white if you can help it. Strong, plain colours are best. Red. Green. Yellow.' So much for the Chanel knock-off. Ally mentally ransacked her wardrobe for strong, plain colours. But Bill Ford hadn't finished yet. 'And no dangly jewellery unless you want to sound like Marley's ghost. Clear?'

As mud, Ally felt like saying.

By the time Matt fought his way through the Monday morning traffic the ideas meeting had already started. When he got out of the lift he found Belinda was waiting for him.

'I've been meaning to ask you. How did it go with Stephen?'

'Fine. He was very receptive. He's going to sort out a trailer every night starting in a couple of weeks.'

'Matt . . .?'

'Yes?'

'We'd better try and have something worth trailing, then.'

97

He knew it was a hint that he hadn't tackled Bernie head on. And she was right. It was time he did.

Everyone looked round when they walked in the room and Matt cursed that he hadn't had the sense to arrive separately. This way it seemed like a conspiracy.

'Bernie, sorry I'm late. I got held up.'

Bernie raised an eyebrow and said nothing while Belinda, deliberately not looking at Matt, sat at the far end of the table. 'OK, but please make more effort.' Seeing who was with Matt, Bernie wanted his pound of flesh. 'These meetings aren't for fun. We were just discussing the line-up for the next couple of weeks. Who's going to set me alight with their guest ideas?'

There was a deafening silence.

Suddenly Matt felt an uncharacteristic flash of depression. Danny Wilde was snapping at his heels because he dared to try the new, while Matt's own producer was terrified of even changing the opening titles in case some granny in Southend preferred them the way they were. The truth was Matt was locked into a show he no longer enjoyed doing. And now even Ally was getting a crack at something new and exciting.

'I've got some ideas, Bernie.' Belinda's voice was friendly and neutral. 'Maybe you'd like to see them?' Matt smiled. In Belinda's terms that was the equivalent of licking his boots.

She passed the sheet of paper over.

Bernie gave it a cursory glance. 'Belinda, how many times do I have to tell you? These people are too heavy. They're just not right for the show.' Even Matt could see that Bernie hadn't really looked at them.

Belinda's face hardened.

'I think they're just right for the show. I think they're what the show needs or it'll be dead on its feet.' She looked up, her dark eyes glinting dangerously. 'And Matt agrees with me, don't you, Matt?'

Chapter 8

Ally woke with a lurch, feeling a sensation of panic as though she were falling in a dream, and sat up. It was six thirty. She never woke at six thirty. And then she remembered. Today was the day of the test.

Matt was sleeping peacefully, his open novel next to him on the bed where it had fallen. What did he think about her testing? For the past week he'd been curiously withdrawn, not talking about the test or about anything much else. She knew he was worried about his own show and hoped that explained his moodiness rather than resentment of her audition.

She realized there was another reason she hadn't really talked to him about it. She feared he might discourage her. And over the last week one thing had taken Ally by surprise: the growing strength of the feeling that she really wanted to do it.

Only yesterday she'd had her biggest buzz in years, going to the medical section of the Marylebone Library to bone up on the Electra syndrome. She'd felt like a student again, excited, carefree. On her way from the underground car park in Russell Square she'd passed a gaggle of sunbathers stripped to bikinis lying like sardines on a pocket handkerchief of grass and had laughed out loud at the wonderful combination of eccentricity and optimism that made up the British temperament.

Inside the library the assistant had dug out a large pile of copies of the *British Psychosexual Journal* plus a vast encyclopedia of psychiatric conditions. As she flipped through the pages of the learned tome, Ally found herself being sidetracked by report after report of people putting their heads in a noose in search of some near-terminal orgasm, peeing on each other without so much as washing their hands afterwards, or tying their lovers up in electrical flex for a lustful lark. Behind their net curtains and their suburban front doors the great British public seemed to be trying it all. Ally had put down the journal and collapsed helplessly with laughter at the extraordinary vagaries of human sexual behaviour. Whether she got the job or not, the research was certainly enlightening.

And then finally she'd found a chapter on the Electra syndrome. She switched her mind for a moment to Jennifer from Birmingham, who went round seducing other people's husbands because they reminded her of Daddy. Bitch, thought Ally. Then she realized being an agony aunt wasn't as easy as it seemed. You couldn't simply jump to conclusions. You had to try and understand *why* people did stupid self-destructive things that threatened to wreck their lives as well as everyone else's. Ally hoped she was up to it.

At lunchtime, clutching her notes, she'd gone to a coffee bar near the University of London Union and sitting there among the foreign students, most of them not much older than Janey, she'd felt young again. Maybe it was because she had a purpose.

And when one of the young men had glanced at her admiringly, she'd even smiled back.

She slipped out of bed and ran a bath. As soon as Matt had left for work, Susie would come to drive her to the studios. She'd turned down Century's offer of a car because driving with Susie's distracting chatter would be less terrifying than an hour on her own in the back of a cab with nothing to take her mind off the ordeal ahead. There was no rush. They didn't want her till eleven.

Ally pulled herself up, and stood naked for a moment as she reached for the shower attachment. She set it to full and turned the dial to blue. Cold water streamed over her breasts making her gasp. Every day since she was eighteen she'd done this and it seemed to have worked. Other bits might not be as firm as they used to be but her boobs wouldn't have shamed a young girl. Suddenly a wave of nervousness swept over her. 'I must, I must,' she echoed the schoolgirl chant, 'not lose my nerve.'

'Hiya, Mum.' Jess was in her dressing gown rifling through the cereal packets like a druggie needing a fix. 'We've run out of chocolate Weetos.'

'Well, have something else. Bran flakes or muesli.'

'Oh, Ma, they're far too healthy. Haven't we got anything that's bad for you?'

'Jess, take this cup of tea up to Dad, would you?'

'Why is it always me who has to do everything?' Jess asked in martyred tones.

'Because you're the extrovert who's always under my feet while Janey shuts herself in her bedroom with The Cure on so loud she can't hear me ask her to do things.'

'Fair enough.' Jess seemed to accept this logic and disappeared upstairs.

To Ally's relief none of them seemed to have remembered the significance of the date. Janey was still fast asleep. As usual she'd been making the most of the summer holidays by staying up till dawn watching videos, no doubt of something highly unsuitable.

Matt gave her a kiss, waved goodbye and drove off. As she stood watching him she felt both relief that she hadn't been teased, but also a pinprick of hurt that her concerns didn't seem to register with anyone in her family.

It was just as well she was looking for something else in her life.

'Hey, you look great! I've never seen you in pink before.'

Ally could see genuine admiration and surprise in Susie's eyes when she came to collect her an hour later.

'Yes. The producer said bright colours. It's funny I never wear bright colours.'

'The producer was right. Mmm. Lipstick, too. Very career woman.'

'Do you think it's too much? I don't want to look like Joan Crawford.'

'Ally,' Susie said patiently, putting her arm round her friend, 'you could never look like Joan Crawford. But you do look fabulous.'

Ally glanced at herself in the mirror as she picked up her car keys and gave them to Susie. And to her surprise she saw her friend was right. She did. Hugging the precious admission to herself she strode out of the house and into the sunlight. Despite her nervousness she had a good feeling about today. And if it turned out to be another disappointment at least she hadn't lost by trying.

'For Christ's sake, who *is* this woman Allegra Boyd?' Maggy Mann, Century's biggest female star, leaned back in the make-up chair and closed her eyes. 'I mean I've never even *heard* of her.' Maggy liked the full treatment. Carmen rollers, false eyelashes. Even if it meant, as it often did, that the rehearsal started late because Maggy wasn't ready to make her entrance.

'I've no idea.' Moira, the show's PA and Maggy's faithful gossip-monger, shook her head until the heavy gold of her necklaces and earrings jangled noisily. 'And neither has anyone else.'

'It's absolutely ludicrous,' Maggy looked up at the make-up girl, a junior she noted with irritation. Why on earth she wasn't allocated the best there was, Elaine, instead of this useless kid she didn't know. 'I suggested my friend Anne Adamson from the *Sunday Examiner* but as usual I was totally ignored. We need someone with a bit of experience, not some raw beginner. What's the betting she's someone that cripple of a producer met at a party and wants to get into bed?'

'He wouldn't dare.' Moira held a tissue out for Maggy to set the scarlet lipstick the make-up girl had just carefully applied. Maggy put it between her lips and opened and closed her mouth, looking to the make-up girl like an overmade-up piranha. 'He's got too much riding on this. Bill Ford's had more pilots than an air hostess. If this one doesn't make a series he's finished.'

'Of course it'll make a series, Moira,' Maggy purred. '*I'm* in it. It's just his choice of agony aunt we're disputing.'

The swing doors opened and Elaine, Century's most respected make-up artist, swept in.

Maggy turned ninety degrees in her chair, so that the girl doing her hair had to turn with her, and swung the full beam of her terrifying charm in Elaine's direction. Elaine had worked here for twenty years. Elaine knew everything.

'Elaine, sweet, you must know something about this Allegra Boyd woman. Who the hell is she?'

Elaine tidied the pots and brushes in her tiered make-up box for a moment. She didn't like Maggy. Maggy was always being girls-together and sympathizing with Elaine about them both being single mothers when their situations couldn't be more different. They both had three kids and no husband. But Maggy had two nannies, an au pair for the evenings and a gem of a cleaning lady from nine to twelve. Elaine did all her own shopping, cleaning and cooking and had three latchkey kids. It was surprising, she told herself, that they'd turned out so well since all she'd been able to give them was love. Maggy's children, on the other hand, had been through family therapy, intermediate treatment and, as a last resort, boarding school. God was clearly in His heaven.

'Yes, I know who she is.'

Maggy put out a restraining hand to stop Elaine wandering off before she told them more. She reminded Elaine of a hungry cuckoo demanding to be fed with the titbits of other people's lives.

'So who is she, then?'

'Allegra Boyd . . .' Elaine spun out the moment of being the only one with this fascinating bit of information for just a fraction longer, '. . . is Matt Boyd's wife.'

Ally pushed her car seat to the reclined position and closed her eyes as Susie drove them both towards Century's studios on Millbank. They'd missed the rush hour. The sun streamed in through the sunshine roof. They had plenty of time to get from Fairlawns to the studios. Ally thought for a moment about reading her notes. No, she wouldn't. She'd only end up sounding like Dr Freud when Bill Ford wanted Dr Ruth.

She smiled and felt herself genuinely relax. This wasn't going to be such an ordeal after all.

Even a faint clunking sound coming from the back of the car didn't disturb her mood. She worried too much. Once she'd nearly had a nervous breakdown because the car started making a peculiar swishing sound and when she'd pulled on to the hard shoulder and opened the door to look she'd found the belt of her mac trailing along the motorway.

'Ally –' She opened her eyes with a start as Susie spoke. She must have dropped off. 'What's that noise?'

The sound was louder now, more distinctive. With a shiver of disbelief Ally recognized it at once. They had a flat tyre.

'Oh, my God, we've got a puncture.'

Susie pulled off the road and they both got out and surveyed the jagged rubber. The wheel was sitting uselessly on its rim.

'Can you change a tyre?' Ally appealed to a horrified Susie.

'Of course not. What are men for?'

'But you're so practical.'

'Not about cars. My idea of a dream car is one where you don't have to open the bonnet. Aren't you in the AA?'

'You can't call the AA out to change a tyre. I'll get the handbook.'

'Ally!' Susie shook her head at her friend's crazy logic. 'Look at you! You're tarted up to the nines.' She kicked the torn rubber. 'This is an emergency.'

But Ally had already opened the door and was rooting around in the glove pocket for the owners' manual. She'd changed a wheel plenty of times before. Then she sat back, defeated. 'Oh, I remember now. Matt took it inside to check the length for some ferry tickets.'

'Better call help, then. There was a phone back a few yards. I always notice them. I'm that kind of person.'

Ally swung her feet out of the car in their pink high heels. Susie looked at them. 'I'd better go and pretend to be you,' she said. 'Where's your card?'

Ally reached for her bag. As she delved into the lucky dip of tissues, pens, make-up, perfume spray and old biros, she thought for a ghastly moment that she'd left her wallet behind. The number of times she'd told herself to get one of those natty little organizer bags with zips and pockets and a place for everything so that she didn't have to turn the contents out on the roof when she was looking for her car keys, incurring those superior smirks from men whose day you made by conforming to the

105

Useless Woman stereotype. No, there it was. She handed it over to Susie.

'Don't worry.' Susie winked. 'I'll tell them we're being attacked by a mad rapist and they'll dash here in under four hours.'

Ally smiled back. Thank God they'd left plenty of time.

She watched Susie walk briskly in the direction of the phone box. Then suddenly Susie stopped. Maybe she thought you had to have money for the phone.

'Ally.' Susie's voice dripped sympathy. 'I hate to tell you this but your card ran out three months ago.'

'Bill, this is outrageous.' Maggy Mann, resplendent in Carmen rollers and salon gown, arrived in the control room like an avenging Valkyrie.

Bill Ford sighed. It had been a very irritating morning. He'd arrived at the studio to find the sparks were running an hour late with the lighting, the colour of the set was terracotta instead of the expected peach and the graphic designer allocated to the pilot had come down with flash flu. One thing he did not need was a menopausal harpie in hot rollers.

'What's outrageous, Maggy darling?' To her fury Bill continued to flick switches and shout orders to the studio crew instead of giving her his full attention.

'Trying out this woman Allegra Boyd on a pilot that's actually going to be transmitted. Bill, she's a *housewife*.' Maggy clearly placed the word on the moral scale somewhere between nymphomaniac and serial killer. 'You can't go ahead. We'll all look ridiculous.' She delved in her bag. 'Why don't I call my friend Anne Adamson and have her standing by?'

'Calm down, Maggy. Ally will be fine. She's got experience in counselling and she used to be on TV. No one expects pilots to be polished, and I'm sure you'll carry her if she isn't perfect.'

'That's not the point, Bill. She's an amateur. She only got the job because she's Matt Boyd's wife. What the hell has *she* got in common with the punters anyway?' Maggy Mann, working-class heroine, clicked her gold Cartier lighter and lit a cigarette. 'Since you clearly won't listen I'm going to see Stephen.'

'Maggy, sit down and put that revolting thing out. There's no point in going to see Stephen.'

'Why not? Stephen understands how to treat his stars.'

'Because' – Bill ignored the implied insult that he didn't – 'Allegra Boyd is Stephen's own personal choice. I had nothing to do with it.'

Maggy sat down heavily in the vision mixer's chair. In spite of himself Bill Ford felt an unexpected twinge of pity. She looked like the old diva sitting in on the auditions for the new. Then he remembered something she'd said that puzzled him.

'What did you mean, she's Matt Boyd's wife?'

Maggy rallied a little. 'What I said, darling. Allegra Boyd is Matt Boyd's wife.'

You bastard, Stephen Cartwright, thought Bill. You bastard for not telling me.

'Didn't you know, sweetie?' Maggy was quick to bounce back. 'Didn't Stephen bother to tell you?'

Bill Ford ignored her, all shades of pity vanished. 'I don't care whose wife she is. She should have been here half an hour ago. Where the fuck is she?'

'Search me, sweetie.' Maggy got up, glorying in her power restored. 'What do you expect from a rich housewife? Probably gone to a tennis lesson.' She swept out of the room, smiling. 'Or having her nails done.'

On the hard shoulder of the A3, Ally looked at her watch

and swore at the nuts which had obviously been welded on to the wheel by a sadistic assembly line worker. She kicked the wheelbrace for the third time. Nothing happened. Behind her she noticed a BMW slowing down and waited for its owner to stroll up and tell her what she needed was an adjustable spanner. Of *course* she needed an adjustable spanner. It was just that she didn't have one.

The driver got out and closed the door. When she saw what he had in his hand she felt like Eve on first beholding Adam's unique tool.

'Here you are, love.' He handed over the spanner, two thousand years of male superiority glinting in his eyes. 'I'd love to do it for you but I've got to run.' He patted her hand. 'You can keep it. I always carry a full set.'

Ally fought back the temptation to say she didn't need his bloody spanner. 'Thanks,' she muttered as the man got back into his car and sped off.

Ally knelt down. With the help of the spanner the nuts finally began to turn and she lifted the punctured tyre off, then rolled the spare along the ground and fitted it on to the nuts. As she tightened the last one she glanced at her watch again. She would be half an hour late, but she wouldn't need to spend hours in wardrobe or make-up. She'd be fine as she was.

She stood stiffly up.

'Oh dear, oh dear,' Susie pointed to her suit. Ally followed her friend's eyes. All down the left side of her new pink jacket was a narrow but distinct streak of oil.

'Don't worry,' Susie reassured her, whisking her into the passenger seat. 'They'll have something you can wear at the studios.' Susie turned on the engine and put her foot down. 'Let's just get there, shall we?'

The next forty-five minutes passed in a blur. Luckily the

traffic going into London kept moving. By the time they reached Century a plump and anxious researcher, who introduced herself as Nikki, was waiting outside the building ready to inform the studio of their arrival. Ally was whisked instantly into make-up as the wardrobe mistress selected an appropriate outfit to replace her oil-streaked jacket.

Ten minutes later Ally stood up. At first she didn't recognize her own face, covered in panstick and topped with iridescent blue eyeshadow and lurid coral lipstick. But it was the suit they'd put her in that really took her by surprise. It was bright orange, a colour she loathed, with enormous gold buttons and a skirt that stopped three inches above the knee, probably more when she sat down. Not something Selina Scott would have selected.

'Nice and bright,' cooed the wardrobe lady. 'That'll cheer them up at home.'

As she tried to pull the suit down to a respectable mid-thigh she took in what the woman had said for the first time. 'What do you mean?' She'd obviously misunderstood her. '"That'll cheer them up at home"? This is just a pilot, isn't it?'

'Absolutely. But it's still going out. That's how they do it these days. Easier to tell if the audience likes it, apparently. Didn't anyone explain?'

As she stood there looking at the gruesome stranger in the mirror Ally felt all her new-found confidence drain away. This was her fault. She'd been the one to try and be clever by insisting they tested her during the pilot.

'They're ready for you, Mrs Boyd.' Ally turned. Nikki was holding the door open. She carried a huge basket of flowers. 'By the way, these came for you.'

Despite the tension Ally felt a smile creep across her face. They had to be from Matt. Clutching her notes with one hand she opened the card with the other.

'You can do it,' said the card, 'for all of us wives at home. Love, Patsy.'

Ally glanced for a last time in the mirror. She didn't know whether to laugh or cry.

Nikki sat Ally down in the small dark gallery attached to the control room by a glass screen. From here, she explained, Ally could see and hear both the producer and director in the control room as well as what was happening on the studio floor.

The audience was already seated and a floor manager was explaining to them what to expect when Maggy Mann made her entrance.

Maybe it was her working-class roots, which she flashed constantly, or the image of the lone mother of three battling against the odds she so regularly promoted, but somehow Maggy had acquired the tag 'one of us'. As one critic trying to pin down her appeal wrote, 'Maggy Mann is seen as the voice of the voiceless shopper in the bargain basement,' bitchily adding, 'Without having ever been in one.'

Ally watched enviously as Maggy walked into the studio to thunderous applause. In spite of her expensive clothes, her vast salary and the fact that she hadn't been home to Rochdale once in fifteen years, Maggy could do no wrong.

She toured the studio, queenlike, with a word for every technician be they never so humble. Forgetting that Ally was sitting in the darkened gallery the director raised his eyes to heaven. They were late enough already. 'For Christ's sake, Maggy,' he muttered impatiently, 'cut the Princess Di act and sit down, will you?'

Ally smiled. Maybe not quite everybody was won over by Maggy's charm, after all. She reached across to a pile of green and yellow scripts to find out exactly when she was due to go on. Part one launched the show and introduced the presenters. Then a quick round-up pre-viewed *Hello*'s regular slots. At the end of part one Maggy would trail the agony slot and announce the topic to be discussed, the letter from Jennifer of Birmingham, then they'd go into a commercial break.

Ally relaxed a little, reassured at knowing exactly when she'd be on, and gazed around her. The technology was different from her days at MidWest Television. The sets and the lighting were slicker and the graphics jazzier, but the biggest change was the autocue.

She watched Maggy for a moment. She might be read-ing the words from a screen in front of the camera six feet away but she couldn't have sounded more relaxed and natural.

'Mrs Boyd, they're ready for you now.' She'd been so immersed in the script that she hadn't noticed Nikki put her head round the door.

Ally got up, her nervousness flooding back. 'Will I get a chance to rehearse?'

'There should be time for a quick run-through, but I'm afraid we're starting so late we'll have to go for it pretty soon. The audience is already getting a bit bored.'

Great, thought Ally. A bored audience. Matt had said so many times that an audience could make or break a show. How on earth was she going to win them over?

She was led to her chair by the floor manager and blinked at the sudden brightness. She'd forgotten how hot and dazzling studio lights were. And in all the rushing she realized she was still clutching her handbag, like an anxious sixteen-year-old at her first party. As she sat in her chair to be miked up she caught sight of a garish stranger on the TV screen to her right and realized with a shock that it was her.

'You must be Allegra.' Maggy leaned towards her with a sugary smile. 'We've all been waiting for you, haven't we?' She turned to the audience as though they were old friends meeting for a coffee. Ally had to admire her skill. 'Did you know Allegra here is married to Matt Boyd – *the* Matt Boyd – so I don't suppose she was stuck at the bus stop like the rest of us.'

Damn the woman. She hadn't wanted them to know she was married to Matt. When was the last time you ever caught a bus? she wondered. Ally could feel ill will oozing from Maggy's every pore. *She's doing everything she can to make me seem like a stuck-up cow who's got nothing in common with them.*

'Actually' – Ally smiled back as warmly as she could – 'I had a puncture.' She turned to the audience, too. 'And I got oil all over my jacket and had to borrow this ghastly suit.'

There was a ripple of laughter. She was beginning to crack their hostility. Suddenly she had an inspiration. 'Have you ever changed a tyre?' She delved into her handbag and pulled out the adjustable spanner. 'If so, carry one of these. I'm taking it everywhere now, even to bed.' A woman in the front row giggled. 'Especially to bed.'

This time the laughter was louder. Ally felt the muscles in her neck relax so she no longer felt as though she was wearing a surgical collar. They were warming to her.

And then they were off. She saw the floor manager hold up three fingers. She checked her watch. There was nothing for her to do in the first part until Maggy previewed her agony slot in about fifteen minutes' time. She just had to listen out for Jennifer of Birmingham.

Two minutes before she got to the agony intro Maggy glanced across at Ally.

Watching the show was so absorbing that Ally had forgotten about the coming ordeal and begun to enjoy herself.

Seeing Ally laughing and relaxed was too much for Maggy. Why should a pampered cow who'd never had to do anything more demanding than brief the housekeeper and pick up the kids in the Volvo be allowed to swan on to *her* show just because of who she was married to? Maggy had sweated blood to get where she was, and although she pretended not to mind that her kids were antisocial little shits, she knew it probably had something to do with never seeing their mother. But what choice had she had?

Sitting two feet away, Ally had no idea of the effect she was having on Maggy Mann. She was simply waiting to be introduced because the sooner she did her bit the sooner it would be over and her heart could stop racing and return to normal.

Already the floor manager was winding up the last interview. Thirty seconds to go. Twenty. Fifteen. Ten. Five.

Maggy swivelled in Ally's direction.

'That's it for part one.' The camera cut from a two-shot and moved in for a close-up. 'In part two we'll be meeting *Hello*'s guest agony aunt, Ally Boyd.' The camera cut to a shot of Ally. She smiled. The audience was friendly now. It was going to be all right.

Maggy was talking again. 'After the break Ally will be advising Sandra from Liverpool.'

Ally felt a flash of pure panic run through her. She'd never heard of Sandra of Liverpool. It was Jennifer of Birmingham she'd been told to advise.

Maggy looked straight to camera. 'Sandra's just seventeen and pregnant. She's keen to go ahead and have the baby but her parents want a termination.' Maggy's voice rang with rehearsed compassion. 'What should she do? Join us and Ally Boyd, our agony aunt, after the break to find out.'

Ally picked up her script and feverishly turned the pages. How could she have made such a ghastly mistake? She knew nothing about teenage pregnancy.

The relief when she found Jennifer of Birmingham in the script was almost physical. The whole thing was a mix-up. Any moment someone would run across the studio floor and give Maggy the right intro.

Then she looked up. From a split-second of intense satisfaction on Maggy Mann's face she saw the truth at once.

Maggy Mann had set her up. She knew perfectly well that Ally knew nothing about teenage pregnancy. And in a couple of minutes so would millions of viewers.

Chapter 9

In the control room Bill Ford swore at the switchboard for putting through a petty call of complaint when the show was on air. For five minutes he'd been harangued by some nutter about Maggy's incorrect pronunciation of the word 'controversy' instead of watching the show's progress. How do you pronounce interfering old bat? he nearly asked.

'How's it going?' he barked at the director, who was forced for a moment to stop shouting at the vision mixer for missing a shot and say, 'Great. Fine.'

So none of them noticed the look on Ally's face as she waited, in vain, for someone to come to her rescue.

Sitting in front of the cameras Ally felt herself go cold in spite of the dazzling heat of the studio lights. For ten seconds she sat with her palms locked together and panicked. What the hell could she do? Complaining to Maggy clearly wasn't possible. She could call someone over and get them to tell Bill what was happening. But what if this was some gruesome sadistic test? Surely, though, no producer would put a newcomer through such a trial? The risk to the show would be too great.

Already the floor manager was signalling the end of the break and *Hello*'s title music began. All her life, Ally knew, that music would bring a surge not of adrenalin but of fear.

She didn't have any options left. There was only one thing she could do. Busk it. *Remember how confident you seem to other people and just be it*. That's what Barbara had told her on the course.

Out of the corner of her eye Ally saw Maggy's small

superior smile as she welcomed the viewers back. And suddenly she felt blazingly angry. How dare she! What right had she to try and wreck another woman's chance at success because she happened to disapprove of her?

Ally pulled herself up so straight that she could feel her back stretch and her chin lift defiantly. If she was going to be an agony aunt she couldn't rely on the *British Psychosexual Journal* to tell her what to think anyway. She was going to have to use her common sense.

As Maggy introduced the imaginary letter Ally closed her eyes for a second, trying to picture what Sandra might look like. She was seventeen with everything in front of her. But how much was that in Liverpool 8? She remembered the images of inner city decay, rundown housing, and unemployment she'd seen on the nightly news. Sandra didn't sound the academic type, so what bite of the apple would she have anyway? A baby would get her a council flat, freedom, perhaps, from parents who seemed to her cold and uncaring, and maybe most important of all something to love. It might also mean the end. The end of dreams of breaking free, of any chance of making something of herself. By thirty-five she'd be old.

For a moment Ally forgot where she was and she wondered what *she* would say if Janey, or worse still Jess, came and sat down at the kitchen table and announced, 'Mum, I'm pregnant.'

'Hello, Sandra.' Ally tried to imagine she was looking not into a camera but into an unhappy face that might be sitting at home, racked by fear and indecision. 'First of all, no matter what anyone says to you, you're a very brave girl.'

In the control room Bill Ford was staring at Ally in utter mystification. 'Why is she rabbiting on about teen-age pregnancy, for Christ's sake?' he demanded, jumping up and pacing around the room. 'She's supposed to be advising some tart on screwing married men!'

116

'How should we know?' The PA turned to him, irritated because he seemed to be incompetent and also because he'd made her miss what Ally was saying. 'You're the producer. That's what Maggy introduced.'

The director was sitting on the edge of his seat, mesmerized. 'Whatever it is, don't knock it.' He pointed to the monitor above camera four. 'Look at the audience. They're crying, for God's sake!' He turned to the hapless vision mixer. 'Quick. Get some reaction shots. This is incredible.'

Bill Ford sat down. He didn't know what the hell was going on. He should have been following it on his script. If the operator hadn't put that stupid call through he would have. He turned to the right page. There it was. The intro, just as he'd written it, to the girl who screwed married men.

He stared up at the monitor again, a ludicrous, crazy thought crossing his mind. Maggy wouldn't. She wouldn't *dare*. But looking at her sullen expression he knew at once that she had dared. She'd read the wrong intro deliberately.

For Ally the rest of the show passed in a daze. She couldn't have named a single thing that was discussed. But she'd survived. Tempted though she'd been, she hadn't dried up or run out or broken down or tried to say the whole thing was a terrible mistake. She'd kept going. And she was proud of that, at least. All she had to do now was sit here and wait for Maggy to wind the show up. Then she could slip quietly off and forget the whole thing. On Monday she'd start looking into voluntary work, as Matt had suggested.

And then, after what seemed like an eternity, the floor manager began to wind Maggy up and *Hello*'s title music began to play. The show was finishing.

As the credits stopped rolling Bill Ford strode across

the studio floor looking like a volcano about to erupt. Ally stood up, then realized she was still attached to her microphone and sat down again. Before she could say anything Maggy expertly unclipped hers and handed it to the sound man.

'I know, I know, darling.' Maggy put out her hands protectively as Ford approached her. 'But let's face it, she needed a real test. This is live television, after all. You have to be ready for anything.'

Ford stopped in his tracks, temporarily stunned by her sheer nerve. 'Well, you certainly gave her one, didn't you?'

But as he turned his back on her to congratulate Ally, he smiled. The full irony had just hit him. Maggy Mann's plan had backfired on her beautifully. Without her little shock Ally would probably have come up with some predictable crap she'd been practising in front of the mirror for days. Instead Maggy had forced her to be spontaneous. And Ally had done it brilliantly. The truth was, no matter who she was married to, Ally Boyd was a real discovery.

'Allegra!' Bill bent down and kissed her. 'You were wonderful!'

'She certainly was,' echoed another voice. Ally turned in amazement to find Matt standing behind her with a huge bunch of roses, and Janey and Jess on either arm.

'Mum, you were unbelievable! I even forgot it was you.' Janey put an arm round Ally and kissed her. 'You didn't really think we'd rush off without saying anything today, did you?'

'Yes, she did,' corrected Jess, kissing the other cheek. 'By the way, Muv, I don't know whether I said' – she grinned impishly at her mother – 'but now that you mention it my period is a bit on the late side . . .'

Jess ducked out of Ally's reach before she could retaliate.

'I don't know about you lot,' Ally said, reaching out a

118

hand to Matt as she felt the tension finally melting away, 'but I feel like a very, very large drink.'

This time Ally only had to wait forty-eight hours to hear whether she'd got the job. Stephen Cartwright rang to say that she'd been brilliant on the pilot and that the job was hers if she wanted it, starting in a month's time. They wanted her in the studio three days a week, with some filming on top of that. And the figure he mentioned as a salary took her breath away. But now they'd offered it to her, Ally was suddenly crippled by doubt.

'What do you mean, you aren't sure whether to accept?' Susie's voice squeaked in horror. She'd come over as soon as she'd heard the news. 'They're offering you your own slot on TV and you don't know whether to take it? You're mad. Bonkers. Round the bloody bend.'

Ally laughed as she removed Janey's jeans from the banisters. Susie was always so certain. Life to her was black and white and no smudges.

'I'm not mad.' She folded the jeans carefully. 'Just worried what it might do to the family. Janey's got her A levels next year and Jess will be having exams soon too. Maybe it's not a very good time for me to be having my little rebellion. Jess is the adolescent. It's her turn to want the attention, not mine. I think maybe I should get a job in a health centre or something.'

'My God, Ally, you'd try the patience of Mother Theresa. Anyone can get a job in a health centre. You've got *talent*. This isn't a little rebellion. You were bloody brilliant. You can't say no.'

Susie followed her into Janey's room as she put away the jeans. Inside the door she stopped in amazement. The walls had been painted black and most of the furniture removed. The raven-haired lead singer of The Cure scowled Byronically down on them.

'God almighty, what's happened here? A fire?'

Ally laughed. 'Janey's redecorated it. She's become a Goth. I drew the line at a coffin as the bed.'

Susie blinked. Last time she'd been in here it had been all frills and Sindy.

In the middle of the tangled mess of fanzines, silver chains and pots of ghoulish make-up Susie spotted a copy of *The Penguin Book of American Verse*.

She jumped on it and leafed through the pages. 'I didn't know Janey was into poetry.'

'English A level. T. S. Eliot.'

Susie whooped when she found what she was looking for. 'There! *He* knew! He understood! Do you want a life like J. Alfred Prufrock's that just passes you by?' Susie held out the book at arm's length and declaimed dramatically:

For I have known them all already, known them all –
Have known the evenings, mornings, afternoons,
I have measured out my life with coffee spoons

'Is that what you want, too? A life measured out with coffee spoons? You're talented. You owe it to yourself!'

'But what about Matt? How will it be for him if I'm out all the time? He needs us as a bolthole.'

'Ah-ha.' Susie shook her head knowingly. 'Now I get it. You're worried about what this will do to his tender male ego. Forget it, Ally. It'll do him the world of good.' Susie put the poetry book down on Janey's messy desk. 'Show him you're more than a bonking chauffeur service. Anyway' – she put her arm round her friend and squeezed her – 'if you're worried about Janey and Jess why don't you ask them? Teenagers can be surprisingly perceptive. They might even tell you what they really think.'

Downstairs Ally saw Susie out with another hug. What

would she do without women friends? She quite often felt sorry for men. They had so much missing from their lives in their race to the top. They worked all hours, hardly saw their children and, worst of all, they didn't have girlfriends. No, rephrase that. They *did* have girlfriends, the bastards, what they didn't have was men friends.

That evening Matt sat flicking through the paper at the kitchen table with Jess reading a book next to him. Janey was at the cooker knocking up a lentil mousse. Jess never sat at the table reading. And certainly not with Matt next to her. In fact this must be the first time the whole family had been in one room together for weeks. She wondered if unconsciously they were playing out some subtle tableau of the nuclear family for her benefit.

'I'm glad you're all here.' She sat down next to Jess. 'Because I wanted to talk to you all.'

'Wow.' Jess put down her book. 'A family conference? This must be serious. Are you leaving us for another man?'

Ally ruffled her daughter's hair. She knew Jess could only ask that because she already knew the answer.

'You're having a sex change. Should we start to call you Alan?' Ally wondered what it was about anything serious that made Jess want to drown it in humour.

'I'm not leaving and I'm not having a sex change. I want to talk about this job offer.'

'But I thought you'd already accepted. Why did that huge bunch of flowers arrive from Century this morning?'

'Tch, tch, Jessy,' corrected Janey from the stove. 'You get the flowers *before* you go all the way, remember?'

Ally looked from Matt to the girls. 'What do you think? Should I take it? It'll mean being out three days a week, maybe more. Bill says there may even be overnights if we do some filming. It'll mean you coming back to an empty house.'

Ally wondered how much they'd mind. She'd always made a point of telling them their home was waiting for them. Not quite a sponge in the oven but certainly the fire lit and the house warm and welcoming. But who did that matter more to: her or them?

'*I* think,' Janey said without looking up from her lentils, 'that you should do what *you* want. You're always doing things for other people. Now it's your turn.'

'What about you, Jess?'

'I say do it. I've always wanted a working mother.'

Ally looked at her in surprise.

'Everyone says they're a much softer touch. So guilty you can get away with murder.'

'Squirt,' Ally said affectionately. 'What do you think, Matt?'

Matt's eyes had unconsciously wandered back to the sports pages of the newspaper. 'About what?'

'About whether I should take the job at Century.'

'Do you want it?'

'I think so.'

'Then do it.' He reached a hand back to Janey. 'We'll survive, won't we, girls?'

Sox shook her head vigorously.

'Absolutely,' agreed Jess. 'Dad can pick up his own suits from the dry cleaner's.'

'Of course I can,' Matt confirmed. 'What's a dry cleaner's?'

'Don't you believe it,' Janey said, from the safety of her place by the stove. 'He'll get his secretary to do it, won't you, Dad?'

'Allegra, I don't know where they get this idea of me,' Matt objected in wounded tones, 'as a helpless, selfish male who can't do anything for himself.'

'Neither do I, darling.' Ally ignored the giggles from behind her. 'Neither do I.'

'I suppose there is one thing.' Matt paused, wondering if he should go on.

'What's that?'

'You don't think people will think you got the job because of me?'

Ally felt her heart sink. He was right. People *would* assume exactly that. But wasn't it about time she stopped caring about what people thought?

'If they do think that,' she said, suddenly surer than ever that she ought to give it a try, 'then I'll just have to convince them they were wrong. Won't I?'

'Right.' On the morning of her first meeting at *Hello* Ally handed Matt a sheet of paper with the day's arrangements written on it in her beautiful italic handwriting. 'Fiona Wilson's mother's doing the school run. It's Thursday so Jess needs her piano music with her, oh, and tell Janey there's a spinach and Quorn quiche in the fridge for tea.'

'You're only going in for a meeting.' Matt pushed her towards the door affectionately. 'God knows what it'll be like when you do a show. Have fun.'

He watched the taxi driver hold the door open for her as she climbed in. She'd thought he was being resentful when he'd warned her about the jealousy she might meet because of who she was married to. But he'd meant it. He knew only too well how bitchy TV people could be. She might be in for a rough time.

But as he waved her goodbye even Matt didn't suspect how rough.

'Now, everyone, I don't really need to introduce Ally Boyd.' Bill Ford smiled at the twenty or so backroom people who made up *Hello*'s programme team.

Ally felt a wave of shyness at meeting so many people at once. Some of them hardly seemed older than Janey. One of the youngest, a fresh-faced twenty-year-old, instantly leaped to his feet and offered her his seat. It reminded Ally of that ghastly moment when even the Italians stop calling you *signorina*. Since she'd already decided, given who she was, that she needed to work extra hard at being one of the boys she smiled no and sat on the floor.

She looked round, recognizing only one or two of the faces. Nikki, the plump researcher who'd looked after her at the pilot, Brian, the director, Malevolent Maggy, of course, and Moira, her watchdog. The others were new to her.

'OK, first the researchers. They're the drones, sorry, backbone of the team. As they'll be quick to tell you, they do the real work round here while we swan off to the Groucho Club.'

'Without your cellphone,' pointed out one of them.

'I never forget my cellphone,' corrected Bill. 'I just keep it switched off. Brian, our director, you know. He's in charge of overrunning in the studio and missing great reaction shots.' There was an appreciative titter from the two PAs. 'I expect you remember Maggy.' He paused infinitesimally before he went on. 'There are our two producers of the day, then there are the most important people in the room – our programme secretaries.' One of them raised a cynical eyebrow and Ally smiled at her. She remembered being patronized just like that when she'd been at the bottom of the heap. Why didn't people like Bill Ford realize it?

'I think that's all our boys and girls, including the odd don't know.'

There was a murmur of dissent from the floor.

'Have I forgotten someone?' Bill gazed round the room

then threw himself from his chair on to the floor. 'Louise! How could I forget our production manager? A vital role. Louise signs expenses and authorizes taxis. I kiss your Gucci shoes in abasement.' And to Ally's amazement he actually did so.

TV types, she recalled, were different from other people.

Once she'd got over the culture shock of meeting so many people at once, Ally relaxed and began to enjoy herself. She'd forgotten how like a family a programme team could be. It had all the undercurrents and sibling rivalries of the average nuclear unit, but there was also a feeling of excitement, a bond, a sense of you against the rest that was astonishingly powerful.

After an hour or so of running through the plans for the current series of *Hello*, Bill Ford closed the meeting. 'Right, who's for a quickie?'

Nikki and Louise exchanged glances. Bill was a notorious lech, well known not just for using his power to get you into bed, but for what was much worse – being a lousy lay. 'That man,' one of the PAs had declared after a night of absolutely no passion, 'thinks a clitoris is something you grow on a south-facing wall.'

'Let me rephrase that.' Bill grinned wolfishly. 'Who would like to join me in the bar?'

Ally thought for a moment about grabbing a cab and reading the big file of viewers' letters they'd had in response to *Hello*'s ads in the paper.

'You are coming, aren't you, Ally?' asked Nikki, holding the door open.

Ally made up her mind. Saying no would look as though she didn't want to join in and be one of the team. Dashing off in one of Century's chauffeur-driven limos to Surrey was exactly what they'd expect Mrs Matt Boyd to do. If she wanted to be accepted she should go with them and buy her round. Besides it would be fun.

'You betcha,' she said. 'Especially if Bill's paying.'

Nikki looked pleased. They'd expected Ally to be stuck-up and difficult but she wasn't at all. 'By the way, sorry about Bill, our talented producer. He's the office grope. He even propositioned Maggy once and when she said no he told her that at her age she ought to be grateful.' Ally giggled. She couldn't imagine anyone being brave enough to proposition Maggy. Working on *Hello* certainly wasn't going to be dull.

As they trooped out of the door, laughing and joking, the phone went on Bill's desk. Maggy, who to everyone's relief had discovered a sudden appointment and decided not to come, picked it up.

'Allegra,' she called. 'It's for you.'

Ally didn't want to spoil the moment by getting stuck on the phone. 'Thanks, Maggy. Could you ask if I can ring them back?'

'Sure.' She picked up the receiver then put it down again, smiling ominously. 'It was Patsy Cartwright, the big boss's wife. She says not to worry to ring her. Just to congratulate you and say how glad she is she suggested you.'

Ally thanked her and closed the door. It was nice of Patsy to ring, but it wouldn't exactly help Ally in her bid to be taken into the fold for everyone to know she'd been Patsy's idea.

A lot of people felt more at home in Century's bar than they did in their own homes, probably because they spent more time there. It was a long, low room running half the length of the building with full-length doors opening on to a terrace overlooking Millbank and the Thames. Some people said you got a wonderful view of the Houses of Parliament from here. Ally wondered how anyone knew as most of them were propping up the bar with their backs to it.

'Right, kids, why don't I get a couple of bottles of house plonk and we can share them?' Bill Ford was renowned for his meanness almost as much as his lechery.

'Sorry, Bill, sweet.' Brian the director, who had developed a camp manner to disguise his heterosexual roots in Ruislip, wasn't being palmed off so easily. 'Mine's a double Malibu. The blood in my alcohol stream's getting a bit high.'

Scowling, Bill tried to memorize twenty assorted orders while the team took themselves out on to the terrace. It was warm for September and they sat in the sun or draped themselves over the low wall letting the glorious weather take their minds off the fact that in a few weeks, when the autumn schedule was launched, *Hello* would be on air daily and they would actually have to do some work.

'Sodding Stephen Cartwright,' moaned Brian into his Malibu. 'He only wants us to be on the air fifty bloody weeks a year. I mean' – he crunched a Quaver angrily – 'whatever happened to nice short runs with a month off at Christmas and Easter?'

'Don't show your age, Brian.' Nikki handed Ally a huge glass of white wine. 'They went out with black and white.'

Ally listened, fascinated. She loved this in-talk. It was amazing that Matt had been with Century for nearly fifteen years and she'd never had an idea who he worked with. Apart from Bernie, of course, whom she'd known from the beginning, unfortunately, and had quite often wished she'd never met. It was funny to think Matt's team was probably rather like this. And sometimes he saw more of them than he did of her. Looking round at the laughing people and the pleasant surroundings she wondered how much of his devotion to duty was strictly necessary.

Without warning George Waites, Britain's most distinguished newsreader, appeared in the French doors and stood there for a moment, glass of wine in hand, his silver hair glinting in the midday sun.

'Hello, my loves.' He peered out at the group of them sitting in the brilliant sunshine then turned back inside muttering, 'Christ, what appalling weather!'

Ally giggled. 'Doesn't he like the sun?'

'He's probably got a hangover the size of the Ritz,' Louise whispered. 'He certainly deserves one. Naughty Georgie Porgie. He's not supposed to drink before the lunchtime news or he slurs his words and the viewers ring in and complain. The duty officer says they don't believe it about the antibiotics any more.'

'Especially after last night,' chipped in Nikki.

'What did he do last night?' Ally was riveted.

'He asked the PA how the hell you pronounce Nagorno Karabakh and then said, "Who cares anyway?" not knowing they were live on air. The ambassador, that's who. He rang to complain. Then Georgie came down here, sang three choruses of "My Brother Sylveste" and took his clothes off.'

Ally sat back, helpless with laughter. The lunchtime news would never be the same again.

Matt sat down in front of the ancient Underwood typewriter in his study and stared at the blank piece of paper. It was crazy to keep using it really. He should have got a smart Apple Mac word processor but it had been his first typewriter and it made a satisfying tap when you hit the keys. It responded best when you were in a bad mood and really gave them a walloping. Ally always said she liked to hear the sound of him banging away upstairs. It reminded her of when they'd met and worked together.

But today Matt couldn't concentrate. He'd taken the

afternoon off to write an after-dinner speech he'd promised to give to an IBM bigwigs conference. Matt Boyd
was always in demand for public speaking, supermarket
openings, giving out pools cheques. People knew the
occasion would go well with Matt around. He was always
funny and he was even prepared to shake a few hands and
chat. He didn't pocket his cheque and push off as soon as
it was decently, or sometimes indecently, possible like
some stars. Matt enjoyed meeting people. All the same
every time he agreed to an occasion like this he asked
himself why he'd done so. He didn't need the cash. He
supposed it was some kind of insurance, rainy day money.
When you came from a background like his, father a
brickie, never enough to go round, it made you very
careful not to look poverty in the face again. And television could be so fickle. He'd been at the very top for
ten years, longer than anyone else, but would he be for
another ten?

Matt got up. He couldn't write the bloody speech.
Even with Mrs O'Shock hoovering in the background it
was too damn quiet. There was a kind of deadness about
the house, a particularly empty quality to the silence he
wasn't used to.

Maybe he'd make himself a cup of coffee.

At the bottom of the stairs he stopped to pick up the
second post from the mat. As he stood up again he
realized what it was.

Ally wasn't there.

When Ally finally settled back in the Ford Granada
Nikki had booked her and headed for home she couldn't
believe it was three thirty. A liquid lunch of white wine
with only a packet of cheesy wotsits as sustenance meant
she felt dizzy and on top of the world by turns.

At half past four her car crunched over the gravel of

their drive. To her surprise Matt was standing outside the front door waiting.

'I see you missed us so much you dashed back.'

Ally grinned as she climbed out of the car.

'You're pissed,' accused Matt.

'I know,' conceded Ally, realizing that attempts at denial were wasted. 'It was great fun. Now I know why you work such long hours. You spend half of them in the bar.'

It was on the tip of Matt's tongue to offer a pompous denial, but he saved himself just in time. 'Damn!' He clicked his fingers in mock irritation. 'She's rumbled me.'

'C'm here.' Ally ignored the grinning driver. 'This is only the beginning. Things are going to change around here, you know.'

There was a fraction of a pause before Matt answered. 'Yes.' He opened his arms to her. 'I'd already noticed. Come on, I'll make you a black coffee to sober you up before Janey and Jess get back.'

'That sounds lovely. Why don't we have it in bed?'

Matt looked at his watch, laughing. 'Because we've only got sixteen and a half minutes, that's why.'

'Tell you what.' Ally took his hand and pulled him towards the house as the driver turned round, chuckling to himself. 'Let's forget the coffee, shall we?'

Chapter 10

'Matt, have you seen this?' Belinda threw a copy of the *Daily Post* down on his desk with such force that his cup of black coffee almost spilled over it. 'Look at the centre spread.'

Matt wiped the drips of coffee off with a pair of musical knickers some misguided PR company had sent in, claiming they would be 'just right for the show', and opened the paper.

From the centre two pages an enormous headline screamed: 'DANNY WILDE REVAMP: Show Needs More Bite, says TV Host.'

'Read the piece.' Belinda's face was sphinxlike but he could tell from the whiteness of her knuckles where she held on to the chair and the intense control in her voice that she was furiously angry. 'They're doing it,' she muttered through clenched teeth. 'They're only bloody *doing* it.'

Matt began to read. Danny Wilde had decided, according to the *Post*, that chat-shows were getting too trashy and trivial and that in the next series they intended to broaden the programme's scope beyond the usual guests who'd turn out for a tenner as long as they could plug their current project. From now on they would invite powerbrokers and politicians as well as starlets and Ivana Trump. It was almost word for word what they had outlined to Bernie Long as the way their own show should go.

'For Christ's sake, Matt, they're stealing our ideas.' Belinda began pacing the room like a caged cat. 'We've got to *do* something. We've got to get in first before their next series starts or we'll look as though we're copying them.'

Matt scanned the *Post* article again. Belinda was right. They had to act. Now. And if they couldn't carry Bernie with them they'd have to go over his head to Stephen.

In her dressing room deep in the heart of Century Television Ally felt a surge of excitement and fear in equal doses. Today *Hello* was going live on air for real with Ally Boyd as its official agony aunt. Dressing rooms in TV didn't have the cosy glamour of the West End where an actress might be resident for three or six months, surrounded by the clutter of flowers, good luck cards and cuddly toys sent in by admiring fans from Clacton. Television dressing rooms were in such short supply that they were allocated daily – one day to the Chippendales, the next to Sir John Gielgud. All the same Ally felt a thrill as she saw her name on the door and punched up the numbers she'd been handed by the PA. It was really happening.

She laid out her dress carefully. Not the ghastly orange suit borrowed from wardrobe this time. This one was lilac with a grey lace collar, subtle without being off-putting. It wasn't Ally who was supposed to be the star, but the viewers who phoned in.

She looked at the formica shelf which served as a dressing table. It was covered in good luck cards from Matt down to their local minicab service. With these good wishes surely it would have to be all right.

She slipped on her dress, touched up her make-up and brushed her hair. She looked at herself briefly in the brilliantly lit mirror and took a deep breath.

It was time to go to the studio.

As she took her place in front of the dazzling studio lights Ally suddenly felt self-conscious and alone. She'd practised all night reading the viewers' letters but now was the moment of truth.

They were halfway through the rehearsal. In less than an hour they would be live on air. Maggy introduced her and, holding her breath, Ally turned towards the red light winking at her from camera three.

And that was when her problems started.

As she tried to read the words rotating slowly on the teleprompter in front of the lens of the camera she felt herself stumble. The rhythm of the sentences was staccato and unnatural. She faltered again.

'OK, OK,' interrupted Bill Ford from the control room. 'Let's start at the top.'

The autocue girl wound back to the beginning and Ally began again.

But this time it was no better. Acutely aware now of how many people were listening and trying to hide their impatience, Ally got it wrong again.

And then panic set in, cold and terrifying. She started for a third time, got through the first few paragraphs fine, breathed a sigh of relief. Thank God, they were the tricky bits. Then she stumbled on the last sentence.

Fighting off her fear she realized why it was. Because suddenly it mattered. When she'd tested she'd never expected to get the job. And she'd been so white-hot furious with Maggy Mann she'd forgotten where she was, forgotten everything except the desire to show Maggy she could do it and get out of there without too much egg on her face. And thanks to Maggy's little trick she hadn't had to read the autocue. She'd had to make everything up.

'Try again, sweetie, *slowly*.' Bill Ford's voice was sugary but she could hear the irritation only millimetres below the surface.

This time she was going to do it.

She plunged in again. Laurence Olivier it wasn't but at least the words were in the right order this time.

She saw the studio crew heaving an almost audible sigh of relief and Nikki giving her a thumbs up from the side of the set.

But that was just the rehearsal. What on earth would she be like when it was the real thing?

'Can Ally go now?' asked the floor manager.

'Certainly.' Ally could hear Bill through the talkback even though she'd taken out her earpiece. 'And tell her to *learn* it for God's sake, will you?'

Nikki appeared, smiling encouragingly. 'Shall I ask the autocue girl if she could run you through again during the teabreak to give you a bit of practice? She's ever so nice.'

'Yes, please,' Ally said gratefully. As she turned to put down her earpiece she caught Maggy's eye. Maggy was far too canny to smile openly, but there was an unmistakable curl to her lips which Ally decided, for the sake of her waning confidence, to ignore.

'Bernie, you *must* listen.' Without noticing it Belinda's tone had become demanding. Bernie looked across his desk at her, his eyes cold with dislike. First she and Matt had come barging into his office, then the cow had started telling him what to do. Bernie knew exactly what Belinda thought of him. She'd made it more than clear. She thought he was a has-been, trying desperately to cling on with his fingernails when he should be letting go and making room for younger, more talented people. Like Belinda.

But unfortunately for her that wasn't how he saw himself. He'd survived a lot of things in his career and he wasn't about to jump ship now. They might have thought Belinda was shit-hot at the BBC and promoted her to being one of the youngest producers ever but that, in Bernie's view, was what was wrong with the Beeb anyway. They wanted to turn everything into a fucking news bulletin.

But what the hell was Matt doing supporting her? Matt and he had been together from the beginning. Matt had been his boy, his discovery. He'd seen that old-fashioned charm and had known instantly that it was the Real Thing, and that it would work on television. And it had.

Matt might be losing a few viewers lately but there was still no one to touch him. No matter what Belinda said, Danny Wilde was no real competition. Danny was too clever by half. He scared the pants off grannies in Grantham, while Matt's charm spanned three generations, teenagers, mothers, grandmothers. Now he and Belinda were suggesting some damn-fool formula which could easily backfire on them and break Matt's career in the process.

'OK, Matt, so you want a change.' Bernie studiously ignored Belinda and spoke directly to Matt. 'Why don't we talk to Stephen about taking the show to Hollywood or the Cannes Film Festival? We could pick up the big names and get out of the studio at the same time.'

'It's not a question of going to Hollywood, Bernie.' Matt knew Bernie wasn't going to understand. 'It's the whole direction of the show that needs to change. You can't be the same for ten years and stay at the top. It's time we moved on. Got sharper. More controversial. OK, so the viewers'll scream. Better than falling asleep in front of the box.'

'Or turning over to Danny Wilde,' added Belinda.

Matt watched Bernie closely. They'd been working together for so long that he knew exactly how Bernie's mind worked. Bernie thought Belinda was behind all this. That she'd ensnared Matt with her short skirts and even shorter manners and was leading him by the prick down the primrose path to professional ruin. But he was wrong. What Bernie couldn't bring himself to face was that the relationship between Belinda and Matt was simply a professional one based on talent, not sex. They shared the same vision. Bernie blamed it on her because it was easier, and maybe less painful. What he didn't want to see was that the person who most wanted change was Matt.

Matt had never been the kind of presenter to throw his weight around or stand on status. But maybe it was time to start.

'Listen, Bernie, we've been together from the start.'

'And it don't seem a day too much,' Bernie quoted the old music-hall song.

'But you know what I've been like lately. The way the show is now I feel I've done it all. I'm bored out of my skull. And it shows. Of course it shows. I know it. You know it. *They* know it, for God's sake.'

Belinda thought of interrupting. She didn't like the way she'd been frozen out of the conversation, but just in time had the good sense to keep her mouth shut.

Bernie shrugged, realizing finally that Matt was serious. 'What are we going to do about it, Matt? This is a pretty fundamental disagreement.'

Matt looked him in the eye. Even though he saw things differently from Bernie he still respected him. 'I've asked for a meeting with Stephen to talk about it.'

Belinda's head shot up. 'You didn't tell me.'

'No.' Belinda detected the faintest note of impatience in Matt's voice. 'I wanted to tell Bernie first. We go back a long way.'

'Boys together,' she muttered just audibly.

'Do you want to come,' Matt asked Bernie, 'and argue your corner?' They both knew what Matt was saying.

Matt was going to tell Stephen he wanted a change or he wanted out.

'Nah.' Bernie took his feet off his desk for the first time since they'd come into his office. 'A man's gotta do what a man's gotta do. You'll probably screw me better in my absence.'

For some reason neither could explain they shook hands.

'Jesus Christ, what's the matter with the woman?' Bill Ford was careful to cover his microphone with his hand so that Ally couldn't hear. He didn't want her to get any worse. Things were going badly enough already. It was a cliché of television that a good pilot means a lousy first show and it looked as though *Hello* was going to prove just how true that was.

And Ally Boyd wasn't his only problem. The scene painters, annoyed about the candid opinion he had expressed of their handiwork after the pilot, had resprayed the set a particularly nasty shade of orange, the lighting director had clearly drawn his inspiration from the London Dungeon, and their gay gardening correspondent had missed his plane from Manchester. Only the thought that he'd never work again stopped Bill from leaving them to it and disappearing to an unknown destination. Rio de Janeiro, maybe. Perhaps it wasn't far enough. He ate three bars of Cadbury's Dairy Milk, as he did before every live show, and wondered if they had daytime television in Tierra del Fuego.

In her dressing room Ally tried to memorize her script for the tenth time. Deep down she suspected that throwing it away might be a better course of action but she didn't have the nerve.

Nikki put her head round the door. 'Time for makeup,' she reminded her. 'And don't let the make-up girl lean over you. I've just seen her eating a spring onion sandwich.'

Ally laughed, grateful to Nikki for trying to take her mind off the ordeal ahead. They'd spent ten minutes rehearsing with the autocue girl during the break, not realizing that Maggy was still in her seat reading an interview with herself in *Harpers & Queen*.

'What do you think?' Ally had asked Nikki when they stopped.

'Why don't we do ourselves a favour' – Maggy's voice had drifted across from the other side of the studio – 'and hire Pinocchio?'

'Well, that didn't go very well, did it, boys and girls?' The closing credits had just rolled after the final show in a disastrous first week. Bill Ford toyed with the idea of being encouraging, but decided putting the boot in would be better for everyone.

The last hour and a half had been among the longest in his life. On the principle that everything that can go wrong will, they had scored brilliantly. Maggy Mann had been about as warm and welcoming as a packet of frozen peas, the live insert to their Fill-Your-Trolley-in-a-Minute contest had broken up into white dots only seconds away from the climax, and a block of wood could have read autocue better than Allegra Boyd. He'd hoped after her first show nerves she might improve. He was wrong. Add to that the distinct impression that the presenters loathed each other, which of course they did, and you had a recipe for a nightmare TV programme. The only thing Bill could hope for was that it would either be better next week or that viewers would recommend it to each other on the grounds that it was so bad it was funny.

★

By the time Ally got home she just wanted to submerge herself in a hot bath and forget all about it. The whole week, which she'd looked forward to with such excitement, had been a complete disaster. She stripped off her studio clothes and attacked the heavy panstick make-up so hard that she left red marks on her face and neck.

Half an hour later, scrubbed clean as a nun and wearing one of her oldest tracksuits, she felt ready to face the eager questions she knew she'd meet downstairs.

'How was it, Ma?' shrieked Jess, abandoning her homework and following her mother round the kitchen. 'Is it move over Dr Ruth?'

Ally filled the kettle. 'I don't think she needs to book her retirement home just yet.'

'That bad?' Jess put her arms round her mother. 'But you were so brilliant on the pilot.'

Ally reached for the tin of Marks & Spencer's Belgian Assortment and selected the perfect biscuit to make up for a disappointing television debut. 'I know. But maybe it was a one-off or perhaps it was because it *was* only a pilot. Now I've got the job I was bloody awful. Even the nice autocue girl was embarrassed at how many retakes I had to do. And Maggy bloody Mann thought she'd died and gone to heaven.'

'Poor Mum.' She took the kettle out of Ally's hand and started making her a cup of tea. 'Maybe it'll be better next week.'

'God, I hope so.' Ally sat down at the kitchen table and closed her eyes. 'I can't stand much more of the nice people feeling sorry for me and the shitbags saying "What do you expect? She's only a housewife?"'

'Come on, Mum, it was only your first week. I bet Sue Lawley screwed up on her first week. It's expected. Otherwise it'd look too easy and all of us punters would think we could do it. Have another biscuit.' She delved in the tin and handed one to Ally. 'Here, you have the one in the gold wrapper.'

Ally smiled. The gold ones were Jess's favourite.

Two hours later, when she heard Matt's car crunching on the gravel, Ally felt a wave of relief at the thought of sharing it with him over a glass of wine. He might even have some useful advice. She jumped up and went outside on to the verandah to wait for him, holding her hand up against the slanting rays of the evening sun. It was so warm they could almost have their drinks out here.

But she knew something was wrong the moment he got out of the car. His face was tight and closed. Usually he came in smiling, opening his arms up to Janey and Jess and telling them bad jokes which made them groan.

'What's the matter, love?' Ally asked.

Matt leaned down and kissed her cheek, then stopped for a moment to drink in her scent. 'Lovely smell. What is it?'

'Matt, you know what it is. It's Diorissimo. I always wear it. What's happened?'

Matt seemed startled. 'Is it so obvious?'

'When you've been married to someone for eighteen years, yes. What is it?'

Matt took her hand and led her into the garden. The setting sun had cast half of it into shadow. 'It's Bernie Long. We finally had a showdown today.'

Ally felt a flash of relief. She couldn't stand Bernie. If Matt fell out with him it wouldn't break her heart.

'What about?'

Matt picked a chrysanthemum and smelt its crisp, pungent perfume. He loved this garden. Whatever mood he was in, however much stress was piling up, it always had the power to soothe him. 'Oh, you know, the direction of the programme. I think we should toughen up and Bernie wants to stick with the old formula.'

He said it casually but she knew at once that it was a crucial difference of opinion. And it explained a lot about the way he'd been behaving.

'And haven't you the right to decide? It's your show. Without you they'd have nothing.'

'True.' He lifted her hand to his cheek and held it there. 'And, of course, I could always walk out. That's one power I do have.'

Ally was staggered. 'But surely it hasn't come to that?'

'No, don't worry. We're not going to be suddenly slung out on the street.'

'I wasn't thinking of that.' She couldn't help feeling offended at his interpretation. 'I only meant I was surprised you were thinking in those terms.'

'I'm not.' He smiled the old Matt Boyd smile, warm as toffee straight from the oven. 'Just rehearsing a bit of sabre rattling for my showdown with Stephen next week.'

'What are you going to say?'

'That the show needs to change or I won't front it.'

It struck Ally with a warm glow of pleasure that they'd hardly ever talked like this before. Matt rarely brought work home, either physically or mentally, and though she knew he didn't mean to exclude her she'd felt excluded all the same. Now it seemed different. Was it her imagination or could it be because she was part of his world now, even if in a small way, that he was actually discussing his problems with her?

'So, how was your first week?'

'OK,' she lied, 'I wasn't too hot on the autocue.'

'No one is at first.' He put his arm round her and squeezed her encouragingly. 'It's a bloody unnatural process reading off a roll of toilet paper and trying to fool everyone you're just talking. You'll improve. Tell them you need some practice. The producer should be suggesting it, not waiting for you to ask.'

Suddenly Ally felt a whole lot better.

'What's for dinner?' Matt caught hold of her and kissed her till she couldn't breathe. 'Or shouldn't I be asking that now you're a working woman?'

'Omelettes.' She laughed and then, freeing herself and pulling him towards the kitchen, added, 'Seeing as they're your speciality, I thought you could make them while I do the salad.' She was now in a terrific mood, despite their problems. And then a thought struck her. 'If you want the show to change and Stephen supports you, what will happen to Bernie?'

'He'll leave the show, I suppose.'

'And who will produce it instead?'

There was a fraction of a second's pause before Matt answered. 'Do you remember Belinda Wyeth, the new producer?' He turned towards the glass cupboard to get himself a whisky tumbler so he didn't see the shadow that crossed Ally's face. 'She's terrifically talented. I thought I might suggest her.'

Chapter 11

Stephen Cartwright closed the door of his office, an unusual step for him unless he was having a meeting, and sat down at his desk. He reached for the remote control and pressed it. A huge, slightly concave screen appeared in one corner of the room. He pressed another button and Maggy Mann in high-definition detail appeared four feet away.

Hello was halfway through its hour and a half slot. Stephen glanced down at the sheet of viewing figures in front of him. Far from being the smash hit they'd hoped for *Hello* was doing worse than the bought-in soap opera it had replaced. At first he'd put it down to teething troubles, but it had been on the air for six weeks now and its sole achievement so far had been to boost the ratings of the programme on the opposite channel.

Watching it this morning Stephen wasn't surprised. The show was a shambles, its set dreary and dated, the lighting depressing and the presenters looked as though they'd rather spend time with anyone but each other. Maggy, wearing a revealing black dress more suited to a singles' bar than a coffee-time TV show, was unsuccessfully trying to liven the thing up by some forced banter with the gardening man.

And Allegra Boyd, who'd been so great on the pilot, was the worst thing of all. She sat staring at the autocue like a frightened rabbit and had about as much charisma as a dental hygienist. Watching her on television and remembering the lovely spirited woman he knew her to be in real life, Stephen wondered what the hell had gone wrong.

Angrily he flicked the TV off. Maybe it had been his fault for following Patsy's hunch and shoving someone so inexperienced into the limelight. One thing he was sure of: if the show didn't improve he'd have to find a new producer. But where would he find someone at such short notice with the flair and talent to rescue it?

The phone on his desk buzzed, interrupting his thoughts which had anyway drawn a blank. It was his secretary Janet.

'Stephen, I've got Alex Williams from Big City Television. He says it's urgent.'

Stephen sat still for a moment, startled. Outsiders thought the BBC was Century's greatest rival, but this was a misapprehension. The BBC didn't compete against them for advertising revenue. The only company that competed directly with Century was Big City Television, and at times it was a dirty war. Big City's salesmen would refuse to sell airtime to companies unless they swore not to advertise on Century. Century, complaining loudly of dirty tricks, did exactly the same. The two companies were not, to put it mildly, the best of friends.

As it happened Stephen found what Alex Williams had to say very interesting indeed.

Everyone in TV knew that Big City's owners, a giant leisure group, had financial problems and wanted to sell. But now they'd found a buyer. And it was his name that made Stephen sit up. Ritchie Page. Ex-porn King. Czar of the video rental business, and currently owner of a satellite outfit called Kids' Club Channel.

Ritchie Page had been one of the first people to understand the power of video. While the experts were moaning that it would never catch on, Page had already started a chain of high-street video shops. It hadn't taken him long to work out that the most popular videos were violence and soft-core porn, the very thing British television prided itself on not transmitting.

On the back of the fortune he'd made Page had decided to go respectable. When satellite had come along he'd spotted another opportunity with his Kids' Club Channel. By clever marketing of Fred Bear, their cartoon presenter, kids all over Europe were blackmailing their parents into buying satellite dishes.

Now he wanted to go a step further and buy a grown-up TV company.

Stephen had never heard Alex Williams so agitated. 'If Page gets his hands on Big City it'll be nothing but stripping housewives.' Williams paused fractionally to let the implications sink in. 'And it won't just be us, mate. You'll have to do it too. Look at the *Mirror* and the *Sun*. It's the way of the world.'

Alex had a point and Stephen knew it. If Page got hold of Big City, Century would find it hard to resist going downmarket too. 'So how can I help?'

'Could you do something on him? We can't because it would look too obvious. But *you* could.'

'Yes, I suppose we could. Let me have a think about it.'

Stephen put the phone down. He could have done without this, at this precise moment in time.

'Why does Maggy Mann loathe you so much?' Susie took her coat off and raised an eyebrow at her friend. An hour ago she'd taken an anguished call from Ally insisting she drop everything and join her for lunch. Ally needed to drown her sorrows. She'd just given her worst studio performance so far. 'It even shows on camera.'

'Have you got a spare day?' Ally poured them both a glass of wine. 'Because I'm Matt's wife, because he didn't leave me and my kids for someone younger like her husband did, because Stephen or, worse, Patsy suggested me when she wanted her friend Anne Adamson to get the job. And worst of all, because she thinks I'm an amateur.'

'But you've worked in television before.' Susie scanned the menu and tried to decide if there were more calories in crespolini with spinach and ricotta or spaghetti carbonara. Spaghetti won hands down, she decided. She'd have that.

'That was before the ark. And before autocue. That's my real problem. I sound like I'm reading out the telephone directory instead of some heartfelt plea.'

'Surely that's just practice.' Susie caught the waiter's eye and asked for more bread. 'After all, you haven't been doing it long.'

'I know,' Ally agreed gloomily, 'but Maggy Mann seems to think it's still too long. Actually' – Ally brightened, remembering that Maggy Mann had smiled wanly at her for the first time today – 'Maggy was a bit nicer to me this morning.'

'Oh, shit.' Susie shrugged sympathetically. 'That's bad news. She must really think you're on the way out then.'

'Hello, Matt, sit down.' Stephen looked up in surprise as Matt and Belinda were ushered into his office. When Matt had asked for this meeting he'd assumed it would be with Matt alone, or perhaps with Bernie Long. He hadn't expected Belinda.

'You know Belinda Wyeth, of course?'

'Of course.' Stephen stood up and held out his hand. He'd forgotten quite how striking she was, with her long hair and dark glowing eyes. She looked as though she belonged on the cover of some magazine, not buried away in a control room. 'You're the new producer on Matt's show. You came to us from the BBC.' He smiled. 'I had a letter from the Head of Entertainment accusing me of poaching his best person with the lure of filthy lucre.'

'It wasn't the lucre.' Belinda smiled back and Stephen

realized she was about half an inch taller than him, even in her flat shoes. 'It was the chance to work with Matt.' Belinda resisted the temptation to add 'so that I could shake up his crappy show.' She must remember to tread carefully.

Stephen glanced at Matt. How nice to have a beautiful and talented girl think you're wonderful. Come to think of it, he'd heard the odd whisper about Matt and this girl, but he'd dismissed them. TV companies would grind to a halt without the engine oil of malicious gossip. Mind you, there did seem to be a frisson between them, though he couldn't say whether it was sexual or simply the spark of shared ideas. Of course, one could very easily lead to the other. Stephen had seen that happen often enough.

'Somehow,' Stephen said easily, 'I doubt that coming to tell me how much you like working together is the reason that you asked for this meeting.'

'Hardly,' Matt conceded. 'Look, Stephen, I might as well be candid. I'm not happy with the way the show's going. It's beginning to feel middle-aged. We're losing viewers because it's getting so dull, but Bernie refuses to take any risks and do something about it.'

'Is that why you've been difficult lately? You're usually so easy-going that a lot of people have noticed.'

Matt laughed. 'You ain't seen nothing yet. Stephen, I'm bored out of my head.' He jumped up and began pacing the room. 'I could recite the guest list for the next six shows, they're all so predictable. We've got to change the format.' He pulled a newspaper cutting out of his briefcase. 'And we've got to do it soon, before Danny Wilde gets in first.'

Stephen picked up the clipping. 'Maybe Bernie isn't just being cautious. Maybe he disagrees with your analysis of the problem.'

'How could he? Even he must see the show's not as good as it was. Stephen, we're not just losing viewers to Danny Wilde, the stars are going too. Last week Tod Brooks was in town, and he went on Danny's show, for Christ's sake! I'm not talking about making the show heavy and serious. I'm Mr Charm, I know that. But I need something to get my teeth into.'

Stephen thought quickly. He hadn't known about Tod Brooks. Matt's was the show the big stars had always chosen. 'So what changes are you proposing?'

'That we try and be a bit more dangerous, push back the boundaries of the chat-show a little. The conventional chat-show's finished. We're in a new era. We need edge.'

'And what does Bernie think of this? I assume, since you're here and he isn't, that he doesn't know.'

'Of course he knows. He just didn't want to come,' flashed Matt. 'Bernie and I have worked together for fifteen years. I wouldn't be here today if I could make him see sense, but he won't listen. I think it's time for a change.'

Stephen glanced from Matt to Belinda. Why had she come when she wasn't saying anything?

'OK, I'm not making any promises,' Stephen said, knowing he couldn't afford to ignore Matt's restlessness any longer. 'But if you work up some treatments of your revamped show I'll have a look at them.'

'You can have them now.' Belinda spoke at last and handed him a folder. It contained three fully scripted shows she and Matt had worked out together. Stephen flicked through them astonished. At the bottom of one a name caught his eye and held it.

'I see you want to interview Ritchie Page.'

'Absolutely,' Matt enthused. 'He's just the kind of bent businessman I'd really enjoy having a go at.'

Stephen had an inspiration. It might work. If Matt Boyd exposed Ritchie Page in front of millions, the man could hardly go ahead and buy Big City Television.

Matt looked at Stephen intently, trying to gauge what was behind his sudden silence. Maybe this was the moment to tell the truth: that he wasn't prepared to go on fronting the show unless Stephen agreed to the changes.

But there was no need to threaten. Stephen was smiling.

'OK, you can try out your new format.' Matt and Belinda glanced at each other in amazement at his unexpected capitulation. 'Providing you get Ritchie Page on the first show.'

Matt caught Belinda's eye and he signalled minutely that they should go now in case Stephen changed his mind. Quickly she gathered up her things, trying with a superhuman effort not to show her delight till they got out of Stephen's office.

'By the way,' Stephen said, addressing their departing backs, the corners of his lips lifting slightly, 'I assume you're not expecting Bernie Long to produce it.'

Matt turned. 'No. I had hoped . . .' He paused for a moment.

'That Belinda here might produce it instead,' Stephen completed his thought. 'OK.' Stephen grinned, telling himself maybe he was mad. But Matt was right. The show was middle-aged. Maybe Belinda would be what it needed to shake it up. Maybe. But how the hell was he going to tell Bernie Long? He had a meeting with him in a quarter of an hour.

As he watched them almost run out, their eyes lit up with excitement, he wondered if he was doing the right thing. And the thought crossed his mind that, given the rumours, he might have done Allegra Boyd a great disservice.

'We've done it, Matt!' Belinda had expected this to be simply the first skirmish in a long war. Instead it was all over. They were still standing outside Stephen's office. She let out something sounding like a rebel yell and Matt grabbed her and pulled her towards the lifts and away from Janet's disapproving gaze.

Outside the lifts Belinda turned to him, still smiling. 'Don't let's go back to the office. Let's go and celebrate.'

Matt smiled back. 'After I've found Bernie. I want to tell him myself before Stephen gets the chance. I owe it to him. Why don't you go over to Studio Five and try and get a table?'

He pressed the button and the lift appeared. Belinda stepped in.

Across the road in the wine bar known as Studio Five – so named to confuse wives, girlfriends or bosses who could be truthfully informed 'he's in Studio Five' – Belinda fought her way through the busy lunchtime crowd and ordered champagne.

Ten minutes later Matt appeared.

'Did you catch him?'

'Yup. Just in time. He was on his way up to see Stephen.'

'How did he take it?'

Matt shrugged. 'You know Bernie. He wished me luck and said I was going to need it with you as my producer. There's only one thing I can't work out in all this.' Matt poured himself a glass and topped up Belinda's. 'Why does it all depend on getting Ritchie Page?'

'Search me.' Belinda shrugged. 'Maybe Stephen's been buying naughty videos.' She sipped her champagne. 'Do you think he means it about only going ahead with the new format if we get Page on the show?'

Matt pictured Stephen's expression for a moment. 'Yes.' He drained his glass and stood up. 'I think he probably does.'

★

Stephen Cartwright was not looking forward to the next meeting. Bernie Long had been Matt Boyd's producer from the beginning and Stephen had been trying to think up a way of softening the blow when he told him he was being elbowed out. And, worse, by a woman. In the event he didn't have to. Bernie did it for him.

'So.' Without being asked, Bernie stretched himself comfortably along Stephen's leather sofa with his hands behind his head, his raddled features restful for once. He looked like every shrink's nightmare. The one who would always get away. 'You're dumping me for a bimbo who's got Matt Boyd's prick in a vice and wants to turn the show into *News at Ten*,' he informed Stephen good-humouredly.

Stephen, who'd been intending to work up to this information carefully, was struck dumb.

'How did you know?'

Bernie grinned. 'Matt's just told me. He was very honest. Said my ideas stank but he'd still be my best friend.' Bernie put his feet on Stephen's Navajo Indian cushion cover. 'Can't say I'm surprised. I'd have to have been blindfolded not to see this coming.'

'You seem to be taking it very well, I must say,' Stephen said, temporarily thrown by Bernie's reaction.

'O Lord,' intoned Bernie, crossing his hands, 'grant me the serenity to accept things that I cannot change.' He closed his eyes in mock devotion. 'The courage to change things I can.' He opened one eye and fixed it on Stephen. 'And the patience to wait until the whole bloody thing falls on its arse. Amen.'

Stephen tried to ignore him.

'It will, you know, Stephen.' Bernie picked his tooth with one of Stephen's matches marked 'Savoy Grill'. 'Fall on its arse.'

'Why?'

'Matt wants to spread his wings, fine. He wants to live

dangerously, why not? As long as he remembers it's his humour people like, and his charm. But this isn't the right slot. That sort of show should be late-night.' He took his feet off the Navajo cushion and poured himself a mineral water, looking at it as though it might be swarming with typhoid. 'Anyway, I don't need to give you a lecture on scheduling. So' – Stephen realized that Bernie had taken the meeting out of his hands completely – 'what crummy consolation prize are you going to offer me? Six weeks in the Bahamas to research a documentary until you want me back to pick up the pieces?'

But Stephen didn't hear him. The solution had just come to him. If he could sell it to Bernie. 'Not this time, Bernie. In fact there's something your style and flair would be brilliant for.'

Bernie held his nose disrespectfully. 'I smell bullshit.'

'Nonsense, Bernie,' Stephen corrected. 'Don't be paranoid.'

'So what is this unmissable opportunity that could so benefit from my inimitable style and flair?'

Stephen paused, then looked him in the eye. 'I want you to take over *Hello* and rescue it.' He sat next to Bernie on the sofa and gave him the benefit of his most charming smile. 'I've spent three million launching that show and I know it's a great concept. I'm not going to sit back and watch it go down the plughole.'

'But that's daytime.' Bernie's voice bristled with outrage. 'I'm not working on some crappy daytime show.'

'Bernie, daytime's changed. It's not three women and a dog talking about cystitis any more. The other channel gets nearly four million viewers, and *Hello*'s almost there. It just needs tweaking a bit and you'll get all the glory.'

'Tweaking?' Bernie laughed rudely. 'The word on the street says it's such a mess it's embarrassing. D'you know what they're calling it?'

Stephen wasn't sure he wanted to.

'*Goodbye*. Because it'll be whipped off quicker than a bride's brassière.'

Stephen declined to comment.

'And do you know the other thing they're saying?' Bernie was beginning to enjoy himself. 'That your own personal choice, Mrs Matthew Boyd, is a complete disaster area who couldn't read a menu let alone autocue. I'm told Maggy Mann's sitting by the guillotine like Madame Defarges waiting for her head to roll.'

'They're right about that, at least.' Stephen looked puzzled. 'What I can't understand is why she was so good on the pilot.'

Bernie shrugged and started to get up. 'I've known Ally Boyd for years, Stephen. For a housewife she probably makes a perfectly good TV presenter ... anyway, there's no point talking about this. I'm not interested.'

'Why not do it for a month? Six weeks at the outside? If you rescue it you get the credit, if it goes down the tubes blame Bill Ford.'

Bernie laughed. 'You're not as dumb as you seem, are you, Stephen? But the answer's the same. Thanks but no thanks.'

'I could make you, you know.'

'I know you could.' Bernie smiled engagingly. 'But you've already had one cynical shit on the show. You don't need another.'

'At least look at a tape and tell me what you think's wrong.' Stephen handed Bernie two tapes.

'What's this?' Bernie asked about the second one.

'That's the pilot. Have a look at Allegra. You'll be quite surprised.'

Bernie took the tapes. He had absolutely no intention of watching them but it was the only way he was going to get out of here and into the bar without offending Stephen.

★

By 1.33 precisely Bernie Long was seated on a bar stool staring into the welcoming smile of a double Martell, thoughtfully laid out, as it was every lunchtime, by Brendan, Century's barman.

Although he would have renounced the demon drink altogether rather than admit it, Bernie had been hurt by the morning's proceedings. His confidence, usually as solid as the rock of Gibraltar and twice as British, had been temporarily dented. Was he washed up on the tide of his own mediocrity, as Belinda kept trying to point out? Playing safe because he'd run out of ideas? Matt's criticism that the show had become the bland leading the bland lodged itself in his brain. There was only one answer.

He'd have another drink.

He was in the act of trying to catch a dry-roasted peanut in his mouth without falling off the bar stool when Maggy Mann appeared at his side and ordered a large Perrier with lime but no ice. She always declined tap water on the grounds that she didn't know who it had been seven times around.

'Bernie, hello.' Maggy Mann glanced at the double in Bernie's hand and the refill already waiting next to him on the bar. She smiled sweetly. 'I hear you've finally been dropped from *The Matt Boyd Show*.' She raised her glass of Perrier to him in a mock toast. 'What happened? Drink problem finally catch up with you?'

Although she didn't know it, Maggy had chosen a very ill-advised moment to accuse Bernie of being a down-and-out. Normally he would have dismissed it as the whinings of a menopausal troublemaker. But today it rankled.

For one long and very enjoyable moment Bernie considered pouring his drink over her. Then he decided it would be a waste of good cognac. Besides, he remembered the job Stephen Cartwright had just offered him. He'd just thought of a much more subtle and effective way of getting his own back on Maggy Mann.

As Ally walked along Millbank after her lunch with Susie she stopped and leaned over the parapet of Lambeth Bridge, feeling the sharp wind that had arrived with the beginning of November. Gulls were wheeling over the river in the wake of one of the pleasure boats, almost empty of tourists now. Big Ben, newly cleaned, stood out disconcertingly honey-coloured against a sharp blue sky. She was used to seeing it black and grimy with the fumes of centuries.

It was three thirty and she knew she'd been putting off going back to the office. Watching the people scurrying towards the tube station eager to miss the rush hour, Ally came to a decision. She couldn't go on like this. She could feel the tension rising almost visibly when she walked into the studio now.

Yet when she'd asked for training Bill Ford had been curiously reluctant. She'd even wondered if he wanted her to fail. And now there was a rumour that Bill Ford was on the way out himself. If she wasn't careful she'd be next. Maybe, if she was really honest, it'd be a relief.

She turned away from the river and walked briskly back towards the studios. A few yards from Century she caught sight of a crowd spilling out of the wine bar across the road, laughing and gossiping. For a moment she envied them their laughter and even more the self-confidence that allowed them to roll back into their offices well after three. She hardly ever did it herself and had been busy formulating an excuse for her own long absence. Then she stopped short. The last two to come out were Matt and Belinda. They looked flushed and happy with either drink or excitement. A sudden fear leapt into her mind watching them. Trying not to let herself be suspicious she waved and quickened her step but by the time she'd run up Century's front steps and into the building they'd disappeared into the lift, only a trace of strong perfume, Paloma Picasso perhaps, remained. Ally felt a momentary temptation to kick the blank wall of steel.

As soon as she walked into *Hello*'s office she knew something had happened. Researchers were huddled into little groups, whispering. Moira, Maggy's friend the PA, looked as though someone had just broken the news to her that she only had three months to live.

'Well!' Ally gazed from one group of people to another. 'What a happy little ship this is!'

'Haven't you heard the news?' Nikki unknotted herself from a group and walked towards her. 'Bill Ford's been fired. He cleared his desk half an hour ago.'

Ally still couldn't understand why the atmosphere was so funereal. Bill Ford, lech and cheapskate, had hardly been anyone's hero.

'So? That's hardly the end of the world, is it? Nobody liked him.'

'No,' Nikki flopped into her chair. Fourteen stone of regret and dismay looked up at Ally pessimistically. 'But you don't know who's replacing him.'

Chapter 12

As Ally opened her eyes she knew that at the back of her mind there was a reason why she wasn't looking forward to today. Then she remembered it. Bernie Long was arriving to take over *Hello*. Ally put her head back under the duvet and decided she never wanted to come out. Maybe if she stayed here in the nice warm dark it would turn out to have been an illusion, one of those nasty pieces of TV gossip, no more.

'What's this I hear about Bernie being your new boss?' Ally could hear the amusement in Matt's voice and she emerged from the covers angrily.

Matt was the other side of the room and to her amazement she saw that he was on the exercise bicycle he'd bought himself three years ago and so far only used to hang his clothes on. It reminded her of the fact that she'd seen him with Belinda yesterday. Why was he suddenly so keen on getting fit?

'Don't sound so damn happy about it!' Ally snapped. 'Just because it got you off the hook and you could have your precious bloody Belinda. You know how much I loathe Bernie Long!'

Matt tried not to smile at Ally's tone of desperation.

'I know you do, but he'll be brilliant. With that cretin Bill Ford you'd have been off the air in weeks. Bernie'll turn *Hello* round if anyone can. As long as he stays sober.'

Ally retreated under the covers again. My God! She hadn't even thought about the drink problem. Matt got off the bicycle and disappeared. In his absence her mind drifted to his sudden energy, the eager look in his blue eyes and the sense of almost boyish enthusiasm she hadn't seen since the old days at MidWest TV. She hoped it was just a new direction for his show that was making him so pleased with life.

Suddenly the duvet was stripped off and Matt, dressed and ready for work, stood by the bedside precariously balancing a tray on one hand.

'By the way, what were you doing having a long lunch with Belinda yesterday?'

'What is this?' He laughed down at her. 'The Spanish Inquisition? Come on, self-pity will get you nowhere. Just because *Hello*'s turning out to be harder than you expected.' He put down the tray and pulled her out of bed. 'Get in there and show him. Show Bernie what you can do. You were brilliant on the pilot. You can be again.' He handed her a cup of tea.

She sat down on the bed and pulled up the duvet again, holding her cup of tea to her like a comforter. 'I thought I might have another five minutes.'

Matt shook his head and stroked her hair. 'Drink up. I'm giving you a lift to work in quarter of an hour.'

'But it isn't one of my days.'

'It is now. Marie rang. Bernie's secretary. He's called a team meeting this morning.'

Ally put down her tea and, despite Matt's exhortations, retreated under the covers again wondering if she should just resign now and save herself the humiliation.

When she and Matt walked up Century's steps, an hour later, she felt as though she were climbing the scaffold. 'By the way,' Matt said as they reached reception, 'you haven't forgotten my folks are coming to stay have you?'

Ally closed her eyes for a second. Amid the drama she had indeed forgotten about it. That was all she needed.

★

In *The Matt Boyd Show* offices things were buzzing. Everyone down to the humblest typist was aware of Matt's excitement and the sense that they were doing something new. Without any prior discussion most of the team had come in earlier than usual and instead of the typical slow start, gossiping by the coffee machine or lazily flipping through the papers with their feet on the desk, phone calls were being made. For once researchers were actually picking up and reading some of the giant pile of press releases sent in by every PR agency in the country with crappy ideas.

Belinda appeared from her office, that had until yesterday been Bernie's, wearing a black wool dress with a white lace collar. It was almost down to the knee and for once there was no air of sexual innuendo about it. It was a let's-get-down-to-business dress. She smiled at Matt, her eyes shining, holding his for a moment. She looked round, raised her eyebrows very slightly, and laughed, sensing like him the delicious and unfamiliar sense of excitement that every one of the thirty team members was feeling.

High above the river in the sixteenth-floor conference room the atmosphere was very different. Small groups stood around in twos and threes waiting for Bernie to make his appearance. Nikki, munching her third custard cream in an attempt to cheer herself up, jumped off her perch in the window ledge when she saw Ally coming in the door.

'I see everyone's taking it well,' Ally said.

'I'm looking on the bright side.' Nikki handed her a cup of coffee and gestured at Maggy sitting hunched at one end of the long table, 'Some people are really worried.' She leaned down to whisper in Ally's ear. 'When she heard she stormed off to complain to Stephen

Cartwright. Said it was Bernie or her.' Nikki grinned. 'Stephen apparently said it'd have to be her then. She soon changed her mind.'

Ally had never thought she'd find it in her heart to feel sorry for Maggy Mann, but today she seemed pathetic rather than her usual spiteful self.

For a moment Ally wondered whether to say something but decided that solidarity, even in defeat, was not likely to appeal to Maggy. But as she turned away she noticed Maggy glance down at a striking brooch made of shiny blue and pink foil and coloured paperclips pinned to her dress, no doubt the expensive product of some postmodernist jeweller.

'Pretty brooch,' Ally, feeling she had to say *something*, smiled and sat down.

Maggy's face softened. 'Thanks. My son made it,' and she touched it like a talisman, as though it might bring better luck. Despite herself, Ally was touched. So there was a person inside there after all.

For the first time Ally saw Maggy's mask drop, revealing the frightened individual beneath. Maybe Maggy really was worried about losing her job with three children to support. In that case she'd have more in common with her audience than she thought. For the first time Ally felt she might have broken through Maggy's spiky exterior and racked her brains for what to say to keep the intimacy going. But at that instant the door opened and Bernie Long walked in.

'Morning, all.' Bernie helped himself to a cup of coffee and sat down at the head of the table. 'Right, shall we get started? Why don't I tell you what I think of the show and my ideas about how it should change, then you can tell me how lousy they are? OK?'

One or two people smiled wanly.

'To kick off, I think the show's absolutely fucking awful.'

'Thanks a lot,' mumbled Brian, the director, under his breath.

'I don't think there's any mileage in beating about the bush. The set's pure *Colditz*, the graphics look like a five-year-old did them and the presenters treat each other as though they're HIV-positive. You may not like the truth, but there it is. If we don't get our act together Stephen says we're off the air at Christmas.' This wasn't in fact true but Bernie liked things to be dramatic.

There was stunned silence. Ally was fleetingly grateful that she hadn't been singled out as one of the show's glaring deficiencies but maybe that would come later. Bernie seemed to be actually enjoying himself, the bastard. Didn't the management books tell you to praise as well as criticize? Bernie clearly hadn't read them.

For a moment Ally wondered if Bernie had been given the brief of closing the show down rather than rebuilding it. She decided that was too Machiavellian for Stephen.

Bernie was talking again. 'So, what are the positive aspects of the show?' He glanced around at the resentful faces, some doodling, some looking at their hands or out of the windows at the stunning view below. 'Well, there's one thing that hits me at once. When you're this far down, you can only go up.'

For some curious reason nobody found this as encouraging as Bernie.

By six that evening *The Matt Boyd Show* offices were still packed and humming. Instead of watching the clock as keenly as a football manager in injury time, almost every member of the team was having to be reminded it was time they went home. It had almost been like launching a new programme.

They already had acceptances from most of the

celebrities for the first two shows. The only major guest who hadn't yet replied was Ritchie Page, and because so much depended on his acceptance Belinda was handling that negotiation herself.

The trouble was he was proving to be tougher to persuade than she'd bargained for. Even pinning down his press agent was harder than getting an interview with Madonna.

Still, thought Belinda as she failed to get through for the third time that day, it's early days yet. She turned to Matt. 'Coming for a drink?'

Matt realized that psychologically today was an important day to be one of the boys. 'Buy a round for me, will you?' He handed her a £20 note. 'I'll be down in a minute.'

Reaching for the phone he called Ally. 'How was it?'

'Wrist-slitting.'

'Go on, Bernie likes to exaggerate.'

'And if half the team jumps off Chelsea Bridge too bad?'

'That's the spirit. Have you cooked yet?'

'No, I was too busy diving into the biggest G. and T. in history.'

'Well, don't. I thought you might need cheering up and I'm bringing something.'

Ally made a unilateral decision to feel more cheerful. And when Matt arrived two hours later with a large carrier bag from Justin de Blank and unpacked foil containers of crab and lobster and Coronation chicken, with side salads of avocado and cracked wheat, rounded off with strawberries and cream even though it was November, she put aside her worries, and settled down to enjoy it.

Matt loved her and tomorrow was another day.

★

As *Hello*'s closing music faded, Bernie Long put his head in his hands and reflected that it had not felt like an hour and a half. It had felt like a lifetime. But maybe he only had himself to blame. He'd hoped that putting a bomb under the team might have galvanized them into searching for new ideas. Instead it was making them cling to the old ones even more tightly for security.

The list of what was wrong with the show was endless. And at the top of it was Ally Boyd.

Bernie watched her unhook her mike and race out of the studio. She clearly knew her performance was lousy. Maybe she'd even resign. Thinking about it, that might be the best outcome all round.

But for the moment Bernie decided there was only one answer. He would go out tonight and get absolutely wrecked. That way maybe he'd avoid admitting that taking on *Hello* might be the worst mistake he'd ever made.

Ally was as grateful as Bernie that she had to rush off so quickly after the show. Mona and Joe, her parents-in-law, were due today and Matt had gone shopping for the kind of no-nonsense food they liked to eat. Knowing him he would have been sidetracked by sun-dried tomatoes and olive bread in the deli and wouldn't be there to meet them. Ally had to admit the thought of coping with her mother-in-law after the direness of today's studio was not a pleasant prospect.

When she arrived home an hour later she was still shaking. And the sight of her parents-in-law's immaculate Vauxhall Astra parked neatly in the drive, but with no sign of Matt's car anywhere, was too much. He'd promised to be back half an hour ago. Mona and Joe would have had no one to greet them and she knew how hurt they must have been by that.

As she opened the front door she heard voices and

followed them towards the kitchen. She put down her bag by the hall mirror and tidied her hair. As she did so she caught the unmistakable tones of her mother and Mrs O'Shock. What on earth was her mother doing here? Then she realized what the topic of conversation was. Her. They were talking about her decision to get a job. She sneaked forward silently and stood listening.

'What do you think of this TV business, Mona?' She recognized her mother's disapproving voice. 'That's why she's not here to meet you.' Typical, thought Ally. Why doesn't she blame Matt for not being back? Why is everything always my fault? But her mother hadn't finished. 'Don't you think that son of yours needs someone to come home to?'

Great. That was all she needed. A discussion group in her own kitchen on whether she was neglecting her wifely responsibilities. She could imagine Mona's views on that. Mona had always put her family first, naturally, and probably had Ally on a par with Joan Crawford in *Mommie Dearest*. Well, after today's performance she probably wouldn't have to worry much longer. It wouldn't be long before she was chained to the kitchen sink again.

Unfortunately Sox chose that moment to notice that her mistress had returned and began to yelp joyously so Ally was destined to never find out her mother-in-law's opinion.

To save their embarrassment Ally began banging about and started to make a noisy entrance. They were sitting with cups of tea around the kitchen table. Mrs O'Shock, she noticed, had found the expensive Belgian biscuits Ally had hidden from her, pointedly putting out Rich Tea for her cleaning lady to have with her elevenses, and was tucking into one of Jess's favourite gold-wrapped wafers.

'Mona. Joe. How lovely to see you.' She kissed them both, hardly recognizing Mona without the flowery pinny which seemed as much a part of her small, plump mother-in-law as her tightly permed hair or the sheepskin slippers she religiously wore whenever she was in the house. 'Hello, Mother. I didn't know you were coming over.'

'I wasn't. Mrs O'Shaugnessy telephoned when Matt wasn't back so that there'd at least be *someone* to meet Mona and Joe.'

Before Ally had time to reply the front door opened and Matt came in.

'Mum! Dad! Great to see you! How was the journey?'

As he strode forward, held his mother and shook his father's hand she noticed how his accent, which normally had only a hint of his origins, took on a more West Country burr in their presence, reassuring them that despite his success and fame he was still the son they'd known. But then he'd always prided himself on keeping the common touch. It was one of the things that made him so popular. Unlike a lot of stars Matt had never made the mistake of forgetting where he came from.

When they sat down to lunch Matt took a mouthful of Newton's Celebrated Meat Pie, brought specially by his mother, and closed his eyes in ecstasy. Mona glowed with pleasure.

After the meal her mother-in-law refused all offers of going into the sitting room with her son, husband and Elizabeth, and insisted on helping Ally stack the dishwasher. Ally half expected her mother-in-law to disapprove of something so labour-saving, but Mona turned out to be a passionate convert, eager to talk about the relative merits of powder versus liquid.

'The only thing is,' Mona said, removing an encrusted pan from Ally's hands which she was guiltily about to load, knowing the heat would bake the remaining food on

165

like iron, and put it firmly in the sink to soak, 'that it's killed washing-up conversation.' Mona ran the sink full of water and put in Fairy Liquid. 'The only chance I got to have a good chat with my mother was when we were doing the washing up.'

Ally laughed. She'd never noticed this unexpected drawback of kitchen technology. Then she remembered her own childhood and saw that Mona was right. She'd always hated doing the washing-up, yet there had been a kind of rhythm between washer and dryer which did indeed encourage the exchange of confidences.

It had been over the intimacy of the washing-up that Ally had made the mistake of telling her mother about fancying her brother's friend. And ever since her mother had never missed an opportunity for teasing her. Ally hung her wet teacloth on the back of a chair. There was a lot to be said for dishwashers.

'How are you finding this television business?' Mona asked.

It was the question Ally had been dreading. 'Fine.' Her brisk mother-in-law wasn't the type to confide in, even over the washing-up.

'I watched you the other day.'

'Oh?' Ally tried to repress the masochistic desire to add, 'What did you think?'

'That Maggy Mann doesn't give you much of a helping hand, does she?'

'No.' Ally put the kettle on to make coffee. 'She doesn't think an amateur like me should be on the show.' Ally paused, the tension of the morning suddenly flooding back. 'Maybe she's right.'

'What rubbish!' Ally was taken aback by Mona's tone. 'She's a cold fish, that one. She treats everyone she interviews as if they were a sack of coal, but only half as interesting. She probably envies you your nice warm personality.' Ally was struck dumb. She'd never suspected Mona of thinking she had a warm personality.

'Actually' – Ally poured water into the coffee pot – 'I haven't even told Matt this, but I'm thinking of chucking it in.'

Ally wondered why on earth she was telling Mona of all people. Mona was bound to be right behind her mother in thinking Ally ought to be at home. Mona had once won an award for having the cleanest dustbins in Bristol. They didn't make housewives like her any more.

'You musn't, Ally love, you really mustn't.' Ally was startled by her mother-in-law's sudden vehemence. Mona was normally so calm that Ally had wondered if she *had* any emotions lurking under her starched bosom. 'That day you talked to the teenager who was having the baby, my neighbour's girl saw that and went and got herself put on the pill because of it.'

For a moment Ally didn't know whether Mona thought this was good or bad.

'So you see, you musn't give up. You're helping people. And people these days need all the help they can get.'

Ally felt an overwhelming temptation to put her arms round Mona and kiss her. Until now she'd just been thinking about herself and how well she came over professionally. But Mona was right. There *was* more at stake.

'Thank you, Mona.' She squeezed the breath out of her astonished mother-in-law. 'You don't know how much you've helped me by saying that!'

The next day Ally was in studio was Friday and she found herself looking forward to the weekend and a large dose of Matt's reassuring presence.

'Bernie's in a good mood today,' said Elaine, the make-up girl caustically. 'He just told Maggy she was a talent-less cow.'

'Maybe it's all a technique like they do in acting schools,' speculated Nikki, handing Ally a script. 'You break down the ego then rebuild it stronger.'

'Well, the first part seems to be working anyway.' Ally sipped her coffee and tried to keep her face still for Elaine to do her eyelids.

When she was made up Ally wandered through to the studio, banishing her nerves by reminding herself of Mona's words. What she did was *useful*. Thinking there was no one in the darkened gallery behind the control room she pushed it open and put her handbag there. In the half-light she caught sight of Bernie Long. He was sitting smoking a Gauloise and drinking coffee from a paper cup. As he raised his cigarette to his lips she noticed through the bluish pungent smoke that his hands were shaking. Then she noticed something else. A powerful smell of spirits. It wasn't coffee he was drinking but brandy.

Ally closed the door and walked through the control room to the studio floor. She looked at her watch. It was nine twenty a.m.

Bernie Long had a serious drinking problem.

'Any news from the Page camp yet?' Matt swivelled round on his chair to face Belinda.

'They've moved from a "No, definitely" to "We'll think about it". And that's after I tarted myself up to the nines and bought his bloody press agent two bottles of Bolly.'

'Well, I suppose that's progress.' Matt smiled his famous crinkle-eyed smile.

He turned back to his typewriter. He'd already started on a draft outline of the script for the first show and it was going brilliantly. The trick was to keep the humour and enough of the Boyd charm not to alienate his faithful fans but to inject some challenging material too. If he could prove that humour could stand side-by-side with tougher subjects he'd have cracked it. And he was sure he could. He hummed as he slotted a new page into the electronic typewriter and turned it on. It winked back at him encouragingly.

Belinda watched him for a moment. It was like working with a completely different person from the Matt Boyd she'd found when she first joined. This Matt Boyd wasn't restless and bored, he was fizzing with enthusiasm. She wondered briefly at what moment she had started to find him so attractive. When they'd walked out of Stephen Cartwright's office and gone across the road to celebrate their new venture? No, it was before that. When he'd turned twelve minutes of drunken Jon Leighton into a hilarious *tour de force*. She turned away and busied herself with opening a letter unnecessarily, and wondered what it would be like to wake up with those eyes, the colour of stonewashed denim, gazing at her across the pillow. She tried to remind herself what they'd been talking about. 'Do you think I should phone them again today?'

Matt shook his head. 'Better not. You know how it is. Nobody loves you if they think you love them.'

'Yes.' Belinda looked across at him levelly. 'I know exactly what you mean.'

Today, finally, things seemed to be picking up for Ally. She read her links without stumbling and gave some advice to a viewer who didn't know how to handle her teenage kids that was both moving and funny.

Maggy, on the other hand, seemed to have lost her spirit, but instead of making her human it seemed to make her pathetic. She seemed to have got smaller and scruffier and to Ally's amazement she noticed that grey roots were showing in Maggy's jet black hair.

And when Bernie bawled her out in front of a studio guest for mishandling an interview she didn't even argue. But it was too much for Ally. Ally had less to lose than Maggy. She leaped to her feet, for once remembering to undo her radio mike.

'Hang on a minute, Bernie!'

Halfway across the studio Bernie turned.

'What makes you think you can talk to us like that?' Ally gestured towards Maggy.

'Because this crappy show will be off the air if you don't put some fizz into it.' Bernie started walking off again. 'Though bloody Lazarus had more life in him, frankly.'

'So you keep telling us. But what are you going to do about it?' Ally was standing just in front of him now, only inches from his face. 'You should be building us up, not kicking us in the teeth. Give us some constructive advice, for God's sake!' Anger was blazing through her now, unfamiliar and wonderful. Barbara, her assertiveness teacher, would be proud of her. 'But I suppose you'd rather be in the bar, wouldn't you, than wasting your time on a failing programme?'

The silence in the studio was complete. The sparks had stopped rattling the lights, the scene shifters stood still, the floor manager pretended not to hear because of his earphones. But he heard all right. And so did everyone else in the studio.

Without a word Bernie stalked out. As soon as the door to the control room closed, the clapping started. Ally watched Bernie's departing back and knew that she'd put the final nail in the coffin of her new career.

Chapter 13

'So how was it today? Any better?' Matt nuzzled up against her in their huge chintzy bed and she felt at once the incredible physical warmth he gave out. In November, even with central heating, having someone as warm as Matt to cuddle up to was a delight.

'Terrible.' She'd wanted to tell him about the showdown with Bernie all evening but his parents had been there and talking shop seemed rude. 'I had a stand-up fight with Bernie.'

Matt stroked her hair. 'What about?'

'He bawled out Maggy in front of everyone.'

'I don't blame him. What was the problem?'

'He's just being so destructive. He may be a good producer but he's wrecking everyone's confidence. So I told him what I thought of him.'

Matt kissed her neck. 'And what was that?'

Ally sighed as his tongue began to lick her ear.

'That he's a pathetic alcoholic and he ought to get his own house in order before dumping on us.'

Matt stopped licking her ear and stared at her in astonishment. She'd never done anything like that before. 'And how did he take it?'

'He stormed out.' She laughed. 'So I expect I'll be out of a job pretty soon.'

'You never know.' He began to kiss her passionately, his hand edging downwards, excited by this new unexpected streak in the wife he thought he knew. 'Maybe he'll respect you for it.'

'Some chance,' muttered Ally before she forgot about Bernie, Century Television and everything else except

Matt's body pushing into hers.

When Bernie Long woke up it took him five minutes to work out where he was. It was pitch dark outside and when he stood up he walked straight into a cold, hard lump of metal, hitting the thin, delicate bone of his shin and making him cry out in pain so intense it made him dizzy. He staggered, holding on to a flat black surface and looked for a light switch. To his puzzlement there were none. As he felt his way round the room a string, like something out of a ghost train, brushed against his cheek. He jumped back holding it. The room filled with harsh, merciless light. Jesus, he was in the office still! And next to his desk, half-hidden in the wastepaper basket, was an empty bottle of brandy.

Bernie sat down at his desk, pulling the switch to off again. He'd never blacked out before. Christ, he hadn't even felt pissed, and there he was laid out on the floor like a corpse in a funeral parlour. And anyone could have come in and found him. The cleaners, one of the guys from security, even someone on the team.

Bernie sat in the dark for five more minutes, then he groped round for his coat. Still not turning the light on he lifted the bottle from his bin, put it in his briefcase and walked slowly towards the lifts.

Ally woke up with a horrible sense that something had happened that she didn't want to face. Then she remembered. She'd insulted Bernie Long and probably talked herself out of a job in the process. Then she remembered with relief that at least today was Saturday. She could leave Janey and Jess to their own devices and take Mona and Joe out to a pub lunch. Maybe by Monday the whole thing would have blown over. Some chance. And anyway the atmosphere on the programme would be just as dire.

In a matter of days Bernie Long had managed to create more depression than Bill Ford ever had.

Maybe it was time to face facts. The job might be useful but there was no point letting herself be humiliated and losing the confidence she'd so carefully built up.

On Monday she'd go in and resign.

Suddenly she felt ridiculously cheerful, as though a weight had been lifted from her shoulders. Television might be exciting and glamorous, but it wasn't for her.

Bernie Long woke up in his over-decorated service flat and faced the day. He loathed this place where everything was toned so perfectly that he sometimes felt the only thing out of place was him. It had been the show flat and Bernie had bought it fully furnished right down to the bed linen and the Portmeirion coffee cups covered with ox-eye daisies. *Saves having to go to John Lewis*, he'd told himself. If Bernie had to describe his idea of hell on earth it would be John Lewis's curtain department on a Saturday morning.

At the end of Bernie's bed was a pile of tapes, one of which was yesterday's show, which Bernie intended to look at to analyse quite how bad it was. Instead the cassette he put in was the one of the pilot, which he'd refused to watch on the grounds that he preferred having ideas of his own.

Staring out at him from the TV screen was Allegra Boyd. Her face was soft with sympathy and her voice rang with warmth, all for some pregnant teenager she'd never even met. And despite his prejudices about her Bernie felt moved.

Watching her he was hit by an unpleasant truth. Ally Boyd wasn't a vicious woman like Maggy Mann. There was a natural humanity about her that beamed out of the screen even to him, the most cynical of viewers. And everything she'd accused him of yesterday was true. His hurt at being slung off *The Matt Boyd Show* had turned him into a bitter, destructive drunk. Now he had a choice.

'Have you heard?' Nikki grabbed Ally as she arrived at Century's studios. 'Bernie Long's renounced the demon drink. He made an announcement first thing this morning. 'It's part of the process, Maggy says. When they give up drink they go all confessional at first. Keep promising everyone from their mothers to the dustman they'll never drink again. Apparently her ex stood up at the end of a board meeting and announced he was a lifelong alcoholic.'

Ally stared at her in astonishment.

'By the way,' Nikki added, 'he said he wanted to see you when you came in.'

Ally summoned up her resolve. Bernie was probably going to fire her after Friday. But she didn't intend to give him the satisfaction.

'That's just as well.' She poured herself a cup of strong coffee from the machine and sniffed the milk. 'Because as it happens I want to see him.'

Five minutes later Bernie emerged from the door of his office and stood looking around the room. When he saw Ally he started walking towards her. Ally noticed that his baggy lived-in face appeared just the same as usual, with no hint of apology in it.

'Ally, do you have five minutes?'

Ally stopped typing the link into a viewer's letter about falling in love with her best friend's husband and stood up.

As she followed him into his office she was determined to take the initiative.

They hadn't even sat down before she started talking.

'Listen, Bernie, I know you think I'm a suburban house-wife who ought to be safely at home doing the school run . . .'

To her amazement he interrupted her. 'But that's why you're so good, that's your strength! You sound like a real person not some expert with a safe answer to every-thing. You let your emotion show.' Ally stared at him, startled, but Bernie was up and pacing the room. There was a suppressed excitement about him she'd never seen before. 'I watched the tape of the pilot over the weekend. I should have watched it before but I was too pig-headed. You were terrific.'

'For God's sake, Bernie, everyone keeps telling me how good I was on the pilot.' Ally stood up and went over to where he was standing. 'If I was so brilliant then what's gone wrong since?'

'That's simple.' Bernie put his hands lightly on the desktop. 'You've lost your spontaneity, that's all. Forget about getting the words right. Tear up your script. Do it from the heart. You've got something, Allegra. Use it.'

In the excitement of the moment Ally felt tears pricking her eyes and she fought them back, feeling foolish. 'So you want me to stay on?'

'Of course.'

'I came in here to resign.'

Bernie burst out laughing. 'The way I've been behaving I'm not surprised.' He took her hand. His grip was surprisingly cool and firm. 'I nearly fucked it up, didn't I? And then I would have blamed you and Bill Ford. But over the weekend I realized something. I *need* to make this show a hit. Not for Century's sake. They can afford a few million down the drain. For my own self-respect. I need something to fight for.' He let go of her hand and walked over to the window. 'I wouldn't blame you if you walked out. But it'll make saving this show much more difficult.' He turned to her, his voice suddenly low and intense. 'Will you stay on and help me?'

Ally looked at the man she'd loathed for fifteen years and smiled. 'On one condition.'

'And what's that?'

'That you don't mention the bloody pilot again.'

'So how the hell are we going to persuade Ritchie Page to change his mind?' Matt tried not to betray the tension he was beginning to feel. The new-look show was due on air in a couple of weeks and Page still hadn't agreed to come on.

'Christ knows,' snapped Belinda angrily. Seeing Belinda losing her cool made Matt realize for the first time that far from being home and dry they hadn't even left the dock yet.

The whole team was gathered in the office Belinda and Matt shared to head-bang ways of tempting Ritchie Page on to the show. Only she and Matt knew quite how important it was that they came up with something.

'Right.' Belinda's voice was calmer now. 'Is there anything we can offer Ritchie Page, anything he really wants which we can help him get?'

'A pair of your briefs?' suggested Paul Wilson, newly promoted and trying to be funny.

Belinda gave him such a withering look that he didn't speak again during the meeting. Even so she made a mental note to put him on lousy stories. Sexism was one thing she couldn't stand in a man. In a woman it was a different matter. Men were fair game. They'd had things their way for thousands of years. Think how many sexist jokes that meant.

'A peerage?'

Belinda laughed. 'Do me a favour! The Honours' List may be as bent as a nine-bob note but they'd hardly knight someone like Ritchie Page, would they?'

'What Ritchie Page wants,' Matt said quietly, 'is respectability. He doesn't see himself as a pornographer. He thinks he's a genuinely misunderstood man.'

There was laughter all round, but Belinda didn't join in.

'That's it. That's what we'll give him. We'll ask him on to talk about Fred Bear. Nothing could be more respectable than talking about a cuddly cartoon character. You never know' – she smiled round at everyone, even the sexist young producer – 'he just might buy it.'

'You're looking very pleased with yourself.' Deeply grateful to be home after a stressful day, Matt came up behind Ally as she pottered round the kitchen putting the finishing touches to a fish pie and slipped his hand in her jumper.

She slapped it away laughing, hoping that Mona and Joe, watching television in the sitting room, hadn't noticed.

'I made it up with Bernie.' She grinned at him. 'He says he's going to make me a star.'

Matt kissed her. 'And exactly how pissed was he at the time?'

'Stone cold sober. Bernie,' she announced dramatically, pouring herself a glass of wine and noticing with mild alarm that the bottle was half empty, 'has gone on the wagon.'

'Bloody hell!' Matt reached for a glass himself. 'I think I need some of this to revive me. So your little homily went home.'

'God knows. Maybe he'd just hit rock bottom and I was one thing too many.'

'Funny. He used to drink, but not like that.'

'I think losing your show was a big blow.'

Matt turned away. 'I know.'

177

'It's an ill wind anyway. Now he's decided *Hello* is the challenge he needs.'

'And all because of Auntie Ally's advice?' He caught hold of her again and took her in his arms, smiling lasciviously down at her. 'You can tell me what to do any time.'

'Good.' She smiled innocently back at him. 'Then how about going and laying the table? Now, this minute.'

'Since you mention it,' Matt glanced at his watch, 'I think the football's starting on the telly.'

'What a pity.' Ally handed him a tray with knives and forks on it. 'That means you're going to miss it.'

Bernie Long nursed a loathsome glass of soda water rendered deceptively pink-gin-coloured by the addition of Angostura bitters and looked down at his script. He'd learned quickly that the trick of being an ex-boozer is to look as though you're still drinking. This stopped everyone trying to buy you double Scotches and also lessened the risk of appearing a killjoy. So far though, he noted with irritation, the expected transformation from overweight boozer to perfect male specimen hadn't materialized. On the plus side he didn't suffer from five o'clock lows and spend half his life waiting for the bar to open. So far the biggest drawback he'd found was that other people's conversation was suddenly so bloody boring.

They were sitting in the small presentation studio where he'd arranged for Ally to have some autocue practice.

'Are you ready, Bernie?' asked the autocue girl.

Bernie nodded. She began to spool the narrow strip of paper with Ally's words on it so that they appeared in front of the lens of the camera.

Bernie held one thumb up to Ally. Her delivery had improved beyond measure in the last few days now that he'd taught her a few tricks of the trade. It was amazing what a difference it made to underline words for emphasis and write in 'pause' now and then so that the operator was able to follow your rhythm instead of dictating her own.

Ally had come on in leaps and bounds and her performance in the studio had improved dramatically. But Bernie had decided training wasn't enough. He was planning something far more dramatic. He grinned into his soda water, wondering what Ally's reaction would be when he told her.

'Have you heard? The whole show's moving lock, stock and radio mike to some godforsaken warehouse in the East End.' Maggy Mann was so outraged that her voice was squeaking like Minnie Mouse's. 'It's miles from anywhere and there are no decent shops.'

'Why are we moving there?'

'Because Bernie Long says it has a view of Tower Bridge and it doesn't feel like a studio. It'll liberate us, so he says, and make us stop acting like stuffed dummies, thank you very much. Do you know, I think I preferred him on the bottle?'

'Oh, come on, Maggy.' Nikki had joined them. 'Just because you can't get to Harrods in your lunch hour. I think it's a fabulous idea. It'll be like launching the programme all over again. I'm really excited.'

Listening to Nikki, Ally felt a burst of excitement herself for the first time in months. Things were really beginning to change at last. Maybe, just maybe, *Hello* was going to work.

And when she arrived at the new set the following Monday she could see at once why Bernie had fallen for it. The space was amazing. The building had once been a jute warehouse and it still kept the bones of its old hoist high in the roof space. But its most sensational feature was a wall of glass looking out directly over the Thames and Tower Bridge.

'It's like sitting in the middle of a postcard!' Ally laughed as she and Nikki wandered round it. The set designer had arranged four different mini-sets, each furnished with cane chairs, bright cushions and bunches of exotic flowers. In the grey of London's winter it was like a shaft of bright summer sunlight.

'Hey, I think it's wonderful.' Nikki plumped up a pink cushion. 'Think of that awful orange Colditz we've been stuck in till now.'

As she walked round the new studio there was only one thing that puzzled Ally. She couldn't find the place where she normally did her part of the show.

'Nikki, do you know where Bernie is?'

Nikki stopped kicking the vending machine outside the studio door and pointed upwards. 'Upstairs, I think. Isn't it fantastic? There's even a suite of offices here.' She paused dramatically. 'And a Jacuzzi. So if the pre-studio stress gets too much –'

'I'm feeling perfectly relaxed, thanks.'

Nikki studied her. She was looking fabulous in a yellow suit, and Elaine, the make-up girl, had tried out a new style which brought out the green tint in her eyes.

Bernie jumped up when she walked in. 'Ally. Great. I was coming to look for you. I'd like to try something a bit different today.'

Ally glanced at him nervously.

'Don't look so suspicious! It's only a live phone-in.'

'A live phone-in!' Ally felt her heart start pounding at the idea.

'Yep. Only four callers. No idea what they're about. Someone will hit the blasphemy button if any of them gets out of hand.'

'But Bernie, I'm not an expert!' Ally's stomach closed up with panic. 'I don't have the information to handle anything like that. I'd give the wrong advice.'

'Then give it. Let people phone in and complain. We'll put them on, too. It'll work as long as you go with your gut. OK, you don't need to be an expert, they're ten a penny. I want someone who understands what they feel, the people at home. And you *did*, Ally, on that pilot. That's why the audience were weeping into their fucking hankies.'

Suddenly the confidence Ally had carefully built up over the last few days drained away. 'Bernie, I'm not sure I can handle it.'

'Of course you can,' Bernie announced, taking her firmly by the elbow. 'That's why I thought of it. Here's a copy of the ITC guidelines. Go down to your dressing room and read them. You're on in half an hour.'

Chapter 14

'Coming to you, Ally, in ten ...' Ally felt her palms sweat as the PA started her countdown. 'Part two in ten ... nine ... eight ... seven ... six ... five ... four ... three ... two ... coming to titles one ... up grams ... zero.'

Maggy was intro-ing the revamped slot and before Ally had time to panic the first caller was on the line.

'Ally, it's Grace from Sheffield. Grace, you're through to Ally Boyd. Go ahead.'

To Ally's immense relief Grace had a relatively straightforward question about adoption, a subject Ally had covered before. The next question was harder. A tangled feud between in-laws which seemed to have been sparked off by an incident five years before so trivial that Ally would have been tempted to laugh if she hadn't guessed the pain it was causing. Then a question from a fifteen-year-old about the etiquette of safe sex, and fortunately for all concerned the girl had a sense of humour.

Ally began to relax. They were on the home straight now. Thank God this was the last caller.

'Hello, Ally? This is Mandy from Castle Millington.'

'Hello, Mandy, what's the problem?'

'It's my husband. He's been having an affair.'

'How long have you been married, Mandy?'

'Three years.'

'Any children?'

'No, my husband says we're not ready.'

He's not ready, thought Ally. Why was marriage so often the same old story of crossed purposes and out-of-sync desires? What was the old saying? Women put up with sex because they want marriage. Men put up with marriage because they want sex.

'How long has the affair been going on?'

'It isn't the first. He's had two others.' Ally thought of Grace stuck with a husband who didn't respect her in Castle Millington. She remembered driving through it once. A dreary industrial wasteland that belied its romantic name.

'And you've just ignored those?'

'Yes, but I couldn't ignore this one.' Ally could hear the pain in Grace's voice and knew at once whose side she was on. Bloody men. 'I came home yesterday lunchtime and he was in bed with her. Right there in our bed. I wouldn't mind' – Grace's voice faltered – 'but I'd only put clean sheets on that morning.'

Maybe it was the thought of the clean sheets that did it. Ally knew what a proper agony aunt would say: 'An affair doesn't necessarily mean a bad marriage. Why don't you ring up Relate and have a chat?' But it was only men who didn't think affairs meant a bad marriage. Women knew they did. It wasn't the sex, it was the betrayal. In fact three betrayals in three years of marriage, and how many more ahead when they had kids and Grace had other things to think about?

What was it Bernie had told her? Follow your gut. But could she trust Bernie? She knew what her gut told her all right. Why *should* men get away with it? Women forgave too often. Papered over the cracks but not over the resentment, which simmered away turning them into nags or bags until eventually he left them anyway when it was too late to make a new life. Suddenly Ally felt very, very angry on behalf of Grace and all the other Graces who put up with shitty men.

'Are you at home now, Grace? And he's at work?'

'Yes, Ally. I'm at home.'

'What I would do, Grace, and of course maybe you won't agree' – Ally felt the devil stirring inside her – 'is go over to the cupboard and pack his case. Then I'd pick up the phone and order a taxi' – she knew there were a million reasons why she shouldn't advise this. The husband might be violent, or drunk, Grace might have no money or she might love him really despite his loutish treatment of her – 'and I'd send his case to wherever he works with a note telling him it's time he decided whether he's really married to you or not.' Maggy was staring at her in horror. 'Then I'd get the locks changed.'

In the control room the phone lines from the switchboard started flashing as the PA announced there were ten more seconds left. Ally saw the floor manager signalling to her to wrap up.

'Then what I would do is go round to my best girlfriend and take her to the pub and get very, very sloshed and leave my husband to stew in his own juice for a bit. What do you think, Grace?'

'Do you know, Ally?' Grace was giggling slightly. 'I feel better already. I'll go and get his case.'

'Bye, Grace.'

'Bye, Ally. Thanks a lot.'

In the control room the PA turned to Bernie, scandalized. 'You'll never get away with it. The switchboard will be swamped with complaints.'

Bernie stood up. 'I know.' This time the smile was unmistakable. 'But Ally just said what a million women think. If men are shits, why should women put up with them?' Ignoring the flashing lights on the phone lines Bernie continued: 'Mark my words, the show'll be a smasheroony. Bye, kids. See you in the office in fifteen minutes. Drinks are on me today. I think it's time we had a little celebration.'

In his new state of grace Bernie had been doing some

soul-searching. When she'd had a go at him last week Ally had been right about more than just his drinking. He'd been lousy to everyone on the show. It was time he started being positive. OK, there was still a lot wrong with the show, but nothing he couldn't get over if he really tried. And if his instincts were right, Ally's advice slot would go from strength to strength. It was a start, and he was going to make sure they all felt good about it.

By the time Ally got upstairs Bernie had got back from the off-licence over the road with a crate of sparkling wine and six packets of Bombay Mix. The wine was warm, but nobody minded. For the first time since *Hello* began there was a buzz of success in the air.

Just before the fizz ran out Bernie banged his glass with a letter opener.

'To Ally Boyd! *Hello*'s very own discovery!' he smiled across at her. 'My prediction is that she'll be a very big star indeed!'

The last dregs were poured into glasses and everyone toasted Ally. Everyone except one. Maggy Mann had decided to cut the celebration and go straight home.

On the other side of London Matt Boyd's leading rival, Danny Wilde, lounged in a large squashy red chair shaped like a pair of lips, a bottle of Grolsch beer in his hand, surrounded by cuttings about the star he would be interviewing later that day. Despite his large – and getting larger by the day – salary, Danny Wilde liked to keep the flat empty apart from his vast collection of '45s and the five or six antique Wurlitzer Juke Boxes he played them on. Those and his prize possession of tapes cataloguing every known performance of his hero and idol, Tony Hancock. It was nothing to do with crappy notions of Buddhism. Danny was not the type to be found with a shrine in the corner of his bedroom intoning some daft mantra. The only chanting Danny went in for was when QPR were playing at home.

Danny liked to keep life simple. A fridge full of beer. Eat out so no shopping was needed. Stick to one-night stands (always with condoms since he'd spearheaded the government's safe-sex campaign) so there was no nagging girlfriend making his bed and ruining the decor with her fluffy Gonks and knickers on the radiator. His only extravagances had been building a closet for the expensive suits he could now afford in every colour and buying a perfectly preserved forty-year-old two-tone Rover 90 with a solid, not veneered, walnut dashboard and an old-fashioned gear stick. Friends were staggered he didn't have a Porsche or a BMW, but none of them suspected the double climax Danny experienced when he persuaded some girl to oblige him on the back seat of the car his uptight moralistic father had driven all his adult life.

Danny was too subtle to want to break every convention he had been brought up with. Only the ones that really mattered.

Bored with reading one sycophantic article after another, he picked up the remote control and channel-hopped, looking for the repeat of *Happy Days*. Instead he got Century Television's dreary new daytime show which Maggy Mann was fronting. Danny's first TV job had been as one of Maggy's 'boys' on her incredibly popular travel show. To Danny, Maggy Mann respresented all that was worst about television. With her concrete hair-do and spray-on smile, and the particular brand of jokey banter she had made her own, she made Danny want to retch. Especially as he knew the truth behind it. He hadn't been able to get away from the show soon enough.

He was about to hit the button when she started to intro their agony slot. Dimly Danny remembered reading that Matt Boyd's wife was doing it.

Ally Boyd had shoulder-length dark hair that waved gently, just touching the collar of her yellow suit and obscuring one greeny-blue eye slightly when she moved her head. Her skin was pale and luminous and she had a warm, humorous smile that almost seemed to send up the curious activity of offering advice to total strangers. But it wasn't her appearance that caught his attention, it was what she was saying. Instead of the usual stuff about talking it through or going to marriage guidance she was telling a punter to stand up for herself and chuck her husband out. And it was like a breath of fresh air.

'Good on yer, Ally!' he found himself shouting at the television. He could imagine the complaints they'd be getting. And, even better, the ratings for next week's show as outraged viewers told their friends to watch. Of course, she'd never be allowed to be this outspoken again. But even a cleaned-up, toned-down version would be worth watching.

Well, well, well! He drained his beer and watched Ally as the credits rolled for the end of the show. Lucky old Matt Boyd. Danny had never fancied older women, but in Ally Boyd's case he might be prepared to reconsider his position. He zapped off the TV and stared at the blank screen for a moment. Was it because she was Matt Boyd's wife? There must be an element of that. But there was something else. He liked his women bolshie and strong and what he'd just glimpsed was a woman who didn't know her own strength. Yet. And he wouldn't mind being the one to show her. Maybe it was time he gave Maggy Mann a call. For old times' sake.

'Wow, Mum, you're really famous!' Jess pointed to an enormous headline on the front page of the *Daily Post*. 'ALLY SOCKS IT TO 'EM, Chuck out Your Man says TV's Ally.'

The reaction to Ally's phone-in had taken everyone except Bernie by surprise. Ever since an outraged viewer had rung the *Sun* to complain, the tabloids had been full of high-toned discussion of the rights and wrongs of Ally's advice. Even *The Times* had run an article on the subject.

The press had been ringing their home non-stop. Matt had refused to talk to them and while Ally was out shopping Mrs O'Shock had given three interviews before Mona took the precaution of answering the phone first and issuing a firm 'No Comment'. Now Ally was back and the phone was still ringing.

The house was in complete chaos. Joe, who never read anything more demanding than the *Sporting Life* was thrilled to have given a quote to the showbiz editor of the *Daily Star*, if only to tell him that Ally had nothing to say. He'd even made a mental note to go and buy a copy tomorrow, in case his name appeared.

The irony was that though their son was one of the most famous men in England, his fame rarely touched Mona and Joe buried away in their semi in Bristol. This was their first brush with his celebrity first-hand and they were making the most of it.

'Mum!' Janey shouted indignantly from the downstairs loo. 'There's a photographer up the apple tree and he's putting me off.'

Matt, about to take Sox for her usual walk, realized he'd have to run the gauntlet of half a dozen reporters eager to know what he thought of having a wife who was a star. Sox would have to have a run in the garden.

As he let the dog out and she started to gambol playfully in the frosty garden he realized that it was something he'd never really considered. And the truth was, although he was ashamed to admit it, he found it surprisingly unsettling. Maybe it was because Ritchie Page was still keeping them hanging on, or maybe it was because to Ally it was all so new and exciting. Whatever the reason Matt recognized in himself a flash of jealousy.

He opened the door to let Sox back in and the phone started ringing again. 'For God's sake,' he heard himself snap. 'It's only telly! Anyone would think you'd discovered the secret of DNA.'

'Don't mind him,' Mona whispered to Ally as she helped her lay the table for their final dinner before they went home tomorrow. 'He was the same when his little brother was born.' Mona nodded sagely. 'Kept hiding his rattle.'

Ally tried not to smile. She'd miss Mona when she left. As she reached for a saucepan to start boiling potatoes for supper she glanced over at Matt. He had buried himself in *The Times* crossword and though he had said nothing, he didn't need to. His body said it all. From the aggressive angle of his shoulders and the way that he avoided looking at her she saw that his mother was right.

She heard the phone buzz on the wall next to the fridge and hoped it wasn't another reporter. This time, thank God, it was only Jeremy for Jess.

To Ally's relief Matt cheered up over dinner and by the end of the meal was his old self. He was even, she noticed, going to some lengths to make sure his parents enjoyed their last evening and took home with them at least a few memories of normal family life.

'Goodbye, Mum.' Matt kissed his mother as she fussed about in the hall the next morning, making sure that Joe brought down all their bits and pieces for their return journey.

'We've had a lovely time.'

'God knows how with all these bloody reporters ringing up.'

Mona looked at him, concern in her eyes. Having watched him growing from babyhood she knew his moods better than anyone, probably even Ally. She knew without being told that he was worried about his career and that the pressure at this moment was intense. She'd meant it when she'd told Ally that he might be jealous of her, but at the same time she hoped that wasn't why he was behaving the way he was. She'd always seen Matt as bigger than that. But with men, you never knew. If you treated them like children and made sure they always got what they wanted you might keep them happy, but it was at the cost of your own satisfaction. Mona knew that only too well. It was what she'd done to make her own marriage work. And it had. They were still together after forty-five years. But Mona also knew that she had a lingering sense of avenues not pursued, doors not opened. Mostly she forgot about it and went on with planting her window boxes or ironing the sheets. But seeing Ally's bid for something more brought it back to the surface.

'Matt,' she asked tentatively, hoping he wouldn't take her words amiss.

'Yes, Mum? I thought there'd been something brewing in that house-proud soul of yours.'

'You don't mind about Ally, do you, love?'

'Mind about Ally what?'

'You know. Going on television. Being in the papers.'

'Mind? Of course I don't mind,' Matt lied. 'I'm very happy for her.'

'I just thought –' She hesitated for a moment, not wanting to sound interfering about a subject he would probably tell her she knew nothing about. 'It strikes me that this fuss would be easier for you if you weren't so worried about your own work.'

'Whatever gave you that idea?' said Matt a shade too quickly.

'Oh, Matt, I'm your mother! I know the signs. They aren't that different now from when you were at home. You're bored and restless like you were when you were fed up with working on the local paper and wanted to get into television. Everything you did suddenly irritated you.'

Matt grinned slowly at his mother. 'You're too acute, you know.' He put his arms round her, his chin resting on her head, his hands feeling the tickly wool of her home-knitted jumper. It was like cuddling a fluffy hot-water bottle case. As a child she'd given him the greatest gifts of all: love and security. And he never forgot it. He knew the confidence to get out there in front of millions had come from her and he loved her for it. 'I'm fine. Really.'

'Are you, Matt? Are you sure, love?' Mona paused, not wanting to break this rare moment of physical closeness, doubly precious because they lived far apart and Mona was almost seventy and knew she could probably count such moments in the future on one hand. 'You seem a bit grudging about it to me.'

Matt's arms dropped. Mona cursed that she had to be the one to say it. But that was what mothers were for, to say the unsayable.

Matt turned away, irritation rising. What on earth was his mother on about? He'd been perfectly supportive. No one would *want* to have their house besieged by reporters. His reaction had been absolutely natural.

Then he caught sight of his mother's expression and saw what it had cost her to say her piece.

'OK, Mum, it's a fair cop.' He grinned and opened his arms again.

Mona sighed with relief. She'd always felt guilty about loving one child more than the other, had believed that you should love your children equally, but Matt was her favourite all the same. And she thanked God he still deserved it.

Behind them Joe struggled down the stairs with a heavy suitcase.

'Here, Dad, let me take that.'

'I haven't got one foot in the grave yet,' Joe said gruffly, hanging on to the suitcase and manoeuvring it clumsily down the stairs.

Matt put his hands in his pockets and stood back. He'd never been able to get close to his father in his adult life. When he was twelve and played Sunday football with his dad as ref, they'd chatted for hours about the game and the league. But now even attempts to talk about Bristol Rovers came out sounding patronizing and forced. So they both left the talking to Mona.

'Come on, Joe, Matt's off to work in a minute. Let's get the car loaded.'

Matt disappeared into the kitchen and came back with a cardboard box. 'Ally left this for your journey. A bit of a picnic. She's so sorry she had to miss you.'

Joe took the cases out to the car as Matt stood watching helplessly, knowing he'd get his head snapped off if he offered to help again.

'She's a lovely woman, Ally.' Mona looked at the cling-filmed packets of home-made sandwiches and little pots of fresh fruit salad. 'It's not like it was, you know, Matt,' she added cryptically.

Matt wondered what his mother was talking about.

'Women,' announced Mona. 'They need more now. And I for one think it's a good thing.'

'OK, Mum.' Matt smiled once more. She was as subtle as a sledgehammer when she had something on her mind. 'I think I get your drift.'

For the first time since she'd started on *Hello* Ally

hummed as she walked up the steps to Tower Bridge House. Maggy might moan but Ally thought the new studio was fabulous.

Across the other side of the vast floorspace she glimpsed Bernie talking to the lighting director. He waved and came over to her.

'How does it feel to be famous?' he asked, taking her by the elbow and leading her towards an area decorated in blues and greens. 'Judging by the papers you must have had half Fleet Street out there.'

'Packs of them.' Ally raised her eyes to heaven. 'And photographers too. At least all they got was Janey on the loo. Poor lamb. She's terrified she's going to be on the front page of the *Post* with her trousers round her ankles.' Bernie laughed, then looked at her curiously. 'How's Matt been taking this?'

'So-so,' Ally lied loyally.

'As bad as that?'

'He's a bit preoccupied with his own show at the moment.' She glanced at him, wondering how he would react since it had been his show too until so recently. 'They're trying to persuade Ritchie Page to come on and he isn't playing ball.'

'I'm not surprised. Anyway, forget Matt, here's Ally Boyd's personal bit of the set. This is where a troubled nation will come and lay its burdens at your feet.'

'Bernie,' Ally began.

Bernie stopped straightening a sea-green hanging and turned round, his eyes small and shrewd in the rhino skin.

'Yes, Allegra?'

Ally hesitated, not knowing how to go on. 'I just wanted to say thanks.'

One small eye winked. 'I could say the same to you.' There was a silence for a while, then Bernie looked away briefly. 'Thanks for trusting me. I've been so shitty over the years that you had no reason to.'

Ally smiled. 'Any more advice you'd like to give me? The last lot seemed to work.'

Bernie studied her face for a moment. 'You still don't believe in yourself, do you, Ally?'

Ally shrugged. 'Sometimes. Sometimes not.'

'Don't worry about it.' He took her by the shoulders and made her look at him. 'Your vulnerability's your strength, not your weakness. It's what keeps you in touch with them.' He nodded at the TV screen. 'Most people are only pretending to be confident anyway. Really they're as frightened as you.'

'Even Maggy Mann?'

'Especially Maggy Mann. She's scared shitless that you're more talented than she is.' He paused. 'And she's right to be. You're going to be a big star, you know.'

Ally glanced at him, serious for a moment, thinking about Matt's reaction. 'I'm not sure I want to be a big star.'

He put his arm round her. 'You may not have much choice. Now get out of here, for God's sake. I've got my reputation as a chauvinist woman-hater to think of.'

Ally started walking slowly across the studio floor thinking about what he'd said.

'Ally?'

'Yup?'

'We're going to make a great team.'

She gave him that warm, lovely, come-on-in smile of hers and as she opened the door, waving goodbye, he wondered whether Matt had any idea quite how famous his wife might become.

Up in *Hello*'s offices the phones were ringing frantically. The moment Nikki spotted Ally she dashed over.

'Have you seen the duty officer's report?' Nikki showed

her the neatly typed sheets of paper recording each viewer's call, and Ally felt like the naughty girl called to see the headmistress. Nearly all calls the duty officer took were negative. By an inevitable rule of thumb people only ever rang in to complain. Phoning in to say fab, great, loved the show, let's have more was almost unknown, and when it did happen the call was immediately suspected as being from the producer's mother in disguise.

Worse still the log was something everyone in Century Television from Stephen down to the post room, enjoyed reading largely because the duty office was manned by resting actors with a nice line in bitchy comments who enjoyed nothing more than some producer's balls being put in a vice and squeezed by Joe Public. Especially if that producer was the one who'd had the bad judgement to turn them down for their last role.

'Were there some calls about us?' Ally wasn't sure she wanted to know the answer.

'A few.' Nikki handed Ally the log and Ally stared in amazement. There were two whole pages of close type, logging more than a hundred calls.

Ally glanced through the first twenty or so, then groaned and handed it back. They were universally negative. How dare she, some pampered rich bitch, tell some poor feckless girl to risk her marriage by chucking her husband out?

'And the switchboard took another batch who couldn't get through to the duty officer. Someone even managed to get through to Stephen.' Nikki giggled. 'Though fortunately that was the favourable one.'

Sitting at the other end of the office Maggy Mann pretended to read her viewers' letters, a task she normally ignored, getting her secretary to read them and answer pretending to be her. Ally noticed that today she was humming.

Nikki was about to put the log back on Bernie's desk, from where she had pinched it, when he appeared at the far end of the office. She guiltily jumped away.

'What's that?' Bernie indicated the pieces of paper Nikki was feebly trying to hide behind her back. 'Has somebody leaked Maggy's expenses to the press?'

Maggy swivelled her chair and gave him the benefit of her most enchanting smile, a sight that would have reduced most men to abject terror. 'It's the duty officer's report. An avalanche of calls about Ally's slot. All of them anti.'

'Oh, good,' said Bernie, removing the sheets from Nikki's hand as he passed. 'Just what I was hoping. Nikki?'

'Yes, Bernie,' Nikki answered nervously, preparing her defence for getting hold of the report in the first place.

'Fax it to Kevin Hudson on the *Sun*, would you?' He handed it back to her and picked up the rest of his mail. 'Anonymously, of course.'

Nikki grinned, sweeping grandly past Maggy Mann's desk. 'It'd be a pleasure.'

'Right, everyone,' Bernie announced. 'Time we went down to the studio and made another ace show!'

Bernie leaned back in his chair in the control room looking like the cat who'd broken into the dairy. For the first time the show was really working. Now that she'd relaxed Ally was right on top of it and even Maggy Mann hadn't been too bad. Boot-faced as usual once the red light went off, but while they were on air she managed the occasional smile. Bernie was surprised her make-up didn't crack. The show, God help them, had actually approached being fun. If they went on like this they were in danger of having a hit on their hands.

A phone on the control desk flashed and a PA answered it. 'Bernie, it's the switchboard. They can't cope with the callers who want to get on Ally's phone-in.'

Bernie grinned. 'Tell them to switch calls through to the office and get some researchers up there to answer them.'

Ally's spot was clearly going to be the most popular thing on the programme, and there was no way they could get all the people who wanted to talk to her on to the air.

By the time *Hello* signed off Ally was buzzing with excitement. She'd actually forgotten she was on air for a moment today talking to a girl who was having an affair with her best friend's husband. And the extraordinary fact was that not only had she enjoyed herself but the girl had sounded as though her advice had made a difference.

'Anyone want a lift back to Century?' shouted Nikki. 'There's a cab outside.'

Ally looked at her watch. Twelve thirty. Matt would be in the office. Maybe she could tempt him out to lunch. She was bursting to share her relief and happiness, finally allowing herself to admit how awful the last few weeks had been.

'Get it to hang on half a mo, Nikki,' Ally shouted, collecting up her things. 'I'm coming too.'

In the taxi she remembered how, when they'd worked together all those years ago, she'd always rung Matt when she felt a real high or low. Those were the days before they were even married and no one knew they were going out, so they'd sneak off to the wine bar round the corner and invariably bump into another illicit couple holding hands under the table as they pretended to talk about programme ideas or long-term planning. Ally smiled, realizing how excited she felt at the thought of seing Matt unexpectedly in the middle of the day.

She walked into Century's foyer and everyone she passed said 'Hello' and congratulated her. Even Bryony the Rottweiler smiled. The security man leaped up and pressed the lift button for her. Yet only a few months ago she'd been excluded from Matt's hospitality because they wouldn't believe who she was.

It was a pretty good feeling.

The Matt Boyd Show office was busy although it was almost lunchtime. The noise level was deafening and Ally was amazed anything got done. Phones buzzed constantly, researchers shouted across at each other, PAs attempted to get the script done and barked questions at one of the directors. Matt had once explained that journalists needed noise to function properly. Complete silence was death to hacks, perhaps because then they could hear the questions they were asking and finally notice their intrusiveness.

The other thing that hit Ally was the untidiness. It would have brought Mona out in goosepimples. There were piles of newspapers everywhere, oddities used on the show, a huge stuffed bear, the symbol of a children's appeal, old paper cups and unread press releases. In the corner a coffee machine had boiled dry. No one noticed.

Through the chaos she glimpsed Matt sitting on the edge of Belinda's desk. He slid off and came towards her.

'Hello, love. What a nice surprise. How was it? Everyone seems to be raving about you.'

Ally looked at him suspiciously but there was no edge to his voice, only pleasure in her success. 'Yes, it went really well. In fact I wondered if you fancied lunch to celebrate.'

Matt glanced towards Belinda's office, about to say that they'd just put in a final call to Ritchie Page and were waiting for the response. Then he remembered his mother's criticism of this morning.

'That'd be great.'

'Good,' Ally smiled. 'I've booked a table at the Savoy in fifteen minutes. My treat.' As she said it she realized what a pleasure it was to mean it. It would be out of money she'd earned herself, not money he'd given her no matter how discreetly.

'Then we'd better get a move on,' Matt said. 'I'll go and tell Belinda I'm off.'

As he walked into their office he sensed something must have happened.

'We've done it, Matt!' she grinned jumping up from her desk. 'He's agreed.'

Matt let out a whoop which made the whole office stare.

'Come on, everyone,' Belinda shouted. 'Let's go to the bar. Champagne's on me.'

As everyone put down their phones and extricated themselves from conversations Ally stayed where she was, screwing up her courage. She'd been here before, shoved out of the way by Belinda's plans. She'd let it happen last time, but this time it was different. She wasn't poor little wifey grateful for any crumb. She was Ally Boyd, TV presenter, and she and her husband were going out to celebrate her success.

'I'm sorry, Belinda,' Ally said clearly and confidently. Behind her she was aware of people stopping to turn and watch. 'But Matt and I are having lunch at the Savoy.'

Belinda stopped and stared at Matt, willing him to contradict her.

Matt wavered for no more than a fraction of a second. 'You did a brilliant job talking Page into it but this is rather a special occasion. Why don't we celebrate after the show tonight?'

'Tonight's out,' Belinda lied, determined not to be trodden on publicly. 'I'm rushing off after the show.'

'Another time, then.' He followed Ally out of the office.

Halfway across the room Ally noticed the punky researcher with the gender symbol earrings who'd been speculating about Matt and Belinda having an affair at that hospitality months ago. She had her thumb raised in congratulation.

Ally smiled back. So she didn't notice the look of sheer dislike on Belinda's face as she turned back into the office and closed the door, her moment of glory ripped away from her.

The lunch was delicious and the setting overlooking the river perfect. After one glance at Matt the head waiter had taken it upon himself to override his junior's decision and place them at a window table. He then proceeded to lavish them with every care and attention. After that, apart from the occasional glance in Matt's direction from well-heeled lunchers who probably disdained owning a television but for some reason instantly recognized Matt, they were left in luxurious peace to enjoy the glorious food, fresh flowers and crisp table linen with just the wine waiter hovering from time to time to refill their glasses.

The only cloud on the occasion was when Matt slipped off to use a phone and then announced that they couldn't stay for coffee. She supposed it must be hard to be with her when there was so much excitement back in the office. Maybe she shouldn't have dragged him off after all. Even two miles away and in these beautiful surroundings he still felt the pull of work. She sighed. Well, it had been nice while it lasted.

But as they walked out of the restaurant, instead of heading for the front door to hail a taxi in the Strand, Matt turned left and walked across the foyer.

'Why on earth are we getting the lift?' asked Ally, confused.

Matt smiled. 'The reason we couldn't stay for coffee' – he pushed the up button firmly – 'is because I've just booked us a suite.'

'Matt!' Ally realized she sounded scandalized. 'But we haven't got any things with us!'

'That's what makes it fun.' He held open the door of the biggest and most highly decorated lift she'd ever seen.

'I don't know why you bothered with the suite,' Ally said, impressed. 'We could just go up and down in the lift.'

Matt put his arms round her. 'Not doing what I've got in mind.'

Ally glanced at the lift attendant, but he stared ahead impassively. He was probably trained like the guards at Horse Guards Parade to withstand jokes, innuendoes, bribes and probably even clients making love in the lifts.

At the second floor he stood aside and let them out. A young bellhop was waiting to guide them to their suite. When he opened the door Ally almost gasped. The whole room was a subtle pink with elaborate plasterwork, cornices, swags of roses and decorative panels picked out in white and darker pink. The furniture was French eighteenth-century and a flower arrangement of scented lilies dominated the sideboard. The floor-length windows were swagged in silk and had a marvellous view of the river. Beyond the sitting room she glimpsed the bedroom with a huge canopied bed covered in crisp white sheets. A bottle of champagne peeped from a silver wine cooler. It was gloriously, deliciously and wonderfully corny. And in the middle of the afternoon too!

To her immense relief the bellhop made no mention of their lack of luggage. Matt gave him a large tip and he backed quietly out. Ally tried very hard to stop herself laughing. She could tell from every gesture of his body language that the last person on earth he suspected her of being was Matt's wife.

Finally Matt turned towards her, his eyes alight with lust and laughter. 'And now, Mrs Boyd . . .'

Chapter 15

Ally lay in the six-foot bath and sipped her champagne. 'What a wonderful idea this was,' she sighed. 'I can't think of anything I'd rather be doing at ten to four on a Wednesday afternoon.' They had made glorious love, the over-familiarity and habit lost in the surprise of finding themselves in such unexpected surroundings.

Matt walked towards her, naked. 'Can't you?' He began soaping her breasts, then lowered himself into the foamy bath, causing water to splash over the side on to the thick white bathmat, 'I can,' he said, and she marvelled at how hard he felt against her. It had been years since they'd made love twice.

'Let the plug out,' she murmured, ever the pragmatist, 'or the fire brigade'll come and break down the door.'

Matt grinned. 'They must be used to it,' he reassured, slipping his hand inside her warm wet legs. 'I read in the advert that the bath fills up in twelve seconds.' She gasped at the pleasure of his caressing hand. 'And overflows in thirteen.' And after that she didn't notice how much water fell on the floor. She had other things on her mind.

'Two cream teas, please. Suite 5516.'

'Matt, how can you possibly want tea? We've only just had lunch.'

Matt turned to Ally, who was drying off after her exertions in a fluffy white bath towel. 'Don't be so suburban.' He started trying to remove the towel and she pushed him off. 'There's more than one thing you can do with a cream tea.'

Ally started straightening the tangled sheets.

'You'd never have made a mistress,' Matt teased. 'You'd be too busy tidying the bedroom.'

She settled down on the smoothed-out sheets and started reading the brochure. 'It says here that the Savoy always tries to make sure you get served by a familiar face.'

There was a knock on the sitting room door and their friend the bellhop arrived with the cream teas, pointedly averting his gaze from the bedroom before he departed with another large tip. 'Who wants a familiar face?' Ally whispered. 'Don't they understand the charm of anonymity?'

'Not everyone's up to no good like us.'

'Just as well. No one'd get any work done.'

Matt laughed. He looked so relaxed and attractive that this time it was her turn to reach towards his towel and start undoing it. 'What was that you said about a hundred and one uses for a cream tea?'

She smeared some strawberry jam round her mouth and slid enticingly downwards, smiling as he stiffened in anticipation.

'Has no one ever told you?' Matt closed his eyes in blissful ecstasy. 'Not to speak with your mouth full?'

For the last five minutes Belinda had been pacing the control room in disbelief and fury. It was 5.59 and they were due to go live on air in under half an hour. What the hell was she going to do if Matt didn't show up?

But Matt did show up less than five minutes later. He breezed in looking calm and cheerful, and charmed the socks off the waiting guests.

'Where the hell have you been?' Belinda demanded. 'We've been having kittens here wondering if we're going to have to get the floor manager to present the fucking show instead of you.'

'Belinda, calm down.' Matt was infuriatingly cool. 'There was never any question that I'd be here. I've never missed a show.'

'So where *have* you been? You can't have been having lunch till six o'clock.'

Matt smiled lazily. 'The service was very slow.'

'At the Savoy?' She stared at him. There was something about him that was out of character. She'd seen him devilish plenty of times, but it had been a sour devil that got into him then. This devil was anything but sour. It was sweet and funny and ludicrously attractive. And then she guessed. *He'd been in bed with his wife.*

Belinda turned away, the pain stabbing at her so hard that she knew it would show in her face. Even though she realized the absurdity of her position she felt a hard, cold fury. It was his wife who should be jealous of *her*! She was the one who was young and beautiful. But why? She had no claim on Matt. She'd always avoided entanglements with married men. She'd sworn on her copy of *Cosmo* it would never happen to her. She'd seen too many friends going down that road and pitied them. The afternoons in five-star hotels paid for six months later by lonely Christmases. The calls from phone boxes late at night as they lay there trying to convince themselves that of course he didn't have sex with his wife. With Matt she wouldn't even be able to give herself that shred of pride.

But today of all days, when they'd finally got the go-ahead from Ritchie Page! It felt like a betrayal. But it wasn't Matt's fault. It was Ally's. She was the one who'd bulldozed into the office and demanded he hang on her coat-tails. Without her today would have been as special as it should have been.

Belinda watched Matt striding across the studio floor charming everything that moved. Suddenly she saw Ally's action in a different light. It had been a challenge. Ally Boyd had been saying, 'He's mine. Keep off.'

Belinda sat in her chair, oblivious to anything going on around her. All right, she thought, fine. If it's war then let's see who wins. She swivelled round so that her face was hidden from everyone in the control room and closed her eyes for a moment. Then she swung back, a look of exhilaration lighting her beautiful features.

'Right, everyone,' she smiled into the microphone on the control panel. 'Let's make this a show to remember.'

'What's up with the wrinklies?' Jess, sitting at the kitchen table, nudged Janey as their mother and father came through the front door laughing. 'Do you think they've been at it?'

Janey choked, almost knocking over the set book of Chaucer's *Patient Griselda* which she was reading as well as watching *Top of the Pops* with one eye. 'Do me a favour, would you?' Her tones rang with disgust. 'I'm trying to eat my Linda McCartney lasagne.'

For days now Ally and Matt had been behaving, in Jess's expert opinion, like lovestruck teenagers. Sneaking off to bed at the first opportunity, holding hands. Dad had even taken to ringing Mum up after the show and asking her what she thought!

'It's like *Portnoy's Complaint* in reverse,' complained Jess. 'Portnoy took so long in the bathroom his mother worried about what he was getting up to. I feel the same about Mum and Dad.'

'Why? You've got your own shower.'

'That's not the point. How can I rebel by getting into sex when my own parents can't leave each other alone?'

'Maybe that's why they're doing it. To put us off.'

'Well, it's certainly working.' Jess glanced at the hall where Matt and Ally still hadn't taken their coats off. 'I'm not sure how much more of this togetherness I can take.'

'I shouldn't worry,' Janey pointed out, without taking her eyes off *Top of the Pops*. 'I don't suppose it'll last.'

'Hi, Mum, hi Dad. How's life in the glitzy world of TV or are you too in love to notice?'

Ally pretended to swat Jess with her wedding ring. 'Fine, thanks. How's life at Hill Hall School? Homework done?'

'Don't ask her,' wailed Janey. 'She *likes* doing homework, the creep.'

'How about you?' Ally leaned down and kissed her elder daughter. 'How's the work going?'

'So, so. Thomas Hardy as the first feminist is fine, but *Patient Griselda*. Yuk!' She threw the book down in disgust. 'How could Chaucer have thought she was an example of perfect womanhood? She's the poorest girl in town until the ghastly lord of the manor decides to marry her. But just to see if she's worthy of him he pretends to kill their children and turns Griselda into a chambermaid. And good old Grizzy takes it until the laird reveals it was all a medieval *Candid Camera* and they live happily ever after. And Chaucer calls her a flower of wifely patience.'

'Sounds like, you, Mum.' Jess took her mother's hand.

'Not any more, buster.' Ally smiled at Matt. 'This flower of wifely patience got plucked.'

Janey and Jess dissolved into mysterious giggles. 'You said it,' they chorused.

Now that Page had agreed to come on the show, the excitement in *The Matt Boyd Show* offices was uncontainable. It would be Christmas in a month's time, but in the sprawling open-plan offices on the tenth floor of the Century building it felt like Christmas already.

Even Stephen Cartwright could feel it when he wandered down on a rare visit to congratulate them about persuading Ritchie Page to come on. As he walked through the busy room, its phones buzzing, people dashing purposefully about, word processors beeping industriously, Stephen felt a twinge of nostalgia for the days he'd worked on programmes himself. He knew this was a common disease in executives. Now and then they yearned to get back to 'hands-on' producing, temporarily forgetting the stress, the long hours, the nail-biting uncertainties producing actually involved. But there was something about the sense of excitement on this show today that was infectious.

Stephen stopped and poured himself a coffee to prolong the mood a moment longer and watched a young researcher approach Matt, sitting at his desk, to consult him. People wanted to please Matt. Stephen had often noticed that in the past. He had a capacity to make them feel good about themselves. It was a textbook management technique, but Matt did it from instinct. The best way.

As Stephen reached the door of the office Matt was sharing with Belinda, the young researcher emerged, smiling. Clearly a word from Matt had made his day.

Matt caught sight of Stephen and stood up. 'This is a rare honour.'

'I came to congratulate you.' Stephen sat down on the chair Matt had pulled up for him. He picked up the draft script Matt was working on for the new show, and burst out laughing. Even in the intro there were two classic Matt Boyd one-liners. He shook his head. 'Where do you get them from?'

'I steal them from other people.' Matt grinned and took back the script. 'And then I improve them.'

Stephen felt a wave of relief. Clearly the sharp, witty Matt Boyd was still going to be there in the new show. But with edge added.

'I suppose you've been wondering why it was I wanted

Ritchie Page on.' Stephen's manner, Matt noticed, was exaggeratedly casual.

'We were intrigued about why he was top of your Christmas list, yes.'

'The answer's simple.' Stephen paused. 'He's trying to buy Big City Television.'

'But that's outrageous!' Matt couldn't believe what he was hearing. 'The man's a pornographer!'

'Big City's parent company aren't too fussy about that. They've got a financial crisis and they need a white knight. Page is offering twenty-one million pounds. You can see why they'll overlook the odd blot on his escutcheon.'

'But they can't sell to someone like him, surely?'

'Yes, they can. It seems as if the deal's going ahead.' Stephen stood up and stared out of the window. A hundred feet below there were only a few boats on the steel-grey river. He turned back to Matt. 'Unless your interview can stop him.'

Ally stood in her dressing room taking deep breaths. In spite of, or maybe because of, all the attention she'd received she was twice as nervous today for her follow-up.

Yesterday she'd even bought all the women's magazines on the bookstalls and watched and listened to every other agony aunt. Jane Spencer was warm and down-to-earth. It amazed Ally how non-judgemental she was no matter what appalling messes people laid at her feet. Doreen Brook was all motherly understanding and talking things through. Eve Brown, maybe because she was younger, went for the no-nonsense, stop-this-whinging approach. What was the Ally Boyd line going to be? The if-in-doubt-chuck-him-out approach wasn't always going to be the solution.

Still, it seemed to Ally from her own experience that taking *some* action, however small, was so good for your self-confidence and that it helped in most situations. How wonderful, she thought suddenly, to have a platform to try and get women to be more confident, to believe in themselves.

Come on, she told herself, if you're going to help other people you can't turn to jelly every time you go in front of the camera. Like Bernie said, don't give in to your vulnerability, view it positively. It's what you've got in common with other people. Use it.

There was a knock on the door and Nikki appeared, telling her it was time to go down. Nikki, she noticed, seemed less hesitant about putting forward ideas since she'd been working with Ally. And she was eating fewer Mars Bars.

Maybe I'm doing something right, Ally told herself as she strode across the studio floor, suddenly keen to hear what today's crop of unhappy callers had to throw at her.

'Don't you think it's time you got some sleep?' Ally gently removed the press cuttings about Ritchie Page from Matt's hands. The big interview was tomorrow and she knew how nervous he was, how he saw it as a test for taking the show off in a new direction. She'd never seen him do so much preparation for an interview before. For days now he'd been immersed in company reports, books on City finance and mountains of clippings about Page's career.

Ally turned off the light and snuggled under the duvet. Outside an owl hooted and in the distance she could hear Janey's CD machine grinding out some ghastly approximation to music, but she was too sleepy to go and tell her to turn it down. Then she heard a click from the other side of the bed and Matt's bedside light went on. She put her hand up to her eyes to shade them from the sudden glare. 'Is everything all right, love?'

'Ally?' Matt reached for her hand. 'What if I'm no good? What if the audience wants the old Matt Boyd?'

'You'll be brilliant.' She lifted his hand to her mouth and kissed it, loving him much more for his weakness than for his strength, and loving him most of all for showing it to her. 'And how do you know the audience won't want the new Matt Boyd till they've seen him.'

'I love you, Ally.'

'I love you, too.' Matt turned out his light again and Ally rolled over until her body was so close to him a cigarette paper couldn't have been slipped between them. She sighed with contentment. She felt at last something bound them together more than simply a home and children. And in a curious way she was privileged that he'd told her his worries. As they drifted off to sleep she knew that though it would be a testing time ahead, she'd never been happier in her life.

Belinda sat in the office with the door closed reading the *TV Times*. Matt's face smiled up at her from the cover, his features as well-known as the Prime Minister's or one of the major royals, his blue eyes glinting with the provocative charm his fans had come to expect. What would they make of the new, tough interview style Matt was going to unleash tonight?

Belinda glanced at the pad next to the magazine on her otherwise empty desk. They'd planned every move a dozen times, thought through every possible way the interview could go. She'd been surprised how quickly Matt had learned the tricks of confrontation after so many years of living on charm and wit.

She got up, opened the door and noticed Matt had arrived and was chatting to one of the PAs at the other end of the room.

'Matt,' she shouted, 'come and see yourself on the front of the *TV Times*.'

Matt strode into the office picked up the magazine and considered his face. The first time he'd ever had his picture in the paper he'd rushed out and bought five copies for his mother but now he didn't even bother to keep track. 'Strong jaw,' he commented, knowing his weakest feature was a slight tendency towards two chins. 'I like that in a man.'

Belinda began striding round the room, unable to contain her restless energy.

'This is the big one, Matt.'

Matt grinned. 'Yes, I had noticed.'

'If we can carry it off it'll show everyone there's more to Matt Boyd than ten Danny Wildes.' She sat down on the edge of her desk and watched him pick up a script to make some last-minute changes. 'How are you feeling?'

Matt looked up at her and smiled. 'Absolutely fucking terrified.'

Chapter 16

Matt glanced up at the clock on his dressing-room wall. It was time he went down to make-up. Ritchie Page was tough and street sharp and Matt had never done anything like this before. He knew exactly what he wanted from the interview: a clear assurance that Page would keep his hands off Big City Television. But what he didn't know were his chances of getting it. He looked in the mirror, took a deep breath and told himself to keep his nerve.

In the control room, the vision mixer ran through the shots as Belinda briefed Roy, the researcher in charge of meeting Ritchie Page, about what to do with him when he arrived. After much discussion with Stephen it had been decided that no details of the show's change of direction should be spelled out to the press in advance. Today was going to be a complete surprise.

'Whatever you do, keep them away from here and the other guests.' Belinda kept her voice down so that they couldn't be overheard. 'I don't want Page or his cronies overhearing anyone give the game away. I want Page coming in cold.'

Roy headed for the door, glad to be away from the tension crackling through everyone from the PA to the floor manager.

'Isn't he going to wonder what's going on?'

'Not if you convince him everything's normal.'

Roy seemed dubious.

'Make something up,' snapped Belinda, her nerves temporarily getting to her. 'After all, you're a journalist.'

Belinda checked her watch. Half an hour till they went on air. The longest half hour of her life. The other guests were already in make-up. Melody Freed, a prima donna of a comedienne, and Dave McGill, a northern football manager with a great line in dry wit.

'How about a cup of tea?' Joan, the PA, asked as they finished running through the shots.

'Joan,' Belinda said, flopping into a chair and suddenly conscious of her nervous exhaustion, 'I worship the ground you walk on. Can I have two?' Joan smiled. 'And a Crunchie.'

'Well,' marvelled Joan, 'this must be a big show.'

Belinda willed herself to keep calm. Behind her she heard voices and turned to see Stephen ushering a party of spectators into the glass-fronted gallery behind the control room. Shit. That was all they needed. She beckoned to him frantically.

'Stephen, what's going on? This is hardly the day for a Rotary Club outing to watch *The Matt Boyd Show* being made.' She jerked her head in the direction of the gallery. 'Can't you put them somewhere else?'

'No,' Stephen insisted. 'Because they aren't the Rotary Club, they're Fleet Street's finest. Every muckraker worth his cheque book's in there.'

'Do they know what's going on?'

'They know they've come to see Matt doing new tricks. But not at whose expense, no. How's Matt bearing up?'

'OK. A bit nervous.'

'I'm not surprised.' He picked up a script. 'I'll be in sound control.' Stephen gestured to the small sound studio next to the control room but visible through a plate glass window. 'With the lawyers. I've brought in a QC in case Page decides to sue the hell out of us.'

After he'd gone Belinda slumped into the high-backed swivel chair so that she was almost invisible. Hacks. Lawyers. Ritchie Page and his merry PR men. She'd thought she was tough but, Jesus, she'd never known pressure like this. What must it be like for Matt?

The door opened at the back of the control room and Matt appeared. He stopped to steal a Camel Light from Joan, the PA.

'I didn't know you smoked.' Belinda handed him a paper plate to use as an ash tray.

'I don't.' He filled his lungs full of dangerous, health-threatening fumes. 'Mmm.' He closed his eyes. 'Wonderful. Where's Page now?'

'In make-up with Roy.'

Then the floor manager was at his elbow. 'Time to go, Matt.'

'Good luck,' Belinda shouted. 'What's your last wish?'

'That this bloody show was over.'

She looked at her watch. 'Forty-three more minutes and it will be.'

As he walked to the studio Matt imagined Ritchie Page sitting in the make-up chair he'd vacated only minutes before, leaning back, relaxed and unsuspecting, for Elaine to dab panstick on to his smooth suntanned skin. Ritchie Page, he'd noticed from the photographs, was the kind of man who flaunted symbols of femininity – moisturizer, blow drys, gold jewellery – but even the poofy hairstyle and the clanking ID bracelet couldn't disguise the toughness beneath.

Matt refused to let himself feel intimidated. Page might be tough but Matt had the advantage of surprise. As the floor manager pushed open the door for him, Matt smiled coolly at the studio crew. This was no time to lose his nerve.

In make-up Elaine fussed over Ritchie Page as though he were Warren Beatty. She consulted him about moisturizer, on which he turned out to be an expert, and on which shade of make-up he liked.

'What do you usually wear?' she asked ingratiatingly. No one had told her but Elaine knew he had to be kept sweet.

Page laughed. 'I don't know. I'm a virgin. Never been filmed before. It's my first time, so be gentle with me.'

Roy listened, amazed. Ritchie Page had never been on television! What a coup for the show. And after tonight he probably never would again.

As soon as Elaine put down her sponge, Page jumped up. 'Right. Where can we watch the show?'

Trying to keep calm, Roy apologized. 'I'm sorry but we aren't allowed in once it's started.'

'Then I bloody well hope you've got a telly in here.'

Roy exchanged glances with Elaine. 'Yes,' she said innocently, 'but I'm afraid I've lost the damn remote control.'

'Jesus,' said Ritchie Page, taking a large sip of the wine Roy had brought him and looking at them suspiciously, 'call this place a fucking TV company?'

Thirty feet away in studio three, Matt willed himself to relax and get the best out of his first two guests. Melody Freed and Dave McGill were good together, his laconic wit a good foil for her outrageous Jewish princess sense of humour. The first commercial break passed and then, amazingly, Matt saw the signal for the second. It was nearly time.

'Three-forty on commercial break, everyone,' announced the PA.

On the other side of the studio Matt glimpsed Page being led across the floor by Roy. And now he was here.

'Matt, this is Ritchie Page.'

Matt stood up, hoping that no sign of his fear was visible, and introduced him to the other guests.

'No walk on?' asked Page in surprise as he sat down. 'I thought all your guests did a walk-on.'

'Walk-ons can be a bit overused,' Matt reassured as the sound man miked him up and asked him to say something for level. Out of the corner of his eye Matt noticed gratefully that the floor manager was holding up three fingers and that the red light on the camera had come on. No further conversation was possible.

In the control room Belinda sat on the edge of her seat. 'Good luck, Matt,' she whispered into her microphone. 'This is the big one.'

Matt held up his thumb in silent reply.

The familiar burst of music played them into part three. They were back on air. Matt kicked off with his familiar, easy charm.

'My next guest' – Matt paused, smiling – 'is probably hated by mums and dads the length and breadth of the country, not to mention the odd Euro mère and père. And all because of this little chap, Fred Bear.'

'Take the graphic, camera three,' yelled Belinda.

'Fred Bear, the presenter of Kids' Club, is a sensation and it's because of him that parents are being told they won't get their pocket money unless they go out and buy a satellite dish. Thanks to Fred 150,000 satellite dishes have been sold already this year. And here's the man behind Kids' Club, video entrepreneur Ritchie Page.'

Ritchie Page smiled as the audience, led by the floor manager, applauded loudly.

'Ritchie, what do you think it is about the little fellow that's caught so many children's imaginations?'

In the gallery the showbiz reporter from the *Daily News* pretended to be sick. Surely they hadn't been dragged off perfectly good kiss 'n' tell stories to listen to Matt Boyd give free advertising to a shitbag like Ritchie Page?

'To tell you the truth, Matt,' Ritchie Page began to relax, his suspicions allayed, 'I think it's their parents that like him even better.' He held up a Fred Bear toy for camera three to get a close-up, which would have been worth about five grand had he been paying for it. 'Fred Bear works on two levels. Rude and ruder.'

In the hospitality suite Page's advisors laughed like drains.

'Now, Ritchie, you're a video man by trade. While the rest of us were trying to understand how to programme the wretched machines you were making millions from renting them out.'

'Only a few millions.' Page was all deprecating charm. 'I bought a high-street video shop, built it up into a chain and sold it.' His gold Rolex flashed in the bright studio lights.

'Didn't you make your own videos at one stage?' Matt's tone was all friendly encouragement.

Page's eyes narrowed. He clearly didn't like the turn the conversation was taking. 'No, not really. Only amateur stuff.'

Matt remembered the pile of soft-porn films in Belinda's office.

'So, first video, then satellite with Kids' Club. What next? A little bird tells me you want to get into commercial television.'

Page's irritability was more apparent this time. He smiled unconvincingly, obviously rattled. 'Rumours of my interest have been greatly exaggerated.'

'Really?' Matt was serious now, any signs of the easy-going chat-show host abandoned. Melody, who'd been feeling left out and was about to come in with a smart remark, held her tongue. In the gallery the hacks stopped whinging. 'I'd heard you wanted to buy a TV company a while ago but feared you'd be turned down as undesirable.' Page's eyes were two slits in his suntanned face. 'You decided to wait till the system changed last year.'

Matt's voice was as soft as silk. 'So that you could buy a TV company without public scrutiny.'

'This is outrageous,' shouted Page's lawyer. 'It's libel!'

'This is fabulous,' said the showbiz editor of the *Daily News*. 'Do you think it's true?'

'And the system has changed, hasn't it? And now you're bidding for Big City Television, the other London franchise, aren't you, Mr Page?'

Page stiffened infinitesimally as he tried not to react. 'Mr Boyd, this is pure speculation.'

'You mean you *aren't* going to buy a TV company?'

Page said nothing.

'You see, I've got a question. Do you think you're a suitable candidate to own the major stake in a TV company?'

In the hospitality room Page's lawyer jumped up and ran to look for a phone.

'As a matter of fact I do, Mr Boyd. All this is the usual whining from TV people whenever they feel their sacred rights to pontificate to the public are being threatened. What did that chap say? There's nothing so ridiculous as the British in one of their periodic fits of morality. Exactly the same applies to TV people.'

'But you're a bit of an expert in morality, aren't you, Mr Page? You see I'd been wondering what kind of programmes you'd show if you did own a TV company.' He reached under his chair for the remote control. 'Would they, I wonder, be anything like this?'

Camera three flashed up freeze frames of a pair of lovers in an advanced state of copulation, though the parts that might offend were discreetly blacked out for family viewing.

Ritchie Page laughed. 'Really, Mr Boyd, is that your evidence that I'm an unsuitable person to own a television company? They show worse than that in schools' programmes now.'

Matt felt fury rising at the towering hypocrisy of the man. 'And how about this, Mr Page?'

The TV screen beside Matt filled with a clip of a girl of no more than twelve or thirteen in baby-doll pyjamas. A man walked threateningly into shot and began to undress her. 'And do they show this in schools' programmes, too, Mr Page?'

Page seemed to be weighing up how bad he'd look walking off the set versus how bad he'd look staying. Matt second-guessed him. 'No point storming off, Mr Page, I'll tell the story anyway. That young girl is about to be rather nastily violated, isn't she?'

Page sat white faced and furious.

'I'd like to ask you again, Mr Page, are you or are you not going to buy Big City Television?'

In the control room even the PA was on the edge of her seat. Behind her the hacks were scribbling furiously or gabbling away to their news editors on portable phones.

Belinda leapt to her feet, raising her fist in a Rocky salute. 'He's got him! He's got him by the short and curlies!'

'I repeat the question: will you or will you not be buying Big City Television?'

There was a moment's silence which to everyone in the control room seemed to go on for ever.

Page glared at him coldly. 'I will not be buying Big City Television.'

Matt turned to camera. 'That's all we have time for tonight. Thank you for joining us.'

As the credits rolled all hell broke loose. Without a word Ritchie Page tore off his mike, threw it on the seat and stormed off into the waiting arms of his lawyer.

His PR man tried and failed to keep the hacks at bay and they ran, tape recorders and notebooks in hand, after Page's retreating back.

'Wow!' declared Melody Freed. 'That was some interview. I thought this was a nice cosy chat show.'

Matt turned to find Stephen standing behind him. 'Congratulations, Matt. You handled him brilliantly. They'll be opening the champagne at Big City.'

Next to him was Belinda, smiling so wide she thought her mouth would split like a melon. 'We did it, Matt! We actually did it!'

Catching her mood, Matt threw back his head and laughed. They'd pinned so much on tonight and it had finally paid off. Relief surged through him and he lifted her up and swung her round. 'I know!' His shout of joy was muffled by her long hair. 'We stitched him up. We stitched him up like a bloody kipper!'

Outside the studios, Ritchie Page finally fought his way through the ranks of hacks, trying to laugh off the incident. Conscious he was failing he climbed into his Rolls-Royce, the reporters still in hot pursuit. He banged on the partition, his usual sign to the driver to start.

Once they were clear he leaned back on the leather upholstery and closed his eyes. His lawyer and PR man exchanged glances. They knew of old that when Ritchie Page retreated into himself he was at his deadliest.

'Right.' Page's eyes snapped open, glinting like sparks from a steel works. 'I'm going to get that bastard. I may have said I wouldn't buy Big City.' He banged his fist on the arm rest. 'But that still leaves Century bloody Television.'

Chapter 17

'Wow, look at Dad! He's everywhere!' Jess held up a copy of the *Sunday Post* with the headline 'Boyd Bites Back!' and a vast picture of Matt opposite an equally huge one of Ritchie Page. The *Post* announced, also in enormous type, 'Matt Shows His Teeth!' The show had gone out too late to catch the Saturday deadlines and the Sundays, delighted at stealing a march on their daily rivals, had gone to town.

'Gosh, Dad,' dropping her usual cool, Janey sounded impressed, 'I didn't know you *could* be more famous!'

Ally reached out and squeezed his hand. 'Hello, star!' She felt nearly as much relief as he did that the interview had come off so brilliantly. 'What next?'

Matt grinned. 'You may well ask. We didn't plan beyond this. This is where the real work starts.'

As Ally got up to clear the table Matt stood too. 'Here, I'll do that.'

'Double wow!' Jess widened her eyes comically. 'Success *is* going to your head.' Matt threw a piece of toast at her.

'Right,' announced Ally. 'Who knows what day it is today?'

They looked blank.

'Stir Up Sunday! Anyone want to help me make the Christmas pudding?'

'Mum,' objected Jess, shaking her head, 'I'm nearly sixteen. I even know there isn't really a Father Christmas.'

Every year since they'd been old enough to hold a wooden spoon this had been a family tradition. Ally had always loved Christmas but this year for the first time the amount of work it involved made her spirits droop a little. Usually everyone came to them. Matt's parents, her mother, even, occasionally, Matt's younger brother whom he hadn't got on with for years. Sometimes she understood why murder and suicide soared during the season of goodwill.

'OK,' Jess capitulated, 'as long as I can choose what charm I get. I'm not having the bloody wedding ring again. I think marriage is an outmoded institution.'

'You can't choose,' pointed out Janey, who believed in these things, 'or you won't get the good luck.'

'I know,' said Matt, as though hit by a sudden bolt of lightning, 'why don't we go away for Christmas?'

Ally put down the cloves and allspice she'd just got out for the pudding wondering if Matt had clairvoyant qualities she'd never suspected. 'Where would we go?'

Grinning, Matt got out a leaflet. 'The island of Rhum. I booked it yesterday.'

'Is it in the Caribbean?' Jess asked hopefully.

'No.' Matt shook his head. 'Scotland. The inner Hebrides.'

'Oh, Dad!' Jess stole one of the dates her mother had assembled for the pudding. 'There won't even be any video shops.'

'Exactly.' Matt smiled beatifically. 'That's why I booked it.'

Matt handed Ally the leaflet. It was from a hotel called Murdo Castle. It looked utterly fabulous. To think: no cooking, no family, being waited on for three whole days. Bliss. She blew Matt a kiss and went on measuring up the fruit and the spices for the pudding together with the brown sugar, the breadcrumbs and the brandy. 'Right.' She reached for the wooden spoon and put it in the vast mixing bowl. 'We'll have this for Easter then. Who wants to stir and make a wish?'

Jess and Janey made theirs and passed the spoon back to Ally. She closed her eyes. As she stirred the mixture a wonderful aroma of cinnamon and allspice drifted up like something out of India or the Middle Ages. And Ally had absolutely no doubt what wish she wanted to make: that they would stay as happy as they were at this moment for ever.

Matt hummed as he drove into Century's underground car park. Jock the security man saluted and waved. As Matt got out of his car and walked towards the side entrance, Jock leaned out of his box and shouted, 'You really nailed him, Matt. Teach him to keep his dirty paws off TV, eh?'

Belinda was busy making a collage of the press cuttings on the noticeboard outside their office when Matt walked in. As soon as they saw him Roy and a couple of the researchers broke into spontaneous applause.

Matt grinned and bowed with mock solemnity. He was rather enjoying this new respect.

'Come on then, people,' shouted Belinda, summoning the team into their office. 'Let's see who else's head should go on the chopping block.'

Everyone got up, laughing and joking, relief that it had come off making them lightheaded. But Matt noticed with pleasure something he could never remember seeing in the team before: a sense of purpose and excitement. It was exactly what he was feeling himself.

When they came out of the meeting there was a message for Matt that Stephen wanted a word. Matt wondered for a second if this meant bad news. Was Page going to sue after all?

But Stephen's face as Matt walked into his office told him otherwise. He was smiling broadly and Century's lawyer, sitting in the chair opposite, was smiling too.

'I just wanted to tell you,' Stephen said, standing and coming out from behind his enormous mahogany desk, 'that Alex Williams from Big City just phoned. Ritchie Page withdrew his offer this morning.' He shook Matt's hand. 'We did it, Matt!'

'What's even better,' added the lawyer laconically, 'we haven't had a writ. And I reckon if he hasn't done anything yet he won't act at all.'

Matt sat down and put his feet up on Stephen's sofa. His grin was wider than the Golden Gate Bridge.

Ally woke up to the clatter of a cup of tea in her favourite china cup being put beside her on her bedside table. She opened her eyes and stretched luxuriously. Matt was beaming down at her. She put her arms round his neck and kissed him. For the last two weeks, ever since the Ritchie Page interview, he'd been happier and more energetic than she'd seen him for years. She watched in admiration as he leaped on to his rowing machine and pulled the handles, giving her a noisy rendition of 'The Eton Boating Song'.

She lay back sipping her tea and closed her eyes for a moment. In less than two weeks they'd be stopping for Christmas. There were a million things to do. Last year she'd counted thirty Christmas presents that had to be bought. Matt had a tendency to think that Christmas presents arrived, gift wrapped, from Harrods without realizing how much schlepping round department stores and trendy boutiques had gone into their selection.

Still, this year she wasn't going to carp. They had Murdo Castle to look forward to.

'Blade on the feather,' warbled Matt offkey, forgetting the next line. 'Ta, ta, ta, ta-da . . . Jolly boating weather.' Laughing, Ally threw a pillow at him, putting him off his stroke just as he was approaching his target. Pretending to be furious he jumped off the contraption and strode towards her, his eyes glinting with dark purposes.

'Sorry!' giggled Ally, retreating under the duvet and holding tight on to her nightdress.

Downstairs in the kitchen Ally's squeals as Matt tickled her mercilessly were audible to both Janey and Jess and to Mrs O'Shock who had started on the ironing.

'Parents!' muttered Jess ominously into the Weetabix. 'Why can't they grow up?'

'The day they do,' commented Mrs O'Shock, reaching for her water spray, 'is when you have to start worrying.'

As she drove to Century TV with Matt later that morning Ally turned on the car radio. They were playing Phil Spector's Christmas tape and John Lennon's 'A Very Merry Christmas' for the 500th time. Christmas seemed to start earlier every year. Ally rubbed a look-out hole on the fugged-up car window. The narrow B road that led from their house to the main road was white with frost, even though it was nine thirty, and the trees were like lacy spiders' webs. Christmas was such a strange time. So longed for and yet so fraught and emotionally charged for many, so lonely for others.

And then she had a thought. She could hardly wait to get to a typewriter to work it up. At Millbank she kissed Matt goodbye and jumped straight into a cab, not wanting to waste a second before rushing to *Hello*'s offices near Tower Bridge.

'Bernie, why don't we do a special Christmas problems show?' Ally was so excited she hadn't even taken her coat and scarf off yet. 'We could invite experts in the studio and have them advise the callers. You know, everything from how to cope with an excess of in-laws to what to do if you have a family row.'

'What a great idea!' chirped Nikki, who was passing

with an enormous armful of letters for Ally. 'We could even have some funnies. Get people to ring in with their hangover cures.'

'I could give you a few of those myself,' Bernie said. He put one arm round each of them. 'Do you know what? I think you might be on to something, Ally. Forget this crap about comfort and joy. Christmas: the Season of Goodwill and Family Tension. We could have a contest for the family who had the worst Christmas.'

Ally grinned. In his laconic way Bernie had turned the idea on its head and made it work far better.

As she sat down at her word processor to bang out some rough thoughts Ally tried not to beam with pleasure. Not only was she beginning to enjoy her phone-in slot, but she'd come up with a whole new different idea!

The next ten days passed in the wink of an eye. She and Matt were so busy that the only time they seemed to see each other was in bed. But it wasn't something that worried her. She could tell from the spring in his step and his relaxed affection towards her that everything was fine. He might be spending more time with Belinda than he was with her but she knew by some deep instinct that there was nothing to worry about.

At that moment Nikki climbed on her desk to stick up a garish gold pom-pom and a banner saying 'Happy Christmas'.

'Why doesn't anyone tell the truth?' demanded Maggy Mann, sitting on the other side of the busy office reading the *Daily Mail*, 'and make a banner saying "Bloody Awful Christmas"?'

Ally laughed. To her surprise, instead of resenting Ally's success, Maggy seemed to be marginally more friendly. Maybe it was because the show as a whole was beginning to take off and Maggy knew better than to rock the boat for her own sake.

'Where are you going for Christmas, Maggy?' Ally asked her.

'Taking the three little shits down to my mother's.' Maggy fingered the brooch her son had made her and smiled. Ally knew that whatever else might be a pain about Maggy, she loved her children. 'How about you?'

'Matt's booked us into a hotel called Murdo Castle on a Scottish island.'

'Ah.' Despite the season of goodwill Maggy couldn't resist a crack. 'So you won't be having a crummy time being worked off your feet producing Christmas dinner for an ungrateful family like most of your punters.'

Ally felt a flash of guilt. How like Maggy to put the boot in. 'Not this year.' She knew her tone sounded defensive. 'But it's the first year I haven't.'

She stood up. It was time to go down for the Christmas problems show she'd spent the last ten days throwing all her energy into. But for once she wasn't nervous. Just excited. To no one's surprise the show was a terrific success. Bernie Long sat in the control room beaming with delight. They couldn't have gone out with more of a bang, especially Ally's phone-in. The switchboard was jammed with callers recounting their catastrophic past Christmases, and the hangover tips were hilarious.

But what had impressed Bernie more than anything was the warm and witty way that Ally had controlled the whole thing. Even he had been conscious of disappointment when it finished. As the theme music ended everyone behind the scenes embraced each other with cries of congratulation. But Bernie sat still. He had had an idea. He didn't want to make Ally run before she could walk, but today he'd glimpsed real potential beyond the confines of a short slot in *Hello*. What everyone in television was looking for was a British Oprah Winfrey. And watching Ally today, Bernie felt a leap of excitement as he wondered if they might just have found her.

On *The Matt Boyd Show* that evening there was excitement in the air, too. With breathtaking skill Matt was somehow carrying off the impossible feat of doing an interview with a stand-up comedian about the average family Christmas, followed by a devastating hatchet job on the fraudulent chief executive of a children's charity.

In his office on the sixteenth floor Stephen Cartwright was watching it, amazed by Matt's surefootedness.

Then the credits rolled. Artificial snow was falling gently on Matt's shoulders and a huge choir appeared singing 'Once in Royal David's City'. Father Christmas arrived from nowhere and revealed himself as Frank Bruno, the boxer. Christmas in TV Land. But Matt had managed to put a spin on it and give it originality and bite.

However, even his pleasure in Matt's performance couldn't take his mind off the call he'd just received from a stockbroking friend in the City of London. Did Stephen know, the friend had asked, the identity of the mysterious buyer of parcel after parcel of Century's shares?

Stephen went on watching the television without seeing it. At the back of his mind was a thought that he couldn't bring himself to face. He might be wrong. He *had* to be wrong. But he knew one thing for certain: he was going to have a bloody awful Christmas.

Ally was relieved when Matt turned down the offer of a helicopter and they opted for the slower and more complicated but infinitely more beautiful route of flying to Glasgow and taking the train that twisted and turned through some of the most spectacular scenery in the world to Mallaig in the west Highlands. From there they would cross via the Small Isles Ferry to the island of Rhum.

The journey was so long, though, that by the time they got there it was dark and cold and Janey and Jess whinged like a couple of three-year-olds on the last leg. When they arrived they all fell into bed without even the energy to eat and Ally found herself wondering if it had been such a great idea to come here.

When she woke the next morning she was surprised how late it was. She slipped out of bed and ran over to the huge windows. The curtains were made of blue brocade and were so heavy that she found it a struggle to pull them until she saw the rope designed for the purpose. Shaking her head at her stupidity, she pulled it. The gesture was somehow so theatrical and the view so extraordinary that she caught her breath. Laid out before her were wild snow-capped mountains sweeping dramatically down to the sea.

She turned to Matt in delight and caught sight of the full beauty of their own room for the first time. It was huge with two sets of sweeping windows, a fantastic carved plaster ceiling and a vast four-poster bed complete with blue brocade hangings. The floor was covered in a thick plum carpet with animal skin rugs exotically thrown to break up its huge expanse. Adjoining it was a marble bathroom with a brass claw-footed bath.

But it wasn't the appointments of the room that made it so special. It was the fact that on every surface there were knick-knacks, family photos, old books lying open, bowls of fragrant pot-pourri, silver-backed hairbrushes. It was as if some Edwardian lady had stepped out of her boudoir half an hour before and now they had stepped in.

'Matt.' She sat down on the bed next to him and kissed him. 'This place is incredible.'

Matt returned her smile with a grin that was endearingly smug. 'I know. Come on, let's get up. I smell sausages.'

Ally laughed, knowing how fond Matt was of a proper breakfast and shrugged off the shoulder of her kimono. A tempting shoestring strap was revealed. 'Don't you want to . . . er . . .' She gestured at the bed.

'First things first, old girl.' He pulled her kimono back up affectionately. 'I might miss the kippers.'

Ally pretended to make a moue of disapproval as she opened one of the many doors of the enormous polished wood armoire looking for something suitable to wear. 'I'm glad you've got your priorities right.'

'I always get my priorities right. Breakfast. A bracing walk in the mountains. A hearty lunch. Then, before tea, a rest and you can ravish me to within an inch of my life.' He smiled. 'Maybe we'll even skip tea. Drinks, then dinner.'

Ally widened her eyes. 'And to think this is only Christmas Eve.'

'Don't push your luck. I probably won't be able to move tomorrow.' He watched her pulling on a pair of sleek jodhpurs and a cashmere jumper then a scarf patterned with saddles. 'You want to watch it, you know.' He got out of bed, came up behind her and slipped his hand down her trousers. 'Dressed like that someone might think you can ride.'

'I *can* ride!' pointed out Ally indignantly. She swatted his hand. 'Keep your mind on the kippers.'

'But Ally' – a provocative smile lit up his blue eyes and she felt his hand slip inside her briefs – 'that's exactly what I am doing.'

They walked slowly down the vast double staircase, holding hands, pointing out the portraits to each other and the vast metal sculpture of an eagle, claws out, that adorned the half-landing.

were out of sight. Mrs Robertson had told her it was the 'country way' to see your guests safely round the corner.

They waved goodbye in return, watching the castle slip out of view with regret and hoping it wouldn't be too long before they could come back. Neither Matt nor Ally had the slightest suspicion of the bombshell waiting for them in London.

'Jesus, Stephen, there must be something we can *do*.' Matt paced round Stephen Cartwright's office furiously. He'd come racing up the moment Stephen had told him what was happening. 'I mean we can't stand back and let Ritchie Page take over Century. Can't the board do something to fight him off, for Christ's sake?'

'They're doing their best. But Page went round nobbling all the institutional shareholders over Christmas.' Stephen looked pale and tired, as though he hadn't slept. Clearly he knew his future was on the line as much as Matt's. 'The trouble is he's made them an offer they can't refuse. I've got a contact at Safe Assurance. Their pension fund owns seventeen per cent of Century. He said Page is paying way over the odds. They couldn't turn him down. It's too good to miss.'

'But surely they wouldn't sell to someone with a reputation like Page's?'

Stephen shrugged. 'Apparently Page has reassured them by promising not to make any significant changes to staff or programmes.'

'Well, he would say that, wouldn't he? He wants them to sell him the bloody company. You don't actually believe him, do you Stephen?'

Stephen sat with his face in his hands thinking of his mansion in Surrey, his 7-Series BMW and his unrivalled health and pension plan.

★

'How's the campaign?' Ally put her arms round Matt's neck and kissed the top of his head as he scanned the papers for any mentions of Ritchie Page. Ever since they'd got back from Scotland he'd been jumpy and preoccupied. 'Surely the *News* or the *Post*'ll do something. They were the ones who splashed the interview all over their front pages. I'd have thought it'd be right up their street. They could have a Save Our Telly From Mr Filth campaign.'

'You'd think so, wouldn't you?' Matt closed the papers in disgust. 'But they couldn't give a stuff. It was one thing showing Page with his trousers around his ankles flogging pornography, but they don't want to stick their necks out about who's suitable to buy a TV company. Too many of them want to get into television themselves.'

'What about the government or the ITC? Surely there must be rules against someone like Page owning a TV company.'

'Page contributes vast amounts to party funds. Besides' – Matt smiled at her wryly – 'they probably think he's showing entrepreneurial flair. He's a notorious union basher, the government always approves of that.'

'Poor Matt.'

'Not poor Matt.' He took her hand and kissed it. 'Poor all of us. You, too. You work there as well.'

Jess looked up from the copy of *Company* she'd been reading. 'Will that mean,' she asked innocently, looking from one of her parents to the other, 'that we'll get Fred Bear on Century?'

When the phone rang at almost midnight Ally had a premonition that it was going to be bad news. Matt picked up the receiver. It was Stephen.

'Hello, Matt, I'm sorry to call you so late.' He sounded terrible, as though someone had picked him up and poured the life out of him. 'I'm afraid it's all over. The chairman's just rung to tell me. He's resigning. As from Monday Ritchie Page will be the majority shareholder of Century Television.'

Chapter 18

Ritchie Page drummed his fingers on his new desk in the chairman's freshly vacated office on the sixteenth floor of Century's tower block, deep in thought. His instinctive reaction on taking over a company was to fire the top men. When that man had helped screw you, as Stephen Cartwright had, you'd be crazy not to. But Century wasn't a typical company. It was full of wimpy creative types who didn't see themselves as employees. They felt you owed them a living. He intended to show them what life was like in the real world. But maybe not yet. For the moment he wanted to get his head down with no more bad publicity.

He thought for a moment about Stephen Cartwright. He had a sneaking suspicion that Stephen Cartwright was a weak man, a man who liked his salary and his share option and his mock-Tudor home in Esher. So far his record at Century hadn't been brilliant, and at fifty-plus he would find it hard to get an equivalent job. And, if Ritchie guessed right, he knew it. Matt Boyd, he reckoned, had principles. But Stephen was a pragmatist. If he was offered a good enough deal he would stay. He'd probably be pathetically grateful.

And he just might be useful. Page could make him the hatchet man. It would be interesting to see how far Cartwright would go to keep his Surrey lifestyle and his swimming pool. By the time he got to the end of his road, if he ever did, he'd probably be expendable anyway.

Page played with some numbers. Fifty thousand pounds should make a decent sweetener. Satisfied, Ritchie Page pressed the buzzer on his desk to ask for a cup of coffee.

'And Lorraine, get Stephen Cartwright to call me, will you?'

Page looked at his watch. How long it took for Stephen to get back to him would be an interesting guideline.

Lorraine returned carrying a cup of coffee in a black and gold cup. 'Your coffee, Mr Page.' She put the cup down in front of him. 'Mr Cartwright is holding on line two.'

Ritchie Page smiled and crossed out the figure on his pad. Maybe the sweetener wouldn't be needed after all.

'How is this going to affect us?' Belinda took a tray and got in the queue for the canteen behind Matt.

'God knows, but I wouldn't book a holiday. Your desk might not be there when you got back.'

They chose their food and sat at a table by the window.

'Will you stay on?' This was the question Matt had been asking himself for days.

'Don't go!' she said urgently when he didn't reply. 'If you do it'll have been for nothing. He'll have won.'

Before he could respond Bernie Long appeared holding a bottle of red wine and one glass. 'Hello, kids. Shall we kill ourselves now or later?' He sat down at their table without being invited and uncorked his wine. Not bothering with the niceties of the glass he took a slug straight from the bottle.

'I thought you were on the wagon these days,' Matt pointed out.

'I was. Two whole sodding months without a drink.' Bernie beamed. 'I've just fallen off.' He raised the bottle to his lips. 'But I think I can plead provocation, don't you?'

As the three of them walked out of the canteen towards the lift they were swept along by a tide of people moving in the opposite direction.

'Where's everyone going? Fire drill?' Matt asked one of them.

'To studio three. Stephen's called everyone to a meeting.'

Every inch of studio three was crowded with anxious faces. On the dais at one end, where the seats would be placed later for *The Matt Boyd Show*, stood Stephen Cartwright.

'Now I know you're probably very worried by this development, but I've just come from a meeting with Ritchie Page and he assures me there is nothing whatsoever to worry about.'

Matt listened incredulously.

'He's been nobbled,' announced Bernie in a loud stage whisper.

Stephen ignored him and continued. 'He asked me to tell you that not a single person will be losing their job.'

'Especially you, you jammy bastard,' heckled Bernie, helping himself to another swig.

Matt stood listening to Stephen pave the way for a bloodless coup until he could stand it no longer. Suddenly he made his way through the crowds on to the platform.

'Stephen knows as well as I do' – Matt grabbed the mike from him – 'that what he has just said is a heap of shit. Ritchie Page is a crook and a pornographer and if he stays in this building then I'll be leaving it.'

Matt's words were almost drowned out by feverish applause.

From his position on the dais Matt could see a woman pushing her way to the front. Finally she broke through. It was Elaine from make-up.

'Now hang on a minute, Matt,' Elaine said, bristling with anger. 'That's a typically bloody male thing to say. You cut and run and get all the glory, not to mention another show with the Beeb, while us poor schmucks with mortgages and kids get lumbered with Ritchie Page. It's here you're needed. The brave thing isn't to go, it's to stay and make sure he does what he says!'

'Good on yer, Elaine!' congratulated Bernie. 'You bloody tell him. It was probably his fault Page is buying Century in the first place.'

'Thanks, Bernie,' muttered Matt, 'thanks a bunch.'

He looked down at the sea of anxious faces, and wondered if Elaine was right. Maybe he should stay. Stay and fight.

Completely unmoved by the fear and loathing he was creating, Ritchie Page called for Lorraine to bring him Matt Boyd's contract. For half an hour he sat reading through the fine print until he put it away with a sigh of irritation. To his annoyance it had more than two years to run. Firing Matt would cost nearly a million. And there was another problem: he hadn't counted on Matt Boyd's popularity. If he fired Matt, Stephen Cartwright assured him there might be a walkout.

Page picked up a handwritten note that had arrived this morning marked 'private and confidential'. He read it for the third time.

The letter was from Jack Saltash, doyen of agents, suggesting that they might have a discreet meeting about his client Danny Wilde. Ritchie Page stirred his coffee thoughtfully. He might be new to dealing with theatrical agents but Page was shrewd enough to understand the subtext. It could only mean one thing. That Danny Wilde was interested in coming to Century Television.

Ritchie Page smiled. It was the perfect solution. Danny Wilde wasn't as popular as Matt Boyd. Yet. But he was ten years younger and, unlike Matt Boyd, he wasn't the type to bite the hand that fed him. With some clever scheduling and good promotion Danny Wilde could be almost as big, bigger maybe. All Page needed to do was find a way of getting Wilde in. And Boyd out.

He put Matt's contract in his briefcase. There was only one solution. He would have to get Matt Boyd to resign. But how the fuck was he going to do it?

'So what happens next?' Belinda sat back in her leather chair and watched Matt intently. 'He's been here a week and he's seen almost everyone from the security guys down to the scene shifters. Except us.'

'We get on with making the programme.' Matt checked the script for tonight's show, changing words here and there. 'You know as well as I do he's doing it deliberately.'

Belinda thought of the call she'd had this morning from her former boss at the BBC asking if she'd be interested in producing a new controversial interview slot. She'd so nearly taken the job. Why hadn't she?

Intrigued by her sudden silence Matt looked across at her and smiled, his blue eyes crinkling at the corners. Despite her mood Belinda found herself smiling back. What was the point of kidding herself? She'd thought about Matt all over Christmas, tortured herself continually with mental snapshots of happy family scenes. She knew bloody well why she'd turned it down. And that she was a mug to have done so. It would at least have got her out of one mess. A mess that hadn't even really started.

But Belinda knew it would.

For the meantime, Matt was right. They ought to be concentrating on the programme. She glanced down at the buff envelope on her desk. It had the ratings for all the shows since they'd started. And the devastating truth was that powerful and controversial though the new show might be, it wasn't pulling in the viewers.

Chip, the post-room boy, chose that moment to arrive with the afternoon's mail. On top was a similar envelope. Belinda tore it open eagerly. It was the ratings for the week before Christmas. Every show had worked well and Belinda was hoping for a breakthrough.

As she read them she felt her stomach begin to knot. They weren't going up, they were going down. She didn't really need to look where they were going to, but she couldn't resist it all the same. To Danny bloody Wilde's show.

Belinda came to a decision. 'Here.' She passed them over to Matt. There was no point trying to protect him any longer. 'Maybe you'd better see these.'

She watched as he read them, his face impassive.

'The show's terrific,' she said, feeling she had to break the silence which seemed to have gone on for minutes, 'but we're not getting the audiences.'

Matt studied the figures carefully. Reading them he felt a sudden and unfamiliar rush of fear. He'd put everything into the new show and it was clear from the figures that they hadn't carried the audience. He scanned the sheets to see where the viewers had gone to. Most had turned to Danny Wilde, a few to the BBC, and some seemed to have disappeared altogether. As he studied the figures his eyes were caught by the one Century programme that was gaining viewers at an incredible rate.

He checked across to the left of the column to see which show it was. *Hello.* And the fastest jump by far was at eleven o'clock on Wednesdays and Fridays. He wondered for a moment what on earth it could be. A cartoon? A superstar interview? And then it dawned on him.

It was Ally's phone-in slot.

'How's it going, love?' Ally kissed the top of Matt's head and sat down at the breakfast table beside Janey and Jess. Matt was hidden behind his copy of *The Times*.

'How's what going?' Matt heard the irritability in his own voice as he lowered his paper.

'Your show.' Ally had been longing to ask him all week but in the last few days he'd clammed up about work and hardly mentioned it. Probably it was because he was nervous about Ritchie Page, but Ally was amazed how much it hurt after the closeness they'd developed since she'd started at Century.

'Have the ratings picked up?' In her enthusiasm to get things as they were, Ally didn't recognize the warning signs.

'They're OK.' He stared at her suspiciously. 'Why do you ask?'

'Don't you think you'd be better off in a later slot?'

'Since when have you been the big expert?' snapped Matt.

Ally felt as though she'd been slapped in the face, and Janey looked at Jess in amazement. She'd never heard her father talk to her mother in that way before.

Once, thought Ally, I'd have apologized and smoothed down his ego. But why *should* I if he talks to me like that? Especially in front of the children!

'Where did you get that idea, anyway?' Matt couldn't resist twisting the knife.

'Just from something Bernie said.'

'Bernie the well-known king of scheduling! If he's so bloody brilliant why did we have to dump him?'

With a flash of surprise Ally realized how much respect she had for Bernie after two months working alongside him. 'Maybe that was your first mistake.' She poured herself a cup of coffee, then, even though she knew she shouldn't, she added: 'After all, Belinda hasn't been up to much, has she?'

Matt flung his paper down on the table and stormed out of the room. Ally resisted the temptation to follow him and calmly loaded the dishwasher. 'Come here, Sox!' she called to the dozing sheepdog. 'Let's get outside for a bit of fresh air.'

Sox bounded to her side as she opened the garden door. 'Back in five minutes,' she said, determined not to let Janey and Jess see how upset she was.

As the door closed Janey looked gloomily at her sister. 'Well' – she picked up her plate and dutifully put it in the dishwasher – 'I told you the togetherness would never last.'

Safe on their little island in the East End, miles from Century's studios, from the tension and uncertainty, the corridor chats and the endless speculation in the bar and the ladies' loo, *Hello* went from strength to strength. Even Maggy Mann continued to mellow, and to Ally's astonishment actually asked her advice after the show one day.

'You're an agony aunt,' she said as she removed her heavy studio make-up. 'Do you think a woman of forty should go out with a toy-boy?'

Ally, wiping off the red lipstick she wore on camera with a Quickie, got the distinct impression there was more to this question than was immediately apparent. Maggy was about as likely to bestow confidences as Madonna was to dress in Laura Ashley.

'Depends what she wants out of the relationship. Sex, fun or something lasting.'

'I'll settle for the first two.' Maggy outlined her lips with a brown pencil and filled them in with lipgloss. Ally had to admit she was looking a lot better lately.

'Maggy.' Nikki put her head round the door, grinning. 'There's someone here to see you.'

Maggy ran her tongue over her lips to make the gloss even glossier. 'Tell him to come in.'

Ally was zipping up her grey wool dress and struggling with the final couple of inches when the zip was suddenly pulled up for her. She turned in surprise and found herself looking into the disarming green eyes of her husband's greatest rival, Danny Wilde.

'Hi.' He put out his hand. 'I'm one of your greatest fans.'

Danny Wilde's reputation for captivating every woman he met was legendary and Ally was well aware of it. Normally she would have treated him with teasing firmness, as if he were the boyfriend of one of her daughters, but she was still annoyed with Matt. So for once she flicked back her hair provocatively.

'Are you now?' She held his hand for just a second too long. 'Then I'm very pleased to meet you.'

Nearly three weeks after he arrived, Matt and Belinda finally received a summons from Ritchie Page to come and see him.

'Is he going to axe us, do you think?' Belinda finally asked the question that had been on her mind for days.

'Your guess is as good as mine.' Matt pressed the button for the lift and they both went up silently to the sixteenth floor.

'Matt, Belinda, hello.' Matt hadn't known exactly how he was expecting Ritchie Page to behave, quietly threatening or openly hostile, but nothing had prepared him for the disconcerting Huggy Bear who stood on the threshold holding out a gold-ringed hand to shake and offering them gin and tonics.

Page proceeded to inform them effusively that *The Matt Boyd Show* was 'real quality television' and that its future was definitely assured. All they should do was go on as they had been doing.

'We had wondered,' ventured Belinda, avoiding Matt's

glance, 'whether the show wouldn't do better in a later slot. Nine thirty, say, after the news.'

'My dear girl!' Page sounded horrified. 'I need you where you are. That's where the viewers expect Matt to be, not hidden away somewhere. People would think I'd lost faith in you.'

There was a certain logic in what Page said, so Belinda didn't push her point.

'And don't worry about your audience figures,' Page informed them as he shepherded them out twenty minutes later. 'Real journalism isn't always popular.'

'Bloody hell!' whispered Belinda as they headed down the corridor. 'That was staggering. He's given us a *carte blanche*.'

'Or enough rope,' said Matt suspiciously.

'What're you getting at?'

'To hang ourselves with. Whoever heard' – he pushed the swing doors open for her – 'of a commercial television boss who told you not to worry about your ratings? The scumbag's up to something. The question is, what?'

As Matt and Belinda waited for the lift, Ritchie Page reflected that it hadn't gone too badly. He couldn't have agreed more when they said maybe the show should be moved to later in the evening. It might actually work at that time. Which was precisely why he wasn't going to move it.

Especially not now. Last night in bed he'd come up with a plan. He'd let *The Matt Boyd Show* run until the summer. By then its ratings would be rock-bottom then he'd take it off the air and replace it with some cheap buy-in. Just for the summer. Or so he'd tell Matt. Being taken off the air wasn't something that had ever happened to Matt Boyd. He might even plant a few 'flagging ratings' stories to put the pressure on. If his assessment of Matt Boyd's personality was correct, that's when he'd resign.

In September, when everyone launched their autumn schedules, he'd replace him with Danny Wilde. Ritchie Page smiled. It was an ambitious scheme, but possible. And he'd always been an optimistic man.

He checked his desk diary. He was seeing Bernie Long, Allegra Boyd's producer, tomorrow. Now that should be interesting.

'How was lunch with Danny the other day?' Ally and Maggy were sitting in make-up waiting for Elaine to finish concealing the treble chin of a famous leading lady.

'Fabulous,' Maggy said. 'We went to Le Caprice. It suits him. He's so charming and so modern. None of those awful hang-ups about being threatened by successful women.'

Ally, naked of make-up under her white bandeau, was conscious of an unexpected frisson of jealousy. Why? she wondered. Danny Wilde was so obvious, so undiscriminating. Otherwise why would he be taking Maggy out to lunch? Suddenly aware of the uncharitable nature of her thoughts, Ally smiled at Maggy sympathetically. 'Isn't it funny going out with someone so much –'

'Younger? He's hardly a babe in arms. He's twenty-eight and I'm thirty-nine . . . ish.' She winked. 'And I get the impression he's made good use of his time, don't you?'

Ally laughed, flustered by this overt sexual reference. 'My daughters adore him. They're always annoying the hell out of Matt by telling him so. So, is it the beginning of a beautiful relationship?'

Maggy appeared slightly glum. 'I don't know. The phone hasn't been exactly buzzing.'

'He must be very busy with his job,' consoled Ally.

'And with his women,' sighed Maggy. 'Ah well.' Her optimism dimmed a little. 'Maybe at my age I ought to be grateful.'

'Maggy,' chided Ally reprovingly, glancing at the celebrated actress who looked like she had three toy-boys for breakfast, 'What kind of talk is that?'

Across a desk the size of the playing fields of Eton, Bernie Long watched Ritchie Page light a cigar without offering him one. Tch, tch. Bad manners. But then Bernie understood. When you came from nothing status was important. They both knew that much. They were Bermondsey boys, often mistakenly called Cockneys. Ritchie Page's father had been a second-hand dealer. He cleared old ladies' houses when they died, telling their grieving relatives it was all old tat, then flogged anything vaguely valuable down at the Bermondsey Market, where everything, even the legit stuff acquired with a proper title, was said to have fallen off the back of a lorry.

Bernie's father was a publican, now retired and contentedly passing his days in a rest home run by the Association of Licensed Victuallers, swapping happy tales of short pints and long odds. His uncle, known universally as Veggy, after the produce on his stall, still manned his pitch in nearby East Street Market and complained, after fifty years of trading, that there wasn't a living in it.

Bernie and Ritchie spoke the same language. Bernie knew Ritchie Page was a shitbag and a con-man. Ritchie recognized Bernie as a boozer and a chauvinist.

'I've come to you' – Bernie didn't bother to disguise his dislike since both knew respect was not relevant to their relationship – 'with a proposition.'

'Be my guest.'

'Presumably you've seen the ratings for *Hello*.' Bernie placed several sheets of viewing figures on Page's desk as evidence. Page tutted and waved them away as if Bernie had offered security in a gentleman's agreement. 'Anyway they're bleedin' amazing. And the most successful part of the show is Allegra Boyd.'

Ritchie Page puffed his cigar.

'I think she should have her own show.'

Page made a small mountain with his ash. Although his face was impassive Bernie got the impression of sudden interest. 'That's a big step. Are you sure she's up to it?'

'Up to it? She's up to it, all right.' Bernie stood and started pacing around the room. 'We're throwing her away on a phone-in. She'd be brilliant if she were face-to-face with the punters. She could be the biggest thing this company's got.'

Page was silent for a moment and Bernie thought he was going to refuse. 'And if she got her own show, how would Matt react do you think?'

The fractional pause before Bernie answered told Page everything he wanted to know.

So Matt Boyd couldn't cope with his wife's success? Well, well, well.

Bernie Long whistled as he walked along Millbank in spite of the freezing February drizzle. God, he hated English winters! Still, he was cheerful today. Page had been very receptive to the idea of Ally having her own show. Now all he had to do was come up with the right format.

And persuade Ally she could do it.

Ally was sitting in the Tate Gallery Restaurant waiting for him, studying the wonderful Whistler murals and wondering what Bernie was up to. The secrecy in which he'd shrouded this lunch was like something out of John Le Carré. Don't mention it to anyone, he'd muttered when he'd invited her yesterday. Maybe Bernie was going to make a pass. Just her luck. Maggy Mann gets Danny Wilde and I get Bernie Long. She giggled, causing the other lunchers to stare surreptitiously.

Ally caught the woman at the next table watching her

and smiled. She probably thought she knew her. Ally realized she was at that precise level of fame where people knew your face but not your name and often thought you were someone they'd met at a party. In a way it was pleasant without being intrusive. Nothing like the universal recognition Matt had to put up with. She wondered idly for a moment what it would be like to be known immediately everywhere you went and decided she'd hate it.

Across the room she saw Bernie arriving. She stood up when he reached the table to kiss his cheek. Three months ago, if anyone had told her she'd be this fond of Bernie Long, she'd have laughed in their face. Even now she didn't know how it had happened. It had just sort of crept up on her. She'd found that underneath Bernie's rhino-like exterior there didn't exactly lurk a heart of gold – he had too strong a streak of self-interest for that – but there was a definite lode of something precious: wit and perceptiveness and a kind of battle-scarred humanity.

'Allegra, have you been waiting long?'

'Whistler was just starting the murals when I arrived.'

He laughed. 'I'm sorry. I've just seen the Porn King and I'm not one to bite the hand that feeds me, especially when it's an iron one inside a sheepskin glove.'

'What do you make of him?'

Bernie scanned the menu. 'Page? Too soon to say. He's keeping his cards close to his chest. Let's say I'm not booking my holidays the year after next.' Bernie signalled to the waitress. 'You know me. Short-term maybe it won't be so bad. He seems open to new ideas.' He didn't reveal yet which new ideas. That would come later. 'What's he said to Matt?'

'That they should go on as before and ignore the ratings.' Bernie raised his eyebrows fractionally. 'Matt couldn't work him out. He was charm incarnate.'

The waitress had arrived.

'I'd like Elizabeth Cromwell's Summer Salet, whatever that is.' Ally was fascinated by the seventeenth-century dishes on the menu. Maybe this was what she gave Oliver after a hard day's rebellion.

'And I'll have the buttered crab then the steak and kidney pud.'

'Watching your cholesterol, I see,' pointed out Ally.

Bernie grinned. 'I have to have some vices now I'm back on the wagon again or I might live till I'm a hundred. God, can you imagine it? Me on a zimmer frame pinching nurses' bottoms at ninety-nine?'

'I can, actually.'

Bernie looked gloomy. 'So can I.'

He poured her a glass of Bordeaux and eyed it enviously. They gossiped gently on through their meal. When Ally told him about Danny Wilde asking Maggy Mann out he choked.

'There must be more to that than meets the eye.'

'He only asked her to lunch.'

'That's a relief.'

'Mind you' – Ally batted her eyelashes at him in mock seduction – 'lunch is always the first step.'

Bernie toasted her in soda water. 'Is it now? I'll remind you of that one day.'

'Now then, Bernie,' Ally was suddenly brisk, realizing she'd have to get home soon, 'what's today all about?'

Bernie laughed. He'd been working up to telling her about the new show gently. But Ally Boyd was far too sharp for that.

'Well,' Bernie teased, 'you've heard the expression "chance of a lifetime"?'

As Ally drove home she tried to keep the excitement at bay and failed. Her own show! And what thrilled her

250

most about the idea Bernie had outlined was that everyone thought she could do it. As her slot on *Hello* had got more and more popular, she'd often felt what a waste it was that they'd had to turn away so many callers. Even before the show went on air people were queuing on the lines to get on. Now that she'd got over her nerves Ally enjoyed doing the slot hugely. Some of the problems people brought were so hopeless Freud himself couldn't have sorted them out, especially in ten minutes, live on air. But sometimes, at the end of the show, she felt she might actually have been some real help. It was a great feeling. But the ten minutes for four callers they had on *Hello* was crazy. With half an hour, they might be able to really get somewhere.

There was only one problem which dampened her spirits. How was Matt going to react? Things weren't going well for him on his revamped show.

'Shit, shit, shit!' Belinda slammed down the phone grateful that the door was closed and the whole office hadn't witnessed her humiliation. Jordan Reed, an American heartthrob with some strange right-wing connections, had just cancelled the interview they'd set up weeks ago. But it wasn't simply the cancellation that worried her. They could find another guest easily enough. It was the reason he'd given. He'd decided to go on *The Danny Wilde Show*. His agent had said candidly that way he'd get an easier ride.

How the hell was she going to tell Matt? He'd been boning up on Reed for days. What's more, they'd already given the billing to the newspapers. Belinda reached for the phone to get the press office to withdraw it. Then she stopped, her finger halfway to the dial. What would the showbiz scavengers make of that, especially when Big City Television rang them later today to say Reed would be on Danny Wilde? Maybe it'd be better to busk it and plead a mix-up later. But then the viewers would ring in to complain in droves. Wouldn't that be preferable, though, to a 'Matt Boyd Loses Out To Younger Rival' story? It was absolutely what they didn't need at the moment.

Matt came in and sat down at his desk. 'Roy's come up with some ace stuff about Jordan Reed's connections with the Ku Klux Klan,' he announced.

There was excitement in his face and she hated the idea of seeing it wiped away by what she had to tell him.

'Matt,' Belinda got up and stood in front of him.

'What's the matter, doctor? Not about to tell me I've got three months to live?'

Belinda smiled wanly. 'Actually it's about Jordan Reed. I'm afraid I've got bad news.'

Matt turned and walked out of the office they shared without a word. He felt sick to the pit of his stomach. He knew there was only one person he wanted to see: Ally. He needed the warm comfort of her presence, to feel her arms closing round him so that he could tell himself, and mean it, that it might be devastating, but it was only television. That it was his home and his family that really counted. It was a crazy idea to go and find her, he knew. He would only have time to dash home and spend half an hour with her before driving hell for leather back to the studio. But today it seemed worth it. She'd be home by now.

The roads were clear and Matt's spirits picked up a bit. On a straight stretch eight miles from home the needle touched ninety. In the distance he glimpsed a police car and slowed down to a Sunday driver's crawl, sweating slightly and cursing as it drew parallel. That was all he needed to make it a perfect day. To his immense gratitude the policeman simply nodded his head in recognition and put his foot down.

Matt felt as though he'd been handed a free gift. What was it Scott Fitzgerald had said? Something like happiness being the moment after the relief of extreme tension. Too right.

By the time he arrived at their turning his relief was tinged with excitement at the thought of surprising Ally, and he was feeling a whole lot better.

But as he parked his car in the double garage he felt the bitter kick of disappointment. Her car wasn't there. She must have gone out somewhere. He sat for a moment in the cold silence, aware of how her presence had come to be his still centre, the point his life was balanced around. And yet he'd always taken it for granted. Until now. Until she wasn't always there any more. For a moment he wondered whether to turn round and drive straight back. Then he heard Sox barking and Ally appeared from the direction of the shed, her arms full of apple logs from the trees he'd cut down in the orchard last autumn, her breath curling in the cold of the afternoon. He felt a weight lifting from his chest at the sight of her.

As she came round the side of the house Ally was amazed to see Matt get out of his car. Today was his studio day. She smiled. Maybe she could tell him her news.

'Hello, stranger. What brings you home?' She held up her cheek, marbled and smooth with the cold. She couldn't ever remember him turning up like this out of the blue before. Then the thought struck her. Her eyes darted up to his.

'Matt?'

'Yes?' He took the logs from her.

'You haven't walked out?'

He laughed hollowly. 'Don't tempt me.' She opened the front door for him and he dumped the logs into the huge basket by the side of the sitting-room fire. 'It's Jordan Reed. He's just cried off.' Casually he threw some

253

logs on the fire, but she could tell from the set of his shoulders how much he minded. He looked up at her for a second. 'He says he's going on *The Danny Wilde Show* because he'll get an easier ride.'

'Oh, Matt.' She held out her arms to him. Bernie had predicted something like this would happen. And as she held him she realized that the last thing she could tell him was about the plan to give her her own show. As they stood silently in each other's arms disappointment fought with the tenderness she felt for her husband. If Matt's career was really on the slide, should she be going ahead and planning to have a show of her own at all?

Matt said goodbye to his last guest after the show and headed up towards hospitality, intending to join the team and knock back a few beers, maybe rather too many beers. But as he picked up his briefcase from the office on the way out he felt a flash of guilt. He'd rushed home this afternoon because he'd needed Ally's comfort and now he was planning to get wrecked to try and drown out his sense of failure. He must pull himself together and not be such a wimp. Why didn't he pick up a nice bottle of wine and a bunch of flowers and spend the evening with Ally instead to thank her for being there when he needed her?

He scrawled a note to Belinda explaining that he'd gone home and stuck it in the middle of the mirror by her desk. She was bound to look there.

In hospitality, Belinda glanced at her watch and wondered where Matt had got to. She knew how he felt today – after all she shared it – and had been wondering whether it might be the time to make her move.

The room was drowned in noise, as it was every Friday. Work was over for the week and everyone let their hair down. It was the classic night for affairs to start. A heady cocktail of alcohol and release of tension. Dynamite.

Quietly Belinda headed down to their office to see if Matt had got stuck on the phone. But the familiar briefcase was nowhere to be seen. She turned and caught sight of the yellow sticker on the mirror. He had gone home to Ally. She pulled it off, threw it into the bin and strode back up to hospitality in search of a glass of wine to drown the bitter taste of disappointment.

Although it was after eight and freezing cold, the flower stall by the station at Fairley Green was still open, as Matt had guessed it would be. The old boy who ran it had to be part-Eskimo to stay open so late in this weather. Matt parked by the station and chose a huge bouquet of red roses. The flower seller surrounded them with delicate white gypsophila and wrapped them up. 'Been a naughty boy then, Matt?'

Matt looked at him blankly, then it dawned on him what the old man was getting at.

'Not in the way you're thinking.' He grinned and handed him a £20 note.

'They'll forgive anything for a bunch of flowers.' The old man's shoulders heaved in conspiratorial laughter. 'That's why there's such a good livin' in being a florist. Mind you' – he surveyed Matt, hopping from one foot to the other – 'they always know why they're getting them.' He gave the bouquet to Matt. 'What would we do without 'em, women, eh?'

Matt laughed and sprinted back to the car, which he'd left precariously parked half on the pavement. Behind him he heard a mutter: 'Be a bloody sight better off, that's what.'

As he turned into their drive Matt felt a warm glow of satisfaction. The house blazed with lights and smoke curled reassuringly from the chimney. When he opened the front door he smelt the delicious aroma of roast pork.

Instead of going straight into the kitchen, he stood in the doorway watching silently for a moment. Jess was sitting at the table reading a magazine while Ally topped and tailed some tiny green beans at the counter. The radio burbled unobtrusively in the background, only the occasional platitude audible. Potatoes bubbled on top of the Aga, the water occasionally splashing out and sizzling on its hot surface. It was a picture of perfect domestic peace. How on earth could he have got so depressed earlier today when he had this to come home to?

They looked up smiling when he walked in, his arms full of roses.

'Matt! Hello darling.' Ally walked towards him. 'I didn't hear you come in. What fabulous roses!'

He handed them over. 'I just wanted to say thank you for being here for me.'

'They're beautiful.' She kissed him, her perfume vying with the roses'. 'Do you want a drink?' She poured him a glass of red wine and he sat down next to Jess at the kitchen table, holding the glass up to the light admiring the wine's ruby glow. Contentment spread through him like the gleam in the glass.

Outside in the hall the phone began to ring and Matt cursed.

Jess leaped up. 'Don't worry, I'll get it.'

Seconds later she put her head round the door. 'It's the *Daily Express*. They want to come and do an interview.'

Without looking up Matt answered, 'Fine by me. Tell them to set it up with Century's press office, though.'

Jess laughed. 'No, not you, Dad. It's Mum they want to speak to. Something about her being given a show of her own.'

Chapter 19

'Susie, Trevor, could you both do me a big favour?' Ally took the bottle of champagne Susie and her husband had brought to congratulate her and put it in the fridge. 'Just don't mention the new show in front of Matt.'

'Hang on a minute, Ally, let me ask you a question.' Susie sat down at the kitchen table and helped herself to a glass of wine. 'If the boot was on the other foot and *he'd* just got a brilliant new show, would he be sneaking around asking his friends not to talk about it in front of *you*?'

'I know, I know.' Ally was mortified. 'But do it, will you?'

But Susie wasn't listening. 'Why is it men can't cope if the woman in their lives actually starts to get a bit successful?' She prodded a cocktail sausage and waved it expressively.

Trevor smiled dazzlingly at his wife. 'I wouldn't mind if you were more successful than me. I'd love to stay at home all day.'

'Yes, darling.' Susie patted him. 'And you'd make a much better wife than me. But we know you're exceptional. We're talking about *most* men.' She turned to Ally sternly. 'Now look, Ally. What would Barbara, our assertiveness guru, have to say about this?'

'No idea.' Ally searched for an oven cloth to put the fish pie in the Aga. 'But she doesn't have to live with Matt and I do.'

'How's he taking it?'

'He keeps saying he's really happy for me,' Ally stirred a saucepan on the stove desultorily, 'then disappearing into two-hour silences.'

'That bad, eh?' Bloody men. 'What I think' – Susie sipped her wine thoughtfully – 'is that you should stop walking on eggshells because of the tender male ego. Why *shouldn't* you be a big success? And if you are why shouldn't you be able to shout it from the rooftops instead of creeping round trying to pretend it isn't happening?'

'Quite,' said Trevor.

Ally sat down next to them, speaking in a low voice. 'But it isn't as easy as that.'

'Yes, it is. You're entitled to your success and if he doesn't like it he can . . .' Susie searched for the right word.

'Bugger off?' suggested Trevor helpfully.

'Learn to lump it,' corrected Susie. 'You've worked bloody hard for this, and you're really talented.'

'Yes, but I want to be talented and still married.'

'And if that involves pandering to the male ego you'll do it?'

'Susie, I'm a realist.' Ally shrugged. 'Marriage is about compromise.'

'Absolutely.' Susie reached for another sausage. 'You compromise and he doesn't.'

Ally grinned despite herself.

'Look, Ally, everyone knows Matt's career is on the slide and yours is on the up, and both of you know it too.'

'Susie, sh! Don't say things like that.' Suddenly she felt furious on Matt's behalf. People were so bitchy, so keen to see even a popular person like Matt fall on his face. 'You can't compare my success with his,' she said sharply. 'Mine's probably just a flash in the pan. Matt's been at the top longer than anyone.'

Ally glanced round. She could have sworn she'd heard the door opening behind them. She got up and looked but the hall was empty. She breathed a sigh of relief. Matt must still be in the bath.

'Mum!' called Janey from the landing. 'Can Adam come and stay tonight, if he sleeps in the spare room?'

Janey skipped down the stairs. She wore a tiny black miniskirt and a long black singlet with no sleeves, even though it was February. On her feet was a pair of shoes so clumpy she must have had to mug a policeman for them. But the most extraordinary feature was her face. It was white as a mime artist's with black lips painted into a perfect arc and eyes slanted up at the corners with eye liner. Ally had to admit she looked stunning, if somewhat bizarre.

'Janey, darling, won't you freeze in that vest?'

'Mum,' said Janey patiently, 'it's the fashion. I don't *care* if I freeze to death.'

Ally remembered the summers when she'd worn knee-length Biba boots in sweltering August heatwaves because everyone else had.

'You look fabulous.' She put her arm round her elder daughter, proud of Janey's sense of style, which neither she nor Jess possessed and which even this strange get-up couldn't quite disguise. Ally had always thought the fairy godmother got it wrong, and instead of giving beauty and wealth she should have given style. It lasted longer.

'OK,' Ally conceded, 'Adam can stay, providing he *does* sleep in the spare room or your father'll have a heart attack.' She tried to look the part of the stern parent and failed. 'He still thinks you're the ten-year-old tomboy he used to drag off to the football.'

'Wow, thanks. Mum, you're brilliant.'

'No, I'm not. I'm a mug who's probably storing up more trouble for herself and who ought to know better.'

'Can I ask him to supper? He's staying with friends in Guildford. He could be here in half an hour. Then Dad could meet him.'

Ally wasn't sure Matt was ready for Adam. Especially tonight. She searched for excuses.

'Is he veggy? It's lamb and I haven't got anything else.'

'No.' Janey seemed a touch crestfallen. 'He's a meat eater. He can't wait to get home for his mum's roast beef. Still.' She brightened. 'Nobody's perfect.'

Oh well, thought Ally, at least he'll have that in common with Matt.

'Who's Adam?' whispered Susie as Janey ran off to ring him with the good news.

'The new boyfriend I told you about.' Ally reached into the rack for more vegetables now there were two extra for dinner. She leaned against the Aga for a moment. 'He's a Goth, too.'

'You mean the ones who wear black from head to foot and more earrings than Madonna?'

Trevor shuddered. 'Thank God ours are into My Little Pony.'

'And you say Matt's never met him? Oh, great.' Susie raised her eyes to heaven. 'This *is* going to be a fun evening.'

An hour later Matt burst into the kitchen. 'What's that thing sitting on the sofa?' He pointed in the direction of the sitting room as though he'd just had a close encounter of the third kind.

'It's Adam. Janey's new boyfriend. He's a Goth.'

'Look at it this way,' Susie said, handing him a glass of wine, 'he could have been a Vandal.'

When Adam and Janey joined them Ally decided to serve the meal as soon as possible to break the ice.

'Adam, why don't you sit there next to Matt?' Ally directed people to their seats at the vast ash kitchen table. 'Janey, you go next to Dad and I'll go here. Where's Jess?'

'Where do you think?' Janey rolled her eyes.

'Go and tell her that if she doesn't switch off her Nintendo I'm coming up to unplug it.'

'Oh, Mum,' withered Janey, 'she doesn't use Nintendo any more. She's into three-dimensional interactive holography these days.'

Susie laughed. 'What ever happened to sex and drugs and rock 'n'roll?'

Ally pretended to swipe her with the wooden serving spoon. 'She hasn't discovered them yet, thank God.' Ally began carving the lamb. 'Though sometimes I think they'd be less anti-social.'

'So, Adam.' Matt looked at the long streak of black leather sitting next to him in vague disbelief. 'What do you do? Are you at college, or working?'

'Neither at the moment.' Adam helped himself to a small mountain of the crunchiest roast potatoes, including the one with the burnt bits Matt had had his eye on. 'I was at Surrey University but I dropped out last term. I don't flourish in hierarchies.'

Matt tried his best not to react. 'What were you studying?'

'American Studies.'

This was the same course Janey had been accepted for at Sussex. Provided she got her grades. 'Just like you, Janey. You'll be able to discuss the future of the great American novel.' Matt filled her wine glass.

'Actually' – Janey took a Coca-Cola-sized mouthful of the ten-year-old claret Matt had just poured her – 'I'm not sure about going to university. Sometimes it seems a bit of a waste of time.'

Matt and Ally exchanged glances. They knew better than to argue. This must be Adam's doing, Matt reflected angrily. Ever since she'd read *Catcher in the Rye* at fourteen Janey had wanted to study American literature.

Diplomatically, he changed the subject. 'What about your parents?' Even as he said it, Matt realized how like a Victorian father he sounded. 'Where do they live?'

'They're divorced. I lived with my mother until she

got married again. I didn't like her new husband so I moved into a squat in Notting Hill. Still there now.'

Matt was horrified. 'I thought that sort of thing went out in the sixties.'

'Tch, tch, Mr Boyd. You need to do your homework. There are thousands of squats. Councils aren't building, you see.'

Of course he knew councils weren't building, opinionated young git. Matt couldn't believe it. He was being patronized by a nineteen-year-old.

'Actually' – Adam winked at Janey – 'it's a very posh squat, isn't it, Janey? Nice flat-fronted Georgian house, running water, electricity. We even have a lock on the front door.' He turned to Ally. 'I love Georgian architecture, don't you, Mrs Boyd?'

All Matt could think of was that Janey had been to this lout's house, squat, whatever, and that she was gazing at him in open adoration as though every word he uttered was a gem of wit and illumination.

Matt felt a sharp pang of – what? Irritation? Resentment at being usurped? Janey had always been his favourite. He adored Jess, too, but she'd always been closer to her mother. Janey had always wanted to be with him. They'd gone everywhere together when she was a child. Football matches. Tree climbing. Long country walks.

Matt got up to take away the vegetable dishes and as he moved out Adam leaned over and held Janey's hand for an instant. A glow of happiness lit up her face that almost stopped Matt in his tracks. He felt a wave of antagonism towards Adam so strong that he wanted to hit him.

You're jealous, he accused himself. You're jealous of your wife because she's becoming a star and you're jealous of your daughter because she's fallen in love. For Christ's sake, what's happening to you? You should be big enough to take a few changes in your life!

Stacking the plates on top of the dishwasher Matt could hardly trust himself to sit down next to them again.

Fortunately he didn't need to.

'Hi.' Jess had finally deigned to put in an appearance. She sat down in Matt's chair and helped herself to the last of the potatoes. 'You must be Adam. I'm the little sister. Why is everyone so quiet?' She looked round the table. 'Let me guess. You've just told them you're sleeping together?'

'What we want in the new show is that confessional feeling you get in phone-ins.' Bernie was bounding round the office like a spring lamb, his small eyes alight with excitement. 'You know, when people admit some terrible thing they've been carrying round inside them for years. Only this time we want them to do it face-to-face sitting there with you in the studio.'

Ally had assumed that the show would be simply a longer version of the slot on *Hello*, but Bernie had grander ideas.

'Of course we'll have to structure it a lot more than *Hello*. And only one topic per show so we can really get to grips with it. Adultery. Alcoholism. Abortion.'

'Come on, Bernie,' Ally giggled, 'there must be more social problems beginning with A.'

He swatted her with his pad. 'Look, gel, take it a bit seriously, will you? Why don't you make some suggestions?'

'OK, then.' Ally stopped laughing. 'Teenage sex. Jealous fathers. Husbands who can't cope with their wives' success.'

'Good girl.' Bernie winked. 'I can see this show's going to be right up your street.'

'You don't think ...' Ally didn't quite know how to put it without offending him '... that this kind of show's been done before?'

'Not with you, it hasn't. The thing is, Ally my love, you're our secret weapon. We did a little survey. Did you know that ninety per cent of callers to *Hello* have never rung a phone-in before?'

Ally listened, her heart beating faster with pleasure. She'd had no idea she was bringing in a new audience. It wasn't so long ago she feared she'd be dropped. But she had to be realistic. 'Do you really think I could handle it? A whole studio full of people and no autocue?'

'Believe in yourself for once, Allegra Boyd! You could do it standing on your head. Besides' – he glanced down at his watch, recalling he had a meeting about their new opening titles in five minutes – 'you're lousy at autocue, remember?'

As Matt drove himself into work he decided it was time to take himself in hand. He didn't like the person he was becoming. The reason he was jealous of Ally was because his own show wasn't turning out to be the success he'd hoped. But that was hardly her fault. It was his.

He either had to make the show a hit or admit he was wrong about the concept. He decided to try twice as hard to make it a hit.

The first thing he noticed when he arrived was that something looked different. Then he realized what it was. Belinda had stopped putting the ratings up on the wall for everyone to see.

He went into their office. 'Belinda, there aren't any figures up for the last two weeks' shows.'

She looked defensive. 'That's because they're so low. I didn't want the team getting demoralized. If they start thinking we've got a problem, then we'll have twice the problem.'

Matt shook his head. 'You're underestimating them. Do you think they don't know why you're not putting the figures up?' He put down his briefcase. 'Forget about the bloody ratings. They're getting at your confidence. You never take a decision now without checking the numbers. Television's not like that. You have to go by instinct.'

'Yes. Well my instinct is telling me that if we don't come through soon we're fucked.'

Matt picked up the envelope containing the ratings and slowly tore it in two.

'From now on we're going to ignore the figures and trust our judgement.'

'And what's our judgement going to tell us? To go back to Jason Donovan?'

Matt grinned. 'No. Not that. Death before that. But we do need a bit of glitz. Perhaps we've frightened the audience. We're going to woo them back with a megastar. An interesting megastar. A megastar with something to say.'

'Isn't that called a contradiction in terms?' Belinda said glumly.

Matt patted her on the back. 'What's happened to the spunky fighter who chewed up Bernie Long and spat him out?'

'She got indigestion.'

Matt laughed. 'Come on. It's not too late. We've got a roomful of talented people working on this show. We can pull round. Why don't we have a head-banging session now, this minute?'

Belinda felt Matt's energy and enthusiasm radiate out towards her. It was irresistible. She got up to go and summon the team. At the door she turned excitedly.

'Matt, I've got it! Syrah Wade!'

'The black soul singer? Isn't he just boring Mr Macho?'

'Not any more. There's been a campaign to "out" him in the States – you know, when the activists force famous gays to come out of the closet, whether they want to or not. I read an interview with him in *Vanity Fair*. He's really angry about it. It would make riveting TV. And he's coming over here soon.'

'What about the big question?'

'Which is?'

'*Is* he gay?'

'I don't know. You'll have to ask him, won't you?'

Matt began to feel his own excitement mounting. 'Do you think he'd talk?'

'I've no idea, but I know his PR person. Why don't I try and find out?'

The small hairs on the back of Matt's neck tickled. If they could pull this off they'd get massive publicity. They'd be back on top. But on their own terms.

'Didn't we used to have people called parents?' Jess was sitting at the kitchen table enjoying the feel of the early spring sun on her back and no parents to fuss over what she had for breakfast. In front of her were two Yo-Yos and a minipack of Capri-Sun.

For the last three weeks Ally had been leaving early for wardrobe fittings and rehearsals for her new show and Matt had disappeared soon after.

'Don't knock it.' Janey surveyed Jess's breakfast selection in disgust. 'It's a whole lot better than the silences and the sulking.'

'Do you think everything's OK between them?' Jess buzzed on the television to catch five minutes of *The Simpsons*, her favourite programme.

'Better than they were a couple of weeks ago.' Janey tried to keep her voice light and chatty. She didn't want to worry Jess. But she suspected all wasn't as well as it should be between them. She knew her father was more rattled than he was letting on by his problems at work.

And she'd never trusted Belinda's intentions where her father was concerned.

And then she remembered overhearing something one of the mistresses at her school had said about another girl in her class whose parents had separated. *They're so selfish, aren't they, the way they go and split up just before A Levels.*

There were another three months to go. Suddenly Janey didn't feel like her muesli any more. Oh God, don't let it happen to hers. Please.

When the day of the first recording of *Tell It to Ally* arrived it was almost a relief. They were to record six half-hour shows, one a week. No one knew yet when they were going out and Ally realized it probably depended on how good they were.

To kick off Bernie had chosen the topic of revenge, inspired by the story of a genteel lady who'd got her own back on her errant husband and his new ladyfriend by painting the word 'ADULTERER' in three-foot-high red letters on the front of his firm's office building. As this turned out to be a respectable firm of City solicitors, the story had ended up on the front page of every newspaper and had kept the nation in stitches all week.

Ally had been nervous that the discarded wife would turn out to be a pathetic victim and that Ally would have to carry the whole show herself. But one glance at Susan Close's patrician features, the twinset and pearls, the baggy tweed skirt and the twinkle in her eye as she was led into the studio, told Ally that it would be fine. Susan Close was a fighter. The kind who built the Empire.

What Ally hadn't bargained for was that Susan was more than fine. She was brilliant. Funny, feisty and yet with a ruthless honesty that made utterly riveting television. She ran rings round the marriage guidance counsellor and the couples' therapist who had come along to advise more cautious tactics.

At the end of the show Ally knew by the thunderous applause from the audience and – even more telling – from the bored and cynical technicians that it was going to be a winner. Unlike the producer or the presenter they had no vested interest and had been known to fall asleep during shows they considered below par. But not this one.

And any lingering doubts were swept away by Bernie. As Nikki led Susan Close off to the green room, he literally ran on to the studio floor and swept her off her feet.

'It's a cracker, gel!' Ally laughed and insisted he put her down. 'You got everything. Laughter. Tears. It was absolutely bloody brilliant!'

'Thanks, Bernie.' Ally grinned as he pulled her towards the lifts and a little celebration he'd planned upstairs. 'But I wish you could think of something nice to say about it.'

'Darling, you were fabulous!' The set designer put down his glass of mineral water to wrap Ally in his arms. Ally looked round and realized that the room was packed with showbiz writers and trade reporters. Trust Bernie not to have a 'little party' without inviting the press.

With the tension of the first recording over Ally felt she could relax and enjoy herself. She stopped a waiter and helped herself to a glass of wine just as Maggy Mann appeared out of the crowd next to her. Trust Maggy to show up at a party.

'So, what does Matt think of your meteoric rise?' Maggy deposited her empty glass on the waiter's tray and took two full ones off it.

'He's fine about it,' Ally lied.

'Is he?' Maggy fluffed the hair she'd made Elaine

backcomb and gel to within an inch of its life. 'Men can be so pathetic. The moment I started to get famous my husband upped and left with his secretary.'

'Matt's not like that. He likes strong women.'

'I see.' Maggy sipped her drink then turned to smile at Ally. 'That probably explains why he's spending so much time with Belinda Wyeth all of a sudden.'

The old Maggy was back. Before Ally had time to think about the implications of what she had said, Bernie banged his glass with a fork for silence.

'I'd like to thank you for coming to celebrate the launch of our new show and to meet our new star, Ally Boyd. I've known Ally for fifteen years – but not as a star herself. In fact the first words Ally ever spoke to me were about her husband Matt.' He smiled across at Ally as she nervously wondered what was coming next. 'She said, "Don't you know he's got a wife and family to go home to?". Ally, quite unreasonably, thought that Matt should have time off occasionally. I knew, of course, that she was just a wife and mum who didn't understand the demands of the job. I thought that was her weakness. Now I know it's her strength. Ally isn't one of us. She's one of them, and that's why they open their hearts to her. And I've got a little confession to add.' From behind his back he produced a huge bouquet of white roses. 'Over the last few months I've fallen in love with her.'

'Well, you're too late.' Ally whirled round to find Matt standing behind her with another bouquet. She reached out her hand to him, relief flooding through her. Coming here could only mean he was really proud of her.

All that had been wrong with Matt was that his show wasn't going well, but ever since Syrah Wade had agreed to come on the old Matt had been back. Funny and sharp as ever. Maggy Mann was wrong. It was going to be fine between them.

On the other side of the room Ally noticed Ritchie Page. Normally he avoided the press like a dose of the clap. Matt caught sight of him too and he stiffened and tried to steer Ally into the crowd as the chairman walked towards them.

'Allegra, Matt, how nice to see you,' Page said smoothly. 'You must be very proud, Matt. Ally's a real talent. She was wasted without her own show.'

Matt was conscious of Page's eyes appraising him.

'I know. I'm very proud of her.'

'I'm pleased to hear it.'

Matt felt an overpowering urge to walk away. The bastard didn't believe him.

'I hear you've got Syrah Wade on the show next week.'

Ally was relieved at the turn in the conversation. 'Yes,' Matt answered tersely. 'It should be a good interview.'

'I hope so, Matt.' Page's tone was silky and unpleasant. 'Because you certainly need something, don't you?'

Behind Page's left shoulder Matt glimpsed Belinda fighting her way across the room towards them. He took a glass from a passing tray and handed it to her, but she waved a refusal. Then he saw her unfamiliar agitation and his stomach turned over. Belinda signalled to him to extricate himself from the conversation and follow her. When they got to a quiet corner she turned to him.

But Matt got there first. 'It's Syrah Wade, isn't it? Don't tell me he's called it off.'

'Not him, he's raring to go. Wants to blow the whole thing sky-high. The man's bursting to come out of the anti-gay closet.'

Matt cheered up. Maybe the game wasn't over yet.

'It's his record company.' Belinda rubbed her hand across her eyes. She was looking wiped out. 'They went spare when they heard what he'd agreed to. They've told him it's them or us.' She tried to smile despite her fury and exhaustion. 'Not surprisingly he's decided it's them.'

'Jesus!' Matt struggled to control himself in front of these people. Rejection might be new, but he was beginning to get used to it. 'Are you sure he can't be talked round?'

Belinda shrugged. 'I've tried every argument I can think of.'

'Is he in London now?' Matt was determined not to give up. 'Come on. Let's have one more try. Where's he staying?'

'The Dorchester.'

'Let's go. I'll just tell Ally I'm leaving.'

They pushed through the tightly packed bodies and eased themselves in the direction of Ally, who was now entirely surrounded by hangers-on.

Seeing his face she freed herself at once.

'Syrah Wade's pulled out,' he explained.

'Oh, Matt. Not again.'

'We're going to his hotel to try and talk him round.'

Ally watched as they squeezed their way out of the room, both looking as haggard as each other. Why couldn't things go well for her and Matt at the same time for once?

As silently as a grass snake, Page appeared by her side.

'Not a problem, I hope?'

'Oh, no.' Ally turned to him brightly. 'Nothing they can't sort out anyway.'

At the Dorchester reception Matt was instantly recognized and the girl behind the desk was happy to call Syrah Wade's suite. She spoke softly into the phone.

'Someone's coming down at once.' She smiled her on-duty-24-hours-a-day smile. 'Would you like to wait in the lounge and perhaps I could order you a drink?'

Matt sat nursing a mineral water in the blue and white terrace bar rehearsing the arguments that would persuade Syrah Wade to override his record company. It was an outside shot, but he had to try.

They didn't have to hang around long.

Less than five minutes later a chic young black woman in top-to-toe Armani walked across the lounge towards them.

'Mr Boyd?' Her voice was firm and clear with all the timbre of a trained singer. 'I'm afraid there must be some misunderstanding.' She smiled sympathetically. 'Mr Wade's already left for Paris.'

Outside the Dorchester Matt felt a tidal wave of depression engulf him. He couldn't believe it had happened again. 'I know what we need.' Belinda hailed a taxi without further consultation. 'Somewhere discreet and anonymous to get absolutely rat-arsed.'

From Belinda's words Matt didn't know what to expect and walking into the intimate, wood-panelled atmosphere of Two Brydges Place, he realized he was feeling slightly nervous. But the place wasn't at all what he was expecting. No louche women on their fifteenth Martini looking for a lift home, the club felt more like an eighteenth-century coffee house or a sophisticated gentlemen's club. But for Matt the really novel experience was that when he walked in no one turned a hair. A young woman sitting at the bar didn't even look up from her copy of the *Guardian*, and when Belinda led him up the narrow stairs to a table on the second floor none of the raffish young drinkers gave him even a second glance of recognition.

'It's because you're television.' Belinda was watching him, sipping a bloody Mary. 'This is a stage actors' haunt, darling. You're a nobody here until you've done Henry V.'

Matt laughed. Sitting here he almost felt like an ordinary person and, though he knew it was probably a myth, it was still exhilarating. He began to forget about Syrah Wade, and the whole damned show.

'Do you know?' he said, draining his glass and standing

272

up. 'I might do something I haven't done for fifteen years.'

Belinda, in the process of extracting the juice from her slice of lemon, sucked a sticky finger. 'And what's that?'

'Go to the bar and buy myself a drink.'

'Sorry, Matt, but you can't.' She wiped her hands on her suit like a bad-mannered child, 'You see, you're not a member.'

Matt looked her in the eyes. She was clearly enjoying putting him at a disadvantage, reminding him this was her patch, telling him he was nobody here. And the extraordinary thing was that, after years of being treated as special by almost everyone he met, he found it curiously exciting. As though this was her game and he had no choice but to play by her rules.

An hour later, when she asked if he wanted to eat in some smart restaurant round the corner in Soho, almost too quickly he said no. The truth was he didn't want to break the spell.

And so they ate there. And as the evening wore on Matt told himself he mustn't give in to this powerful but false magic. Outside the small, insignificant front door, more like a strip-club entrance or a walk-up-and-wait joint, the world was just the same as when he'd come in. It was the real world, the world with Ally in it. And Janey. And Jess.

'What a bloody awful week.' Belinda held up her glass of red wine as she talked to him, so that it reflected a pink glow on to her face like an Egyptian temple at sunset. It was a theatrical gesture and he knew it. She was trying to charm him. 'But at least we're in it together.'

For a fraction of a second he brushed her hand with his. Then, as if coming to some decision, he stood up.

'Time I went. Ally will be home by now.' He laid the name down between them like a bolster in the middle of a bed.

'Fine.' Belinda knew she had to be casual, sophisticated, cool. But that wasn't how she felt. She wouldn't get another chance like this again. Matt's guard had been slipping tonight and both of them were aware of it. She stood up and quietly followed him out.

They walked silently down the dark crevasse of Brydges Place, almost Dickensian in its darkness and narrowness. Neither of them tried their usual banter. Just before the alley broke through into the bright lights of St Martin's Lane they both stopped instinctively.

She put her hand on his shoulder and stood a foot away, her stance almost swaggering. 'It's true what they're saying, isn't it?' Her eyes were level with his, dark holding blue. 'You preferred it when Ally was little wifey. Now that she's changing you don't really like it, do you, Matt?'

It was a direct challenge to his masculinity, pure and simple, and there was only one way he could answer it.

For a fraction of a second he thought of Ally earlier today, her face concerned, wanting things to work out for him. Ally the star. And Matt the failure.

His body pressed Belinda's against the cold railings and his hard lips closed over hers.

Chapter 20

Matt woke up suddenly, moving in a split second from being totally asleep to totally awake. He glanced at the figure by his side and saw to his overwhelming relief that it was Ally, not Belinda. Yet as he turned over to try and go back to sleep he found he couldn't. His mind, like a dog digging for a lost bone, kept returning again and again to the same thought. A thought that brought both unease and excitement.

He had kissed Belinda. He closed his eyes, trying to blot out the memory. But there it was again. Belinda challenging him, deliberately he knew, but somehow all the more provocative for that. No come-hither looks or off-the-shoulder straps. More threat than invitation. The way her mouth opened like a yawning lioness's under his. No soft, feminine yielding. She took.

In her sleep Ally stirred and rolled next to him, her warmth against his. Matt reached out a hand to hold back the curtain of her hair and look at her face.

In all their years together he had never felt a need to prove his masculinity through sleeping with someone else. He had never, as many men around him did, equated power with sex. The irony was that now, when suddenly he doubted his capacities and his talent, he kept thinking of Belinda.

Ally's eyes opened for a moment. Half awake she seemed to sense some need for reassurance in him and rubbed herself against him, her nipples hard against his chest through the thin silk of her nightdress.

As she caressed him, her hand slipping down between his legs, he felt himself respond. Sleepily she looked up at him and smiled. He felt a stab of guilt so hard at the sweetness of her smile that it punctured his erection like glass under a tyre. Kissing her softly and pushing her gently away he tried to avoid her eyes. This wouldn't last. It meant nothing. It was just that, now, today, she was the last person who could reassure his flagging masculinity.

Still half asleep, Ally turned over and snuggled under the duvet. But instead of falling into a comforting sleep her eyes snapped open. Something was very wrong.

Belinda woke up and stretched. Tonight she was supposed to be having dinner with a news journalist she'd met at a friend's party last week. Suddenly she didn't want to go any more. She knew she'd spend the whole evening thinking about Matt.

She jumped out of bed, full of energy, and pulled back the heavy plush curtains of her bedroom window to look down at the street below. People were scurrying off to work. It was a time Belinda liked best. She never left till the nine-to-five brigade had long departed. She might work terrible hours but they didn't start early like these poor wage slaves with their dull time-serving jobs.

Belinda smiled. She looked round her bedroom at the huge polished mahogany bed with its white lace bedspread, painstakingly sewn by some prospective bride as part of her bottom drawer, the wallpaper covered in tiny bunches of violets, the potted palms in elaborate jardinières, everywhere pictures and knick-knacks. She had created in this room, and this flat, a little slice of Victoriana. And what never failed to give her a thrill was the sense of being a modern girl, making her own choices, free to do exactly what she wanted in surroundings from an era where women had none of those options. She was her own person, neither mistress nor wife, and that was the way she liked it. Didn't she?

The thought of Matt flooded back. Should she go ahead and get involved? He wouldn't want to leave Ally and his children.

She closed her eyes and remembered the feel of his kiss and the flash of intense excitement when his hand had touched her breast in the darkness of Brydges Place. Never, not once since she was fifteen and had felt an exploring touch for the very first time, had she experienced an electricity like that. She saw the risks she was taking. Matt was no wham-bam-thank-you-mam philanderer. Having an affair with him might be the beginning of a big adventure. Or it might be an invitation to desperate heartache which would leave her alone, leading her life in the margins of his.

And why should she, who had always wanted powerful men, men on the way up, have fallen for Matt Boyd when his star was falling? Closing her eyes she saw his face again, the laughing blue eyes, the razor-sharp wit, and underneath it all the capacity for tenderness. And she knew she was prepared to fight to get him.

'Right. Got everything?' Ally stood on the doorstep to wave goodbye as Matt took the girls to school. 'Jess, have you packed your piano music? I'll be back today to drop you off.'

'You don't have to, you know.'

'I know. But I enjoy it.'

'Well,' Jess reassured, 'if it helps with the maternal guilt . . .'

Ally swiped her, laughing. 'Get in that car!'

She leaned down and smiled at Matt through the open window, trying not to think about last night. That little problem had never happened to them before. Tiredness on his part. Occasional unwillingness on hers. But not that. Poor Matt. He must be under so much pressure at

277

the moment. And yet he wouldn't talk about it. Every time she even asked obliquely he brushed her off. Bloody television! She'd thought it would bring them together and instead it seemed to be pushing them apart.

In the car Jess chattered on as usual, but Janey, always sensitive, sat in the back silently. Without even being aware that she was doing it, she had started to watch her parents closely for signs of the thing she dreaded most. And for weeks now, ever since Mum had started working on her new show, she knew something was wrong between them.

When Matt pulled the car to a halt in the usual place round the corner from the school, Jess got out and ran ahead while Janey stayed on in the car trying to pluck up courage.

'Dad.' She leaned forward through the gap in the two front seats and kissed him on the cheek. 'I love you, Dad,' she said simply.

Matt turned to her and felt his heart lurch. She had a look of apprehension in her eyes he'd never seen there before. She couldn't know anything. There was nothing to know. Not yet.

'Dad?'

'Yes, Janey?' He took her hand and squeezed it.

'Why don't you and Mum go out to dinner tonight? Did you know,' she continued quickly before he had time to answer, 'that you and Mum have only spent one evening together in the last three weeks?'

'Don't be silly, darling,' Matt smiled at her seriousness. 'It's much more than that.'

'No, it isn't,' she insisted. 'Jess worked it all out. She made a chart on her computer. You had a meal together last Wednesday week. Even Mrs O'Shock's noticed, though she says she and Mr O'Shock find absence keeps the spice in their marriage.'

278

Matt burst out laughing at the irresistible thought of Mrs O'Shock in black negligee and tartan bedroom slippers waiting for the hero to return from an absent night at the Coach and Horses.

He squeezed her hand again. 'That's a delicious idea, Janey love. We'll do it soon.'

'Why not tonight?'

Matt was touched at the urgency in her voice. 'Darling, I don't even know what Mum's doing tonight.'

'She's free. I checked in her diary. Dad?' She fiddled with her spiky fringe. 'Promise? I'll make the booking in case you forget.'

This time Matt didn't laugh. And his eyes were troubled as he watched her walk slowly towards school. What had he been thinking of, fantasizing about Belinda? Janey trusted him absolutely. How could he have ever thought of betraying them all? When he got into work he was going to explain, gently and firmly, to Belinda that it had been a crazy mistake.

'What's the matter, angel?' Bernie had been watching Ally stare at her script without appearing to see it for five minutes now. When a drop of water fell on to the yellow paper he decided to speak up. As if he didn't already know the answer.

'It's Matt. I can't seem to get through to him. It's as though he's always thinking about something else.'

'Maybe he is. He's having a tough time, after all.'

Ally looked up, unsure how much to tell him. He was watching her and she could see the concern in his small, sharp eyes.

'He doesn't want to make love any more.'

'Maybe you should be understanding. Watching your career go down the tubes isn't much of an aphrodisiac, is it?'

'Bernie?'

Without being asked Bernie knew what was coming next and dreaded it.

'Yes, my love?'

'He's not having an affair with Belinda, is he?'

Along with everyone else at Century, Bernie knew how much time Matt spent with her. But that was hardly evidence.

'I don't know. Do you want me to go and talk to him?'

'Would you?' Ally felt a sense of relief. Matt closed up whenever she asked him anything. Maybe Bernie could find something out.

'Anyone seen Matt?' Bernie shouted round *The Matt Boyd Show* offices later that morning, half-hoping he'd be told Matt had gone on a daytrip to Land's End.

'In their office,' said Roy. One phone slung round his neck and the other in his hand, he nodded his head towards the closed door. Bernie could hear angry voices.

'I'll try later.' Bernie turned on his heel.

'Bernie, what brings you here?' Matt opened the door of the office, clearly eager to get away.

Bernie hesitated a moment. He could hardly have the conversation he wanted to with Belinda around. Then she appeared and grabbed Matt's jacket, trying to pull him back in until she noticed Bernie standing there.

Bernie knew immediately something had just happened between them. It was in the way neither of them looked in each other's eyes, the way they tried to hide it with a kind of neutral jocularity he knew to be false to both their characters. He'd seen it a hundred times before, even done it himself. Matt and Belinda were trying to throw him off the scent and there was only one possible explanation.

Ally was right. They were having an affair.

At that moment one of the secretaries arrived and handed Matt a message. 'Who's it from, Sue?' he asked.

'She didn't say. Just to tell you that she'd booked a table for two at nine o'clock at La Pomme d'Amour.'

Matt smiled and Bernie felt a sudden temptation to hit him. Had Matt gone mad? He was obviously involved with Belinda and now it sounded as though there was some other woman too. My God, poor Ally. Talk about not coping with your wife's success. Failure must be going to his prick.

He took his time before going back to their studio in the East End, standing for a moment on Tower Bridge, the cold March wind whipping up off the steely water, and wondering how the hell he was going to tell Ally.

But by the time he got back to the studio Ally was smiling as though she didn't have a care in the world.

'You seem very cheerful.' Bernie could hardly bear to look at her happy face. She was positively glowing.

'I am.'

'Why's that?'

'Matt and I are being sent out to dinner tonight by Janey.' She laughed as she picked up her script for tomorrow's show. 'The children don't think we see enough of each other. She's booked the restaurant herself.'

'Don't tell me,' Bernie grinned. 'La Pomme d'Amour at nine o'clock.'

'How on earth did you know that?'

'Didn't I ever tell you' – Bernie winked at her – 'that my grandmother was pyschic?'

He took her hand and stroked it affectionately. Maybe it would be fine. He hoped to God it would. They were both people he cared about.

Ally waited for Matt at the small bar of La Pomme

d'Amour surrounded by pastel murals and felt almost shy, as though it was a blind date set up by a mutual friend and she wasn't sure that they would hit it off. But the moment Matt walked in and smiled at her she could see he was as self-conscious as she was and she relaxed.

Once the waiter had taken their order and brought them each a glass of kir royale, Matt took her hand and kissed it. For a moment he was tempted to tell her about Belinda, but he wasn't sure of his own motives in confessing. Confessions, he knew, could often be easier for the giver than the receiver.

By the time they rolled out of a taxi three hours and two bottles of wine, plus the odd brandy, later their house was in darkness. Even Sox was asleep. Very quietly Matt opened the front door and fell over the bowl of water Janey had left out for Sox in the hall. He and Ally disintegrated into giggles. In a gesture of wifely concern Ally insisted he sit on the stairs while she removed his wet trousers.

Upstairs Janey knocked softly on her sister's door. 'Jessy, you don't think that's burglars, do you?'

Jess sat up in bed listening. She'd heard their taxi arrive. 'Not unless they came in a minicab and raided the drinks cabinet.'

'It must be Mum and Dad,' Jess said.

'Let's go and see.'

Gingerly they crept on to the landing and peered down through the banisters.

On the bottom step, minus his trousers, sat their father clutching a bottle of Remy Martin in his left arm and their mother in his right.

'Janey, you're brilliant,' Jess whispered. 'I think it might have worked.'

'I hope so.' Janey put her arms round her younger sister so that she couldn't see the tears that were pricking

282

in the corners of her eyes. 'I certainly bloody well hope so.'

As the unruly sun fought its way round the edges of their heavy bedroom curtain the next morning Ally woke and stroked Matt's hair lovingly. For a moment she wondered what they were doing lying on the floor. Then she remembered and smiled.

Sleepily she nudged Matt and coaxed him into the bed, dragging the duvet behind her. On the bedside table the phone rang and Ally looked at her watch. Nine thirty!

'Oh my God!' she exclaimed. 'That's my mother. I promised to fetch her and take her to the station.' She picked up the phone. 'So sorry, Mum, but I've been struck down by some kind of flash flu,' she lied as Matt began very slowly to caress her inner thighs.

'Tell her,' he instructed, as his mouth slipped downwards, featherlight and exquisitely tantalizing, 'to get a bloody taxi.'

With superhuman willpower Ally tried not to moan. Her mother didn't believe in sex after marriage.

'Are you all right, Allegra? Who was that talking?'

'Didn't I tell you, Mum? I'm under the doctor.'

With his face buried between her thighs, Matt still managed a laugh.

Ally's mother sniffed. 'Well, he doesn't seem to be taking it very seriously.'

This time Ally gasped. 'Oh, I wouldn't say that.' Her back arched in almost intolerable pleasure. 'I wouldn't say that at all.'

'Goodbye, Allegra. I hope you're better soon.'

'Good . . . bye . . . Mum. I'm sure I will be.'

After they'd made love Matt lay next to her, stroking her hair. How could he have ever thought about being unfaithful when his life was so rooted in Ally and his family?

★

'Drop Matt Boyd from the Telethon?' Stephen Cartwright's tone couldn't have been more horrified if Ritchie Page had suggested dropping the Queen from the annual Christmas message. 'You can't be serious!'

For more than ten years Century Television had co-hosted the Telethon, ITV's charity fund-raising evening, together with their rival Big City Television. It was the most prestigious and high-profile event of the year, watched by twelve million people. For one night at least the rival TV companies stopped worrying about whether they were outdoing each other in the ratings and concentrated on trying to outdo each other in raising money for a good cause. Ever since it began it had always been hosted by Matt.

'Why ever not?' Page tapped his cigar impassively. 'It's time for a change.' The idea had come to Page fully formed as he lay in the bath last night.

'But Matt always does it. He *is* the Telethon.'

'People get bored with the same face. I think we should find someone new.'

Stephen wondered what the hell Page was up to. 'So who do you suggest?'

Ritchie Page did his best to make his voice as casual as possible. 'As a matter of fact I've been thinking about Danny Wilde.'

Stephen looked at Page coldly. This time he was going to rebel. 'But he doesn't even work for Century. Our presenter's always been the main one.'

'What I had in mind' – Page smiled his perfectly capped smile – 'was a little break with tradition. A two-hander. Danny Wilde as the main presenter and someone from Century to co-present.' He paused fractionally. 'Maybe a woman.'

Stephen was puzzled. 'Maggy Mann, you mean?'

'No. Maggy would never take second billing to Danny

Wilde.' The personal fax machine on Page's desk suddenly jumped into life, disgorging a piece of paper which Page picked up, read briefly and put in a drawer of his desk while Stephen tried to think what other woman at Century was well known enough to front the Telethon. After a moment he began to get Page's drift.

'I don't suppose,' he asked, for once showing a bit of spirit, 'that the woman you have in mind happens to be Allegra Boyd?'

'Exactly.'

'But she's not well enough known just from *Hello*.'

'She will be soon. Bernie Long says she's a star. She'd only co-host. I think she'd be brilliant.'

Chapter 21

Janey watched her parents closely for the next few weeks and was grateful that their life seemed to settle down into a comfortable pattern. They were both busy but at least they found some time for each other.

'I hope that between your two dazzling careers you haven't forgotten the importance of the twenty-second of April,' she announced one morning.

Ally clapped her hand over her mouth. 'It's the first day of spring. And I haven't even washed my Druid's outfit.'

Janey laughed, knowing that her mother wouldn't really have forgotten. 'My eighteenth birthday.'

'Of course it is,' said Ally, as though she'd just remembered. 'And how do you want to mark it?'

'Well,' Janey announced solemnly, 'I was going to go to the cinema and donate the money I would have spent on a party to Greenpeace.'

'*We* would have spent,' corrected Matt, catching Ally's eye and winking. 'But?'

'But I've decided to go ahead and have a party instead.'

'Ah, well,' said Ally, bowing to the inevitable. 'What sort of thing have you got in mind?'

'Oh, you know, nothing special, a band, disco, food, drink, marquee for about three hundred.' She noticed Ally's horrified expression. 'Or I could always hire a club for the night,' she suggested hopefully.

Ally thought of the pitch dark, spray-painted caverns throbbing with deafening music Janey liked to frequent and decided a marquee in the garden was the less terrifying option. At least they'd know what everyone was getting up to.

Jess came in with the morning post. 'Bills for Dad,' she said, 'and some fan mail for Mum.'

She put a handwritten white envelope down in front of her mother. Ally was surprised to see it was from Century but the writing was unfamiliar. Maybe it was the press office sending something on.

She opened it with Jess hanging over her shoulder, eager to read what her mother's admirer had to say. To her astonishment it was from Ritchie Page. Ally read half the letter then tried to fold it up and stuff it back in its envelope. But not before Jess had already got the gist.

'Wow!' Her voice rang with excitement. 'You'll never believe this! Mum's been asked to host the Telethon! And guess who with, Janey . . . your hero Danny Wilde!'

Ally closed her eyes feeling a flash of anger at Jess. How could she be so stupid and tactless? There was a beat of silence when everything seemed suspended in time.

'I'm not going to do it.' Ally picked up the letter and tore it in two. 'I'm telling Page it's out of the question.'

Matt's face was impassive. 'It's an extraordinary opportunity. It would be ludicrous to turn it down.' He gathered his post up, not looking at her. 'Besides,' he added, and she could hear an edge of suppressed anger in his voice, 'if you turn it down it'll look as though you're protecting me. You don't have any choice. You've got to do it.'

Jess glanced from one parent to the other, gradually realizing the impact of what she'd done.

Matt walked from the room and Ally watched him, not knowing what to say that wouldn't make things worse. How could Page have done this to her and Matt? What the hell was she going to do?

She heard the front door slam and Matt leave without saying goodbye, not even coming back to offer the girls a lift to school. She fought back the tears and wondered if she should run after him, but what would she say? Everything she said about his work these days seemed to sound wrong. Patronizing or falsely cheerful.

Matt's car door slammed. Maybe she should just tell him she loved him? But then Jess suddenly burst into tears and sat down at the breakfast table with her head in her arms.

'Oh, Mum,' she sobbed, 'I'm so sorry. It was all *my* fault.'

'No, it wasn't.' Unable to go on being angry at Jess when she was in such distress, Ally stroked her hair. She could hear Matt starting his car and she desperately wanted to race after him, but she knew that Jess needed her too. Bloody Ritchie Page.

Outside the gravel flew in the air as Matt spun the car round and drove, very fast, down their front drive towards the lethal junction with the main road. He was doing fifty by the time he came to the end of the drive and he knew there was barely enough space for him to get out in front of the next car but he did it anyway. He couldn't remember when he'd felt angrier or more humiliated. After ten years neither Ritchie Page nor Stephen had had the courtesy to even warn him that he was being dropped from the Telethon. And to put Danny Wilde in his place when he didn't even work for Century was a deliberate snub.

Matt pulled off the road down a country lane and stopped in the entrance to a field. He got out and leaned against the gate. He had to admit there was more to his reaction than simply being replaced by a man ten years younger than him. All right, so it might make him feel one step closer to the scrap heap, but television had to change. It was a fickle medium. It chewed people up and spat them out and that was why they were paid so well.

Television needed new faces. And this year one of the new faces would be Ally. He had no doubt that she would be terrific.

But there was something else he was going to have to face: what he really felt about her sudden success. The truth was that it had bitten deep into his ego, his sense of himself as the breadwinner, the provider. Ally hardly needed him now.

Men were supposed to have changed, to enjoy letting the woman have the hunger and the ambition. But Matt knew that in his deepest self he wanted to be more successful than his wife. It might be unacceptable for a New Man, but it was the truth for him and, he felt sure, for many men.

And yet, wasn't Ally entitled to her own life, to use her own talents? Wasn't he being a selfish shit? Matt closed his eyes. He didn't know any longer what was male and what was selfish. Susie would no doubt say they were the same thing.

He thought for a moment of his parents. It had been so much simpler for them. His father had gone to work and his mother had stayed at home. Every Friday his father had handed over his wage packet and his mother gave him pocket money. She hadn't worked, yet everyone knew who had the real power. She had.

But now women wanted to be more than simply the power behind the throne, and who could blame them?

A cow came up, chewing the cud in utter disinterest only a few inches away. It nuzzled up to him. I suppose you'll be next, he said, stroking it. Cow's lib. Fed up with standing around being milked and wanting to do something interesting with your life.

He turned back to the car, realizing that even to think things like this was probably beyond the pale and to say them was impossible. Perhaps it was even unfair. There was no going back for Ally or for women. Either he had to come to terms with the new Ally, or their marriage would be over.

By the time he drove into Century's car park he knew he was directing his anger at the wrong person. It wasn't Ally's fault, but Ritchie Page's. He smiled breezily at Bryony on reception and took the lift to the executive floor.

Lorraine, the secretary Ritchie Page had brought with him seemed disconcertingly calm when he demanded to talk to her boss. Almost as though she'd been expecting him. She picked up the phone on her desk and a couple of minutes later Page was standing at his open door smiling broadly.

'Matt, what a pleasant surprise!' He held out his hand like a timeshare salesman one deal away from his bonus. 'What can I do for you?'

'You know bloody well.' Matt walked past his outstretched hand and into his office. Behind his back Ritchie Page winked at his secretary then followed. 'What the hell do you mean by asking Danny Wilde to front the Telethon when I've done it for ten years?'

Page looked ingratiating. 'Don't you think that after ten years people might like a change? That it's time to give someone else a crack of the whip?'

'It's in my contract.'

Page smiled. 'It's in your contract that we pay you.' He reached into his briefcase. The bastard had clearly been through it already. 'But not that we use you.'

'What are you up to, Page?' Matt refused the offer of a chair. Sitting down would signal this was a cosy chat. 'Why are you trying to rope in my wife?'

'Because she's so talented. Because the viewers love her.' He paused, pretending to shuffle some papers on his desk. 'Because I thought she and Danny would make a great team. After all, the Telethon isn't about egos, is it, Matt? It's about collecting money for sick children.'

Matt felt an almost uncontrollable urge to stuff his cigar down the sanctimonious scumbag's throat.

'There is one solution, Matt, if you feel so strongly.' Page sat down in his massive grey leather chair and swivelled so that he was looking not at Matt but down at the river. 'You could always resign. We wouldn't hold you to your contract.'

So that was what this was about! Without another word Matt turned and walked out of the room. For a fraction of a second he had been tempted to take Page at his word and throw in the towel. Except that Page had played his hand too obviously. He'd made it clear he wanted Matt to resign. The only thing that would really annoy Page was if he stayed.

And that was precisely what Matt intended to do.

'Is it true, Matt?'

Belinda grabbed him after the show and pulled him into the darkened gallery.

'Is what true?' Matt felt his irritation rising at the thought that he'd probably have to get used to this.

'That Danny Wilde's fronting the Telethon with Ally?'

'You'd better ask her.' Matt tried and failed to sound disinterested. 'Or him.'

In the darkness she took his hand. 'Poor Matt.'

He found her sympathy both wildly annoying and yet at the same time deeply comforting.

'I think they're making a ludicrous mistake. Danny Wilde hasn't got a tenth of your talent. It's just like Page. He's only trying to undermine you, Matt.'

Without warning she leaned forward and kissed him swiftly on the lips.

In spite of himself, Matt felt both touched and

reassured by her faith in him. He hadn't felt a lot of either lately. He smiled down at her, 'Thanks a lot. I've always thought you had good taste.'

It was an ill wind, Belinda thought. And if she played her cards right this could bring them closer together while it put a wedge between him and Ally.

For a moment she wondered whether she should tell him that a reporter from the *Post* had rung their office and tomorrow they would be splashing the story over their front page. She didn't want to spoil the moment. Then she imagined him seeing it cold tomorrow and how much more painful that would be.

'Matt,' she said gently, 'there's something you ought to know.'

Ally lay in bed aware that Matt was only two feet away from her, yet they might as well have been separated by a cricket pitch. Instead of the usual warmth, his body radiated coldness and stiffness.

It was ludicrous. She didn't even want to *do* the bloody Telethon. Of course it was an incredible career opportunity and in other circumstances she would have killed to have a crack. But not at the cost of Matt's pride and self-respect. Maybe in the morning she'd ring up Ritchie Page and turn it down.

Fitfully she slept for a few hours. When she woke Matt was already up and dressed. She went down to breakfast, hoping things might have mellowed between them, but she could tell from the set of Matt's shoulders that nothing had changed. He sat at the table, a huge pile of newspapers at his elbow.

'Nice headline,' he commented, holding up the front page of the *Post*. 'MOVE OVER DARLING,' it announced, 'ALLY ELBOWS MATT OUT OF TELETHON.'

'The sods!' shouted Ally furiously. 'I haven't even made up my mind.'

'Haven't you?' Matt's voice sounded icy. 'Then why did you tell them it was a fantastic opportunity and you were longing to work with Danny Wilde?'

Ally looked at him for a moment. What had gone so wrong between them that he believed she'd be so insensitive just to further her own career?

'As a matter of fact I didn't talk to the *Post*.'

'So who did you talk to? The rest of the gutter press? No doubt you're learning to give good quotes like every other minor celebrity.'

He stood up and walked out of the room, leaving the pile of papers behind him. A few minutes later his departing car crunched on the gravel. He hadn't even said goodbye.

Ally picked up the papers and, without reading any of them, dumped the lot in the bin.

Fifteen minutes later she called the girls and got into the car to take them to school. As they went down the drive Ally noticed a crowd of people at the end of it. She stopped the car and peered. On the other side of the entrance were about twenty or thirty journalists and their photographers. The ratpack had landed.

And then they saw her. A dozen flashes went off and Ally heard cries of, 'Ally! Ally! How's Matt taking it?'

Ally resisted the temptation to tell the truth: that he was taking it like a six-year-old. But she made up her mind about one thing. If this was the way he was going to continue to behave, she was going to go ahead and do the Telethon.

In the end, Ally had to phone Susie and get her to brave the shock troops and take the girls to school.

When they finally drew up outside it nearly an hour late, Janey looked round nervously in case there were any more reporters lurking about. It had been bad enough when she'd had one famous parent, but having two was far worse. Everyone would have read the story and she'd get teased about it all day.

She wished to God her parents could sort this out. The atmosphere at breakfast had been poisonous. The saying she'd overheard from one of the teachers drifted back into her mind again, a terrifying litany. Why are parents selfish enough to split just before A levels? Her A levels were in eight weeks' time.

When Bernie Long saw the headlines in the papers he picked up his phone furiously and demanded to see Ritchie Page.

'Look, Page, why the hell didn't you discuss this with me? Allegra Boyd's my star.'

Page watched him impassively. He'd expected something like this.

'No she isn't, mate, she's Century's star.'

'She's not ready for this. Six months ago she'd never been in front of the camera, apart from reading the news. Now you want her co-hosting the most complex show we do.'

'I'm sure she'll manage.'

Realizing he was getting nowhere, Bernie threw in his last card. 'Well, if you are going ahead with this ridiculous scheme, at least let me produce it.'

Page swivelled gently in his chair.

'All right, Bernie. I don't see why not. You produce the Telethon.'

Things didn't improve between Ally and Matt over the next few days. It was almost as though they were living in separate houses. He seemed to be timing his comings and goings not to coincide with hers. And every night he seemed to be coming back later.

After a week it was too much for Ally. She'd made supper for eight thirty and now it was after ten. She scraped the contents of Matt's plate angrily into the bin just as she heard the front door open.

'Look, Matt, where have you been?' She was determined not to sound like a nagging wife, but she was damned if she was putting up with this. 'With *la belle* Belinda again, I suppose? Was she soothing your fevered brow as usual?'

'As a matter of fact I was having a few beers at Century.' His voice was cold and hard. 'But it wouldn't be surprising if I was with Belinda. At least she's got a bit of humanity as well as ambition.'

'And I haven't?'

Matt stood watching her like a hostile stranger and despite herself Ally began to feel defeated. Nothing she said seemed to break through to the Matt she loved.

What the hell was happening to their marriage?

To her enormous relief Ally was too busy to do much agonizing. They had three more shows to record for *Tell It to Ally*, one of them a tricky hour-long special on guilty secrets, when everyone in the audience would have something different to confess to and Ally had to remember what each secret was.

But now that she had got her bearings and become less nervous, professionally at least she'd never enjoyed herself more in her life. *Tell It to Ally* had an energy and sense of excitement, of confidences exchanged, and of people recognizing their capacity to change which was at times nothing short of inspiring.

And Bernie was ecstatic over the show, telling her time and time again that they were really on to something. The only bitter thought that crept in was that she couldn't seem to get her professional and personal life working at the same time.

And in the few spare moments off from *Tell It to Ally* she was dealing with the endless arrangements for Janey's party.

So by the time the first meeting for the Telethon came along she'd almost forgotten about it.

As she walked into Ritchie Page's outer office, she was startled by how much it had changed. The last chairman had been from the old school, all hunting prints and Persian rugs. Page couldn't have been more different.

True to his reputation, here was a man who liked to be surrounded by skin. Only – in this case – of rare animals. Clearly, environmental issues didn't keep Ritchie Page awake at night. The sofa opposite his secretary's desk was covered in leopard skin with black suede cushions perfectly positioned at half-metre intervals. Next to it was an elephant's foot and a glass coffee table.

When Ally arrived, Lorraine, Page's secretary, apologized that he and Bernie would be late.

'Can I get you a drink, Mrs Boyd?'

She opened an enormous Chinese lacquered armoire revealing more bottles than Stringfellow's bar. Ally refused the offer of a cocktail, though she was almost tempted to ask for a Pina Colada just to see if she'd get a little umbrella in the top. In the end she settled for spritzer, though even that came in a fancy glass with a gold swizzle stick in it.

When Lorraine led her into Page's office proper she couldn't help an involuntary gasp of amazement. It was the size of a warehouse with every flat surface black and shiny, even the floor and ceiling. The only furniture was Page's desk and three enormous zebra skin sofas, each lit with a spotlight.

It was so unnerving that at first Ally didn't notice someone sitting behind the desk. So when he spoke she jumped.

'Taste isn't our Rich's strong point, is it?'

Ally wheeled round to find someone watching her, drinking a beer from the bottle, his feet on Page's desk, an irreverent smile lighting up his familiar features. It was Danny Wilde. She reddened, remembering that last time she'd met him he'd done up her dress.

Lorraine was smiling at Danny unperturbed. Obviously he could do no wrong in her eyes – even taking over her boss's desk and putting his feet up on it while slagging off his décor.

'Do you know Mrs Boyd, Danny?' she asked. Ally noticed that tough Lorraine had become almost kittenish in his presence.

'Absolutely. We've already met. We have a friend in common.' Danny got up as though he were welcoming her to his own office. 'As I told her, last time we met, I'm one of her greatest fans.' His tone lost the faintly mocking edge and sounded genuinely enthusiastic. 'I never missed a show when you were on *Hello*.' Ally listened in disbelief as Britain's number two chat-show host reeled off the reasons why she was a fabulous agony aunt. He really had watched every show. 'What I love most' – he flicked back a strand of dark brown hair from in front of his eyes as if in emphasis – 'is the way you tell them to get off their arses and take *control* of their lives.'

Ally felt a glow of pleasure that he understood what she was trying to do so well. And he was serious, too, without even a glint of the patronizing air she sometimes got from Matt. 'And I hear the new show's even better. Your new PA used to work with me and she says the ones you've recorded are sensational. When are they going out?'

Ally found herself amused by his roller-coaster enthusiasm. 'We don't know yet.'

'In prime time, I hope, not hidden away somewhere.'

Suddenly he walked towards her. Ally, standing by the window, involuntarily took a step back. His physical presence was overpowering. He somehow filled your space as well as his own. 'You're a dangerous woman, Allegra Boyd,' he said, leaning over her. She couldn't help breathing in his aftershave. She recognized Chanel's L'Egoïste. Susie had once given it to Matt for Christmas. 'It means charming shit,' she had announced, clearly hoping for a reaction. Matt had just laughed and said she must have bought it for the wrong person then. Danny smiled at her. 'I could easily tell you all my secrets myself.'

With a shade of embarrassment Ally realized that not only was she being treated to the famous Wilde charm, but that it was working. Nothing had prepared her for his powerful attraction. The way he looked directly into your eyes when he talked to you. The flick of his dark hair. The disconcerting intensity of his green eyes. Danny Wilde was a charmer.

What's more he was making it very clear that he found her attractive. She sensed that with Danny her success, instead of being threatening, was part of her appeal. Maybe it was because he was ten years younger. With a shock Ally realized what a good feeling it was.

She glanced up at him and found that he was still looking at her, holding her eyes with his, as though he could see right into her to the place where she kept the key to herself. It was an unnerving experience.

As he watched her Ally thought she saw in his ironic green eyes a brief flicker of desire. And to her absolute horror, Ally, sensible, straightforward Ally, whose marriage seemed to be lying around her in pieces, felt an answering flame.

And the no-nonsense, Susie-part told her to stop it at once. *This you do not need!*

So when the door opened and Ritchie Page came into the room with Bernie, Ally forgot how much she resented him. Instead, as he walked towards her, relief flooded through her at being rescued from the dangerous currents she felt unexpectedly swirling around her.

When Ally got home two hours later she was conscious that she hadn't even thought about what she was supposed to be doing in the Telethon. What if Matt or the children asked her about the meeting? She sat for a moment in the darkness of the double garage, but no matter how she tried to concentrate on the meeting her mind kept darting to the sight of Danny Wilde flicking back his lock of hair and smiling his long, slow smile. And despite herself she couldn't help wondering what it would be like to make love to him.

Ally shook herself, appalled. She never thought about sex. She wasn't the type to have affairs. She was far too bad a liar. She'd watched friends who were cheating and known she could never cope with the guilt and the constant fear of discovery. Some of them said they even found that exciting, but she knew she wouldn't.

And for the first time she could ever remember she dreaded going into the house. Dreaded the tense atmosphere and Matt's grudging attitude. Meeting someone who clearly thought she was wonderful had been heady and unnerving. She told herself he probably had that effect on every woman. Then she remembered the way he knew her every show, how he had understood what she was trying to do.

Picking up her bag she locked the car and walked briskly to the house, putting Danny Wilde firmly out of her mind. Thank God for children. Matt might be being a pain, but she still had Janey and Jess to think of. Consider how they would react if they could read her thoughts.

As soon as she walked through the garden door into the kitchen she realized something was different. When she'd rushed out this morning in a panic because she had a day so busy it would have had even Margaret Thatcher reaching for the Lucozade, the room had been a complete mess. Now it was tidy. Or almost tidy. Yet it hadn't been Mrs O'Shock's day. Would Janey or Jess have done it? But there was something about its not-quite-finished quality that wasn't their style. A lonely smear of grease remained on the wiped work surface. Someone had put a bunch of daffodils from the garden in the middle of the kitchen table, but they were in a milk bottle while the dresser was full of vases. She opened the drawer of one of the units. Everything was there but in the wrong place. Then she saw the note. *I'm sorry, I've been a bastard. Matt.*

Holding it Ally felt unutterably moved. It was the sort of thing a lot of husbands probably did, unsung, every day. But from Matt it was more touching than if he'd taken her out to dinner or bought an expensive present. Things like that cost no effort. Ally walked to the sitting room, all thoughts of Danny Wilde lost in the power of this simple, ordinary, everyday gesture.

Chapter 22

For the next two weeks Ally ruthlessly excluded any thoughts of Danny Wilde. Once, when Susie dropped round for a chat, she felt an almost overwhelming temptation to confide in her. But what was there to tell? That she'd met someone who'd made her feel talented and clever and wonderful? She'd sound like a menopausal housewife falling for the tennis coach. It had been a silly fantasy. After all, what would she tell one of her own punters if they were in this position? Don't risk your marriage unless you're really sure it's over. Affairs sometimes put the spice back in marriages, but just as often they simply put the boot into them.

Fortunately her life was full to exhaustion with recording *Tell It to Ally*, preparing for the Telethon and getting everything ready for Janey's party. She might have a nervous breakdown but no way was she going to have time for an affair.

Bernie Long watched Ally hammering away at her keyboard, a phone to the wine suppliers for the party balanced round her neck. For the last two weeks it was as though she'd been trying to fill every corner of her life with activity. She'd gone home every night loaded down with briefing papers for *Tell It to Ally*, and when she wasn't busy with that she was up to her eyes in the last-minute details of marquees, bite-sized pizzas and recalcitrant rock bands for Janey's party. Just watching her made Bernie feel tired. But more than that, concerned. If she went on much longer like this she'd collapse.

He stood up. 'Right. Time for the Telethon meeting.'

'My God!' Ally glanced at her watch in apparent amazement. 'Is it that time already? . . . Bernie' – she gave him her most enchanting smile – 'there's no *way* I can get to this meeting tonight. Could you possibly make my excuses and plead a crisis on *Tell It to Ally*? The truth is I'm absolutely cream-crackered and I won't take a word in.' That wasn't the truth at all. The truth was that she was absolutely terrified of meeting Danny Wilde again.

Bernie looked at her with his sharp eyes that never missed a trick. 'That's not like you, Ally.'

For a moment Ally felt her stomach knot up in panic. But Bernie couldn't possibly guess she was avoiding Danny.

'I know, but suddenly everything's happening at once. I just hope I can cope.' She hated pleading weakness, it was so female, but couldn't think of anything else to convince Bernie.

His rhino-skin features softened into something approaching but just missing tenderness. 'OK, but for God's sake go home and get some rest.'

'I promise. I'll just finalize a few details for Janey's party and be off in five minutes.'

'See you tomorrow then.'

It was nearly an hour before she got off the phone, yawned and began to pack her briefcase, fantasizing about a long hot bath. As she gathered up her things and stuffed them in a voice behind her made her wheel round abruptly.

'It must have been a pretty big crisis to stand up your boss.' The tone brimmed over with amusement and she could tell even without turning exactly who it was. He stood in the doorway smiling his familiar lopsided smile, with a disconcerting hint in his green eyes that he'd guessed the real reason why she hadn't turned up for the meeting.

'Feel like a drink?' Her hesitation only seemed to deepen his amusement. 'Purely between colleagues, of course.'

Ally didn't answer for a moment. She knew she shouldn't spend time alone with him, yet if she said no it would sound as though she were reading too much into the situation.

His smile widened. She guessed with a flash of irritation that Danny Wilde thought he'd got her taped. And then she saw a way of getting off the hook and showing him that she wasn't fazed by him at all.

'I'm afraid I can't.' She returned his smile, but without a trace of flirtation. 'But my daughter's having her eight-eenth birthday party next week. I'm sure she'd be thrilled if you could come.'

For the first time in their brief acquaintanceship Ally had the pleasure of seeing Danny Wilde thrown. But not for long.

'I'd like that very much.' He held the door open for her.

As she walked through, deliberately avoiding his eyes, she had a moment's misgiving about how Matt would react. But Matt had nothing against Danny personally, and Janey would be in seventh heaven. It would make her party. Anyway, he would never come.

'How many people are you expecting tomorrow?' Matt grabbed the list from Janey's protesting hand. The print-out looked a mile long. 'Half the London phone book seems to be here.'

'There's only about three hundred actually.' Janey lunged unsuccessfully for the list.

Janey was her happy smiling self again, Ally noted, now that she and Matt were at least talking to each other.

'Plus gatecrashers,' pointed out Jess. Janey looked at

her quellingly. Trust Jess. 'A party isn't cool without gatecrashers. They're usually the most interesting.'

'Mum?' Janey smiled winningly. 'Could we have tequila really watered down? It's the crucial drink this year.'

'No, you couldn't. Punch. So I can dilute it with lots of orange juice when you're not looking. I'm not having your friends driving their minis into next door's swimming pool.'

'Oh, Mum, that was in the sixties.'

'We behaved very well in the sixties, thank you,' corrected Matt.

'What about all that free love?' asked Jess innocently.

'Nonsense. They once proved the sexual revolution only happened to six people in Chelsea.' Matt helped himself to another piece of toast. 'And I wasn't one of them. In fact at my twenty-first my father went round with a torch looking for unsuitable behaviour.'

'And did he find any?'

'Only my friend Larry in the toolshed with a girl.'

'And were they at it?' Jess was enthralled at this bit of quaint social history.

'Of course not. They were standing there like butter wouldn't melt in their mouths. There was only one problem.' Matt sipped his coffee, grinning at the memory. 'Larry's tie was caught in the back of her zip.'

Ally laughed. 'And was that all he found?'

'Absolutely,' Matt replied pompously. 'We knew how to behave in those days.'

'Rubbish!' Jess covered her toast with half an inch of marmalade. 'They were probably upstairs bonking on the coats.'

Matt pretended to look shocked. 'Thank God I'm not young any more.'

'What are you going to wear tomorrow, Mum?' Jess's

question brought Ally down to earth. She'd been too busy to even think about it. 'Something understated,' she answered vaguely. 'It's not done to upstage the birthday girl.'

'You'll have a job.' Jess laughed raucously. 'Have you seen what she's planning to wear?'

As Janey walked down the wide staircase, which the florists had draped with flowers and greenery for the occasion, Matt was speechless. She was wearing the shortest black silk microdress he'd ever seen. Her face was painted white, her lips black and her long hair was piled high adorned on the top with an open fan. She looked stunning but to Matt's protective fatherly eyes frighteningly like the kind of doll you probably got in Chinese sex shops.

'Thank God we're not going out,' he mumbled finally. 'If we did you'd get arrested.'

'Adam chose it,' announced Janey proudly.

'Well,' Matt gulped, 'at least it can't have cost much. There's only half a yard of material in it.'

'Appearances can be deceptive.' Janey smiled benignly. 'Anyway' – she planted a huge kiss on his cheek – 'you'll soon find out. I put it on your bill at Harvey Nichols.'

Matt closed his eyes in mock acceptance as Ally appeared from the kitchen where she'd been checking that the caterers had everything under control. He tried to catch her eye on the subject of extravagant daughters but she was busy chatting to a waiter.

When she stood on the stairs next to Janey to admire her daughter's outfit Matt's heart turned over at the sight of Ally, subtle and sophisticated, next to Janey's exotic jailbait. And all the more because she seemed unconscious of it.

He was about to tell her so when the doorbell rang.

The first guest had arrived.

From then on in it was chaos. Not only were there the three hundred official guests on Janey's print-out, but Ally had erased from her own memory of being eighteen the teenage predilection for gatecrashing. From the casual, 'Oh, my third cousin's friend was staying and I *knew* you wouldn't mind if I brought her along' to the full frontal assault with a rope over the garden wall. Matt even caught one climbing in the window of the downstairs loo. 'I'm a friend of Adam's,' the leather-clad youth had explained amiably. In fact, Matt reflected, all the most unsuitable looking types seemed to be friends of Adam's. He clearly demanded high standards of undesirability.

But Janey was loving every minute, especially the formal major domo Ally had hired to announce the guests. Ernie Dowden, king of MCs, was certainly having his horizons broadened.

'Mr Mojo Williams,' he announced sonorously. 'Mr Sting Edwards . . . Miss Yazz Mcmahon-Wilson.'

Ally watched, laughing. She remembered Mr Mojo Williams when he'd been Mark and wore nappies. Now he had shoulder-length hair, a nose-stud and wore a Zodiac Mindwarp T-shirt under his borrowed DJ.

To Ally's amusement one or two guests lost their cool when confronted with Matt and asked him to autograph the labels on their Sol beers.

When Bernie Long was announced Ally fell upon him with gratitude. Not only was it great to see his raddled face amongst all this youth and beauty, but he could keep Matt company.

Bernie had brought an autographed album by The Cure for Janey.

'Wow! Mum! Look at this!' Janey rushed off with it to show Adam.

'How come you understand the teenage mind so much better than we do?' Ally asked, handing him a Perrier.

'Because he wants to make money out of it.' Ally turned to find Matt standing behind her.

Bernie laughed. 'What motive could be higher than that?'

The music was blaring in the marquee. Everyone seemed happy. It would soon be time to serve the soya-bean hot dogs, vegie-burgers and pizzas that Janey had chosen as the height of culinary aspiration within her social circle. Matt had just refilled Ally's glass from the private supply he was keeping under the hall table when the major domo strode back to his position at the top of the reception line, spotting a few last stragglers.

'Mr Zit O'Brien and Miss Mandy O'Brien,' he declaimed, managing to make himself heard above the music as their next door neighbour's two ghastly children sauntered in. There was a lull as the band conferred momentarily on what to deafen with next and into the silence the major domo proclaimed another two guests.

'Miss Petronella Harvey.' An anaemic blonde shrouded in more layers of black than Morticia Addams appeared. 'And Mr Danny Wilde.'

For a fraction of a second there was total silence in the room until Janey ran towards her mother, screeching at the top of her voice, 'Mum, you never told me Danny Wilde was coming.'

'No,' echoed Matt, a hard edge of anger in his voice, 'you didn't tell me either.'

'I asked him casually because I thought it'd be fun for Janey.' Ally didn't look at Matt as she spoke. 'I didn't think he'd actually come.'

Danny Wilde, a strand of dark hair falling across his eyes, walked towards them.

'Hello, Allegra, it seems to be a wonderful party.'

'Hello, Danny.' Ally decided the safest course lay in extreme formality. 'Have you met my husband, Matt?'

'Only in the ether.' Danny smiled his most disarming smile. 'Good to meet you, Matt. I'm sorry about this crazy Telethon business. I think they're probably making a big mistake.'

'Don't mention it.' Matt found a glass and poured him some champagne. 'TV needs new faces. You're the flavour of the month.'

'Danny, you know Bernie, of course.' Ally hurried to change the subject, knowing the last thing Matt would want was Danny Wilde's sympathy.

'Absolutely, but I haven't said how chuffed I am you're producing us. You were one of the greats.' Matt almost burst out laughing at the expression on Bernie's face. 'Must rap with you about the future of chat-shows.'

He'd only been here two minutes, Matt reflected, and he'd managed to get up both their noses already. Some going.

'Come on, Bernie, let's you and I ex-greats go and crack a bottle of Perrier water in the conservatory.'

Bernie sat on a cane sofa and closed the door so that the music was marginally less deafening. 'Did you mean any of that? About not minding?'

'Up to a point.' Matt sat opposite him. 'TV does need new faces.'

'Bollocks! You mind like hell.'

'What I like about you, Bernie, is that you're strong on subtext.'

'What I reckon,' Bernie said, gazing at Matt over the top of his glass, 'is that you think he's a Jack the Lad with a nice line in patter but no substance.' Bernie held out his glass for a refill. 'And you're hoping like hell he'll fall flat on his arse at the Telethon so everyone sees what a pro you are.'

Matt opened the mineral water with a loud fizz and poured some into Bernie's glass. 'I'll drink to that.'

Matt glanced over at the dance floor in the marquee. Danny Wilde was clearly being a hit. He'd danced with Janey and nearly all Janey's best friends. There was only one person who hadn't fallen for his charm. Adam. Matt saw him watching Danny Wilde disdainfully. The boy had better taste than Matt had suspected.

The next time Ally had a moment to look at her watch it was almost midnight. She looked round contentedly, catching sight of Jess and Jeremy squeezing each other like two tubes of toothpaste on the dance floor. The evening seemed to have been a success, thank God. A hand touched her lightly on the shoulder. She jumped as if it were a red hot poker. It was him.

'Great party. Time I went, though. No stamina any more, I'm afraid.'

Ally was grateful for the conventions of being a hostess. 'It was very kind of you to come. Did you have a coat?'

'Somebody in a French maid's outfit took it upstairs.'

Ally looked for one of the helpers, but none was in sight.

'I'll find it. What was it like?'

'Camel. It's my "Wide Boy Trying to be a Stockbroker" coat.'

Ally laughed and started walking up the flower-draped staircase. Halfway up she realized that he was still behind her and that they were alone. Everyone else was either downstairs or in the marquee. She felt her breath quicken as she struggled to keep calm.

His coat was on top of the pile, and as he picked it up she was conscious of how close he was to her. There was a second frozen in silence when neither of them moved. Then very slowly he took her hand. For a moment she thought he was going to kiss it and she held her breath. Instead, in an oddly formal gesture, he shook it as though they'd just been introduced.

'Thanks for the party.' He slipped his coat over his shoulders. 'I'll see myself out.'

She stood where she was, ashamed to acknowledge a sense of disappointment so strong it almost physically hurt. He had behaved perfectly, damn him. But what had she expected? That he would throw her on to the coats and make passionate love to her amid the fake furs at her own daughter's birthday party?

For a moment she couldn't face the bright lights and the fresh optimistic faces trying to be cool and laid-back downstairs. Inside she was burning with a bright, dangerous fire.

She turned off the light and sat on the edge of the bed in the darkness.

Downstairs in the hall, Matt searched under the table for another bottle of champagne, where it was safely hidden from Janey's marauding friends. So he had a good view of Danny Wilde's face as he came down the stairs and walked out of the front door, smiling broadly. A few minutes ago he had walked up the stairs with Ally.

Matt stood transfixed with pain. He knew that look. It was the unmistakable male glint of conquest.

Chapter 23

Ally woke up three days later knowing that today was the biggest challenge of her career and wishing it wasn't happening. She looked across the pillow at Matt and told herself that no matter how charming he was, no matter how much he seemed to understand and appreciate her, she was going to resist Danny Wilde.

She got quietly out of bed, had a quick shower and searched through her wardrobe. Normally she would have flung on a tracksuit for a gruelling day of rehearsals, knowing that Elaine and Century's wardrobe mistress would do their fairy godmother act later. But today she caught herself reaching for something sexier. Grinning at her own transparency, she made herself put back the slinky cashmere cardigan and choose a tracksuit.

In the kitchen she only had time for a quick cup of coffee, but because Jess had microwaved six croissants into a passable imitation of granite in honour of the occasion she felt she had to have one.

When the doorbell rang announcing the arrival of her cab Matt still hadn't put in an appearance. Ally wondered if it was deliberate, so that he wouldn't have to wish her luck. Oh, well. What did she expect?

'Bye, all,' Ally mumbled to the girls, her mouth half full of indigestible croissant, 'I must rush. See you later.' She picked up her suitbag and briefcase and headed for the door.

Just after she went through it, Matt appeared, almost as though he'd chosen his moment.

'Aren't you going to wish Mum good luck?' Jess inquired.

Matt's conscience had already been pricking. He followed Jess out to the front of the house but they were too late. Ally's car was already turning out of the top of the drive and on to the main road.

When they got back into the kitchen Janey was there.

'Where's Mum?' she asked.

'Gone. Today's her big day, remember?'

'They all seem to be big days at the moment.' Janey heard the bitterness in her own voice and tried to cut it with a smile. It was just that Mum seemed so strange at the moment, so caught up with work, as though sometimes none of them existed any more. And this tension between her parents had gone on too long.

'You know what you two need?'

'Oh, God!' Matt put his head in his hands in mock horror. 'Not two agony aunts in the family.'

'A weekend away together. Why don't you go once this silly programme's over?'

'Barbara Cartland says you should go away alone together at least once a year,' pointed out Jess pompously, 'for the sake of your relationship.'

'Why don't you book something?' Janey put her arm round her father and nestled in. 'Without us. Rediscover sex in the afternoons.'

'Or at least sport on telly in the afternoons,' corrected Jess, grabbing his other arm.

Matt laughed. 'Oh, well, if Barbara Cartland says so, what choice do I have?' He looked down at his elder daughter. 'You know, Janey, you're absolutely right.' Somehow when he and Ally were alone things did get back in perspective. 'Just as you were about the dinner. You're a very wise girl.'

'That's not surprising.' Janey reached up and touched his cheek. 'I was taught to think by a pretty amazing man.'

The love and admiration in her voice were almost his undoing. Matt felt his throat tighten with emotion. He and Ally had lost touch with each other lately and they'd both forgotten how much it would affect Janey and Jess. It was probably his fault. It was crazy to feel threatened by Ally. OK, so it was tough that she was doing so well when he had problems of his own, but he ought to be bigger than that. And at Janey's party he'd even suspected her of getting involved with Danny Wilde. It was probably his paranoia. And anyway, the way he'd been behaving, no wonder she'd got fed up with her husband.

'So' – he grinned at his daughters, resolving to take their advice and try and make amends – 'who knows what's happened to *The Good Hotel Guide*?'

Any embarrassment Ally might have felt at seeing Danny so soon after the party was dissipated by one glance at the schedule. The programme was so complex and demanding that the rehearsal would take up every second of the day with no time for polite conversation.

There were pre-recorded packages and live inserts from nearly a dozen local stations, all with the possibility of losing picture or sound at any moment, when Ally or Danny would have to fill. Ally would need to know the names of each of the regional presenters and enough about them to chat in an emergency. On top of that she had six different groups to interview in the studio as well as supervising a bank of stars on telephones taking pledges from viewers.

'Just remember,' Bernie reminded her, handing over the biggest script she'd ever seen, 'the main thing is the fund-raising. We want to collect more than £20 million and it doesn't really matter if there are a few slips along the way.' He squeezed her arm reassuringly. 'You know how the public loves cock-ups.'

From then on in, there wasn't even time to think. The vast studio was ablaze with light, three different floor managers barked orders at her, the number of moves she had to remember was mind-blowing and the sadistic director made her practise ad libbing for ten whole minutes when one of the VT machines jammed. But after two solid hours, even though she could feel the distant rumble of a headache, Ally realized she was enjoying herself. The venture was so vast and complex it carried you along on its own energy.

To her relief the only time she even exchanged glances with Danny was when one of the lights suddenly exploded above her head and she found his arm round her for a fraction of a second, pulling her away from the risk of falling glass. Almost as soon as she looked round he had taken it away again. *Pull yourself together*, Ally told herself. *There's nothing between you and you ought to be grateful for it.*

Matt smiled to himself as he put down the phone. He'd just rung the beautiful Manoir aux Quat'Saisons and they'd had one room left. It seemed a good omen. He thought about phoning the Telethon offices and leaving a message but he knew how busy they'd be. He'd tell Ally when she got back.

He had a free morning and decided to make the most of it. Cheerfully he went out to tie up the daffodils, which were just finishing in the garden.

'Right, that's it everybody. End of rehearsal. We're breaking for tea now.' The floor manager relayed the message from Bernie, hidden away in the control room, to everyone on the studio floor.

Ally breathed a sigh of relief. She could never remember such a gruelling day. 'How long have I got till you need me again?' She was conscious of the headache getting closer and was longing for a brief lie-down in her dressing room.

The floor manager spoke into his mouthpiece.

'Bernie wants you back here, made up and ready to go, in forty-five minutes.'

Ally groaned, realizing that ruled out the precious rest she'd been fantasizing about.

'Oh, and Ally, Bernie says well done. Rehearsed like a trouper.'

'Right then, Allegra.' Elaine sat her down in the make-up chair and covered her in a white cape. 'What can I do for you?'

'A new head would be nice.' Ally swallowed two para-cetamol extra strength. She looked in the mirror. After staying up so late the other night she looked like some-thing out of a Hammer film. Bride of Dracula, perhaps. No, too flattering. Dracula's mother-in-law? 'Just make me look like someone else, would you?' she said to Elaine. 'Meryl Streep would do.'

Elaine laughed and reached for the foundation. She put a white hairband round Ally's hair and told her to lean back and close her eyes. Utterly drained by the efforts of the day and the stress of the challenge ahead, Ally gave in to the luxuriousness of being pampered. In seconds she'd fallen asleep. When she woke up she had a strange sensa-tion that she was looking at someone else. Someone far sleeker, more glamorous and a lot less tired than she was.

'Elaine, you're a miracle worker! Where did that woman come from?'

Elaine surveyed her work. Ally did indeed look stun-ning. Elaine's experiment with rose and tawny colours instead of the usual bright red lips had taken years off her. She was positively glowing.

'It's amazing,' Elaine said, enjoying Ally's obvious delight, 'what you can do with a bit of panstick.'

Back in her dressing room Ally looked at her watch. God, she only had ten more minutes. She quickly stripped off her clothes and flung them on the daybed. Where on earth had the wardrobe mistress gone with her suit? She swore. There was no phone in this dressing room. She couldn't even call Nikki and ask her to hurry the woman up. And she could hardly chase down the corridor stark naked to get it herself.

Trying to keep calm she took out a pair of briefs and some ten-denier black tights from her bag and pulled them gently on. She felt her heart thumping from nerves, and began to take deep breaths to keep calm.

Outside the door she could hear someone pressing the combination lock. Thank God, it must be the wardrobe mistress bringing her suit back.

The door opened just as Ally had put her foot on a chair to smooth out the sheer black tights. The unexpected silence made her look up and stare into the brightly lit full-length mirror in front of her.

In the doorway Danny Wilde stood calmly watching her. Ally's hands flew to cover herself.

'I'm so sorry,' said Danny, not sounding it. 'I think I must have the wrong combination.'

Slowly he closed the door, leaving Ally's pulse racing and a red flush of embarrassment creeping down her neck to her naked breasts.

She closed her eyes, trying to regain her composure, suddenly aware that her headache had completely disappeared.

Ten minutes later Ally sat down in the gallery at the back of the control room grateful both that she had stopped shaking and that no one appeared to have noticed her sitting here in the cool darkness.

OK, so she'd had a shock. But it had been a mistake, that was all. The sort of thing that could happen to anyone now that Century had this silly system of combination locks on the dressing rooms. The best thing was to forget about it and get on with the show.

She flicked on the light and picked up a script sitting next to her on the banquette. She skimmed through it looking for her first link to camera.

'Ally?' Ken, the assistant floor manager, put his head round the door. 'You haven't seen Danny's script, have you? He's lost it and it's got some notes he needs on it.'

Ally sympathized. It was infuriating to lose the script you'd written on. She leafed through the pile. None was his.

Sitting down on the bench again she flipped over the script she'd just been checking through. It had something scribbled on the front. She stood up to shout after Ken, and then she noticed what it said. Across one corner, in Danny's distinctive scrawl, were the numbers 3215. Ally bit her lip. 3215 was the number to the combination lock on her dressing room.

Ally turned the light off again and sat in the total darkness for nearly a minute. She knew she should be angry, that she should feel outraged and invaded. Instead she felt a wave of heat start spreading through her whole body. She recognized it immediately. It was the unmistakable heat of desire.

'What time does it start, Dad?' Janey had suddenly materialized from her bedroom and taken possession of the sofa.

Matt looked round from attempting to set the video, a skill that, to his enormous embarrassment, still eluded him after an entire career in television. Jess, away for the night at a party, had made the request and Matt had been wrestling with himself as to whether he could cop out tonight and watch it with her tomorrow. Somehow that would be less painful. And yet he knew he couldn't do it. He had to watch it live – for Ally's sake.

'I thought you were out.' He smiled, not knowing whether it would be harder or easier to have her there.

'Adam's gone to his mother's, so I thought maybe I should show a bit of self-sacrifice and watch mine.'

'Big of you.' He sat down beside her, suddenly glad of her presence, and pressed the button on the remote control.

Despite his misgivings, after five minutes Matt found himself engrossed. Only one thing puzzled him. A lot of the tricks Danny Wilde used – the roguish look to camera, the off-the-cuff quips, the self-deprecating jokes, the way he made the whole thing seem effortless when it was deeply stressful – reminded him of someone. And then he realized who. Danny Wilde's technique was pure Matt Boyd.

A couple of minutes later Ally came on wearing a pink suit he'd never seen before. She looked startlingly beautiful, but not with the usual groomed-to-death, shrink-wrapped glamour of the average female presenter. Ally seemed real.

And when she interviewed the mother of a child with leukaemia you forgot that this was television. To Matt's amazement, when it was over Ally simply got up and put her arms round the other woman, mother to mother. Matt felt a tear in the corner of his tough pro's eye and realized he could never have made that gesture. For all his warmth he would never have exposed himself like that. And he saw that this was precisely Ally's secret. She got involved.

Matt sat back and watched the Telethon from start to finish. Ritchie Page had been right in putting Ally and Danny together. There was a kind of electricity between them that crackled out of the screen. They had even managed to weave the ultimate magic of making him, the man who had presented the programme for ten years, forget that he was different from any other viewer.

To Janey's amusement he even rang in after the interview with the mother of the sick child and made a pledge, secretly hoping no one would work out which M. Boyd he was.

Janey yawned and looked at her watch. It was already ten thirty. 'I think I'm for bed.'

'Aren't you staying up for the grand totals?'

Janey shook her head. 'Not my scene. Mum was great, though. I'll watch the rest with Jess tomorrow.' She kissed his cheek and headed for the stairs.

As the show wound towards its close for the night and the totals rose from fifteen to twenty and up to twenty-three million, Matt noticed Danny Wilde wink at Ally in one shot, and saw her smile of acknowledgement in the next. Somewhere in the back of his subconscious another alarm sounded as he remembered Danny's smile from the other night.

The celebratory crescendo of the title music signalled the end of the show and the credits began to roll. The total flashed again and again as the crowd roared its approval and delight.

Matt saw Danny Wilde lean down and kiss Ally on the cheek. It could have been a comradely gesture from one satisfied presenter to another. But with a sense of something finally understood, Matt knew that it wasn't. His instincts had been right.

Ally and Danny were falling in love.

'Darling, you were brilliant!' The director rushed up to Ally in hospitality and kissed her on both cheeks. 'Putting your arms round the mother with the sick kid was inspired!'

319

'That's called spontaneous kindness,' Bernie pointed out to him. 'Not an emotion you'd recognize, darling.'

Ally laughed. She was still adapting to showbiz bitchiness. She was just deeply grateful she'd got through the Telethon without disgracing herself. All around them champagne corks were popping and people were laughing and holding each other, both out of professional pride at having raised millions of pounds and from the wonderful sense of release at having survived one of the most technically demanding ventures on television.

Suddenly, down the other end of the room, Ally heard what sounded like a child crying. She wheeled round to find Danny Wilde coming towards her with a little girl of about six years old, weeping her heart out. It was the first time she'd spoken to him off-screen since the dressing room incident and she felt herself begin to redden, but any sensitivity was soon forgotten when she saw the child's tearful face.

'She wanted to pledge her pocket money,' Danny explained, 'but she didn't get here in time.'

'Oh, darling.' Ally lifted the little girl up and held her, the small determined face reminding her painfully of Jess at that age. 'You can give it to us now. We'll add it in. How much have you got?'

'Fifty p.'

Ally put the child down and clapped her hands. Everyone turned. 'Listen,' Ally announced grandly, 'we have a new total. Twenty-three million two hundred thousand pounds – and fifty p.'

There was a huge round of applause as the girl's mother came and picked her up to take her home, glowing with pride.

Ally turned back to find herself looking into the smiling face of Danny Wilde. 'You're amazing, you know.'

His voice was soft and caressing. 'Has anyone told you how amazing you are?'

'Not lately.' Ally knew she should change the subject, but couldn't bring herself to.

Then one of the researchers, a jolly, likeable girl called Sally, almost completely covered in Telethon badges and stickers, bounced up. 'Ally, Danny, you're both coming to dinner, aren't you?' She stuck a sticker on Ally's suit jacket. 'There's a Telethon cake and the champagne's on Century.'

Ally shook her head regretfully. This was the first she'd heard of any dinner. Looking round at all the happy faces she realized how much she'd like to go. Saying no would look as though she wasn't putting her heart and soul into the evening. But there was Matt. She knew he might be feeling down and that she ought to get back.

'Sorry, I'd love to come.' At least her voice sounded genuinely regretful. 'But I have to get home.'

'Is Matt waiting for his cocoa and reassurance, then?' Ally was shocked at the sarcasm in Danny's voice. 'Sorry,' he apologized almost at once. 'I shouldn't have said that. I just couldn't stand the thought of you going back and ministering when it should be such a triumph for you. Everyone thought you were brilliant.'

Ally smiled, flattered in spite of herself at his obvious jealousy.

'It's hard for him losing the Telethon to you.' She didn't want to sound as though Matt needed sympathy, but some explanation seemed necessary.

'It's even harder for me losing you to him.'

Ally was grateful she didn't have time to reply before Sally was back chivvying people downstairs into waiting taxis.

Her indecision only lasted a moment before she knew

she was doing the right thing. 'I'm sorry, folks, I really am, but I've got to get home.' There was a general groan from everyone standing nearby. 'Have fun.'

Ally walked out of the room as quickly as possible and went to her dressing room to gather up her belongings. It would only take her five minutes to pack up and get her cab. In an hour she'd be home.

Matt sat with the television still on, staring at it but not taking it in. He felt totally replaced. Not just on the programme, but in life. His reason told him that the kiss on the cheek could still mean absolutely nothing, but his instincts screamed something different.

After so many years in television, he knew how easily it happened. You were thrown together. You had the excitement of sharing an enterprise you both believed in. You worked late. People around you were doing it. It wasn't as though you went looking for it, it found you. It was too hideously predictable.

He switched the television off. He must pull himself together. All this was about power. And he saw for the first time that it was the one without the power who imagined the worst because they had most to lose.

Suddenly angry with himself, Matt made a conscious effort to believe that in an hour Ally would walk through that door and he'd laugh at his stupid suspicions and tell her about the weekend he'd booked. It would be fine. Feeling more cheerful, he pushed Sox's head off his knee and went to make himself a cup of coffee.

When the doors of the lift opened ten minutes later Ally was surprised to see that a small group of people from the programme were still in reception. They turned sheepishly when she appeared and one of them pushed Sally, the noisiest of the PAs, towards her.

'Oh, Ally, *do* come! It won't be the same if you're not there.' Sally knew she was laying on the blackmail, but she couldn't bear the thought of them going off without her. 'Think how hard we've worked. There's even going to be a present for you!'

Ally knew when she was beaten. She'd resisted Danny because she had to, but she couldn't resist this onslaught.

'OK,' she said and grinned, 'but I'll have to phone Matt.'

'Tell him to put your slippers by the fire and your dinner in the dog,' offered another of the PAs, who was clutching a bottle under her arm.

Ally went to the phone at the reception desk. There was no sign of Danny. He'd either gone ahead or gone home. She wondered which she'd prefer.

As soon as Matt heard the phone ring he knew who it would be. He'd been in the same position so many times. The excitement of the show. The euphoria afterwards. Then too many drinks too fast and someone suggests dinner. How often, in her situation, had he remembered his wife and children and politely declined?

'Hello, Matt, it's Ally.' He could hear the faint note of apology in her voice and the girlish laughter in the background. 'Everyone's going out to dinner to celebrate. We made twenty-three million pounds!'

'I know,' he said, sharing her pleasure. 'I was watching.'

Ally was surprised and touched. She hadn't expected him to.

Go on, he was about to say, *enjoy yourself*.

Out of nowhere Danny Wilde appeared.

'Come on, star,' he said, slightly louder than was strictly necessary, 'everybody's leaving.'

At the other end of the phone Matt put down the receiver and closed his eyes, feeling engulfed by jealousy.

And as he sat there in the semi-darkness, he recognized another feeling – powerful and unfamiliar – of being the one who's left behind.

On the pavement outside Century Ally discovered that Sally and the noisy group of PAs had somehow evaporated in search of taxis or their own cars and that she and Danny had been left alone together. Spotting a passing taxi she put up her hand.

'Don't worry, we can take my car.' He gestured towards an old-fashioned Rover parked a few yards away.

Ally was amazed to find him driving something forty years old, and relieved that it would give them a talking point on the way to the restaurant. He held the door open for her, saluting and giving her the kind of knowing look that chauffeurs in porno movies give the wives of their employers before climbing in behind them.

'Isn't it wonderful?' Ally laughed, suddenly as nervous as a schoolgirl, trying to avoid his eyes in case he could read what was in her own. And it was an extraordinary car. She remembered driving in one like this with her uncle. It had been a Wolseley with a polished walnut dashboard that she could still picture vividly, and a little glove compartment that opened with a silver handle like a chest of drawers. Next to her she discovered an old-fashioned arm rest and pulled it down, grateful that the seats were so wide there was no danger of accidentally touching him. Even so, she was completely aware of his nearness.

As they moved off she didn't notice that someone was watching them from the desk in reception. Belinda had been working late and had come down to phone a taxi. Changing her mind, she got back in the lift and returned to her office. This was one call she needed to make in private.

Fortunately for Ally the journey was very short. Ten minutes later they were outside Down Mexico Way.

'Oh, look,' she pointed out brightly, trying to conceal her relief, 'there's Sally getting out of a taxi. And there's a parking space right outside the restaurant.'

But Danny went past it and on round the block till they were out of sight. Twenty yards further she saw the familiar yellow hoarding of an underground car park.

'I don't like leaving it in the street.' Danny rolled down his window by hand and took a ticket. 'I'm too fond of it to let some joyrider nick it.'

They drove down into the concrete depths of the car park and Ally was relieved at the sudden darkness. She was desperate to hide the waves of dangerous excitement which were flooding through her, stronger with every second.

As the car stopped she scrabbled for the catch. But in an old car it wasn't in the usual place. Smiling his slow, lazy smile, Danny Wilde leaned over, pushed up the arm rest, and undid it. Then, without a word, he turned and kissed her hard and long on the mouth, pressing her body back against the cool leather of the old-fashioned car seat.

Sitting alone in the dark Matt knew he had to talk to someone or he'd go mad. At moments like this women scored over men every time. If this had happened to Ally she'd have been on the phone to Susie half an hour ago and by now they'd have downed a bottle of Chardonnay and put his character through the shredder several times over. After two bottles they would have concluded, as usual, that all men are bastards and moved effortlessly on to righteous indignation swiftly followed by reassuring pity for men's pathetic inability not to follow their pricks.

He tried to imagine calling Bernie and confiding to that lifetime cynic that he feared his wife was having an affair with Danny Wilde. Bernie would probably laugh out loud and say, 'You should buy the talk-show rights.'

Matt put his head in his hands. He'd never felt such pain. He reached behind him and got the bottle of brandy out of the drinks' cupboard, but after one slug he put it back. What would be the point? If he drank the whole bottle, and in this mood he would, he might forget for tonight, but he'd have the mother and father of hangovers and the problem would still be there in the morning. Instead he stood up and walked upstairs. Janey's door was slightly open.

He saw that she had thrown off her duvet and very gently he pulled it over her again. She was sleeping peacefully, her pale skin luminous against the black sheets. He noticed that she was wearing the T-shirt he'd given her for Christmas. ASK A TEENAGER, it advised, THEY KNOW EVERYTHING. Tenderly he knelt by the side of the bed and stroked her hair. He loved them both so much. But tonight, for the first time, he had the premonition that he might lose them.

Downstairs he heard the phone and wondered who would be ringing after eleven o'clock.

Chapter 24

Bernie watched Ally and Danny arrive, five minutes later than everyone else, and wondered. There'd been times today when he'd asked himself if there was something between them. Odd little moments when he'd sensed them watching each other. But in Bernie's experience there was only one sure way to tell: colleagues having an affair always ignored each other in public, often to the point of rudeness, to throw everyone off the scent.

Danny sat down amid cries of welcome and picked up a menu as the Mexican waitress slammed a tiny glass of tequila topped up with lemonade in front of him. It fizzed over the top as he drank it in one gulp. The girl took another glass from the leather cartridge belt she wore slung round her shoulders and repeated the gesture. Tequila slammers were this year's 'in' drink.

Next to Danny was an empty seat. The only other one was at the far end of the long table next to the dragon of a production manager. Without a moment's hesitation, Ally turned her back on Danny and chose that. At the far end of the table Bernie raised an eyebrow as he poured himself another Aqua Libra.

The meal was fun, especially when Ally was presented with a plastic mini-Oscar and a slice of cake to take home like a child's birthday treat, but she still found herself waiting for the first opportunity she could decently sneak off. She needed time to think.

As she stood up to say goodbye, everyone else did too, but to her relief no one followed her. She was so eager to get out into the fresh air that when she found she had no change she gave the hat-check girl a fiver and made her evening.

It was no surprise to Bernie when Danny Wilde stood up five minutes later. Ah, the wonder of lust. It convinces people that no one will notice their strange behaviour when they might as well just fax the details to everyone they know. Bernie watched Danny hand his ticket over and retrieve his camel coat. He wasn't sure about this development. Ally was always so level-headed, so down-to-earth. Matt may not have been the perfect husband. He'd taken her for granted and then he'd grudged her her success, not to mention firing Bernie from his own show. And then there was Belinda. Yet to his immense surprise Bernie found that it was Matt he sympathized with. Maybe it was because Danny Wilde dressed himself up as a New Man with all the right-on sympathetic attitudes. But if Bernie knew anything about it, underneath it all he was a wolf in wimp's clothing.

Matt got to the phone on the tenth ring. Part of him was hoping it would be Ally saying she'd changed her mind about going out to dinner and would be coming home instead. The last person he was expecting was Belinda.

'Matt, hello. Are you on your own?'

'Apart from Janey, who's gone to bed, yes. Why?'

'I thought you would be. I've just seen Ally . . .' Belinda paused dramatically.

Matt jumped at the bait as she knew he would.

'Where?'

'Outside Century. Getting into Danny Wilde's car.'

'I know. She called me. They're going out to dinner with the rest of the team.' Matt could hear the defensiveness in his tone and felt annoyed with himself.

'That's not what they looked like.'

'And what did they look like?'

'Like young lovers on their first date.' Matt felt himself flinch. So he hadn't imagined it. The pain was so awful

328

that for a minute he didn't hear anything Belinda was saying.

'Matt!' She interrupted his thoughts which were scrabbling back for the image of that kiss. Belinda was talking again. 'Look, Matt, why don't you come over? You shouldn't be alone tonight.'

'Did you watch it? What did you think?'

'I didn't think Danny was a patch on you.' That wasn't what Matt meant but he let it pass. 'Ally was good, though. It's all crappy emotional blackmail, but she has a knack for it.'

Matt smiled. Belinda was nothing if not honest. And listening to her he knew that what he wanted was the honesty of her reassurance that he had done it better.

'Come on, Matt. You don't have to stay. Just for an hour. You can be back before she is if you want.'

Suddenly Matt weakened. 'OK. Just for an hour. See you soon then.'

Belinda put down the phone. She'd be home in ten minutes and could put a bottle of wine on ice. Or maybe even two.

Wrapping her coat round her as a chill wind blew off the river Ally stood at the cross of Victoria Street and Vauxhall Bridge Road waiting for a cab. She still had the unenviable task ahead of convincing a cabbie that it was worth his while to take her to deepest Surrey, but at least the recession had improved her chances. A few years ago when Britain was booming even the most mildly inconvenient journey would be pooh-poohed as being beyond the six-mile limit. But now times had changed.

Except that tonight there weren't any cabs. She even walked down towards the river hoping that some cabbies might be on the look-out for after-theatre diners, but there was nothing. She was beginning to feel conspicuous standing on the pavement and was wondering whether to turn back towards the station when a car slowed down behind her. She walked faster. It really would be too much if someone was trying to pick her up.

As the car approached the first thing she noticed was that it had its windows down and that Jess's favourite record, rejoicing in the subtle title 'Let's Talk About Sex, Baby', was blaring out. Just her luck. Not just a kerb crawler but an underage kerb crawler.

'Want a lift, lady?' She recognized the voice immediately.

He leaned over and opened the door of the Rover invitingly. She was cold and tired and it needed more resolve than she had to resist. But once in the car she came back to her senses.

'You can drop me at Victoria Station. There's bound to be a cab there.'

Two minutes later he stopped opposite the station and looked at her, his disconcerting smile making her feel hot and bothered again. This time he made no attempt to kiss her, but he wasn't going to make it easy either.

'Sure I can't tempt you to come back to my nice warm flat to phone for a cab from there?'

For a moment Ally almost said yes. She imagined what it would be like to pick up the phone, sitting on his sofa. He might reach over and slowly undo her buttons, caressing her breasts until she forgot her name, address and anything but the pure excitement of his touch.

'No, thanks,' she said eventually, hoping he couldn't hear the quaver of indecision in her voice.

'You could have real coffee and croissants,' he said, his tone breathy and inviting. 'In the morning.'

'I can have real coffee and croissants at home.'

'Ah, but you've never tasted *my* coffee.' He smiled lazily. 'It's famous all over London.'

'I'm sure it is,' she said drily. She'd recovered now. She would be all right. 'It's just that I prefer tea.' She opened the door and got out.

He leaned over and shut the door behind her then wound down the window. 'I'll tell you what, Mrs Boyd' – across the other side of the road she'd caught sight of a taxi with its light on and was about to dash towards it – 'I prefer you without your clothes.'

Without answering she ran across Victoria Street. As she got into the taxi Ally felt a wave of desire so strong that all she could do was sit there mute.

'Where to, darlin'?' asked the cabbie.

Danny Wilde, she decided, wasn't safe. Not safe at all.

Danny sat in silence for a moment watching the cab do an unauthorized U-turn and drive at speed back down towards the river. It wasn't often he felt real disappointment, but he was feeling it now. These days, with his fame and money, almost no woman refused him. But Ally had. And he couldn't decide whether it was that, or her undoubted attractiveness, that made him want her so much.

He turned on the engine and headed back to his empty flat, and then remembered the phone call he'd had from Ritchie Page two days ago. Ritchie Page had invited him and Jack Saltash, his agent, to a secret meeting to discuss replacing *The Matt Boyd Show*. Danny had no idea whether the proposition was simply a flyer to scare Matt or a genuine option. Either way it would certainly be better not to get emotionally involved with Matt's wife, or things could get unpleasant.

As he drove round Hyde Park Corner Danny recalled the sight of Ally's beautiful breasts and how vulnerable she'd looked as she tried to cover them. And he wondered if it wasn't already too late for both of them.

★

The cabbie agreed to take Ally home without the usual rolling of the eyes and the deep sigh. As it happened he'd been thinking of knocking off, and he lived in that direction.

Ally got in gratefully. The demands of the show and, even more, of resisting Danny were beginning to get to her. Without even being aware of doing it, she surrendered to the tensions of the day and fell asleep.

'Here you are, lady.' The cabbie slid across the partition and turned to Ally. 'That'll be twenty-six quid.'

Ally sat up, astonished that they were home when she'd only closed her eyes ten seconds earlier.

She had a curious feeling as she opened the front door. The lights were off and the house was strangely quiet. Even Sox was silent. She looked at her watch. After one a.m. What did she expect, a reception committee?

She wandered into the sitting room on the off-chance that Matt had fallen asleep on the sofa, as he sometimes did, but it was empty. He must have gone to bed.

Upstairs she checked the girls' rooms first, forgetting for a moment that Jess was away. Janey was lying on her side, her duvet tucked right up to her chin like a little girl, one of her set books hidden by a Jilly Cooper novel. Ally knelt beside her for a moment, relief washing over her that she hadn't done anything stupid, that she'd remembered Janey and Jess just in time and hadn't given in to the temptation she knew would risk her marriage and their security.

She walked softly across the thickly carpeted floor to their bedroom and opened the door, a half-smile on her face, expecting to see Matt's form under the duvet, familiar and reassuring.

But there was no sign of Matt anywhere. She tiptoed downstairs. His coat was gone. She opened the front door and ran across the moonlit terrace to the double garage. Matt's car wasn't there.

There has to be some perfectly reasonable explanation for this, she told herself. *It's just that I don't know it.*

Matt drifted back into reality slowly, aware at precisely the same moment of a splitting headache and the embarrassing realization that he was in Belinda's white lacy bed minus his clothes. What's more he knew for a fact that it couldn't have been he who removed them. They were folded on a cane chair as neatly as if they were on the shelves in Benetton. He wouldn't have done that sober, let alone pissed. For a moment he ducked beneath the crisp white cotton. He wasn't sure he was ready to deal with this development.

'Good morning,' Belinda's voice prompted from the doorway.

Jesus, was it morning? He'd meant to go home, not spend the night here. What would Ally have thought when he wasn't there?

'I'm sorry to have to ask this,' he said sheepishly, 'but what happened last night?'

Belinda watched him for a moment, wondering which would worry him most. To hear that they'd made love five times or the truth – which was that they hadn't made love at all because Matt, either from too much drink or too much guilt, hadn't been able to get it up? She suspected it would be better for her to say that they had, but an unexpected streak of honesty made her tell the truth. She sat down on the edge of the bed and took his hand.

'You mean what *didn't* happen.' She smiled wryly.

Matt put his head under the cover. 'You mean we tried?'

'*I* tried,' she corrected. 'But nothing seemed to do the trick.'

'How did I get undressed?'

'Think of me as a nurse.' Belinda patted his hand.

He dismissed the smart answer he was about to give and decided to confide in her.

'I suppose this business about Ally and Danny Wilde's getting to me.'

Belinda wasn't going to waste an opportunity like this. 'Look, Matt, if she's behaving like that so publicly it wouldn't be disloyal if you moved in with me – at least for a while.'

Matt was grateful for the offer and the genuine emotion behind it. Gently he stroked her hand and tried to work up the courage to tell her that in spite of Danny Wilde, Ally was still the one he loved and that he had to fight for her.

Ally sat at the kitchen table watching the minutes tick by on the clock above the dresser and facing the hard truth that for the first time in their marriage, Matt had stayed away for the night without leaving an explanation. She'd been awake since seven and it was now after nine and there was still no sign of him. She'd been through the usual fears that he might have wrapped the car round a lamp post and could be lying in a ditch somewhere, and now she drank her fourth cup of coffee tasting only cold anger. She had rehearsed countless versions of what she was going to say to him and knew that when he walked in the door she would say none of them.

At first she'd thought of phoning Bernie or someone at Century. Then she'd realized what a fool she'd look. She felt a cold shiver of humiliation as she imagined the brief, wounding silence on the other end of the phone as Bernie thought, poor cow, doesn't she know? And the truth was she did know. She knew as well as anyone else where Matt had to be. The bitter truth was that while she had been resisting Danny Wilde, Matt had been giving in to

Belinda. Her only relief was that neither Janey nor Jess had yet put in an appearance and asked where he was.

Then the garden door opened and Matt stood there, looking uncomfortable. There was something about his unfamiliar gaucheness, the set of his shoulders that told her everything she needed to know.

Ally looked at him steadily. 'So where were you last night?' She loathed herself for the cliché.

'I could ask you the same question.'

Watching her sitting there, Matt realized she still had her make-up on from the show. She looked as though she'd been crying. He felt as guilty as hell.

He knew he should apologize and searched for the words. But Ally got in first.

'So you finally surrendered to the lovely Belinda. Oh, well. I suppose she deserves some marks for trying hard.' The anger in her voice scorched him. 'You just can't take it, can you?'

'Take what?'

'I thought you were big enough. I thought you'd let me have my bit of success.'

'I have.'

'Come on, Matt. You're as selfish as ever. Tidying the kitchen every six months doesn't turn this into an equal marriage! I thought maybe you could change. I was wrong. You're only happy when the whole house revolves round you. As soon as I stopped waiting on you hand and foot you couldn't deal with it and ran off to Belinda.'

Matt's innate sense of justice struggled with his male pride. The pride won. A righteous anger spurted up in him. How dare she accuse him when she was involved herself?

'So you found yourself a New Man to cry on.' He thought of Danny Wilde and the suppressed longing he'd caught in their eyes. 'Does he make you cups of tea after you've screwed?'

Ally felt sick. How did Matt know about Danny?

'He makes me feel good about myself,' she flashed. 'He respects my talents, which is more than you've ever done.'

Matt couldn't bear the pain. She hadn't even bothered to deny it. 'Of course he does! He wanted to get you into bed.' Matt was so angry he didn't know if he believed what he was saying. 'And why did he want to get you into bed? Because you're a warm and wonderful human being – or because you're my wife?' Matt knew he was lashing out, trying to hurt her, and couldn't stop himself. 'Can't you see what he's up to? He got my show, now he wants to be able to boast he's screwing my wife.'

The moment he said it he regretted it. It was just that in some part of him he'd expected her to deny it, if only for form's sake. But she'd made no attempt.

'That's exactly the kind of thing you would think.' Ally was numb and wounded inside. She couldn't believe what she was hearing. 'You think the whole bloody world revolves round Matt Boyd.' She was angry too now. 'I don't suppose it's ever occurred to you that Danny Wilde was offered the Telethon because he's talented.'

Too late she saw the implication of her words.

'And I'm yesterday's man, you mean,' he added. 'Well, maybe I should relieve you of my second-rate presence and leave the field open for the greater talent of Danny Wilde.'

Outside in the hall Janey removed the Walkman she'd borrowed from Jess. She'd never heard her parents shout at each other like this. She opened the door of the kitchen a couple of inches, then stopped transfixed.

Neither Ally nor Matt, engrossed in their anger and self-justification, noticed.

Ally was furious at Matt's male pride which blinded him to the fact that someone might be attracted to her not for the effect on him but for her own sake. She knew that she had to shake him up. Right now he wasn't a man she wanted to share her life with. 'Maybe you're right. Maybe we'd better part till we know what we want.'

'Don't worry.' Matt was already heading for the door to the hall. 'I'm going. You can have all the time to work it out you want.'

Ally closed her eyes as she heard the front door slam. Did she really want him to go? They'd both said some bloody stupid things. Why didn't she run after him and tell him the truth? That she had never been to bed with Danny Wilde, that she'd refused him because she loved her family. And him.

Finally coming to a decision, she turned towards the door to find Janey, white-faced and shaking, standing there in her T-shirt and bed socks. She looked about six.

'Hello, Janey love.' Ally tried to pretend to be calm. 'Would you like some breakfast?'

Outside Ally could hear the crunch of the gravel as Matt drove out of her life.

Janey turned away. Instead of them both going off for a romantic weekend as her father had planned, they had had a bitter quarrel.

Matt drove fast down the A3 towards London trying to exorcize his anger by hooting at weekend drivers and jumping lights on amber. He was finally brought to his senses by the sight of a cabbie and dispatch rider coming to blows because one had cut the other up, and realizing his own behaviour was equally juvenile, he slowed down to thirty and pulled into the middle lane.

He slowed down even further. Ahead the road forked off to a ring road which would take him back round the way he'd come and eventually to his home and Ally. The other went into Central London and Belinda's Battersea flat.

He could still turn off at the next crossroads. But why should he? Ally had made no attempt to deny she was having an affair with Danny Wilde. Gripping the wheel till his knuckles whitened, he realized how much more he minded about that than about any professional rivalry.

Then he thought of Janey and her A levels. And Jess who tried to be so tough, but wasn't underneath. And he knew he couldn't walk out like this without even a goodbye.

His mood lightening a little, he moved into the inside lane and took the ring road back towards his home and family.

Chapter 25

When Matt woke up the next morning he knew he was glad to be in his own bed. Ally might not have exactly welcomed him home with open arms – in fact they'd come to a rather uneasy truce – but there was one thing he'd convinced himself of: it wasn't so much her success as his unexpected failure which was souring their marriage. And doing something about that was certainly within his grasp.

Lying in bed last night he'd even had a brilliant new idea for his show. Now all he had to do was talk Belinda round. But, given her reaction when he'd phoned last night to tell her he was staying with Ally, that might not be too easy a task.

Bernie Long sat in edit suite three at Century Television and watched as the editor laid the final piece of music on the guilty secrets edition of *Tell It to Ally*. It was, quite simply, one of the most riveting pieces of television he'd ever seen.

'What did you think?' he asked the grey-faced editor, who was busy rolling up the sleeves of his nylon shirt. Video editors were a secretive breed. When Bernie had started in television most programmes were still shot on film. The old editor was a colourful type and rather too free with his opinion, in Bernie's view. But video editors never gave a view. You had to prise information out of them with a can opener.

'Well, I –'

'Come on, Chris, put yourself on the line for once,' interrupted Bernie impatiently.

'Well . . . I – think it's bloody amazing.'

'Thank you, Chris.' And it was. Ally had managed to get the participants to forget they were on television and really open up. The result was dynamite.

And there was one thing he was equally sure about. He wasn't going to let Ritchie Page bury this in daytime. It needed a grown-up prime-time slot. If Bernie's instincts were anything to go by *Tell It to Ally* was destined to be a monster hit.

'Look, Belinda, I think it's time I admitted that I've made a few mistakes.' Matt and she were walking together along one of Century's endless corridors towards the studio.

'You don't need to remind me of that, Matt.' Belinda's tartness reinforced the fact that she had in no way forgiven him.

'OK, OK, I know, but I mean professionally. Since we're stuck with this transmission time and Page won't let us change, maybe we've made the show too heavy. What we need is a way of making it sharp and different, but funny at the same time.'

'And how do you propose to do that?'

'By rethinking the format again. Instead of three mediocre guests, have one superstar and do a really in-depth interview. Someone we invite specially, not some passing star who happens to be in the country at the moment.'

'But they only come on because they want to plug. How will we get them if they're not pushing anything?'

'We'll flatter them by the scale of the venture. Sell it as a kind of tribute. We could even get people in the audience to ask them questions.'

She could hear the eagerness in his voice and, despite her anger with him over deciding to stay with Ally, it was infectious. It wasn't a bad thought. And they needed something.

340

'OK. Let's give it a whirl. Have you got anyone in mind to kick off with?'

'As a matter of fact . . .' He smiled tantalizingly. 'I was thinking about Meredith Morgan.'

'But she doesn't give interviews at the moment.' The legendary Hollywood sex goddess was now nearly eighty, on her eighth husband and was rumoured to have a drink problem.

'She will,' Matt assured her remembering the instant rapport they'd had when he'd bumped into the star at a Hollywood party. Matt had rescued her from a group of non-drinking bores and shared his secret stash of whisky with her. She'd pledged eternal devotion and an appearance on his show. 'When she knows it's me.'

To Bernie's annoyance, Ritchie Page was due to go to New York for two weeks and the first appointment he and Ally could get was when he returned. But at least it would give them the chance to get two more shows shot and edited. Between now and then Bernie could make up a really sensational tape of highlights from all the shows. Someone like Ritchie Page probably only had the attention span of an average ten-year-old so there was no point in expecting him to watch a whole show. 'He's like President Reagan,' Stephen Cartwright had once advised Bernie on the art of memo-writing to the new chairman. 'He doesn't like having to turn the page.'

Bernie thought about Stephen for a moment. Lately he'd been looking a lot happier. Rumour had it he'd been moved to Head of Corporate Relations and that instead of resigning as everyone had expected, he'd decided to take the money and settle for an easy life. All right for some.

Bernie turned his mind back to the job at hand. Before he showed anything to Ritchie Page, he had to see what Ally thought of it herself. He was pretty sure she'd be interested. He picked up the phone. 'Look, sweetheart, you have *got* to come in and see the tape before we send it upstairs. When can you manage?'

'How about the day after tomorrow?'

'Fine.' He was a shade disappointed that she hadn't insisted on jumping in the car and coming there and then. 'By the way, when's your birthday?'

Ally sounded puzzled. 'In November.'

'No, it's not. It's the day after tomorrow. And you couldn't ask for a better present.'

When Ally sat down in front of the tape she was afraid she wouldn't like it as much as Bernie. But she needn't have worried. From the moment it started it was so gripping that she was utterly absorbed.

When it was finished there was a beat's silence as Bernie, grinning broadly, waited for her reaction.

Ally searched for the words. Finally she hugged him and shouted, 'It was so good I forgot it was me!'

'You, my modest superstar, are about to be a very hot property.'

Ally smiled and hugged him tighter. At last she'd done something she was really proud of. If only they could persuade Ritchie Page to give it a decent slot.

When they eventually got to see Page, Ally found the occasion deeply unnerving. Page, fresh in from the Red-Eye, was jet lagged and apparently bored. Ally even saw his eyes close bang in the middle of Bernie's sales pitch. Her excitement evaporated as she sat there. Then it got to her.

'Look, Mr Page.' She stood up as though the meeting were at an end. 'Why don't we just leave the tape with you as you're obviously far too busy to judge it properly now?' Her voice, abrasive as sandpaper, seemed to get through to him.

'No, no. I'd like to see it. Put it in the machine.'

As he watched it Ally saw Page's body language gradually transform from polite boredom to almost as much enthusiasm as they were feeling.

'But this stuff's fabulous!' He was sitting right up in his seat now, looking like a tout being offered a lorry load of fake watches. 'Absolutely amazing!'

'That's what I've been telling you,' Bernie pointed out. 'Fabulous. Riveting. Wonderful. People will be talking about it in every pub in the land, prising out each other's secrets. The tabloids will run double-page spreads. It will be mega. If, *if*, you give it a decent slot. The question is, do you have any?'

Page was as quiet as a sphinx. A solution so perfect had just occurred to him that he couldn't quite believe it. This show deserved a great slot. He'd always planned to take Matt Boyd off the air for the summer and replace him with cheap buy-ins. Why not – he practically climaxed at the beauty of this scheme – why not replace him with *Tell It to Ally*? He could put it out on Friday and stick something else in on the other two days.

'There is one slot coming up.' He put up his feet on his desk in an exaggeratedly casual gesture.

'And that is?' Bernie asked.

'Seven o'clock on Fridays, starting in six weeks' time.'

'Hey!' Bernie jumped up, his mind racing. It was one of the best slots of the week.

Ally's heart leaped for an instant, but then she worked it out. She looked Page directly in the eye. 'That's Matt's slot.'

'Jesus!' Bernie shook his head at his own stupidity. 'I produced the fucking thing for ten years. Of course it is!' So that was what Page was up to, the devious bastard.

Page shifted his feet on his desk fractionally, his voice calm and reasonable. 'Yes, but I'm taking *The Matt Boyd Show* off for the summer. It's crazy to keep it on all year.

No other TV companies do.'

Ally's bubble burst as she listened to Page. 'Does Matt know?' She knew the answer already. He would have told her if he'd known.

'Not yet. I'll tell him once this is sorted out.'

'No.' Ally desperately wanted a prime-time slot; but not at this price. 'I'm sorry, Mr Page, but I couldn't do that to Matt.'

Page shrugged. 'I'm taking his show off whether you replace it or not, so it won't make any difference.'

Bernie watched mesmerized, torn between sympathy for Ally's dilemma and a lifelong sense of self-interest. It was the most amazing bloody opportunity. 'What else could you offer if we don't go for that?'

Page reached in his drawer and removed an enormous chart. He studied it for a moment. 'I might be able to clear Tuesdays at three thirty, subject to agreement with the scheduling department, of course.'

'But that's crap! The mums will have gone out to pick up their bloody kids from school and not even a man and a dog will be watching.' Bernie knew it was useless to argue. This was all for show anyway. Page wanted them on Fridays at seven o'clock and anything else he offered them would be shit.

Page shrugged. 'The choice is yours.'

'We'd better talk about this.' Bernie picked up his papers.

'There's nothing to talk about, Bernie.' Ally's tone was adamant. No matter how much she wanted her show to work, she couldn't betray Matt like that.

'Look, Allegra.' Page took his feet off the desk and smiled his perfectly-capped-tooth smile, so immaculate it was somehow threatening. 'It's about time you realized that you're the one who's on the up. Matt's finished. His ratings are lousy. This new show is a disaster. If he'd been a smaller star I would have taken it off months ago, but I wanted to be fair. To give him his chance. Well, now he's had it.'

Ally closed her eyes. She didn't want to hear this. It was like listening to obscenities being spoken about someone you love. It was so unfair! Why did her success seem somehow to depend on Matt's failure?

'Come on, Bernie, let's go.' She grabbed his arm and almost pulled him from the room, fighting back tears of anger and frustration and sorrow for herself and for Matt.

'You think it over.' Page decided to leave the door open a few inches, no matter what Ally might have said. He stood up and leaned on his desk, smiling again. 'By the way,' he said. 'I don't need your consent, you know. Your job is to make the programme. Neither of you has any say about scheduling.'

As soon as the door of Page's office closed Ally turned to Bernie. 'That's not true, is it? He can't just stick *Tell It to Ally* out without our consent, can he?'

'I'm afraid the truth is' – Bernie held her against the roughness of his old tweed jacket in a rare gesture of tenderness – 'that he can do whatever he bloody well likes with it.'

'Jesus, Bernie!' Ally leaned against the comfort of his shoulder. 'What the hell am I going to do?'

Bernie battled with himself for a moment. If they did nothing Page would go ahead with his plan and very likely they would end up with one of the best slots on television, but it might be at the cost of Ally's marriage. If they objected, they might be lumbered with some crappy afternoon slot.

He looked at Ally. He knew which solution she would want to go for. 'I think you'd better talk to Matt before Page does.'

*

Ritchie Page sipped his cappuccino and smiled. Things were going better than he'd expected. The negotiation with Danny Wilde to take over from Matt in the autumn was satisfactorily underway, and now Allegra Boyd had presented him with a perfect way of putting the screws on her husband. What's more, the show was so great there could be no suggestion of foul play on his part. He took a deep breath of satisfaction and leaned forward to press the buzzer on his intercom. 'Lorraine, could you find Matt Boyd and ask him to come up here immediately?'

Although Matt's offices were humming with activity when Ally went to look for him she couldn't find him anywhere. Belinda emerged from the office she and Matt shared and acknowledged Ally's presence with a frosty smile.

'I'm looking for Matt. Do you know where he is at the moment?'

Belinda did know, but she was damned if she was going to tell Ally. Let her find him herself. ''Fraid not. He was here a few minutes ago. He must have popped out.'

Ally's pulse raced. 'Could you tell him I need to see him when he comes back? He can page me. I won't leave till I've talked to him.'

Belinda watched her as she hurried away, and wondered what was going on.

Ten minutes later her secretary interrupted the meeting she was having to tell her that Ritchie Page was also looking for Matt urgently.

'He's down in STU having a new earpiece fitted.' Belinda was so intrigued she finished her meeting before it was scheduled to end. Something was definitely going on.

★

'Matt!' shouted the sound engineer, putting his hand over the mouthpiece of the phone. 'The Porn King wants to see you sharpish. "Can you go up now?" his secretary says.'

Matt looked annoyed. 'Tell her I'm tied up. I'll ring when I'm free.'

The sound man was impressed. Ritchie Page scared the wits out of him. Matt had nerve, all right. 'She says to go up as soon as you're free. Mr Page is waiting for you.'

Reluctantly Matt put down the earpiece he was testing, fascination struggling with a hint of fear in his mind. Page had never summoned him out of the blue like this before. He slipped into the gents' outside STU and splashed his face with cold water, then he stood for a moment in front of the mirror steeling himself. Whatever it was, he was up to it. Last night he and Belinda had decided to go for the interview with Meredith Morgan as soon as possible – provided, of course, she agreed to do it. And Matt was sure she would.

Feeling more optimistic, Matt opened the door and strode towards the lifts. Just as the doors closed behind him Ally arrived in Sound Transfer. It had taken her half an hour to find out where Matt was. Five minutes too long.

In his shiny black office on the sixteenth floor Page waited, savouring the moment until his secretary showed Matt in.

When there was a knock on the door he sat down behind his desk. 'Come in. Ah, Matt. Sorry to tear you away from such a vital fitting.'

So the bastard had known where he was all along. 'My pleasure.' Without being invited, Matt sat down on one of the zebra skin sofas. They really were utterly naff. 'So, Ritchie, what can I do for you?'

Page looked up, annoyed. He didn't like anyone trying to assume control of his meetings. 'It's about your show.'

'I guessed it was.' Matt's tone was laced with the faintest sarcasm.

'Dropping all the froth has been a brave experiment, but let's face it, it hasn't worked.'

'I know.'

Page paused for a moment, thrown. He'd expected Matt to fight him every inch of the way.

Matt took advantage of the gap and jumped in. 'I couldn't agree more. The heavy stuff isn't working, we both know that. That's why we're kicking off a whole new format. In-depth interviews with really big personalities. We're setting the first one up already with Meredith Morgan.'

'I'm sorry, Matt.' Page leaned forward and fixed Matt's eye with his. 'But I'm afraid that won't be possible.'

'Why not? It's a great idea and I can guarantee our old ratings, plus some, especially if you give us some on-air promotion . . .'

'I don't think you're getting my drift, Matt. I've decided to take *The Matt Boyd Show* off for the summer.'

Matt listened in disbelief. In anyone else such a plan might seem reasonable. Century was the only TV company who kept their major chat-show on throughout the summer anyway, but nothing was ever straightforward with Ritchie Page. Watching him sitting there, shiny-suited and deceptively reasonable, some instinct told Matt that if his show came off it would never see the light of day again.

'You're axing the show, aren't you?' Matt's blue eyes were suddenly chips of steel.

'Nonsense, Matt. I'm merely putting something more suitable out in its place for the summer months.'

'Another Aussie soap opera? The public won't stomach it, you know.'

'Maybe one night. And a nice cop show on another.

I've always felt there wasn't enough violence on TV.' He laughed at his little joke.

'There'll be an outcry if you just put out crap.'

'I don't think so.' Page paused. Like sex, you had to hold back to get the greatest pleasure. 'You see I've got something lined up that'll be a critical success as well as a monster hit.'

'And what's that?' Matt knew Page had to be bluffing. Century hadn't made anything like that for years.

'*Tell It to Ally*. Bernie and your wife came up this morning to beg me for a prime-time slot, and I promised them yours. Just for the summer, of course.'

Matt listened silently. He felt winded. As though he'd been smashed in the gut by some giant punchball. How could she have done this to him when she knew how hard he'd been working on his new concept, how optimistic he'd been feeling?

'Don't worry, Matt.' Matt's silence told Page he'd won, that Matt had given in in the face of overwhelming odds. 'You can still try your new format. I won't take you off till the end of June. Maybe it'll give us some ideas for your autumn relaunch.'

Matt stood up. He knew as well as Page that there would be no relaunch. His career at Century was ending, and right at this moment he didn't care. Because it wasn't just his career that was ending in this room today. Page had tossed their marriage on the bonfire for good measure.

'Matt, what's up?' Belinda had been about to brief one of the producers about an upcoming show, but after one look at Matt's face she sent him out of the room. 'What on earth's happened?'

Matt sat down heavily. 'I was summoned for an audience with the Porn King.'

'And?'

'He's taking us off the air for the summer.'

'But we've got all these shows planned!'

'They can still go out. He's giving us till the end of June.'

Belinda collapsed on a sofa next to him. She wasn't altogether surprised. Their ratings had slumped to an all-time low. She looked at Matt. 'Is it so awful? It'd be nice to get the chance of a breather. Time to plan a cracking new series.'

'If there is a new series planned.'

'What do you mean? He wouldn't axe us altogether, surely?'

'He can do what he bloody well likes, as he told me in no uncertain terms.'

'Then we'll just have to show him how brilliant we can be in the next few weeks and make him change his mind, won't we?'

Her optimism made him smile for a moment.

But Belinda had got to know him too well over the last few months. 'There's something else, isn't there, Matt?'

'You could say that.' She heard the bitterness in his voice.

'What is it?'

'You'll never guess what Ritchie Page is planning to replace us with.' The tone changed to forced gaiety. It struck a false note. Belinda waited. '*Tell It to Ally*, for God's sake. Page had Ally and Bernie up this morning to give them the good news.'

So that was why Ally was searching for Matt so enthusiastically. To soften the blow.

'Oh Matt, how terrible!' Belinda realized she was furious with Ally on Matt's behalf. 'You must feel so betrayed. How could she live with herself?' She turned and delved in the huge duffel bag by the side of her desk and then like a child winning the lucky dip, she pulled out what she'd been rummaging for. It was a set of keys on a Bart Simpson key ring. Matt looked away for a second. Ally had put a similar key ring in Jess's stocking last year.

'Take these.' She tossed the keys to her flat on to his desk. 'I don't need them anyway, I've got plenty.' She gazed at his anguished face. 'You don't have to use them. It's just your security.' She was careful to keep her tone light and breezy even though she desperately hoped he would come. 'Everyone needs a bolthole.'

Matt regarded them for a moment, undecided. Then he put them into his pocket. 'Thanks, Belinda.' He looked away, frightened that if he didn't hold on to himself he might break down. 'Thanks a lot. I think maybe I'll go home now. Ally and I have a lot to talk about.'

As she watched him gather up his things and walk slowly through the office, Belinda bit her lip. She knew with absolute certainty that this was her best chance yet. Surely now he'd decide he'd had enough and come to her?

When he got home Matt was glad the house was empty. For nearly an hour he sat in his study, staring into space, trying to think his way out of this awful bloody mess. Finally he stood up. All the solutions were painful. He would hurt his family if he went, but he'd hurt them and himself if he stayed. The truth was Ally and he had been growing apart for months. She had been spending more and more time engrossed in her programme and he was already marginal to her life. The real question was how to do it without hurting Janey and Jess more than he absolutely had to. He looked at his watch. They wouldn't be back for another hour at least. By then he could have his suitcase in the car so they didn't see it.

Slowly and painfully he went up to their bedroom,

reached for his bag and started packing. He wouldn't want much. He just needed a few days to think, away from Ally, even away from Janey and Jess. He felt too hurt to stay here and pretend none of it mattered. For a moment he wondered whether to leave a note, but that was the coward's way out and Matt wasn't a coward. Neatly he folded a row of shirts, a few pairs of trousers and a couple of his working suits. Then he went into the *en suite* bathroom to get his sponge bag.

So he didn't hear the crunch of Ally's car on the gravel as she turned into their drive exhausted, and with her temples grinding with pain as the headache she'd been fighting off all day finally engulfed her.

Chapter 26

'Matt, what on earth are you doing?' He whipped round to find Ally standing in the doorway.

Matt had watched this scene in so many films. Now it was happening to him and he didn't know what to say.

'I'm moving out for a while. I came back last time because I didn't want to hurt you, but it's no good. It isn't working. We're miles away from each other. We don't even pass in the night.'

Ally watched him silently, torn between wanting to lose her temper and making one last attempt to save their marriage. She sat on the bed next to his suitcase, remembering that the last time she'd seen it they'd been going to Scotland for one of their happiest times ever. She reached her hand towards him, choosing her words carefully. 'Matt, don't you think what's been happening is really just bad timing? One of us is up while the other feels down. Isn't that what's been making it hard for us?'

But she could see he wasn't convinced. His face closed in on itself in anger, with no sign of the teasing, ironic Matt she'd loved.

'Don't patronize me, Ally!' he snapped. 'I don't need your sympathy.'

The coldness of his tone finally lit the touchpaper of her deeply buried anger.

'Go, then! Why don't you just *go*?' The coldness in her voice more than matched his. 'It'll be better in the long run to make a clean break. I can't take any more of this.'

Matt glanced at her for a moment then shut his suitcase with the finality of a blade on the chopping block.

'Goodbye, then. I'll phone soon to sort out seeing Janey and Jess. I want to tell them my side of the story.'

Ally nodded without looking up. She wanted him to go and yet she couldn't bear to see him actually walking out of the door. Instead when he closed the door she rolled over on the bed and stared at the wall.

Belinda cancelled her final meeting and went home. She couldn't concentrate. She felt almost girlish with excitement, as though she was waiting to go out on her first date. It was crazy, she knew, wildly speculative. But all the same she stopped off at the off-licence and bought a bottle of good wine. Then a quick foray into Marks & Spencer. In the chill cabinet two half lobsters looked up at her plaintively. They were wildly extravagant but she put them in her basket all the same. What if he doesn't come, you silly cow? You could have bought yourself a new pair of trousers for the money you've thrown away in here.

'Celebrating something?' asked the nice young cashier.

Belinda smiled. 'I certainly hope so.'

She had been in the flat just long enough to unpack the shopping, stuff the wine into the fridge and think about running a bath when the door bellrang.

She did up her bathrobe, suddenly frightened that her confidence had been misplaced. If it were Matt he would have let himself in with the keys she'd given him, not ring the bell. It must be someone else.

Putting the chain on the door she opened it a couple of inches. Matt was standing there leaning on the lintel, a hesitant expression on his face.

'Hello,' said Belinda, a wide smile of triumph and of excitement lighting up her strong features. 'Why didn't you use the keys?' She opened the door and stood back.

'It seemed a bit presumptuous.'

'That's OK.' She touched his face, her eyes alight with anticipation. 'I like men who're presumptuous. It saves having to make decisions.'

Matt put his suitcase down on the floor of her hall, pushed her against the wall and kissed her.

After a few minutes Belinda closed the front door, took Matt by the hand and led him upstairs to bed. Before he had the remotest chance of changing his mind.

Without speaking she began to undress him, conscious that she might have to be patient, that it might be holding, not sex, he needed now. And for the first time in her life she realized she was prepared to give, not take.

Matt understood and was unbearably touched that this tough, assertive woman could show such tenderness and concern. Somehow he'd expected her to be as brash as she was at work. Demanding even in passion. Instead he found sweet sympathy. And it was almost his undoing. For a moment he thought he might break down and admit the jealousy and the sense of failure he'd been trying to bury inside. Maybe he'd fail even in this.

But as she began to run her lips softly across his neck he found himself harden in response, and when he looked in her eyes he saw the pupils widen with desire. And to his blessed relief he knew that he wanted her, urgently and with a longing that obliterated every other emotion.

Together they fell back on to the lacy bed and began to pull at each other's clothes with an annihilating passion that blocked out any thought of regret on his part or of future pain on hers.

When Belinda got out of bed next morning, ravenously hungry, she opened the fridge and remembered that she hadn't dared plan this far. There were no croissants waiting to be warmed or bagels with cream cheese and smoked salmon as there had been in her fantasies. Buying any had seemed too much like tempting fate. The two lobsters stared out at her balefully but they didn't look like breakfast. Otherwise there was nothing. Belinda wasn't into cooking. She occasionally cut out and kept those 'dinners for six in thirty minutes' menus in *Cosmo* but they were just as much a fantasy as a copy of *Playgirl* would have been. Lately she hadn't even had time to boil an egg.

Fortunately there was a deli round the corner which did perfect food for lovers. Italian *ciabatta* bread, spicy dressed olives that left you with an exciting challenge as to what to do with the half-inch of fragrant oil in the bottom of the tub, vegetable samosas from India and meze from Greece. A gastronomic feast just made for a picnic in bed.

'Matt?' She gently poked him as he dozed. 'The cupboard's bare so I'm just nipping round to the deli.'

'Great idea,' he threw back the duvet. 'I'll come with you.'

In Da Gennaro's Deli Matt was struck by how unmarried the atmosphere was. Round every corner were couples who'd clearly met only the night before and were trying desperately to remember each other's names as they loaded their wire baskets with taramasalata and Italian cheeses. The air was thick with naked hope and taken-for-granted disappointment.

For a moment he thought about Janey and Jess. What would Ally have told them? Probably she would have stalled, no more sure of what to do next than he was. What the hell *was* he going to do?

His thoughts were interrupted by Belinda asking his advice on whether to go for the linguine or the spaghetti. Unconsciously Matt removed his sunglasses as a woman appeared from behind the shelves, her hair scraped back, eyes hidden behind huge dark glasses, pushing a trolley with two bottles of wine and an individual bread roll.

'Hello, Belinda.' The woman did an almost comical double-take when she saw who was with her. 'Aren't you going to introduce me to your friend?'

Belinda became uncharacteristically incoherent and mumbled something about writing a script together. She dragged Matt towards the check-out.

'Shit, shit, shit!' she muttered as she delved in her tote bag for her purse.

'Why shit?' asked Matt, unloading the basket and avoiding the immediate look of recognition on the check-out girl's face. 'Who was she?'

'Only Gloria Mizzi.' Belinda looked glum as she handed over the money. 'She's the gossip writer on the *Sunday Star*. And she'll never forgive us for catching her without her eyelashes on. Look, Matt.' Suddenly serious, she steered him towards her flat the back way. 'We've got to sort this out. If you and Ally really have split up you're going to have to tell Century's press office. Once the tabloids get a whiff of this they'll be crawling out of the woodwork with lenses bigger than an Italian waiter's pepperpot.'

As they unpacked their shopping in Belinda's kitchen Matt knew she was right and he cursed being the kind of name people wanted to read about over their cornflakes. He sat at the table and wondered what the hell to do. He didn't want to go making public statements about his marriage. He didn't even know what was going to happen to it. If he was anyone else he'd be allowed some time out of the public gaze to make up his mind. But Belinda was right. In five minutes the ratpack would descend on Ally and probably even on Janey and Jess. He had to warn them.

Ally got up slowly the next morning, conscious of the unfamiliar silence in the bedroom. No sudden songs from

357

Matt, no easy chat, no arguments about him wanting breakfast television and her preferring to listen to the radio. And last night she'd hardly slept at all. Before when he'd been away for a few days she'd gloried in his brief absence, spreading herself deliciously across the bed and eating boiled eggs and toast for supper. But now that he'd gone permanently, even though she'd been blindingly angry with him, she missed the warmth of his body, the sense that there next to you in bed was another human being, fast asleep but somehow on your side in a lonely universe.

The only way she'd been able to sleep at all last night was to stuff a bolster down the bed and lean her back against it, as though it were Matt.

Now as she stood in their bathroom she saw he'd left a small bottle of aftershave. She undid the lid and sniffed. The sharp spicy smell made her close her eyes. It was so vividly Matt that he could be standing there next to her. Quickly she did it up again and tossed it in the bin. How much of this, she asked herself ruthlessly, was anything to do with Matt himself rather than habit or the simple fear of loneliness? For answer she fished the aftershave out of the bin and hid it behind the medicines in the back of the cupboard.

Downstairs, after her two-minute bath, Ally made herself some coffee and wondered what the scratching noise she could hear at the side door was. An ecstatic bark from Sox reminded her. She'd invited her mother round before any of this had happened. Ally stared at the door appalled and wondered if there was any way she could pretend to be out. But Sox was already scrabbling shamelessly at the wood and her mother's face appeared peeping through the glass and calling her name.

Ally sighed. The one thing she could do without was her mother's disapproving analysis of why her marriage had broken down. To her it would be just another thing Ally had failed at, in a long list of disappointments. And, knowing her mother, she'd probably derive some sort of twisted satisfaction from it. Ally had finally lived up to expectations. Success and happiness had simply been a blind alley off her destined road of failure and disappointment. Her only hope was that in her usual state of self-absorption her mother wouldn't notice.

Steeling herself she opened the door with a bright artificial smile on her face. 'Muv, how lovely to see you!'

Elizabeth looked at her curiously as she tried to stop Bitzer jumping on to Sox. 'You seem very cheerful.'

'I'd forgotten you were coming.' Ally stood back to let her in.

'And finding me on the doorstep's made your day, has it?'

Ally glanced at her mother to see if she was being ironic. She wasn't. 'Sit down. Have you had breakfast?'

'A bit late, isn't it? Where's Matt? Not still in bed, surely?'

Before Ally had time to answer Janey appeared, a kimono half covering her T-shirt, wearing Jess's Walkman since hers was broken and Jess was still asleep. Ally was grateful for the distraction.

'Hello, Granola, I didn't know you were coming.' Janey kissed her grandmother and stroked the revolting Bitzer's ears.

'Neither did anyone else, apparently,' Elizabeth commented tartly. 'You all seem to be in bed. Even Matt.'

'No, he's not,' Janey corrected her. 'I've just been in your bedroom looking for the paper.' She concentrated on plugging in the kettle. 'He hasn't gone to work on a Saturday again, has he?'

Ally felt her palms go damp. She couldn't tell Janey the truth. Not with her mother standing there. She'd have to stall her and talk later.

'Opening a leisure centre or something,' she mumbled. It was the first thing that came into her head.

Janey, unsuspecting, accepted her story without suspicion but Elizabeth sniffed her disapproval. 'How tacky. Doesn't he earn enough already without renting himself out?'

Janey caught her mother's eye and grinned. 'Can I take Bitzer and Sox out for a run?'

'In your dressing gown?' Ally tried to smile back.

'Only in the garden. Come on, Bitz! Sox, heel!'

The two dogs bounded out of the French windows, barking joyfully, with Janey running after them, her hair flying behind her.

Five minutes later she bounced back in chasing Bitzer. 'Bitzer, down boy!' she tried to stop him putting his muddy paws over Ally's white slacks. They'd just persuaded him to get down when the phone rang.

Ally jumped up, hoping it might be Matt. Maybe she should leave the door between them open, even if only a few inches.

But Janey got to the phone first. The smile on her face froze as she listened.

'It's for you, Mum.' She turned to her mother brusquely, holding out the phone. 'Someone from the *Sunday Star*. She says can you confirm or deny that Dad has moved in with his producer, Miss Belinda Wyeth?'

Janey handed the phone to her mother and ran up the stairs.

Ally closed her eyes for a second as the truth she'd tried to avoid slapped her in the face. She slammed the phone into its cradle, not caring what the bloody woman thought. How could anyone be so callous?

'Muv' – she turned to Elizabeth, who was standing in the kitchen doorway, looking appalled – 'could you unplug the extensions in the kitchen and the sitting room?

I'll do the bedroom.' She made no attempt to explain or deny, but ran after Janey.

Upstairs she unplugged the bedroom extension and the one in Matt's study, then went at once to Janey's room. Jess was still asleep. Thank God for teenage sloth. Through the door she could hear Janey sobbing and she cursed journalists for their crass insensitivity, the way they delighted in giving you bad news so they could report your distress at hearing it.

Janey didn't look up when she came in, but went on sobbing into her pillow.

Ally sat down on the edge of her bed and began to stroke her hair.

Finally Janey struggled to control her sobbing. 'It's true, isn't it, what that woman said?'

'I don't know.' Ally said. 'It might be. We had a quarrel last night and he stormed off. He didn't say where he was going.'

'It was about you being on the Telethon, wasn't it?' Janey looked up at her suddenly disturbingly calm.

Ally reached for her hand. It would probably be easier for her, if she believed that. 'Yes, in a manner of speaking.'

Janey shook her off. 'Why did you ever agree to do it? You must have known it would hurt him.'

Ally closed her eyes, a wave of pain sweeping over her. Janey was right in a way. Only not in the way she thought. She had hurt him. She could see that now.

'It's all your fault, you know. You're the one who's changed.' Ally was staggered by the white-hot loathing in her daughter's eyes. But then she'd always been so close to Matt. 'We were happy till you got this stupid job in television. Now look at us! But we weren't enough for you, were we?'

Ally couldn't believe what she was hearing. For

eighteen years she'd stayed at home to be there for them, not as a martyr but because it had made her happy as well as them, and in the end she'd only looked for a job because she and Matt were drifting apart and she'd needed to get back some sense of herself, for her sanity and for the sake of her marriage, too. She'd felt that if she was someone in her own right maybe their relationship would be enriched. Instead it had gone disastrously wrong. But would Janey understand any of that?

'Janey, that isn't fair. I took the job because I had to let go of you two. In a year you'll be gone. Off to university.'

'Oh, will I?' The bitterness in her daughter's voice cut her to the quick. 'What happens if I fail my A levels? Which I may well do, thanks to you.'

'Janey, how can you say that? I've always been right behind you.'

'Except when you were too busy handing out advice to total strangers to notice what was going on in your own family.'

Tears of anger and injustice pricked at Ally's eyes. She'd taken the job because neither child seemed to need her and she'd somehow believed they'd all benefit. Janey had just kicked that illusion out from under her.

'You've wrecked our family! Get out!' Janey began to cry again. Picking up her copy of T.S. Eliot, she threw it on the floor. 'Get out of my bedroom. I hate you!'

The pain was almost too much to bear. Ally could cope with Matt's anger being directed at her. She could even cope with him leaving. But not her children blaming her and hating her for it.

Wearily she walked out of the room and closed the door. At least she'd learned one thing. As soon as she'd composed herself she was going to have to tell Jess the truth. Before anyone else did.

★

Sitting hunched up in Belinda's tiny study, Matt tried to get through to Ally to warn her that the ratpack might be about to descend.

He tried the number nine times, grateful for the last number recall facility on Belinda's phone, but each time it was busy. After the tenth time he called the operator and asked her to check the line. Five minutes later she rang back.

There was no one talking on the line. There could be a fault or it was possible the phone had been left off the hook.

'Hiya, Ma.' Jess was playing with her Game Boy in bed when Ally knocked on her door. She didn't look up, cloaked as players of this electronic game always are behind an iron wall of concentration which drives their parents insane. Finally she glanced up. Seeing her mother's face she switched it off at once.

'What's the matter with Janey? Did Adam find himself another Goth?'

Ally smiled despite herself. If only it had been Adam who had found himself someone else instead of Matt. Janey had more chance of recovering from that.

'I'm afraid it's more serious than that, darling.' Ally sat down next to her. 'It's Dad. He's moved out for a little while to think things over.'

'Oh, Mum.' She reached out her hand but didn't seem surprised. 'It's been brewing for ages, you know.' Jess put her arm round her mother. 'He hasn't gone off with Belinda, has he?'

Ally was staggered by Jess's perceptiveness.

'Don't worry. He'll get sick of her.' Jess patted her mother protectively.

Ally was dangerously close to tears, and only the knowledge that she was the adult and that Jess must have pain of her own to cope with kept her from crying.

'Jess, Janey says it's my fault.' She knew she shouldn't be doing this, that she was pulling Jess into the mess because she needed reassurance, but she couldn't help herself just for a moment.

'Janey's always thought Dad was perfect.'

'And you don't?'

'I love him to pieces, but he has to let you have your success. You put us first for all these years. Now it's your turn. Fair's fair.'

'And do you think he'll see that?'

'I don't know, Ma.' Jess squeezed her arm lovingly. 'You know what they say: behind every great woman is a man who tried to stop her.'

'Thank God for one thing' – Ally held her daughter tightly, laughing and crying at the same time – 'at least I've got you two.'

When she went downstairs Ally had almost forgotten that her mother was still there. Now for the recriminations.

But to her astonishment Elizabeth had taken herself discreetly off to the sitting room. When Ally walked in she stood up. 'Poor Allegra, how completely bloody awful for you.' She held out her arms to her daughter.

For the first time Ally could remember since she was a small child she flung herself into them and sobbed her heart out.

'Men,' murmured her mother as she patted her gently. 'They're all the bloody same. Even the nice ones.' Together they sat down on the sofa and her mother stroked Ally's tear-stained face. 'Do you want him back? I have to admit, I've always liked Matt. He may be selfish, but he's fun. Most of them are just selfish.'

Ally smiled faintly. 'I didn't know you were a feminist.'

'That's just life.' Elizabeth smiled back. 'Life makes you a feminist.'

'Yes, I suppose it does.' She looked at her mother. 'I don't know what I want. Things haven't been good between us lately.'

'But is that enough reason for ending a marriage?' She hesitated, aware that her words might not be popular. 'It's been hard for him, you know, you spreading your wings so suddenly.'

'But why shouldn't I? Aren't I entitled to some freedom too?'

'Yes but it's happened so quickly and so publicly. I think he may be a little jealous of your talent.'

'Matt jealous of *my* talent?' Ally laughed bitterly. 'Oh, Muv, don't be ridiculous! Matt's the biggest thing on television.'

'I'm not sure *he* thinks that at the moment. I think he's feeling pretty insecure. He's taken a big risk and so far it isn't really paying off. But your career's soaring.'

Ally closed her eyes and covered her face with her hands. *Had* she been too caught up with her own success? She simply didn't know any more.

'Look, darling' – her mother's tone was almost humble – 'would you like me to go? You probably want to be alone.'

Ally gazed into her mother's eyes. All her adult life she'd been trying to get away from her mother, and her mother's damning opinions. But suddenly now she desperately wanted her to stay.

'Oh Muv,' she said, struggling against the tears which were once more flowing unstoppably down her cheeks, 'please, whatever you do, don't go.'

For a second her mother held her tightly without saying anything, and there was a catch in her voice when she spoke again. 'You know one thing I've learnt about you lately, Allegra?' Ally half expected some ghastly homily but her mother was proving full of surprises today. 'You'll survive, whatever happens. And do you know why?'

'I've no idea.'

'Because you're much stronger than you think.'

The next morning Elizabeth was the first one down and she hummed to herself as she made herself a cup of coffee. For the first time in years she felt needed. She sat at the sunny breakfast bar with an armful of papers. On a fixed income she only allowed herself the *Sunday Telegraph* and splashed out with the *Mail on Sunday* when she felt really extravagant. Here they got everything, including all the scandal sheets. Elizabeth settled down with pleasure and anticipation and reached for the *News of the World*, leaving the rest in an enormous pile for Ally. So she didn't take in the banner headline in the *Sunday Star*.

'I think you'd better read this.' Belinda passed the *Sunday Star* across the white wooden table on her patio to Matt. Her emotions were fluctuating wildly. She'd known this might happen but now that it had she saw how much pain it was going to cause.

Without looking up from 'Relative Values', his favourite Sunday newspaper feature, Matt took the copy of the *Sunday Star* and glanced at it.

'Jesus Christ, she's written it!' He felt his stomach tighten. 'Without a shred of evidence.' He quickly scanned the lines then flung the paper on to the table. 'Terrific journalism. There's not one fact in the piece. All unnamed colleagues who've seen you and me "growing steadily closer." He read on. 'Oh, great! Here's the parallel with *A Star is Born*. As Ally's sun rises mine is apparently setting. It's all my fault because I can't cope with my wife's success and my own declining ratings. Thanks a bunch, Gloria Mizzi!'

'No one'll believe it.'

'Janey might. Jess might. I've got to talk to them.'

He went to the phone, but to his irritation he still couldn't get through. Ally must have kept it off the hook. But had she seen the *Star* or not? With a sinking feeling he remembered that they had it delivered at home.

The first thing Ally noticed when she woke was the unfamiliar sensation of being alone in the bed. Fighting off a sense of dread at facing the day she had a long bath while listening luxuriously to *The Archers* bumper edition and tried not to think about what she was going to do next.

Lying in the comforting water she decided that she might do precisely nothing. She would wait and see. It was too soon to think about the consequences of a permanent split and anyway they were too awful to contemplate. The effect on Janey and Jess. Splitting their possessions. Leaving Fairlawns. For the moment she would go with the flow. The thought was comforting somehow.

She pulled herself out of the bath, towelled herself vigorously, splashed her boobs with cold water, towelled herself again.

She noticed that the loo roll in the bathroom had finished and fetched a new one from the cupboard on the landing. Halfway through the gesture she stopped and laughed. Her life was falling about her ears and she was changing the bloody lavatory paper! But then, wasn't that women's strength? Their capacity to stick to little rituals? Sometimes she thought it was changing the loo rolls that kept women sane.

When she got downstairs her mother was chuckling at the saucy stories of transvestite vicars and corrupted choirboys that made the *News of the World* sell in its millions.

Ally reached for one of the colour supplements, dislodging the *Sunday Star* at the same time. Her own face stared up at her from under an enormous headline proclaiming, 'ALLY AND MATT MARRIAGE IN RUINS'.

Chapter 27

Ally felt herself turn cold. She'd thought by not giving them any comment they could hardly go ahead. But they had. Gloria Mizzi even cited Ally slamming down the phone as near-conclusive evidence of breakdown.

She sat down, wanting to tear the rag up but was mesmerized by the web of innuendo and hearsay that claimed to chart the end of her relationship. She tried to push her humiliation aside and assess the article simply in terms of how far it would hurt Janey and Jess if any of their schoolfriends were to read it. And then she came to the most devastating quote from a 'close colleague on *The Matt Boyd Show*'. This colleague, said the paper, was not at all surprised at the revelation. 'Matt and Belinda have been in love for months. Everyone knew. This was just a matter of time.'

Ally picked up the paper and flung it across the room, startling her mother and the two dogs. She'd been far too sympathetic to Matt by blaming everything on her success. If half this were true it had started months ago. Even Jess could see that. Forgetting her humiliation or her fear for the girls' reaction Ally knew that she was furiously, blisteringly, consumingly angry.

Danny Wilde and his agent, Jack Saltash, didn't know whether to be more amused or impressed by the lengths Ritchie Page was going to to keep the meeting he'd called for this Sunday morning secret. They'd been flown to Loxley Green Country Club in his own helicopter, then shown through a side entrance to a private room. Danny was beginning to wonder whether maybe Page worked for M.I.5.

'Good morning to you, gentlemen,' Ritchie Page was all twinkling smiles and expensive leisure gear. He looked out of place in it, as though relaxing was somehow very hard work. 'Have you seen this?' He handed a copy of the *Sunday Star* to Danny.

Danny read it quickly. Poor Ally. She'd never mentioned anything about Matt having an affair. Maybe she hadn't even known. Jesus, what a way to find out!

'Well, well, well,' commented Jack Saltash. 'The perfect marriage crumbles. Is this going to be bad for business?'

'On the contrary.' Page smiled. 'The punters will switch on in droves to see how they're taking it.'

'Do you think it's true?' Danny tried to keep his tone neutral. 'After all it's only the *Star*. They could have made it up.'

'No smoke, as they say.' Page looked like Christmas had come early. 'He's always been after Belinda Wyeth, if you ask me.'

'It's not something recent, then?' Danny didn't want to sound too interested, but he couldn't help wondering if the Telethon business had been a catalyst.

'Christ knows.' Page, losing interest, put the paper to one side. 'Anyway, to business. As you know I'm looking for a way of getting Matt Boyd out and you in.'

'And how will you do that?' Jack Saltash was eager to discover how Page intended to get round Matt's contract which, he was reliably informed, had nearly two years to run. 'Buy him out?'

'Not if I can help it. As a matter of fact I have a little plan. I'm hoping to get him to resign.'

'And that's why you asked me to do the Telethon.' Danny Wilde was beginning to understand a number of things that had been puzzling him. 'With the greatest of respect . . .' Danny noticed Page's face suddenly become wary; in his experience people always insulted you after they'd said that. 'Why are you trying to dump Matt? OK, his ratings are taking a bashing, but he'd be all right in a different slot.' Danny Wilde didn't want to shoot himself in the foot but he couldn't work out what Page was up to. 'After all, he's still the most popular face on television.'

'He's also,' Page said slowly, pouring freshly-squeezed blood orange juice into three glasses and topping them up with vintage champagne, 'the shit who screwed me in front of eight million people. I bought Century to get him out.' He handed each of them a glass. 'And that's what I intend to do.'

'I see.' Jeez, Page was a devious bastard! Danny loathed the man, yet he had a certain grudging respect for him, too. Danny hadn't grown up in Liverpool, where the Fly Man and the Hard Man were heroes not villains, without it brushing off on him. 'And what would you be offering to his successor?'

'Would you be interested, by any chance?' Page flicked an invisible crumb off his cashmere cardigan.

'I could be,' Danny exchanged glances with Jack Saltash. His agent had warned him to give nothing away at this meeting. 'My contract with Big City runs out in a couple of months and I haven't signed the new one yet.' He smiled his famous cheeky smile. 'For negotiating purposes.'

'Well don't.' Page raised his glass to Danny's. 'Give me a month. I'll find some way of getting him out by then, trust me.'

Danny, who had an instinctive dislike of anyone who said 'Trust me', shrugged. 'I'll watch this space then.'

'Do.' Ritchie Page walked to the door. 'It's going to be an eventful time for Matt Boyd.'

Danny picked up Page's copy of the *Sunday Star*. 'In every way.' He slipped the paper unobtrusively under his jacket. It wasn't a bad likeness of Ally, but with a face like hers she probably couldn't take a bad photo.

Walking out to the helicopter it struck him for the first time that all this could land him in a right royal mess.

Ally and Elizabeth were picking at a cobbled-together lunch with Jess – Janey was still refusing to leave her room – when there was a knock at the side door.

Ally jumped. 'Mum, could you answer it? If it's anyone from the press, tell them to get lost.'

Elizabeth opened the door gingerly and Susie tumbled in, closely followed by her husband Trevor.

'Jesus, it's war out there! There must be twenty of them and more arriving every minute!' Susie swept the hair out of her eyes and plonked herself down at the table, pouring herself a glass of wine without being invited. 'Ally, I'm so sorry. We had to come when we saw the *Star*.'

'Poor Ally.' Trevor patted her hand, his voice oozing gleeful sympathy. 'You've had to put up with a lot from Matt, haven't you?' Ally felt an irrational desire to leap to Matt's defence. Especially if Trevor was the alternative. Ally remembered how he'd won a prize for the best breathing at their ante-natal classes. Susie had lived in fear that he'd be better at the birth than she was, but by a stroke of luck he'd put his back out reaching for the Vichy spray and had to spend the rest of her labour flat out in the hospital corridor. It had been the most tremendous relief for Susie.

What was it she'd read the other day? A quote from a maverick feminist pointing out that if we went on emasculating men we wouldn't be able to get hot sex from them. Ally tried not to smile. It was impossible to imagine

372

having hot sex with Trevor. Or, indeed, sex at all. He'd be forever asking you what you wanted him to do next. Matt, at least, had had a few ideas of his own.

'Anyway,' chipped in Susie, 'the other reason we came was to tell you he rang. He can't get through because your phone's off the hook so could you call him? Here's the number. He says that even if you don't want to talk to him, he wants to explain things to Janey and Jess.'

'Ally –' Trevor leaned forward helpfully. 'That sounds a very risky thing to do. Would you like me to talk to him for you?'

'No, thank you, Trevor.' Ally tried to imagine the conversation. 'I'd rather talk to him myself.'

Trevor and Susie made no move to leave, evidently hoping she would make the call while they were still there. But since Ally clearly wasn't going to, they eventually left.

As soon as they were out of the door Ally went upstairs to her bedroom and dialled the number she had been given. To her relief it was Matt who answered. She couldn't have borne to talk to Belinda.

'Ally, I'm sorry. I've been trying to get through ever since I saw the piece in the *Star*. How are Janey and Jess taking it?'

Ally paused, trying not to use them as a weapon and failing. 'It was Janey who took the call from Gloria Mizzi asking if we could confirm you'd moved in with Belinda.' As she said it she knew how much it would hurt him. And why not? Let him suffer a bit. She was. 'So she's pretty cut up.'

'Oh, my God!' Ally could hear the guilt in his voice and felt bad, but only a little. 'Poor Janey.'

'Jess seems OK. You know Jess.'

'Ally?'

'Yes?'

'At least let me see them. Tell them how things are myself.'

No matter how angry she was, Ally knew she couldn't refuse him this. 'All right. As long as they want to.'

She knew they would. What made this so hard was that they loved their father. Maybe too much.

Not for the first time Ally was grateful for the consolation of hard work. She still had the final show for *Tell It to Ally* to record. And by a supreme stroke of irony the subject was divorce.

Thank God even the press was getting bored with the Matt and Ally story. There were fewer of them outside the front gate every day.

'It's such a waste,' sighed Susie as she helped Ally choose her clothes for the last show, 'to have all those hacks here and never talk to them. Why don't you open up your heart to them? You'd get brilliant publicity for the show.' Susie smiled beatifically. 'And you could put the boot into Belinda at the same time. Everyone'd be on your side.'

Ally had to admit it was tempting. She remembered when a famous playwright had left his wife for a glamorous author. 'He didn't need to take any shoes,' the discarded wife had pointed out bitchily to the press. 'She has very big feet, you know.'

For the first time Susie noticed that Ally's eyes were red.

'Are you OK?' She put her arm round her friend. 'Are you missing the creep?' She looked into Ally's face. 'Are you hoping he'll come back?'

Ally stared in the mirror. The sixty-four-thousand-dollar question. 'It wouldn't be any different. This isn't just about Belinda. It's about the kind of person I've become.'

374

'I know. You're not little wifey any more. Thank God.'

'I've changed, but Matt hasn't.'

'Men don't.' Susie gave her a quick hug. 'Remember what Natalie Wood said? The only time you can change a man is when he's in nappies.'

Ally laughed.

'The big question,' Susie went on, 'is why are women so much nicer than men? It's enough to turn you gay. Almost.'

Ally decided on a suit. It looked fine and she didn't feel like agonizing over her appearance.

'You've lost weight,' pointed out Susie.

'Worry. It's brilliant for the waistline.' She stared in the mirror and put on her best hardsell accent. 'Yes, viewers, I can highly recommend the thirty-day-marriage-break-up diet to anyone. Just chuck him out and try it now.'

'How's Mum?' Matt hadn't intended to ask about Ally so soon – they were just sitting down at the table in Joe Allen's and he'd meant to keep everything neutral for a while – but it had just come out. All around them, he noticed painfully, were Sunday fathers trying to keep up the intimacy with the kids they'd lost, exactly as he was. Yet he'd only been gone two weeks. Would they still be meeting like this after two years? He put the dreadful thought out of his mind.

'Fine,' Jess answered quickly, not wanting her mother to be seen as the rejected one. 'Busy being a star as usual.'

The waiter stopped to offer Jess a menu. She turned it down. They'd often been here together and she always had the same thing. 'I'll have eggs Benedict with extra hollandaise, please, then pecan pie. And a Diet Coke.'

Matt smiled at this final gesture of optimism. At least

unhappiness hadn't dampened her appetite. 'What about you, Janey?' He looked at his older daughter with concern. She'd hardly spoken at all.

'A Waldorf salad, please.' She fell silent again.

Matt decided this was the moment to speak. 'I wanted to tell you both . . .' He paused, searching for the right words.

'That you still love us even though you aren't living with us,' interrupted Jess rudely.

'As a matter of fact, yes.' Jess's blistering scorn burned through his careful defences like spilt acid.

'Do us a favour, Dad.' Jess gazed round at the people sitting at the bar and at other customers, anywhere but at Matt. 'If you really loved us you wouldn't have buggered off with Belinda, would you?'

'Jessy, this isn't really about Belinda. It's between Mum and me.'

'In other words Mum still thinks you're a selfish shit and you won't admit it and try and change.'

'I am not a selfish shit.' Matt began to sound angry and defensive. 'Your mother's the one who changed.'

'You mean she stopped waiting on you hand and foot. You never used to do a thing. She did all the shopping and the cooking and held the home together. But you lost interest, didn't you, because she was merely a housewife and not an exciting TV producer like Belinda. And then when she got herself an exciting job you couldn't take that either. You're pathetic, Dad!'

For a second, through his pain, Matt felt the truth of Jess's accusations. Then he thought of Danny Wilde. 'Listen, Jessy, it isn't as straightforward as that.'

'Oh, yes it is. And please,' she added as the waiter arrived with her Coke, 'don't say marriage isn't easy.'

'Come back, Dad.' Matt looked up. It was the first time Janey had spoken since they'd arrived. 'It's not the same without you.'

Matt felt himself crease up with guilt and pain. None of this was their fault. And there was no way he could explain the complexities of what had gone wrong between him and Ally.

'I can't, darling. I really can't.'

Grabbing her coat from the back of her chair Janey stood up and ran out of the restaurant. Matt got up too, chucking his wallet at Jess, and went after her.

At that moment their orders arrived. The waiter looked at the chairs, one of them empty and the other lying on its side. He was one of those nice American boys, usually out-of-work actors, Joe Allen's is full of. 'Hi!' He put down the food. 'Typical family outing, huh?' He picked up the chair. 'Enjoy your meal.'

Out on the street Matt couldn't see Janey anywhere. She must have disappeared into Covent Garden market. They were so different. Jess with her barbed put-the-boot-in-before-you-do manner and Janey struggling to contain her raw emotion. But there was one thing they had in common. He'd hurt both of them. Feeling like the shit Jess had accused him of being, Matt went back to face more of her relentless criticism.

Thank God for work, Ally repeated to herself. It was absorbing, demanding, tiring and gave her the solace as well as the friendship she needed as a balm to her mangled emotions. Even Maggy Mann was being nice to her, a mixed blessing which involved extended confidences on the working title, 'Men: Are They Worth all the Hassle?'

And she needed all the help she could get. Ever since the lunch with Matt, Janey had stopped speaking to her altogether. There had been a wall of silence she couldn't break through. And it terrified her, especially since Janey was supposed to do her A levels in two weeks' time.

She picked up her script and headed off for the studio.

It was a difficult show where there would be a gruelling confrontation between a woman divorced against her will by her ex-husband because he'd fallen in love with someone else, and an interview in the studio with their children.

Ally hoped she was up to it.

The first part, between the husband and wife, went beautifully. Ally found that to her relief she didn't warm much to either of them. They were both difficult people who would always have had problems in any marriage. But when she came to the children it was a different matter. The youngest was a boy of six, a spunky little thing worth ten of his parents in Ally's view. He did a touching interview with Ally, telling the story of the breakdown from his point of view. Then, out of the blue, he turned to his unattractive parents, his voice cracking with emotion, and pleaded with them to get back together.

Ally found tears blinding her eyes and when her link to camera appeared on the autocue she couldn't even read it.

'Sorry, Bernie,' she whispered into her microphone, 'but I'm afraid I'm going to have to stop.'

In seconds Bernie appeared on the studio floor and led her into a quiet corner. 'I know, Ally love, I know.' He patted her clumsily. 'I thought this stuff might be a bit near the bone for you. But if it's any consolation it's making you even more sympathetic than usual. They're really responding to you.' He hugged her. 'Only a couple more minutes now.'

Ally smiled through her tears at the irony of television, where emotion was the most desirable currency. The more pain she felt, the better she performed. With her breaking down and the child's appeal, she thought bitterly, it would probably be the most powerful programme in the series.

'OK, Bernie, I'll be all right now.'

Somehow she got through the rest of the show and stumbled back to her dressing room. Five minutes later Bernie appeared with a cup of hot, sweet tea.

'You're like an old auntie,' she scolded him.

Bernie laughed, his small eyes almost disappearing in his leathery skin. 'I care about you, Allegra Boyd. Not just because of all this' – he waved his arm in the direction of the studio – 'but also because I feel responsible for the split with Matt. If we hadn't gone to see Page –'

'Don't worry, Bernie, it's been a long time coming. It isn't anything to do with you.'

Bernie smiled a sad smile, not convinced. 'Now, the really important question is: are you up to coming to the end-of-series party?'

Going to the mandatory party that marked the end of the run was about the last thing on earth Ally felt like doing. But it would have been unheard of to miss it. So she resigned herself to grabbing a quick shower at Century and borrowing a dressing room to change into her black silk shift dress. She'd lost half a stone since the break-up and she was looking terrific. She wondered if those stick-thin models who made you feel like a 73 bus were actually suffering deeply inside. It was a cheering thought.

It was a rule of thumb for end-of-series parties that they had to be at some highly inconvenient venue. This one was no exception. In a sudden spurt of nautical enthusiasm Bernie had hired the battleship HMS *Belfast*. Even though it was docked not far from Tower Bridge, it was in such a well-hidden backwater that it took Ally half an hour to find it.

By the time she finally climbed on board there were at least a hundred people gathered on deck in party mood. As Bernie helped her down the last three steps they turned and gave her a spontaneous round of applause. She resisted the temptation to look round and see if there was someone behind her and surrendered to the moment. This was for her. Even in her usual state she would have been moved, but given how hard she was struggling just to stay in control it was almost too much.

Bernie put a glass of champagne in her hand and pushed her into the crowd.

'Go on, gather a few rosebuds. The dancing starts soon.'

Nikki, standing a few feet away, pulled her into their group. She was in the middle of describing the early morning call Maggy Mann had given to a young pop star she'd taken home with her after interviewing him on *Hello*.

'So she said to him, "Do you like being woken up by fellatio?" And do you know what he said? "Actually my mum usually brings me a cup of tea."'

Ally laughed with the others. Everyone seemed to be having a good time. There was nothing like the party after a series everyone knew had worked out brilliantly.

'Ally, I wondered if . . . you might like to dance?' Ally turned to find one of the newest young male researchers standing next to her, obviously having had to pluck up his courage to ask her.

Her immediate instinct was to refuse. Then she smiled and nodded and he guided her towards the crowded dance floor. At first she felt self-conscious, then she told herself to relax and let the champagne, the loud music and the pleasure of being under the fairy lights on a fabulous dark blue night aboard this ludicrous battleship get to her. She hadn't really danced for as long as she could remember. Even at Janey's party she'd been too busy. Nikki waved at her and she waved back, relieved that she felt absolutely no threat from her partner. He was just having a good time, too. And, looking round her, she realized how close she'd got to people on the team. They'd become real friends.

Half an hour later, exhausted, the sweat running down between her breasts, she excused herself, laughing. She hadn't had such fun in years. She searched for Bernie but he was nowhere to be seen, so she helped herself to another drink and wandered up the other end of the ship, past the lifeboats and the gun barrels, to where it was quiet and dark. Leaning over the rail she looked down into the still waters and over the other side of the Thames at the lights of the City of London. Suddenly her depression flooded back, the awful sense of waste, and of pain caused to Janey and Jess through the failure of their marriage. Matt had gone for ever. Soon they'd have to think about divorce and what to do with the house.

But there was one thing she had to be grateful for: at least she'd be able to earn her own living. And yet, would they still be together if she hadn't got the job on *Hello*? Shivering a little, she tried to convince herself that regret was pointless and destructive. And yet it took an incredibly strong and determined person not to indulge in it. She willed herself to walk back towards the life and the music. She must look ahead.

This time Bernie was standing by the bar, grimacing into his orange juice. He saw her at once, taking in in one swift glance the pain under her taut smile.

He put his arm round her. 'You seem a bit peaky under all the warpaint.' He'd been watching her over the last few weeks and was worried about her, especially after today in the studio. Damn Matt. And damn Life. This ought to have been her greatest moment, instead of which she was losing weight and looking miserable, with great black smudges under her eyes.

'It's Janey. She's being a bit difficult at the moment. She blames me for the breakup.'

'What you need is a bit of pampering. And Uncle Bernie knows exactly the place.'

'Where?'

'A health farm. A nice massage, a facial or two, swimming pool. Just what you need.'

Ally smiled gratefully at his concern. She didn't know what she would have done without Bernie. He'd been wonderful. But she still couldn't go.

'Bernie, I can't. Janey's A levels are in two weeks.'

'Ally love, I'm worried about you.'

'Well, I . . .' Ally stopped. A familiar figure in a chic suit had just sauntered up the gangway. A flush of red spread across Ally's face. It was Danny Wilde. Bernie watched her curiously, remembering how Danny had followed her out of the restaurant after the Telethon. There was obviously something between them but by the look of things it hadn't gone too far. He felt a slight pang of misgiving. There was something he distrusted about Danny Wilde. He suspected that under the obvious charm and the trendy espousing of the female cause, Danny was a loner, someone who didn't really want the hassles of real commitment and average family life. Just as he didn't himself.

At that moment Danny saw them. Immediately he extricated himself from the group he was talking to and came towards them.

Ally steeled herself to appear normal, even though she was feeling ridiculously embarrassed. So much had happened since that night in his car that she'd forgotten the physical effect his closeness had on her.

'Danny, hello.' Bernie handed him a drink. 'You seem to specialize in unexpected entrances.'

Danny grinned. 'Actually, Nikki rang up to invite me and I'd heard such incredible things about the show I had to come and congratulate you all.'

Greaseball, thought Bernie.

Danny turned to Ally, his voice a symphony of sympathy. 'Allegra, I was so sorry to read about you and Matt.'

Like hell, thought Bernie. 'I was just saying' – Bernie gazed at him appraisingly – 'that Ally is exhausted and ought to have a day or two at a health farm.'

Danny looked at her. 'Bernie's right.' His voice was caressing. 'You do seem tired.'

'All right, all right!' Ally put out her hand as if to ward off further pressure. 'I give in.' Maybe if she got out of the house for a night it would take the pressure off Janey.

'I can highly recommend Langdon Hall,' Danny said, 'I go there a lot. An hour up the M1, turn left at junction eight and there you are in paradise.'

'Thanks for the tip.' Bernie sounded unenthusiastic, as though he didn't want to take advice from Danny and Ally wondered why. 'I think I'll get my secretary, Marie, to phone round a few on Monday.'

'Good idea,' agreed Danny, making a mental note to find out from Marie which one they decided on.

Matt read through the fax from Meredith Morgan's agent that Belinda had just handed to him. It was perfectly clear and polite. It stated simply that Miss Morgan was not doing any television shows at present owing to other pressing commitments. She had asked him to convey her thanks that they had invited her.

'Maybe we'd better think up someone else.' Belinda had got so used to rejection lately that she wasn't even surprised.

'Nonsense.' Matt was delving into his briefcase for his address book. 'What's the betting this creep hasn't even asked his esteemed client if she wants to do it?'

'But he's her agent.'

'So what?' Matt was glancing at his watch. It would be

mid-morning in Beverly Hills. Just about acceptable. Meredith would be on her second Martini. He dialled the number she'd given him at the party.

A man answered the phone. Presumably husband number eight.

'Hello. This is Matt Boyd calling from London. I wonder if I could speak to Miss Morgan.'

'I'm afraid Miss Morgan is with her trainer now. Could I take a message?'

Matt debated whether to leave a message – always dangerous since it gave all the power to the other party – or whether to call back. Maybe Meredith Morgan gave her phone number to everyone and then pretended not to know who the hell they were. Matt decided to trust his instincts.

'Yes. Please could you tell her I would very much like to devote my entire show to a tribute to her one day in June. When do you think she would be able to come to London?'

The young man drew in his breath dubiously. 'She has a *very* busy schedule.'

'Ask her anyway, could you?'

'OK, we'll call you when Miss Morgan is free.'

Matt toyed with the idea of holding on, but drew back in time.

'Fine. And tell her I'm looking forward to singing "The Wild Rover" with her again.' Meredith Morgan had Irish ancestry and at their meeting they'd ended up singing rebel songs by the side of a Bel Air swimming pool.

For the next half hour Matt and Belinda both tried to pretend they were extremely busy with other things. When the phone rang and Belinda's secretary answered, they looked at each other and said nothing.

'Matt,' shouted the girl, 'it's Meredith Morgan's husband. She'd love to do the show. She says to call her agent.' Meredith's husband relayed another message. 'And she says to forget the tribute. She's not dead yet.'

Matt whooped and ran three times round Belinda's desk without stopping until Belinda caught him by the hand and made him sit down.

'Matt?' She bit her nail so a thin strip of skin hung from it. 'You don't think this is all banging our heads against a brick wall? That Page has decided to give us the chop anyway and nothing we do will make a blind bit of difference?'

As a matter of fact, Matt had confronted this thought in himself already and instantly dismissed it. They had to keep fighting.

'Nonsense, my girl, what kind of talk is that? When he sees this interview he'll be begging us to come back in the autumn.'

Belinda smiled, basking in the warm glow of his infectious confidence.

It was time to go to the studio, and Matt stood up. It struck him that they'd heard no more from Page about taking them off and replacing them with *Tell It to Ally*. Even the thought of it and of Ally's betrayal still stung him to the quick. He stooped for a moment and glanced down at the sunny early-evening river and wondered what she was doing at this moment.

Ally lay back on the reassuring firmness of the beautician's table and pulled her fluffy white bathrobe close round her. This was bliss! She'd never been to a health farm before. She'd always had vague objections to the places, suspicious of so much dedication to bodily perfection and unable to rid herself of the belief that you could have a holiday in the sun for the same money – and be allowed food and drink, too. But this time she needed it.

And now, lying here, she understood. Health farms weren't about self-sacrifice, they were about self-indulgence.

'You've never had a facial?' the beautician asked incredulously when Ally confessed this was her first, as stunned and shocked as if Ally had just announced she was a transvestite. 'Well, aren't you in for a treat, then?'

And she was. From the moment the girl placed damp eyepatches over her eyes and directed the steam at her stressed-out, clogged-up pores she began to relax. By the end of the afternoon she'd had a manicure, a pedicure, half an hour on the sunbed, a rest in the Jacuzzi and had swum twenty lengths of the pool, watched sedately by a row of mock-Greek statues. At six o'clock she returned, tired but more relaxed than she'd felt for weeks, to her room.

She hummed as she turned her key in the door, looking forward to a quiet supper in her room and an early night. But as she opened the door she realized that someone was in her room. Her pulse raced with fear and she pulled her bathrobe tightly around her.

On the double bed, wearing a bathrobe identical to hers and a teasing, provocative smile, his suntanned skin glowing against the white of the towelling, lay Danny Wilde, reading a copy of the *Guardian*.

Chapter 28

Ally jumped. 'How on earth did you get in here?' she demanded, trying to make her voice as outraged as possible.

'I lied.' He seemed infuriatingly unperturbed by her reaction. 'I'm a good liar. It's one of my redeeming features. Have you had a massage yet?'

'No.' Ally put down the magazine she was carrying realizing she was being deliberately sidetracked. 'If I wanted a massage I would have had one. Now what the hell are you doing in my room?'

'Calm down. You're supposed to be here to relax. What I'm offering is a genuine, *genuine* massage. You don't even have to take your clothes off. Now lie down, there's a good girl.'

Ally knew she should refuse. That she should chuck him out of her room now this minute, that his presence here was disgracefully presumptuous. But she'd been feeling so incredibly lonely since Matt went, and with even Janey turning against her, the teasing tenderness in his voice was too much for her.

Obediently she lay down on the towel he laid on the bed, her pulse thumping in her head, and shrugged the bathrobe discreetly off her shoulders, agonizingly conscious of his nearness but overwhelmed with a sudden desire to forget everything and to feel his golden skin against hers and his arms around her. You could only be strong for so long.

Lying on the bed she closed her eyes as Danny massaged aromatherapy oils into her taut shoulders. The effect was miraculous. She began to feel that all the pain of rejection and of betrayal, of failure and of regret, had somehow transferred itself into her nerve-knotted back, to be pummelled and kneaded and rolled away by Danny's expert fingers.

She kept her eyes tightly closed and abandoned herself to the pressure of those insistent fingers, kneading her back in an ecstatic sensation of pleasure mixed with pain until a moan of release escaped her.

'Wakey, wakey. Dr Wilde's magic show endeth here.'

She opened her eyes and smiled, almost regretful that the wonderful sensation was stopping.

'You can do it!' she said in surprise. 'You really can do a massage.'

'I've got a lot of skills you don't know about.' Very lightly he brushed the nape of her neck with his lips. 'Yet.'

She looked up over her shoulder at the famous lopsided smile. Danny leaned down and kissed the top of her back. Then, very gently, he turned her over and began to undo the belt of her towelling wrap.

'I can honestly say, Ally Boyd' – he kneeled down in front of her and slipped the robe slowly down inch by inch till it fanned around her on the bed – 'that I've never waited for anyone as long as I've waited for you.'

Ritchie Page leaned back in his deep leather chair and smiled. The Boyds' marriage breakup hadn't featured in his scheme of things but it had done him nothing but good. Matt Boyd's halo had slipped more than a little in the public eye now that he'd abandoned his family and gone off with Another Woman. The fact that Belinda had been portrayed by the press as a hard-bitten career woman hadn't done any harm either. Even some of the hitherto loyal members of the programme team were mumbling complaints at Matt and Belinda working and living together.

Things were cooking nicely. Page reached into his pile of post, ignoring various important-looking letters, and pulled out *The Matt Boyd Show*'s ratings. Down another point.

He knew that their offices were buzzing with a new excitement. Bernie Long had told him that he thought Matt's new idea was a cracker. But it was too late. If the format worked he'd give it to someone else.

Nothing could save it now.

Ally woke up, stretching luxuriously, and reached across the bed. There was an empty space. Her eyes snapped open. Danny wasn't there. It was only her sense of loss, of having failed at something that mattered, still so sharp in her memory that was making her overreact like this. He'd probably gone swimming.

Two minutes later the door opened and Danny appeared holding a spare bathrobe and grinning broadly. He removed it to reveal a bottle of white wine and two packets of frozen carrots.

Ally burst out laughing. 'Where did you get that? It says no alcohol on the premises.'

'From the kitchen. It's cooking wine. I told the chef I'd interview him on next week's show.'

'And will you?'

Danny winked. 'We're off the air next week.'

'And what are the carrots for?'

'Cooling the wine, of course. What did you think they were for?'

Ally laughed again. She had no idea any longer of whether what they were doing was mad or utterly sensible. All she knew was that she didn't feel desperate any more.

Danny put down the carrots. 'Come here, agony auntie. I've got a problem that needs sorting out.'

'So I see.' Ally undid the belt of his robe. 'It's a very big problem, isn't it?'

He reached for her. 'I've never had any complaints before.'

As she drove home after her night at the health farm Ally realized she had a silly giveaway smirk and a tendency to giggle at the slightest encouragement, both highly unsuitable to a woman in her position. She parked the car in the double garage and forced her features into some sign of seriousness, then got out and lifted her overnight bag from the boot.

Jess was waiting on the steps.

'Mum! Wow!' Jess grabbed Ally's bag and carried it in for her. 'You look as though you've been on holiday!'

'Wonderful things, sunbeds,' Ally lied. 'Where's Janey?' She was desperately hoping Janey would be less hurt and angry.

'Round the back reading *Middlemarch* with Adam.'

'That sounds encouraging. Has she been doing any work?' She kept her voice low, knowing Janey would hate her checking up.

'Not so's you'd notice. She keeps saying she doesn't want to go to university anyway.'

Ally sighed and put her arm round Jess. 'Let's go and find them.'

On the sloping back lawn Janey and Adam lounged still wearing, to Ally's amazement, black leather despite the glorious weather. Adam stood up.

'Hello, Mrs Boyd, you look well.'

'Hello, Adam. Yes, it was very restful.'

Janey held her hand up against the sun and surveyed her mother. 'Hello, Mum. Was it fun?'

There was no smile, Ally noted, but no open hostility either. Definite progress.

'I must say, you really *do* look fabulous.' Jess was watching her curiously. 'Are you sure you didn't meet some gorgeous hunk in the Jacuzzi?'

Despite herself Ally felt herself go red and tried to change the subject.

But not soon enough for Janey. Without another word she jumped up and ran into the house.

'Did I put my foot in it?' Jess looked at her mother bemused.

''Course you didn't,' said Adam, turning to follow Janey into the house. 'It's just Janey. She's a bit sensitive at the moment.'

As she lay in bed with Danny three nights later, Ally was beginning to realize how hard it was going to be to keep their relationship secret. Instead of meeting in public she'd come to his flat after recording the voiceover for her final show, and she intended to leave soon. There was no way she could stay the night because of Janey and Jess.

'Do you know,' Danny said, stroking her back, 'you're the first woman I've been to bed with whose phone number I don't have? Will you give it to me?'

Ally smiled. 'Of course. But for God's sake don't say who you are. Janey couldn't cope.'

'OK.' Danny kissed her. 'I'll say I'm Tubby the Tuba if you want.'

Ally giggled. 'Just say you're from the show.'

'You know, Ally' – Danny's face was suddenly serious – 'You'll have to decide what you want. If we're going to go on seeing each other you ought to tell them. Before someone else does.' He touched her cheek gently.

As she curled, suddenly silent, in the crook of his arm it struck him that the same argument applied to him. When was he going to tell her that he was negotiating with Ritchie Page to replace *The Matt Boyd Show*? He, too, ought to do it now before she found out some other way.

But charming though he was, Danny was a coward and he knew it. And he didn't want to spoil the moment. So he curled up next to her and within minutes they were both asleep.

Ally sat up aware of the total darkness in the room. Jesus, it was two a.m. She scuttled out of bed and into her clothes. She looked down at Danny's sleeping face and decided not to disturb him. Then she remembered how bereft you felt on waking when you expected someone to be by your side and they weren't. Gently she shook him.

'Got to go. I've left my number by the bedside. See you soon.'

Sleepily he raised himself on to one elbow. 'Hey, this is like "Wake Up Little Suzy" in reverse. You're scared in case your kids find out you've been out all night.' He blew her a kiss and disappeared under the duvet, grateful for one thing at least. He didn't have to drive her home.

Ally parked as quietly as she could, wishing for once that they'd settled for something quieter than gravel in the drive. She turned the car lights out and tiptoed towards the house. With luck Janey and Jess would have been asleep for hours.

In the kitchen everything was silent. Ally cursed that her brain was suddenly racing and decided to make herself some hot milk. She had just put on a small saucepan to boil when the front door opened again. Ally stood stock still, imagining a burglar. She should have locked it. In a shaft of moonlight she made out the shortest skirt she'd ever seen, almost but not quite covered by a black leather jacket.

'Janey!' The fear she'd felt made her voice sharper

than she'd intended. 'Where the hell have you been? It's three o'clock!'

'At Adam's. He's just dropped me back.' Janey walked towards her mother. 'And isn't that a bit rich coming from you?' Her voice was cold and insulting. Ally had never heard her speak like this before. 'I mean, whose bed have you crawled out of?'

Cut to the quick, Ally raised her hand and slapped Janey across the face. The sound rang out, sharp and echoey, in the empty kitchen as the milk boiled over in the saucepan.

Janey turned and fled, sobbing, from the room.

Ally removed the pan from the Aga and sat at the table with her head in her arms. She'd never hit Janey before, even when she was a child.

Finally, twenty minutes later, she dragged herself miserably up the stairs. She climbed wearily into bed and buried her face in the pillow. Not only did she have to cope with her marriage breaking up and trying to keep her affair a secret as well as fending off the press and doing a demanding job. But now her daughter despised her. As she finally drifted off into an uneasy sleep the phone beside her on the bedside table began to ring. Ally groped for it, furious, guessing that it might be Danny pulling some stupid joke.

But it wasn't Danny. It was Matt's mother Mona. Ally had never heard Mona other than unflappably calm. But not tonight. Joe had been rushed into Bristol General Hospital and no one was sure how long he would last. Mona obviously knew about the breakup, but not where Matt was staying. Ally could hear her struggle between tact and panic as she tried to ask for his number.

Ally knew it off by heart. And as she gave it to Mona, irrationally she begrudged Belinda the right to be the one who was with Matt when he needed to be comforted.

As Mona repeated the number. Ally could hear the hysteria rising in her voice.

'Do you want me to ring him for you?'

'Ally love, would you?' Mona sounded relieved and grateful. 'I must get back to Joe.'

'Absolutely.' Ally tried not to sound as reluctant as she felt. 'What ward is he in?'

'The Clifton Ward. It's on the second floor.'

Ally said goodbye and put down the phone. She waited a moment before dialling Belinda's number.

It was Belinda who answered. 'Yes?' Her voice was angry and sleepy at the same time.

'Can I speak to Matt? It's Ally.'

'Christ almighty!' The anger won. 'Do you know what time it is?'

'Yes, I do know what time it is. His father's been taken ill.'

Matt came on the line, his voice alert. 'Ally? What's this about Dad?'

'Your mother just rang. He's in Bristol General Hospital. Clifton Ward. Can you go?'

'Oh, Jesus! What's happened?' She could hear him struggling to stay calm.

'She didn't say. She was a bit upset.' Ally felt inefficient that she hadn't got more details. 'Just that they were worried if he'd last. Do you want me to come?'

There was a fractional pause. 'Better if I go alone. But thanks for the offer. I'll keep in touch. I must get moving.'

'Matt –' Ally paused, searching carefully for the right words. In recent years Matt and his father had had a relationship that was both distant and uncomfortable. 'I know you find it hard to get through to him, but he loves you.'

'I know.' Matt's voice softened. 'I just hope I'm not too late to tell him I feel the same.'

As she listened, propped up on the other side of the bed, her dressing gown pulled round her, Belinda couldn't help feeling jealous and excluded. When they talked to each other they still sounded like a couple.

Matt put the phone down and Belinda almost said, 'What about tomorrow's show?' but thought better of it. Someone else could stand in if necessary. Instead she also asked if he wanted her to come with him. She was learning fast. But Matt shook his head. It would be better alone.

Matt got out of bed and fumbled in the wardrobe for some comfortable clothes. It wasn't light yet and the air was cold and damp even in the flat. His heart was thumping as he pulled on a pair of jeans. Oh, God, let there be time!

Outside her mother's door Janey stood in the dark, trembling. She had been about to knock and apologize to her mother for what she'd said when she'd heard the phone ring. Then she'd heard the conversations about her grandfather.

Everything, it seemed, in her world was suddenly crumbling. All the security that had seemed so rock solid. The parents who loved her and each other. Her grandparents. Now the whole thing was tumbling down leaving her alone and shivering in the dark. Next it would be Adam. And she would fail her A levels, and have to give up her place at Sussex University. She knew she would. She ran back to her room and buried herself under her duvet, sobbing.

From her bedroom Ally thought she heard the faintest sound and decided she was imagining it. She wondered for a moment if she should check it out, but she was dog-tired and she couldn't face another confrontation with Janey.

As she sat in the darkness listening, she came to a decision. She was going to have to stop seeing Danny till Janey settled down. She couldn't risk her finding out about them. It was only two weeks until Janey's A levels. It would be unutterably selfish not to wait until they were over. She turned over to go to sleep, and she knew she'd made the right decision.

She'd talk to him and explain that they'd have to put things on hold. But as she closed her eyes, she felt a sudden sense of loss. After all, someone like Danny might not be prepared to hang around.

And there was one other thing she'd have to do. Make a lightning visit to see Joe. She'd always loved Joe for his gentle kindness, and if something did happen and she hadn't said goodbye it would be on her conscience for the rest of her life.

As Matt drove through the night down the empty motorway, sharing the road with nothing but a few long-distance lorries, he felt wide awake. He was filled with an urgency bordering on desperation to get there and make his peace before it was too late. He'd heard so often of people leaving in the morning with angry words and never seeing each other again, a heart attack at the bus stop, a random car crash. Or parents and children, like him, grown distant over the years with all the things they'd never said and too many that they had.

He drew into a motorway service station for a quick coffee. The neat lady sweeping the floors reminded him briefly of his mother.

For more than forty years of marriage she had been the rock they had leaned on, his father most of all. The perfect wife and mother, her aspirations channelled into giving her children the things she'd never had.

And as far as Matt could tell, they'd been happy. Even though the words 'I love you' had never been spoken, they rang out even so, disguised as, 'More tea, pet?' or hidden in the offer of the last slice of cake on the plate.

Suddenly Matt felt choked with emotion and he ran back to the car. He could be there in an hour.

He stopped for petrol just outside Bristol and to buy flowers. Recognizing him, the lady gave him the best bunch and called him 'Matt'. He liked this West Country openness. No elbows in the ribs and whispers, just, 'Good morning, Matt.' Her voice had the soft burr of Bristol, where the greeting for men and women, friends and strangers, is 'All right, my duck?'

Matt got back in the car. The hospital was ten minutes away. He looked at his watch. Seven fifteen. He wondered if they would let him in.

The reception area was empty. So much for hospital security. Above the lifts a maze of signs indicated the wards. Matt got in.

When he finally found Clifton Ward it was alive with activity. Breakfasts and blanket baths. Matt looked round for someone in authority. Eventually a tall, well-built Sri Lankan nurse in dark blue noticed him and walked over. 'I'm sorry, but visiting hours aren't till nine o'clock. You'll have to wait outside.' Her face changed almost comically when she realized who she was talking to. 'Mr Boyd?' Her voice lost its irritation and became brisk and reassuring. 'I didn't know you were *that* Mr Boyd. We're all fans of yours here. I'm the ward sister, by the way. Your father's over here.'

Matt was relieved it wasn't going to be a battle to be allowed to see him. At least there were some advantages to a famous face. He followed in her efficient blue wake, suddenly nervous about what he'd find.

'How is he?' Matt stepped past a breakfast trolley of rubbery scrambled eggs and bloodless sausages. The over-cooked smell made him almost retch. 'What happened?'

'He had a stroke.' The sister stopped and lowered her voice. 'He hasn't regained consciousness yet so we don't know the effects. Your mother's with him.' She began walking again. 'We're hoping he'll come round soon. Maybe you being here will do the trick.' She glanced around the ward, and Matt noticed for the first time that everyone was watching him. 'It's certainly working for everyone else.'

At the end of the ward Matt saw a small figure, frail, almost childlike, propped up against the pillows on a high bed. His eyes were closed and no life flickered in his face. By his side sat Mona, calmly knitting, and as the tears of emotion fought into Matt's eyes he remembered how during every childhood illness – whooping cough, flu, fevers – he had looked up and found his mother knitting by his side.

And then she saw him. 'Matt, love, you've come.'

Matt held her as the sister quietly pulled the curtains round the bed and their sorrow.

'Of course I came, Mum. How is he?'

His mother's face was pinched. 'They don't know yet. I wish he'd wake up.'

Matt sat down by the bed and took his father's hand, fuelled by the absurd fantasy that his presence might jolt his father back into life. 'Hello, Dad.' He squeezed the cold hand gently. 'It's Matt.'

Nothing happened. There was to be no miracle. Life, after all, wasn't Hollywood, even for Matt Boyd.

There was a sudden coughing fit from the bed next door and a querulous request for a urine bottle.

Matt stood up, feeling helpless, wanting to be able to make a difference. 'He should be in a private room. I'll see about it.'

'No, love.' His mother pulled him back down. 'We're ordinary people. We believe in the National Health. Your father wouldn't want to go private. The treatment's the same out here or in there. We've always been proud of that.' She took his hand. 'Besides, when he wakes up he'll like it better here. Plenty to look at. People to swap symptoms with. Stuck in a private room he'd only have the telly.'

Matt laughed in spite of everything. *Only the telly.* Somehow it put the shenanigans over his show into rude perspective. His mother was right. It was, after all, only telly.

And suddenly tiredness and the shock caught up with him and his eyes began to close.

'You should go and sleep. Nothing's going to happen yet. I've been trying to get hold of Tim.' Matt's younger brother worked for Shell and spent most of his time flying round the world. 'They're trying to track him down. I hope he'll be in time.'

'Come on, Mum, don't talk like that. Dad's going to get better.' His mother smiled wanly and patted his hand. Matt thought longingly of staying in a five-star hotel and knew his mother would be deeply offended. 'Have you got room for me at home?'

'Of course. I made up the spare bed.' His mother smiled. 'Just in case. Matt?'

'Yes, Mum?'

'We're so sorry about you and Ally.'

Matt felt a stab of guilt. He'd meant to come and explain in person instead of sending them the short note he'd ended up writing a few weeks ago.

'Don't worry, love. Tell us about it when you feel like it.' Involuntarily she glanced at the bed. She was so used to there being two of them. A small tear slid down the side of her face until she sniffed it into submission. 'Off you go. Come back after you've had a good sleep.'

★

'No, Ally, I *don't* understand.' Danny's voice had a puzz-led petulance about it as he opened the front door of his flat to let Ally in. 'I don't understand why you don't want to go on with our relationship, and I certainly don't see why you've got to chase after Matt down to Bristol.'

Ally sighed as she sat down on his ridiculous squashy-lipped sofa. Clearly, until now Danny's life had not been vexed by complex questions of divided loyalty. 'Duty' or 'family responsibility' were not words in his vocabulary. As he said, he hadn't seen his own family for five years. Families, to him, were something to get away from.

'Look, Danny –' Ally knew she probably sounded like his mother, but what the hell? 'I've got obligations. I can't just drop them or pretend they don't exist. If Janey fails her A levels it'll be my fault. I can't risk her finding out about us. And it isn't Matt I'm chasing after. My father-in-law may be dying. I want to say goodbye.'

Danny looked at her sceptically. 'You'd better go, then.' He remembered sourly that he had changed the sheets when she'd called earlier. 'But don't expect me to be waiting when you get back.'

Ally took a last sip of the wine he'd given her. She was too old for this. At eighteen this sort of behaviour had made her want to kill herself. Now it was just irritating.

'Goodbye, Danny.'

'Goodbye, Ally.'

As he watched her leave it struck him that maybe it was for the best. It was getting too deep for him. And at least this way he wouldn't have to tell her about trying to take over Matt's show.

Matt lay back in the narrow plastic bath with its built-in bathmat to stop you slipping but which was sticking uncomfortably in his back. The bathroom was freezing and smelt faintly of Izal, a product he didn't know still existed. He realized how much he missed his *en suite* bathroom with deep pile carpet. Except that it wasn't his any more.

Downstairs the phone began to ring. Matt jumped out on to the fluffy bathmat and reached for a small rough towel from the unheated rail.

It was his mother and her words made him forgot any minor discomforts he might be suffering.

'He's come round!' Her voice was overjoyed. 'Oh, Matt, he's woken up and he's all right!'

'Mum, that's amazing!' He raised one hand in a fist of victory and his towel fell off. He hardly noticed. 'I'll come straight away.'

As he walked across the ward half an hour later carrying a copy of the *Daily Mirror*, his father's lifelong paper, and at least six different paper bags of fruit, Matt was conscious of nervousness as well as joy. He and his father had always had a difficult relationship. They'd never talked much and Matt's success had only widened the gulf.

'Dad.' Matt bent down to kiss him. 'Thank God you're OK.'

Joe patted him, looking round in embarrassment. Mona watched them for a moment and decided to leave them alone. She knew that if she was there they'd rely on her to do the talking instead of having to face up to their own emotions.

'I think I'll go and see if the tea bar's open and bring us back a cup.'

Matt sat down, appalled that he, the great chat-show host, couldn't think of anything to say. Unconsciously he reached for his father's hand. As it lay in his he was aware of how few times he'd actually ever held it. He remembered its roughness, and the chapped, split skin. His father had spent a lifetime mixing cement on icy scaffolding. Gloves were impractical for a bricklayer. But he'd never complained, just run his hands under cold water from time to time when they started bleeding.

Joe looked down at his hand, held tight in his son's, and broke the awkward silence.

'I was always ashamed of me hands.' He tried to pull his away but Matt held on. 'Brickie's hands. I didn't hold yours often. I thought you might be shy of touching mine.'

Matt felt his eyes blur over with tears. All those years he hadn't known why his father never touched him. He'd thought him distant and unloving.

'Oh, Dad.' Matt held his father's hand up and kissed it, the tears now running down his face, glad of the screen surrounding them. What a waste! What a waste of all that time they could have shown some tenderness.

'Hang on, lad.' Joe patted his arm 'I haven't died, y'know. I've recovered!'

Matt looked at his father and smiled. It was true. He could have gone without them ever getting a chance to talk like this. But he hadn't.

'I love you, Dad.'

'And I love you too, son.' Joe's watery blue eyes were smiling in a carbon copy of Matt's own. 'Now for pity's sake let's change the subject.'

'First or second?'

Recognizing Ally at once, the booking clerk at Paddington Station was already punching up a first class ticket. She didn't usually travel first class, but ever since the Telethon, to her surprise, a few people recognized her and struck up conversations. Just at the moment she didn't feel up to it. First class at least gave you some protection.

'Platform three in ten minutes.'

Ally scuttled off, bag in hand, avoiding everyone's gaze and making straight for the train. Then at least she could hide behind a paper. Though with her luck she'd be next to someone whose idea of a good journey was telling their life story, no holds barred, to a total stranger.

Once on the train, instead of reading her paper, she drifted off to sleep, imagining Matt's face when she turned up. Maybe Danny was right. She should be asking herself who she was going for.

'So what was this rubbish about you and Ally splitting up?' Joe drank his cup of tea with relish as his wife chatted with the Sri Lankan sister at the far end of the ward. 'We got your letter and Mona showed me some article in the *Sun*. Of course, I don't believe a word I read in the Tory press.'

It was the question Matt had been dreading. 'I'm afraid it's true, Dad. We're living apart. Trying to decide what to do next.'

'Whatever for, Matt? We always had you down as happy.'

'I wish I knew, Dad.' Matt was conscious of how unconvincing this must sound to his father, married to one woman for forty years. 'Somehow we drifted apart. It seemed to go wrong when she started in television. We were both so busy. I suppose I'd got used to having her at home.'

'She stopped putting you first, you mean?'

Matt glanced at his father quickly, searching for signs of irony. But his father wasn't an ironic man. Joe gazed across the ward at Mona.

'We've been married forty-three years, your mother and I, most of it happy.'

'And?'

403

'There's one thing she's never forgiven me for.'

Matt was intrigued. He'd never noticed any rifts in his parents' marriage.

'When you were eleven she decided she wanted to be a teacher.' Joe drank the last of his tea and put down the cup on the bedside locker. 'She didn't want to be a helper in a primary school. She wanted to be a proper teacher. She wanted to teach maths. At secondary school. But she needed more qualifications.'

Matt listened, amazed. His mother had never mentioned any of this.

'And to get that she needed to go to teacher training.' Joe picked at the threadbare hospital bedspread.

'Yes?'

'I said no.'

Matt was beginning to understand. 'Because she wouldn't put you first any more?'

Joe looked away, clearly struggling to find the right words.

'No, not because of that. I could cope with that.'

Matt smiled at the implication *he* couldn't.

'I said no because I thought she'd leave me behind.'

Matt felt a shock of recognition. He'd always thought his father and he so different, but weren't they talking about the same emotion? Suddenly Matt recognized it for what it was: insecurity. The need to be at the centre of his family's universe not because he made them secure, but because they gave *him* stability. But at what cost to themselves? Hadn't he fallen into a habit at least as narrow as his father's way of life, needing everyone to revolve round him as Ally had said? Except that unlike his father he hadn't had the honesty to admit it.

'And do you know what?' His father hadn't finished yet. 'It's been the only cloud in our whole marriage. If she asked me again tomorrow I'd say go, we can manage, spread your wings a little. We want you with us, but we want you happy! Not feeling you've missed out. That life's somehow passed you by.'

They both saw Mona bustling towards them, her brisk, efficient self. All those years he thought she'd been happy with her lot, always there for them because she wanted to be. Now he realized there was another dream she'd been harbouring but had never had the chance to make it come true.

'Matt' – Joe took his hand again, dropping his voice so Mona couldn't hear – 'don't make the same mistake I did. Don't wreck your marriage because you're not big enough to let Ally have her dreams.'

Matt sat with his eyes closed. His father had put his finger so precisely on what had gone wrong with their marriage. 'You know, Dad,' Matt said, opening his eyes, 'I think I might take your advice.'

Joe smiled gently. 'It'd be the first time.'

'What are you two on about?' Mona looked at them both affectionately.

'Men's talk,' Joe said gruffly.

'Oh, is that all?' Mona turned to straighten the fruit in the bowl while behind her back Joe winked. 'I thought it might be something interesting for once.'

As Ally got off the train at Temple Meads Station and hailed a cab, Matt was being reassured by the senior registrar that his father would be discharged in a few days' time. It was an incredible relief.

A few hundred yards from the hospital Ally's taxi drove past a Radio Rentals shop and she caught sight of Maggy Mann's face being beamed out on eight screens. It gave her a sudden inspiration.

'Could you stop here a moment, please?'

In one corner of the window was a tiny TV, small

enough to carry round with you – and perfect for watching television from a hospital bed. It was just the thing to cheer Joe up.

Ally had a lot of faith in Joe. In his quiet way he was a fighter. By buying this she'd be making an act of faith in his recovery.

To Ally's amazement the salesman explained it was not only a television but a video too, a sort of video Walkman. Perfect! She imagined Joe's pleasure as he showed it off to his fellow patients.

Sitting in the car outside the hospital Matt remembered what his father had said. *Don't make the same mistake I did.* And he admitted for the first time exactly how much he'd been missing his home and family. Suddenly they seemed incredibly, irreplaceably precious. And he came to a decision. He'd go home. He would apologize to all of them, to Janey and Jess as much as to Ally. He'd admit it had been his fault. He'd turn over a new leaf and be a New Man.

He imagined their smiles of affectionate cynicism. Reality dawned for a moment. Maybe the cynicism would be just cynicism. Pushing the thought from his mind he accelerated out of the car park and headed for the ring road out of the city towards Surrey and home.

Ally's taxi-driver hooted at the pinstriped consultant in a Range Rover who was in the act of parking so selfishly that no one else could reach the dropping-off point outside the hospital.

'All right for some!' yelled the taxi-driver rudely. He'd been clamped parking in the staff parking area last week when he'd only nipped inside for two minutes to pick up a fare and was feeling particularly bitter.

The consultant, acting as though he owned the place, which he more or less did, ignored him and took his time.

It was another five minutes before Ally was deposited in front of the hospital. Finding no one to ask where Joe's ward was she ran apprehensively up the stairs and down endless confusing institutional corridors until she eventually found the right one.

To her delight, Joe was sitting up chatting to the man in the next bed. 'Ally, what a lovely surprise!' Joe's face broke into a smile of genuine pleasure.

'Joe!' Ally leaned down and put her arms round him. He felt heart-wrenchingly fragile. 'You don't look ill at all.'

'He did it just to keep us on our toes.' Mona stood up and kissed Ally warmly. 'Wanted to remind us how much we'd miss him.'

Joe smiled. 'Seems to have worked, too.'

'I brought you something to keep you amused.' Ally handed the box she was carrying to Joe. 'I had a feeling you were going to pull through.'

Joe's face lit up like a kid at Christmas as he opened it. 'It's a telly. Bloody hell! I've never seen such a small one.'

'And not only a telly.' Ally laughed and produced some tiny tapes. 'It's a video too.'

'My God!' Mona grinned. 'I hope you haven't bought him anything racy. He'll have a heart attack as well.'

'I think we should be safe with *Two Hundred Greatest Goals*.'

'Oh, I don't know.' Mona shook her head dubiously. 'Didn't they have *Pigeon Fancying for the Over Sixties*?'

Joe patted the seat next to him. 'Thanks, love. It'll make all the difference. All I've got so far is Jeffrey Archer and poetry.' He looked at Mona accusingly.

'I thought he might as well improve his mind.' Mona touched his cheek. 'There's plenty of scope.'

Ally watched them tease each other affectionately and noticed for the first time that Matt wasn't around.

'Where's Matt? I thought he'd be here.'

Mona and Joe exchanged glances.

'He's gone, love. Once he knew I wasn't going to peg out, off he went. I must admit' – Joe tried not to sound too knowing – 'I rather thought he'd gone to try and find you.'

Ally looked startled. Joe took her hand for a moment, and studied it. 'You've nice hands, love.' He looked up. 'Matt's all right, you know, Ally. He might do stupid things sometimes but basically he's a good man.' He patted her hand, wondering if she knew what he was talking about. 'That means more to me than all the fame rubbish.'

Ally stared into his faded blue eyes, once as sharp and alert as Matt's, and he could see that she understood. She smiled, thinking of Matt's bright blue eyes.

'I think it does to him too.' She felt a sudden lurch of excitement. 'Maybe I'd better get home, then.' She grinned at her father-in-law and stood up.

Danny Wilde paced restlessly in his dressing room. When he'd said goodbye to Ally he'd felt a certain relief. It was getting too complicated for him. And he didn't like the way he was the one who was being pushed to the margins of her life. In his other relationships Danny was used to being centre-stage. But today the prospect of not having her at all had hit him full force. And Danny had come to a reluctant conclusion: he couldn't let her go that easily.

The problem with Ally, he'd concluded, was that she didn't want to make up her mind. She wanted Danny to stay on hold, but she wanted Matt in the picture too. The stalemate could go on indefinitely.

Unless he did something to unbalance it.

Almost hesitantly Danny reached for the phone and dialled Ally's number.

Chapter 29

As Matt turned off the motorway with only another twenty miles to go until he got home he felt a ludicrous sense of excitement. Ludicrous, he knew, because he'd had absolutely no sign that anything had changed from Ally's point of view. Maybe it was his father's recovery and the sense of life being so valuable that made him push all that from his mind. He was also, he had finally to admit, absolutely terrified.

At least the weather seemed to be on his side. He'd only been away for a day or so but it seemed almost like coming back to another life. The golden light of late afternoon was casting shadows over the fields on either side of the winding road. In Fairley Green roses dazzled from the small suburban front gardens. For a moment he envied the people who lived in the neat rows; their predictable, settled lives.

Then he realized what a stupid assumption that was. There was probably as much mayhem and passion and tragedy behind those neat façades as there was in his own life.

Then he thought of Ally sitting in the garden in her favourite place under the tree. Maybe he was being irrationally optimistic. Maybe she'd throw him out like she did last time. In less than half an hour he'd find out.

When the phone rang Jess was in the garden and Janey was upstairs in her room desultorily reading her notes. Jess got to it first and as she picked up the receiver she noticed the answering machine was on. *Hello*, said Ally's voice, *we can't come to the phone at the moment. Please leave a message after the tone.* Jess sensed uncertainty in the person on the other end of the line and almost said something, then decided against it. She loved the power answering machines gave you to listen in and decide if you wanted to speak to the caller.

'*Ally,*' a male voice said, so low it was almost a whisper. 'It's no good. You've got to ring me.' There was a definite pause and Jess wondered if the caller would finish the message in the space provided. 'I love you.'

Jess stood transfixed, not only by the message but because she recognized that voice. But who was it?

'Janey!' she shouted, running up the stairs two at a time towards her sister's bedroom. 'Come and listen to this.'

Janey allowed herself to be dragged reluctantly down to the phone. Anything was better than revision.

'Mum's got an admirer. I know the voice but I can't work out whose it is.' Jess rewound the tape and pressed the incoming messages play button. 'Do you recognize it?'

Janey listened, the blood draining from her face as though she were in shock. 'Yes, I recognize it.' She stood in complete silence for a fraction of a second.

'Well who is it then?' Jess demanded impatiently.

'It's Danny Wilde.'

'Don't be silly!' Jess stared at her sister incredulously. She had to be wrong. There was no way Danny Wilde could be in love with her mother. They hardly knew each other and anyway he was ten years younger. Janey had to be wrong. Maybe it was some kind of joke. As she reached for the button to play the tape again, the doorbell rang.

They both jumped.

At Century Television Belinda cracked a bottle of champagne and handed it to everyone on the team in plastic cups. Matt's call had definitely worked. Meredith Morgan's agent had just huffily faxed them to confirm the travel arrangements. Miss Morgan was expecting a suite at the new and vastly expensive Lanesborough Hotel on Hyde Park Corner but Ritchie Page could afford it.

Last time she'd been on a chat-show, according to Matt, she'd charged a Gucci handbag to room service. When challenged she'd replied waspishly that men put hookers on room service but she preferred something with a little class.

And already the *Daily News* had heard about her appearance. They wanted to splash it across the whole of their centre spread. Things were going brilliantly. *The Matt Boyd Show* would be back where it belonged in the ratings. And watch Ritchie Page drop it after that!

Belinda closed the door of the office and wondered what time Matt would be back. He'd only been away one night and she'd missed him incredibly. And it was only when someone else did the show that you realized quite how good Matt was. The stand-in they'd hired had been perfectly competent, but he reminded you of the difference between skill and charm. Matt, by some lucky gift of fate, had both.

She sat down and tried to put Matt firmly out of her mind. Tonight they'd go out to dinner. She'd tell him all about the show. And then maybe they'd go to bed early.

Belinda smiled.

'Dad! Jess flung her arms round Matt's neck and squeezed the breath out of him. 'It's Dad, Janey!'

Suddenly his other arm was full too. Matt closed his eyes and held on to both of them, feeling the same flood of love he'd known when they were small children.

They stood locked together for almost a minute before Jess untangled herself and pulled him inside.

'Why did you ring the doorbell?' she asked. 'It's your house.'

There was no answer to that. He looked round. 'Where's Ally?'

'In Bristol.'

'But I've just come from there.' He tried to hide his sharp disappointment. Maybe she'd gone to see his father. That would be like her. 'What's she doing there?'

'She didn't say,' Janey replied. 'Just that she'd be back later. Is Grandad all right?' It struck Janey with full force that her mother hadn't even trusted her with the truth about where she was going. She'd treated her like a child or an impossible adolescent.

'He's fine. Really on the mend.'

'What's happened to Grandad?' Jess asked, confused. This was the first she'd heard of it.

'He had a minor stroke.'

'Mum didn't say anything.'

'No,' Janey said spitefully. 'But then maybe she didn't go to Bristol at all. Maybe she went to see her lover.'

Matt was startled by the bitterness in Janey's tone. He felt a slash of pain and then the duller edge of disappointment. 'What's this about a lover?'

'Oh, come on, Dad.' Jess signalled madly to Janey to stop before it was too late but Janey, hurt by her mother, wanted to hurt someone herself. 'You can't be the last to know about Mum and her toy-boy.'

Matt felt thunderously depressed as he parked his car in Century's underground car park. Until Janey had spoken he'd had the illusion in some part of himself that he'd been wrong about Ally and Danny Wilde. After all, in the malicious, gossipy world of television people knew you were having an affair before you'd even put your clothes back on. Yet he hadn't heard a single whisper linking

Danny Wilde with Allegra Boyd. Sitting here in the gloom he realized he'd let himself hope for the best. And he'd been wrong. He was stupid to have thought about a reconciliation. It was only the fear of his father dying that had made him so unrealistic.

When he walked into *The Matt Boyd Show* offices the atmosphere visibly cheered up. Matt's arrival was like turning a light on. Everyone rushed to him with their pieces of good news about stars booked, feedback from the audience, plans for the Special.

Watching from the door of their office Belinda smiled. It was only when he was away that she understood how much people respected him. She could see them now, queuing up eagerly for his approval, hoping for a word of encouragement, because from Matt it really meant something. Almost like children to a father.

Quickly she pushed that image out of her mind as she walked forward to meet him, conscious that just like the others she craved his approval too.

'You stupid idiot, Janey!' Jess flung the magazine she'd been reading down on a chair and let out all the emotion she'd been sitting on so carefully ever since her father left. 'Can't you see what you've done? You've screwed it up! He was going to come back. I'm sure he was. Till you mentioned Danny Wilde. It's all your fault! If it wasn't for you they'd probably have got back together. You've spoilt it all!' And calm, phlegmatic Jess threw herself down on the sofa and wept.

It was too much for Janey. She hadn't seen Jess cry for years. 'Why is everything always *my* fault?' She ran to her room and banged the door shut.

Was it really because of her their father had gone? She flung herself on the bed, devastated by sudden doubt. She'd missed him every day since he'd left. Sometimes even more than her mother had, she believed. She wanted him back desperately.

Suddenly the pain and the hurt, and the terrible suspicion that Jess might be right, broke out of her in great racking sobs until her throat felt sore and swollen and her eyes ached.

She wondered for a moment if she should go to her father, try and persuade him to change his mind. But he might just send her away. And then she remembered someone else she could go to. Someone who really loved her.

She jumped off the bed and turned her stereo up till the noise blotted out all her thoughts, even her pain. And reaching into the back of her wardrobe she pulled down her backpack and started to stuff her clothes into it.

By the time Ally got home from Bristol it was almost midnight and she was bone tired. After what Joe had said she'd half expected to see Matt's car in the drive. Although the leap of excitement she'd felt had died down into something more realistic during the three-hour train ride, she'd persuaded herself not to prejudge the issue but to hear him out.

Instead what awaited her was a tearful Jess slumped in front of the television.

'What on earth's the matter?'

'It's Janey.' Jess pulled herself up on her mountain of cushions. 'She's locked herself in her room.'

'Why? Not a row with Adam?'

'No, with me.'

Ally felt relieved. If it was between Janey and Jess it couldn't be too serious.

'What about? You haven't been borrowing her 501s again?'

Jess went quiet. 'Actually it was about Dad. He came

414

here earlier and Janey told him about you and Danny Wilde. So I had a go at her.'

Ally froze. 'What do you mean she told him about me and Danny Wilde?' Ally tried to keep the panic out of her voice. 'What is there to tell?'

'Oh, Mum, come off it.' Jess shrugged and turned up the volume on the television. 'You'd better go and listen to the answering machine.'

Her heart racing, Ally pretended to walk casually out to the hall. There were three messages on the machine. The first was from her mother. The third she never got to. The second, as Jess had told her, was from Danny Wilde. She listened in disbelief to the brief message and stood wondering in the dark if it was indeed a gesture of love or of something far more destructive.

In the cool of the silent hall she thought of Janey, locked in her bedroom upstairs. Poor Janey lying there feeling she'd screwed up the thing she wanted most. Ally's body ached for sleep and escape from the emotional tangles enveloping her, but she knew first she must try and break through the walls of her daughter's hostility for both their sakes. She turned and ran upstairs, unsure of her welcome and certain that this was yet another sin that Janey was bound to lay at her door.

Buried deep in the cushioned depths of her wing chair, Jess listened to her mother's footsteps and felt a bitter pang of jealousy that Ally had gone to Janey. What she'd hoped was that her mother would turn off the answering machine and come back into the sitting room, teasing and laughing and dismissing the ridiculous idea that she was having an affair with Danny Wilde.

Jess realized that not only was she angry with Janey for crassly telling their father about the message, she was angry with Ally too. The truth behind her flip comments and worldly-wise attitude was that she wanted her father

415

back desperately. Without him the house was dead, waiting. It felt rented instead of owned, as though the rightful inhabitants had moved out when Matt did. Oh, God, Dad, she muttered tearfully into the fat, disinterested cushion. Please come home.

When Janey heard someone coming upstairs she knew it would be her mother and she pushed the backpack under the valance of her bed.

There was a knock on the door. Janey turned down the music. Now that she'd made her decision she felt powerful, in control. She'd intended to go tomorrow morning, but tomorrow was Saturday and that would make it easier for her parents to come after her. No. She'd wait a few days. Next week. When it was her father's Special. Her A levels weren't till the week after. If she took them at all. Next week would be the time. That way she'd have a fighting chance of getting away with it.

'Janey!' She heard her mother's voice, struggling to be reassuring but not judgemental. 'Can I come in?'

As she pushed the door open Ally was taken aback to find her daughter lying serenely on top of her duvet reading *Tess of the D'Urbevilles*.

'Are you all right, darling?' She was suddenly aware that she hadn't been into Janey's room or talked to her for more than five minutes in weeks. Partly that was just coping with a teenager, but she felt guilty all the same.

'I'm fine.' Janey smiled neutrally as though this was a silly question, reminding Ally of a punk Barbie doll with her fixed, unnatural brightness. Still a smile was better than nothing. Ally wondered if she should say anything about Danny. Maybe now wasn't the moment. They were both overwrought. She leaned down to kiss Janey's forehead. 'I just wanted you to know I love you.'

'Do you, Mum?' Janey looked up from her book for no more than a fraction of a second. 'That's nice.'

Ally sat down on the bed. This polite restraint wasn't like Janey. Janey had always been the emotional one. Every time you told her you loved her when she was a child she would instantly demand, *More than Jess?* This cool, distant person wasn't like Janey at all.

There was no point pushing it. She'd try again tomorrow. She must clear more space in her life for both Janey and Jess. What did success matter if you lost out on closeness to your children?

Feeling reassured, Ally got up. Her eyes were almost closing and her body was screaming for rest, so when she stumbled on Janey's backpack stowed out of sight under the bed, she had no suspicion of what it might mean.

To Ally's immense relief life returned to relative normality over the next few days. She rang Mona often and was delighted to hear that Joe was continuing his recovery and would go home soon. Both girls, she knew, were angry that she hadn't told them about his stroke, but at least they seemed to accept her explanation that she'd felt they had enough to cope with without worrying unnecessarily.

Although she still seemed reserved, Janey was getting on quietly with her revision and Ally didn't have any of the expected requests to stay out late or borrow the car. Janey was more like the model student. At this rate, she would get her grades and go to university in October after all.

Jess, too, had clearly heaved a sigh of relief that she wasn't being made to pay for her outburst. Now that things were calm again Ally knew she had one more challenging task ahead: to lose her temper with Danny for the behaviour that had almost been so damaging to her family.

*

'But I was only telling the truth.' Danny smiled his most winning smile down the telephone, wishing she was standing next to him so that he could persuade her in person of the genuine depths of his feelings. The truth was he was surprised himself. 'I really do love you.'

Despite herself, Ally smiled too. The bafflement in his tone was both touching and revealing. Danny Wilde was obviously unused to loving someone else more than himself. And she could tell from the shadow of uncertainty in his voice that he wasn't entirely sure he liked it.

Still, she told herself sternly, loving her hadn't stopped him doing something potentially damaging to her happiness. Love was quite capable of being as destructive as Semtex. This was a subtlety that Danny, new to the emotion at all, didn't appreciate.

'I'm glad you love me.' She paused. Was she really? Wasn't it going to make life ten times more complicated? 'But you shouldn't have left that message. My daughters heard it and one of them told Matt.'

Danny said nothing.

'Danny, you can't go round behaving like that. Janey was really upset.' She paused. 'And I still can't see you so it's all for nothing.'

'Ally, please.' The hurt rang in his voice. *Like a child when you take their toy*, she told herself, *and they're fine in five minutes*. She wasn't going to let herself get caught up. 'Don't finish it like this. Let me at least see you to say goodbye.'

'It isn't goodbye. We're only talking about a couple of weeks.' And she knew she should refuse. That it would be safer if she did. But she was so lonely, so tired of being strong, she just wanted to be held, for someone to think she was wonderful. And Danny Wilde really did, for some crazy reason, seem to think she was wonderful.

'All right.' She felt weak and pathetic even as she said it. 'Just one last time.'

'Great!' Danny's voice swooped like a gull. 'This week-end?'

'No, I can't leave the girls.'

'Monday?'

She couldn't help smiling at his eagerness. 'Tuesday.'

'Tuesday it is. You won't regret it.'

Oh, won't I? thought Ally as she put the phone down. She had a feeling it wasn't going to be as simple as that.

'So, Jan darling, fill me in on the gossip. Who's screwing who in the glitzy world of showbusiness?' Maggy Mann leaned back against the red plush sofa in her agent's office and waited, savouring the enjoyment of being represented by one of London's bitchiest negotiators.

Jan Green was fiftyish, blondish, chicish. She could, on occasion, be little girlish, but only to hide the fact that she had a mind like a steel trap. Early in her career Jan had found a tendency for producers' nuts to shrivel in her presence. Being a bright girl she had disguised herself from then on under ten layers of mascara, a dose of peroxide and several yards of cleavage. It had been remarkably effective and Jan now had a villa in Marbella, a white Mercedes and some very famous clients. Last year she had joined forces with Jack Saltash, who represented even more stars than she did. The very name of their agency cast fear into the heart of the cost planner, and caused executive producers to add another nought to their budgets.

'Well, you know Sonia Shaw's sleeping with Tim Winterson.' Jan's laugh rippled through the office as she named a leading female newscaster and the head of entertainment at one of the big commercial companies. She could afford to be indiscreet about Sonia. She was one of Jack's clients, not hers. 'And Sonia's started demanding that Tim checks through all her contracts before she signs them.' Jan rolled her eyes and shrugged. 'So Jack had to say, "Look darling, if you want him as your lover, fine, but *I'm* your agent, savvy?"'

They both laughed.

'Coffee, darling?' Jan's secretary had just put her head round the door to take orders.

'Lovely. Black, no sugar.'

Jan looked at her shrewdly. 'Yes, I thought you were looking a little jowly on *Hello* last week.' She ignored Maggy's scowl. Clients had to be told these things, especially after forty. It was a young business. 'You'll have to take up those exercises. Eurythmics? No, that's the pop group. Cindy does them.' She name-dropped a blonde client who looked twenty years younger than she deserved. 'Unless it's the oral sex. Very good for the jaw, I'm told.' She patted her own as though in confirmation.

Maggy giggled. Chance would be a fine thing.

As the secretary opened the door to bring in the coffees Maggy glanced in her direction and saw Danny Wilde come swiftly out of an office opposite. Maggy reddened slightly and sat back in her seat so that she was invisible. Since Danny had ditched her after only a few dates she'd avoided him whenever possible.

'I didn't know you represented Danny Wilde.'

'Jack does.' Jan leaned forward. 'He's about to pull off something mega.'

'Who with?'

'Darling, my lips are sealed.' She smiled smugly. 'But somebody very big better watch out.'

'Not Matt Boyd, surely?'

Jan's smile widened almost imperceptibly.

Maggy sipped her coffee. She wondered if anyone had bothered to tell Matt.

'Don't you think you're being a bit hard on your mother?'

420

Janey had been thrilled when Adam called her from a phone box to see how she was, but she was less keen on the way the conversation was going now. 'I got the impression she really loves you.'

Adam had liked Ally from the start, and for obvious reasons could see less wrong than Janey in being consoled by an attractive younger man.

'She has a funny way of showing it, then. Having an affair with Danny Wilde.'

'She's probably lonely since your father left.'

'God, I don't want to even think about it. It's disgusting.' Janey winced.

'Janey, my money's about to run out. Why don't you stay at home till after your A levels? Then, if you still want to, come to my place. Maybe you should talk this through with your mother, tell her how you feel about her and Danny Wilde. I don't think running away's the answer before your exams. You'll just fuck up your life.'

'OK.' Janey hoped he wasn't putting her off. But it was only three weeks till her A levels were over.

She'd give her mother one last chance. When Mum got home tonight, she'd try and apologize and talk it through. Maybe Adam was right. She had been a bit unfair.

'Matt, could I have a word? Wilf Steel, Century's most popular production manager, came into the office Matt shared with Belinda and looked grateful that she wasn't there. He was carrying a thick sheaf of papers.

Wilf Steel had been at Century for as long as it had existed, but even though he'd lasted longer than most, he had never been a company man. He was too subversive by nature. Today, Wilf, plump, cheerful and given to losing his temper when people underestimated him, seemed uncharacteristically serious.

'I just wondered' – Wilf paused. He had a lot of time

for Matt Boyd and didn't like what was happening to him – 'if you'd seen the scheduling plans for the summer?'

He handed them over.

Matt glanced at them curiously. Scheduling plans weren't normally things he paid much attention to. And then he saw what Wilf was getting at.

Ritchie Page had meant what he'd said. In four weeks' time *The Matt Boyd Show* was to come off the air. He realized that though it was what Page had threatened he'd never really believed the man would go through with it. But there it was, spread over a concertina of computer print-outs. No more *Matt Boyd Show*. He glanced down at the sheets of paper again. It had been true. The programme that was going to replace him on Fridays was *Tell It to Ally*.

As Wilf closed the door behind him Matt felt his resentment boiling up into frustration and anger. He knew that presenters had no real power over when their shows went out, but there must have been *something* she could have done. And if not her, then Bernie. Between them, surely, they could have stopped this happening if they'd wanted to.

Matt stood up. He needed to know if she'd at least tried.

When he burst into Bernie's office, Ally and Bernie were in a meeting with the PR department about ideas for promotion. Ally had rarely seen him so angry. His eyes were glinting dangerously, and she felt her stomach tighten involuntarily. The PR people took one look at him, instinctively gathered up their things and prepared to leave.

'For God's sake, Matt,' Bernie snapped, 'we're in the middle of a meeting.'

'I won't take much of your time.' He waited until the PR people had left, exchanging glances with Bernie as they quietly shut the door. The story would be all round the building in five minutes.

'So,' Bernie looked nearly as furious as Matt. 'What's the big problem?'

'Your show's the problem.' Matt waved the schedule at them. 'You know how hard we're fighting for our life and now we're being pulled off the air to make way for your bloody programme.' He turned to Ally. 'Ally, how could you do it? Are you so eager to be a star that loyalty doesn't matter any more?'

Ally almost laughed out loud. The irony of his words, coming from someone who'd just walked out on his wife and family after nineteen years was too much for her.

'Loyalty!' She jumped up furiously. 'What do you know about loyalty? Was it loyalty that made you turn your back on a perfectly good marriage just because you weren't the centre of attention any more? Was it loyalty that made you move in with Belinda and humiliate me all over the front pages of the tabloids?' Ally strode towards the door, grateful she had to go and do a voiceover. If she stayed here she might hit him. Even so, she couldn't resist one more jibe. 'Has it ever occurred to you that the only person you've ever been loyal to is Matt bloody Boyd and his stupid chat-show?'

She stalked out, glad for once that she'd had the nerve to simply get up and go.

'Well.' Bernie watched her disappearing back. 'You certainly screwed that up. What intrigues me' – he undid a paperclip and began cleaning his nails with it – 'is that you could be married to Ally for so long and understand her so little.'

'So you're the big expert on Ally now, are you?' Matt glared at Bernie, amazed he could have considered him a friend all this time. 'You were the one who used to go on about her suburban values.'

'That was before I knew her. You don't have the same excuse.'

'So, o guru of the airwaves,' Matt asked nastily 'what don't I understand?'

Matt's incapacity to admit he was even a little in the wrong began to annoy Bernie. 'Ally. Your own wife. You really think she'd betray you out of ambition? Even when you've walked out on her for that executive tart of yours? Come to your senses, Matt. Shake yourself out of your bitterness, for Christ's sake. Page offered it to her all right. One of the best slots on television.' He fixed his small eyes on Matt mercilessly. 'Just think what a perfect revenge it would have been for her. And she turned it down. She didn't even think about it. I did, I assure you. But Ally said there was no way she would take your slot. Page just rode roughshod over her. We didn't even know he'd finally made up his mind.'

Matt dropped his head into his hands, feeling hideously ashamed. It was jealousy of Danny Wilde that was making him behave like this. Yet the truth was he was driving her into Danny's arms. 'Christ, Bernie, I'm sorry. What's the matter with me? I had no idea.'

'No,' Bernie replied crisply, slinging his paperclip into the bin with consummate aim. 'Of course you didn't. But you could have guessed. All you've ever done is begrudge her her success. Danny Wilde may be a greaseball but at least he's made her feel good about herself.' He looked at Matt unsympathetically. 'I used to like you once. Anyway, it isn't me you should be apologizing to.'

He thought for a moment Matt might go for him. Instead Matt stood up and walked towards the door. Before he got to it he turned, and for the first time Bernie saw a shadow of pain in his eyes. 'Thanks, mate. For pointing out what a stupid shit I've been.'

Bernie's face wrinkled into a vestige of a smile. 'Any

time. You could book some sessions. Just talk to my secretary.'

Ally sat fuming in Century's car park. When Matt had accused her she'd thought of telling the truth. That she'd turned down Page's offer. But why should she be the one who had to explain? She'd been the one who'd always apologized in their marriage and she was damned if she was going to do it now it was over.

She drove up the ramp and remembered that tonight was the night she'd promised to go to Danny's. The night she'd decided she had to say goodbye. For a moment she regretted it. It would have been cleaner to have done it on the phone.

All at once she felt utterly lonely. And the thought of Danny and his frank admiration seemed impossibly tempting. She only needed to stay a little while. Anyway she'd promised Janey she'd be back. Janey had said there was something she wanted to talk about. She wondered for a moment what it was. She'd been so strange lately. And then, remembering the feel of Danny's hands on her breasts, undoing the buttons, kissing her as he did, Ally forgot about Janey and drove off towards his flat.

As Danny opened the door he had a look of such smug expectation that she almost turned round and left. But then the expression was instantly replaced by humility and even, Ally thought in surprise, the merest hint of gratitude. Either Danny was thrilled to see her or a very good actor indeed. She followed him in and reflected that though she'd known him for several months now she couldn't have sworn which it was.

'You seem tired, love.' The tenderness in his voice caressed her fraying nerves.

'I am. Bloody Ritchie Page is putting us out in Matt's slot and Matt stormed in to blame me for it.' Ally suddenly felt in need of sympathy.

425

Danny looked embarrassed. Wait till she knew it wasn't only for the summer. Should he tell her? It was a God-given opportunity. No, he'd wait till she was more receptive.

'Come here.' He led her gently towards the bedroom. 'What you need is a Danny Wilde special.'

This time the massage was even more heavenly than before. He somehow knew exactly where the knots of stress had gathered in her back and her neck. As Ally surrendered herself she decided this was almost better than making love. Almost.

As Danny pummelled and stroked and kneaded he could feel Ally coming alive under his fingertips and he smiled. Now was his moment.

'Ally, there's something I've got to tell you.'

But Ally wasn't listening. Her eyes had a veiled faraway light in them as she turned over which Danny recognized immediately as desire.

Janey looked at her watch. It was nearly midnight and she'd been waiting to talk to her mother since eight fifteen. Suddenly starving, she took herself out to the kitchen and made a fried courgette in pitta bread sandwich, one of her favourites. Where the hell had Ally got to? She slipped off the stool of the breakfast bar to put her plate and knife in the dishwasher, smiling at the sign saying 'IN NOT ON'. Then it struck her. There was no way her mother would be this late unless she was doing something else. How stupid of her! She knew exactly where her mother had gone. To Danny Wilde's.

Suddenly all the anger she'd been feeling at the way both her parents were behaving surfaced in a tidal wave of pain and fury, pulling her down into its depths. What was the matter with them both? Didn't either of them care how she and Jess felt? Maybe their children didn't

426

matter any more now that their own lives were so exciting.

Janey looked at her watch one final time and came to a decision. After tomorrow her mother wouldn't have to be burdened with her tiresome presence any longer. Adam was the only one who cared what happened to her and she'd go to him in the morning. If she failed her exams and didn't get into university what did it matter? Maybe it would teach her parents a lesson.

Feeling scared but exhilarated at finally coming to a decision, Janey ran up the stairs to her bedroom to finish packing her rucksack.

Ally always liked Danny's bedroom. It managed to have character even though it was almost empty. Danny had resisted all those male greys and graphites usually thought suitable for single men trying to impress. His bedroom was a subtle shade of lavender, too blue to be grey but grey enough to be masculine. It reminded her of the colour of an Ossie Clarke crêpe-de-Chine dress she'd had years ago, which she'd always seen as the height of sophistication. And the biggest surprise was the Empire bed, shaped almost like a boat. But it wasn't a boat she was going to let herself drift out to sea in tonight. She knew if she went to sleep she'd be lost. Danny's eyes were firmly closed with a smile on his face which, she noted, was dangerously close to a smirk. This time she let it pass. It seemed to be from pleasure not one-upmanship.

For a moment she sat on the bed watching him. He seemed in his way to love her. But would a life with him be possible? Was he capable of understanding she couldn't be everything to him, that other people needed her too, sometimes at just the wrong moment? By the side of his bed she noticed a CD of Janey's current favourite record. She remembered with a start of guilt that Janey wanted

427

to talk and had probably been waiting up for her. God, why was life always so complicated?

Quietly she reached for her clothes.

When Ally turned the front door key an hour later the house was completely silent. She could detect the faint smell of frying and she followed her nose, half hoping to find Janey munching a pizza at the kitchen table. She noticed the dirty pan and the single plate on top of the dishwasher and, ignoring her smart clothes, bent down and put them in. The pan was still warm, so it couldn't have been long since Janey went to bed.

On her way to her bedroom she put her head into Janey's room, but she was fast asleep. With her hair fanning out across the pillow and her white T-shirt against the black of the sheets, she looked almost like a child.

In the morning, Ally decided, she'd make a point of taking Janey breakfast in bed to say sorry. Tomorrow she'd have all the time in the world to listen.

At five o'clock the next morning Janey woke up before her alarm clock, as she always did when she was nervous. Someone at school had told her if you hit your head on the pillow five times you'd wake at five. But this time Janey hadn't needed to. She knew she would wake anyway. She dressed quickly and picked up her back-pack.

The floorboard creaked outside Jess's open door, but Janey paid no attention. Jess was impossible to wake even when you wanted her to.

Grabbing the A–Z street map from next to the tele-phone and her parka from the pegs by the back door, Janey crept out and began the two-mile walk to Fairley Green Station. With luck it would be too early for any of her schoolfriends' commuter fathers to spot her and ask her where she was going.

At the station she bought a single to Waterloo. There was a train just about to leave. Rushing under the underpass, Janey took it as a good omen. God, or the Great Green Spirit in the sky, was on her side.

When she got off the train at Waterloo she felt lost. Commuters surged passed her in great waves. Half a million people a day, she'd read, and all of them seemed to be there now. She hung on to her backpack grimly and made for the Casey Jones' takeaway. She turned her face away at the sight of the double sausage specials and the bacon 'n' sausage sizzlers and settled for a blackcurrant muffin and coffee. As she wandered off a young man, unnervingly cheerful at seven forty-five, asked her if she would like to do the Pepsi Test. She almost laughed.

In the huge, modern cathedral-like station British Rail, eager to cut the wino count, had reduced the seating to about six. Janey squatted by a pillar to eat her muffin, suddenly overcome with panic.

She'd run away from home.

She remembered Adam's tone of voice advising her to stay at home and patch up things with her mother. Maybe he wouldn't want her turning up out of the blue, invading his space. Maybe he'd have someone else there. Perhaps she should go home after all.

She finished her coffee and went to find a bin to throw away her paper cup. It was next to the entrance to platform fourteen. On the platform she glimpsed a small brown-haired girl of about three playing an ecstatic game with her father. Janey watched as the child ran towards the edge of the platform then stopped, waiting for her father to scoop her up and carry her back, certain in every atom of her small being that she would be saved. Tears pricked Janey's eyes. She must have looked a lot like that. Had her own father run forward to save her? And if he loved her, where was he now, when she needed him?

For a moment she thought of running towards the platform's edge too. But there would be no one there to stop her. Screwing up the cup and throwing it in the bin she headed off for the tube station and Adam's squat.

Ally took the croissants out of the freezer and put them in the microwave to defrost. She'd already set a tray with a lacy traycloth and a cup and saucer. They didn't match but they were Janey's favourite, painted Italian earthenware in glorious pinks and yellows. Deciding the tray needed a final touch of luxury, Ally opened the French windows and went out into the garden in search of a rose.

She stopped for a moment and looked round at the dozens of different varieties, then headed for a great sweep of one of her favourites, Madame Grégoire Staechelin, bowing fragrantly down in her direction. She cut three of the delicate pale-pink blooms with her secateurs and breathed in their heady perfume. Although it was after eight this part of the garden was still shady, and they were damp with dew.

As she headed back into the kitchen Jess appeared, the ends of her blouse sticking out of her school skirt. Even though she had such good taste for other people, Jess herself was a Bermuda triangle of style. No matter how much you spent on her she looked like an urchin five minutes later and always had. Ally remembered taking her to France on holiday, where the little French girls wore tartan frocks with white collars and perfect white tights. Jess had stood out by insisting on wearing old jodhpurs and a jumper of Matt's four sizes too big.

'What's that for?' Jess indicated the tray.

Ally looked faintly guilty. 'It's for Janey. I got home too late last night to chat and I wanted to say sorry.'

'You never do that for me.' Jess's lower lip stuck out so comically Ally laughed.

'I'll do it for you tomorrow. Now get on with your breakfast.'

'Are there any more croissants?'

'In the freezer.'

'But they'll be frozen.'

'Highly likely,' conceded Ally. 'Put in microwave. One minute on medium. Press start.'

Jess continued to look aggrieved and switched on the television. Disconcertingly Matt's familiar smile filled the room, trailing the interview on his show tonight with Meredith Morgan. 'Hey, Mum, they're trailing Dad's Special.'

Ally was pushing the door open with her foot and glanced round abruptly, but by the time she did it had finished. It was a real coup to get Meredith Morgan. Hoping Janey wouldn't be too angry with her she went upstairs.

Outside Janey's door Ally balanced the tray in one hand and knocked. Janey must be still asleep.

'Janey?' Ally called softly, opening the door with her free hand.

It was dark in the room and it took Ally a second or two to take in that Janey wasn't in bed. She put down the tray, only slightly thrown, and pulled the curtains. There was no one there. Ally pushed to one side a sense that there was something strange about the room, a kind of unfamiliar emptiness. Maybe Janey had gone for a walk with Sox. But Sox had been in her basket.

The first glimmerings of worry began to flicker at the back of her mind. She looked in Janey's cupboard. It was only half full. She pulled out the drawers. All Janey's black sweatshirts and leggings, the things she wore all the time, were gone. Speeding up her movements, Ally searched through the rack of clothes. None of her favourite things were in the wardrobe, her black leather jacket, even the minidress she'd worn the night of the party. At the end of the rack, symbolic in its continued presence, was the school uniform she should have been wearing.

Ally rushed across to Janey's desk, the antique pine one they'd bought her when she was thirteen and had announced that she needed some privacy and wanted to do her homework in her room. Matt had chosen it himself and hidden a present in each of its many drawers.

Ally knew there was one in particular where Janey kept all her important documents: her cheque book and her building society stuff. It was empty.

Ally stood still, beginning to feel sick with fear.

There was only one possible explanation.

Janey had run away.

Chapter 30

'Oh, Mum, it's all my fault!' Jess wept over her half-defrosted croissant. 'I shouldn't have had a go at her the other day.'

Ally put her arms round Jess and patted her. Her daughter's panic was having the unexpected side-effect of calming her down. If Jess had been her usual wry self Ally would have been in hysterics by now.

'Let's just think about it for a moment.' She sat down next to Jess. 'Where would she have gone to?'

'To Granola? Joe?'

Ally shook her head. 'Janey'd know they'd send her back. And she couldn't have gone to Mona and Joe because Joe's still in hospital.'

'No.' Jess looked up. 'Poor Janey. She was still upset you didn't tell her about that when you went to Bristol.'

Ally closed her eyes, feeling everything was her fault not Janey's or Jess's. Maybe she'd been trying to protect too many people.

'What about friends?' Ally racked her brain for who was close to Janey.

'I doubt it. Janey's got loads of friends, but none of them really close. Mum?' Jess hesitated, knowing her question might hurt. 'You don't think she's gone to Dad, do you?'

'Of course.' Ally sighed with relief, not offended, only relieved. 'Maybe that's where she's gone.' She reached for the phone.

There was no answer from Belinda's. She waited a beat then dialled Century, glancing at her watch as she did so. Nine a.m. Probably too early for TV types, but finally someone answered.

'Hello, is that *The Matt Boyd Show*? Is Matt there?' She didn't wait to be vetted. 'It's Allegra Boyd here.'

'I'm sorry, Mrs Boyd. He isn't in yet. It's our Special today. He's laying down some commentary in Soho, but he should be arriving soon. I'll tell him the moment he gets here.'

'Thanks. Could you ask him to call me at home? It's urgent.' She paused. 'No, make that very urgent.'

As she put down the phone she realized Janey couldn't have chosen a worse day. With his Special today there was no way she'd be able to rely on Matt to help her find Janey. For the first time she wondered if she should tell the police. But they wouldn't pay any attention yet, would they? A missing eighteen-year-old wouldn't rate much of a priority with them.

'There is one other place she might have gone to.' Ally was so preoccupied she almost jumped when Jess spoke.

'Where?'

'She might have gone to Adam's.'

Ally felt a weight being lifted off her chest. It made sense. If she wasn't at Belinda's, or at Century looking for her father that was the obvious place she'd make for.

'Where does Adam live?'

Jess looked stricken, knowing she was about to take away half the crumb she'd handed out. 'That's the trouble. I don't know. All I know is that it's Notting Hill. Somewhere near Portobello Road.'

Ally felt like a punchbag someone had put their fist into. She hardly knew that part of town except for an occasional visit to the antiques market. What she needed was someone who did. She thought for a moment. At the back of her mind was the certainty that she'd heard about Notting Hill recently. Then she remembered. There'd been an item on the news about the Notting Hill Carnival. And Danny had told her that when he'd first come to

434

London, he'd lived there. Ally started to feel better. Danny would be perfect. Even the young people would want to help Danny.

'Hello, could I speak to Danny Wilde please?' Ally tried to keep calm. If she sounded hysterical they'd put her down as a nutty fan and refuse to put her through.

'Who's calling, please?'

Ally paused for a moment. What the hell was she going to say? No one knew about her and Danny apart from her family. Oh, what the hell? This was an emergency. 'It's Allegra Boyd. Could you tell him it's very urgent? I'll hold on.'

The girl on the other end clucked in irritation. 'Are you sure? It might take me a while to find him.'

'That's OK.' As long as she was holding on to the phone Ally felt reasonably calm. She was doing something.

Danny was buried in the bowels of the sound transfer unit recording the voiceover for a promo when they finally tracked him down.

'Can't I call her back in ten minutes?' Danny's voice rang with annoyance. Unlike him, he'd screwed up his commentary three times and was blowing his reputation as First-take Wilde. An interruption was the last thing he wanted.

'She's holding on. She said it was very urgent.'

Danny swore under his breath. He hoped Ally wasn't becoming the clinging type. Up till now she'd been the one who was obsessed with secrecy. He wasn't sure he liked the abrupt change-around. The two sound engineers were already exchanging knowing looks.

'We can always pick up later,' smirked one, 'if you've got more important things to do.'

'No, we can't,' corrected the other. 'This promo's going out in two hours.'

Danny sighed. 'Can you put the call through here?'

The PA was equally irritated. She couldn't remember which extension Ally was on. Now she'd have to go all the way upstairs to find out and get her transferred.

Finally after various clicks and silences Ally was put through to STU. The engineer handed Danny the phone, glancing meaningfully at the clock on the studio wall as he did so.

'Danny, thank God!' The relief in her voice startled him.

'Ally, what's the matter, for God's sake?' From her tone he half expected to hear that Matt had taken her hostage with a sawn-off shotgun and was threatening to shoot the whole family.

'It's Janey. She's run away. I was supposed to get back and have a chat with her last night and I came to you instead.'

Danny sensed the engineers and researcher hanging on his every word. He turned away.

'Is that all?' He almost laughed at her overreaction. 'She's eighteen, Ally. She's not a child any more.'

Ally listened, shocked. 'But she's got her A levels next week, and I've no idea where she is. She's taken her things.'

Danny smiled. 'You'll probably get a call from her later telling you everything's fine. Calm down, Ally.'

'I think she may have gone to her boyfriend's squat in Notting Hill.' She paused, suddenly unsure that he would understand the request which had seemed so logical to her five minutes ago. 'But I don't know the address. So I wondered if you could come and help me look, since you know the area.'

This time he did laugh. 'Ally, I'm in the middle of doing a promo.'

'When you've finished, then. Danny, she could be lost, broke, not knowing where to go.'

'Don't you think you're going over the top on this? Why don't you go and sit outside in the sunshine and wait for her to ring you? She'll soon come home if she runs out of money.'

'Danny, I can't just do nothing.'

'Look, love' – this time she could hear the impatience in his voice – 'I'm sure she's fine. In fact you'd better get off the phone in case she's trying to ring you now. I'll call you later, OK? Bye.'

Danny put the phone back in its cradle, avoiding the expressions on the sound engineers' faces.

'Right.' He went back into the voice booth and tapped the side of the mike. 'Shall we get on and finish this bloody promo?'

Ally sat holding the phone for a moment. Some of what Danny had said made perfect sense. Janey probably *would* ring if she was in real trouble. But the dismissiveness in his voice! He hadn't given two thoughts to the way she might be feeling, hadn't even cared. Suddenly the age gap between them, which had seemed unimportant, appeared so wide it was unbridgeable. The reality was that Danny's life was a blank page dedicated only to himself. He hadn't the slightest inkling what it felt like to know that your firstborn child, whom you have loved from her first breath, is wandering alone in the streets of London, feeling lonely and rejected.

In a way he'd done her a favour by opening her eyes.

'Thanks, Danny,' she said to the dead phone. 'I'm really glad I asked.' Then she replaced it, realizing that Danny was right. Janey might be trying to ring.

One thing was getting clearer. If she was going to search for her, she'd have to go alone.

'Mum, do I have to go to school today?'

In her concern for Janey, Ally had forgotten about taking Jess to school. Then it struck her that if Janey did

437

phone it would be useful if Jess stayed nearby to answer it.

'OK. Just for today.' She put her arm round her daughter and tried to smile reassuringly. It helped to have someone depending on your being strong. 'I'm sure we'll find her. Now, what about Adam? Does he have any family we could get his address from?'

Jess thought for a moment. 'His parents are divorced and his father lives abroad. I don't know where his mother lives. Somewhere in Somerset, I think he said.'

'What's his surname?'

Jess shrugged. 'I haven't the slightest idea.'

Ally sighed. She didn't think Janey had ever told her. He'd always been Adam the Goth.

'We'd better go and check in her room.'

'You'll be lucky,' Jess said. 'Knowing Janey, she'll have flushed any clues down the loo.'

Ally looked through every inch of Janey's room, but it was useless. It was like checking through an empty hotel room. Janey had taken everything important with her. The only vaguely useful piece of information was an invitation addressed to Janey and Adam from Mojo Williams. Mojo, aka Mark, was the son of some old friends of theirs so at least she could follow that up.

To Ally's surprise, when she tried the Williamses' number a child answered the phone.

'Hello, who's speaking, please?'

Ally decided she'd rather not say who she was and have Mojo's parents running to the phone.

'Is Mojo in, please?'

'OK, I'll go and see if he's there.' The child, a boy, sounded bored, as though most of the calls in the Williams household were for Mojo. She heard him pad off and shout upstairs. 'Mark! Somebody's mother for you!'

Despite her worry, Ally smiled.

438

'Hello?' The voice sounded like a bored pop star, with only the faintest hint of schoolboy. It also sounded highly suspicious. Obviously Mojo wasn't used to having people's mothers ring him.

'This is Allegra Boyd, Janey Boyd's mother.' Ally tried to sound as casual as possible, certainly not like an over-protective parent spoiling her daughter's fun. 'I wondered if you know her friend Adam's address.'

'Shacked up with him, has she?' Mojo asked laconically. Why was it that if you beggared yourselves sending your children to expensive private schools, which she knew the Williamses had, the one thing you guaranteed was that they'd sound like they went to a secondary mod?

Mojo thought about it for a moment. 'Divinity Road, I think he said.'

The relief Ally felt was as heady as a large brandy. Thank God she was beginning to get somewhere. Divinity Road even sounded familiar, though she couldn't remember why.

Mojo clearly had nothing further to add. 'Would you like to speak to my parents?'

'No, thanks.' Ally couldn't face the prospect of half an hour from Bunty Williams on the subject of what's the matter with kids today. 'Thanks a lot, you've been very helpful.'

'Have I?' Mojo sounded, in Ally's view, a shade disappointed.

It was just after the rush hour by the time Ally, a giant-size A–Z sitting next to her on the seat, headed round the big roundabout at the end of Westway, past the Kensington Hilton, known locally by the less flattering title of the Shepherd's Bush Hilton owing to its proximity to that insalubrious area, and along Holland Park. She didn't know this part of town and hoped she wouldn't get lost. At least she'd recognize one landmark: Portobello Road.

Years ago, when they moved to London, she and Matt used to come to the antiques market to browse and look for bargains. Silver napkin rings, gilt picture frames, pretty pottery by Clarice Cliff. They'd hardly had any money, but had enormous fun spending what they had. Matt's new job in London had seemed to both of them so exciting and yet unpredictable, and for the first year they'd both seen it as a fairground carousel which might grind to a halt and fling them off at any moment. So they'd held on to their flat near MidWest TV and rented in London – a big old mansion flat in Victoria, near the cathedral, that came furnished with the most hideous furniture either of them had ever seen.

One Saturday near Valentine's Day they'd wandered down Portobello Road and Matt had found a heart-shaped mirror made entirely out of shells on one of the stalls and insisted on buying it for her, even though it cost a week's rent. She still had it in their bedroom. Except that it wasn't their bedroom any longer.

Driving slowly along, Ally pushed the happy images of her and Matt out of her mind. She was supposed to be trying to find Janey.

She passed a phone box near the corner of Notting Hill Gate tube station and pulled in. Maybe Matt had rung. Or Janey.

Jess answered on the third ring.

'Jess, darling, has anyone phoned?'

'Only Granola. I palmed her off, otherwise she'd have the police out from seven counties. Oh, and Bernie Long. You were due at some meeting or other.'

'What did you tell him?'

'That you were out and must have forgotten.'

'Good girl.' It struck Ally that if she got really desperate she could probably draft Bernie in. 'Nothing from Janey or Dad?'

'No. Shall I call him again?'

'Yes, why don't you? I'll phone later to find out how you got on.'

She returned to the car and drove down the top end of Portobello Road, impressed by its bijou smartness. It was like a pastel palette, every house a different shade. Pale sugar-almond pink, pistachio, ivory, Wedgwood blue, primrose. Ivy-leafed geraniums tumbled from terracotta window boxes and hanging baskets, tangling with trailing lobelia and bright red petunias. Each front door shone with gloss paint and polished brass. Ally began to feel reassured. It was all so quietly moneyed. Surely Janey could come to no harm round here.

At the cross with Westbourne Grove the houses changed to antique shops, boarded over during the week with steel mesh covers, and pubs distinctly grimier than the area she'd just driven through. Then the antiques gave way to the fruit and veg stalls of a conventional street market.

Ally spotted a meter and decided to park. According to the map, Divinity Road wasn't far from here. As she stopped the car she realized how hungry she was. Walking towards the flyover past the refurbished rococo glory of the Electric Cinema, Ally felt she'd almost walked into a timewarp. Indian prints and batik clothes hung from hangers outside every shop, flapping gently in the wind, record stalls sold old LPs by Tangerine Dream and the Grateful Dead. In the Portobello Road hippy days were here again. In the distance she could even hear the faint chant of 'Hare Rama, Hare Rama, Rama Rama, Hare Hare' from a wandering orange-clad group of Hare Krishnas. She should be grateful for small mercies. At least Janey hadn't joined them.

Almost unconsciously Ally scanned their faces as they passed. They were all young men, undernourished and

441

smiling beatifically. No one had remembered to tell them the sixties ended before they were born.

After this burst of exoticism the familiar drabness of Woolworth's seemed positively welcoming, but instead of dipping inside to look for a Kit Kat, as she'd intended, a waft of new-baked bread pulled Ally a few shops further along to Ceres Bakery. Lyons and ABC might come and go, but Ceres had kept on baking its solid stoneground selection since the days of flower power.

As she came out a stallholder interrupted his cry of 'Strawberries are lovely. Two punnets a pound!' to greet her cheerily. 'Don't worry, Ally,' he grinned, 'it might never happen.' He went on building a pile of the huge, glossy fruit. Ally felt an overwhelming temptation to knock it over and shout, 'For your information, sunshine, it already has.'

Instead she screwed up the Ceres bag from her wholemeal bun and handed it to him. Then she opened her A–Z.

'Loved the Telethon,' he commented good-naturedly. You and Danny were great together. Where're you lookin' for, darlin? One of them posh shops up Westbourne Grove?'

Ally hesitated. 'Actually I'm trying to find Divinity Road.'

The man exchanged glances with his mate on the neighbouring stall. 'Nah, nah, nah.' He shook his head discouragingly. 'You don't want to go round there, darlin'. Nasty road. Nasty people.'

'*Very* nasty people,' endorsed his friend.

'Not your sort at all, Ally.'

'Listen.' Ally had had enough friendly advice. She wasn't about to tell them her life story just to get a few directions. 'Tell me where it is, would you?'

'All right, all right, suit yourself. Take a right down

that road over there.' He pointed to a turning the other side of the street. 'You can't miss it. It's the one with the coppers on every corner and syringes in the dustbins.' He and his friend both laughed.

Ally crossed the road nervously and turned right. In marked contrast to the moneyed chic of the top end of Portobello, and the noisy multi-racial buzz of the street market, the atmosphere changed abruptly. Bags of rubbish littered the pavements, their contents spewing out everywhere. Dogs nosed around in them looking for food. Instead of sugar-almond façades, here the stucco was peeling with huge lumps of plaster missing from the front of the buildings. Many of them were boarded up against squatters. Others were crammed with bedsits and had ten or twelve bells by their entrances.

Ally remembered dimly that it was round here that Rachmann, London's most famous slum landlord, had operated, packing in the first wave of immigrants back in the fifties and breaking their arms if they complained about the conditions.

On the front steps groups of youths sat silently watching her. Ally shivered, feeling she was entering an alien world where her preciously held values would be scorned and laughed at. She could hardly believe that five minutes away the bijou paradise of Portobello even existed. It was as though the Yuppies who'd colonized so much of the inner city had drawn a line south of here beyond which they would not venture, no matter how cheap the property prices.

Ally saw another group staring at her from the steps. Even from across the road she could smell the strong, sweet scent of marijuana. She'd hoped there would be someone friendly to ask on the street. But she could hardly trot out her story of teenage rebellion here, hoping for a sympathetic murmur of 'kids these days' and a helpful finger pointing to where her daughter might be found. They would shrug or laugh in her face.

Suddenly Ally felt a wave of helplessness and fear. Looking at the unwelcoming eyes following her, she remembered why the name of the road rang such a bell. She'd seen it on the news. Janey had chosen the heart of London's drugland to run away to.

Turning, she ran back towards the teeming life of Portobello Road and the relative safety of her car.

She was almost surprised to see it still there, but as she came closer she saw a yellow parking ticket stuck to the windscreen. In her excitement at finding a space she had forgotten to put any money in the meter. A crowd of drinkers on the pavement outside a nearby pub cheered as she pulled it off, though whether out of commiseration or pleasure at her bad fortune she couldn't tell.

As soon as she had unlocked the door and sat down in the driver's seat Ally dropped her head on to the steering wheel and felt the tears start to run down her face.

It wasn't the ticket, though that seemed like the final straw. The truth was she didn't know where to start. She wished desperately Matt were with her, but with his show today she might as well forget about him.

She was on her own.

She made herself sit up, comb her hair, clean up her tear-stained cheeks and get out of the car. This time she remembered to put some money in the meter. She walked slowly round and round the block for nearly an hour until finally a policeman, who'd seen her three times in the last twenty minutes, pulled in and asked if she was lost.

When she explained what she was doing he shrugged. Half the properties round here were squats. Looking at her forlorn face, which he vaguely recognized but couldn't put a name to, he at least tried to make suggestions.

'There's two places you could try. One's the Notting Hill Housing Trust. They own a lot of this stuff' – he gestured at the better properties around them – 'and they know the housing round here backwards. The other place is the council. It's their property that often gets squatted.'

Ally felt a flicker of hope. This was the first encouraging thing she'd heard all day.

Matt whistled as he walked down Wardour Street from the dubbing suite where he'd been recording the final piece of commentary for tonight's show. They'd only finished editing the film about Meredith Morgan at midnight and it was brilliant. In fact Matt realized he'd enjoyed the last few days of frenetic activity more than anything he'd done in years. It had been like his early days in TV when everything was challenging and exciting. The irony was that just as Ritchie Page was proposing to drop them, Matt had come up with a formula that finally seemed to work and be different as well. Surely when he saw it even Page would have to change his mind, despite his prejudices. And if he didn't – Matt smiled to himself – maybe Matt would take the format somewhere else.

He was about to hail a cab when he noticed the mouth-watering display of pastries in Patisserie Valerie's window. He decided to go in and buy some cakes to take back for the team to eat this afternoon. Everyone had been working so hard it would cheer them up.

Even though it was almost midday Patisserie Valerie was crowded with people breakfasting on coffee and croissants, hiding behind their copies of *Screen International*. Matt remembered that Soho was the haunt of film editors, beavering away in endless tiny cutting rooms and edit suites. Patisserie Valerie was their canteen. They sat here in their leather jackets, winter or summer, reading monographs on Eisenstein as they cut their commercials for Pepsi.

Matt ordered a takeaway coffee as the girl boxed up his selection and tied it with ribbon. The bill came to a staggering amount. No wonder commercials cost so much to make these days

Sitting by the phone, Jess felt almost as helpless as Ally did. She'd tried her father's office and had been told brusquely that he was out and wouldn't be back till after midday. Then she'd called every friend of Janey's she could think of who might know where she'd gone. But none of them seemed to have any idea. Then she realized maybe she'd better stay off the phone in case Janey or anyone was trying to ring. Just waiting felt worst of all.

She looked at her watch. It was twelve fifteen. She decided to try her father again, determined to make them look for him if he wasn't there. This time she was put through to someone much more helpful, but even so the level of noise in their office, people shouting to each other, other phones ringing and a TV set that seemed permanently on maximum volume meant that Jess only hoped the woman had understood the urgency of the situation.

Feeling overwhelmed by the responsibility, and a recurring sense of guilt that this was all her fault, Jess began to sob into the cushion of the sofa, hoping desperately that her father would ring soon.

Ally's first mistake when she went to the Housing Department was the naïve assumption that they might be helpful to someone whose face had been seen on television. The lumpen young woman behind the counter made it clear she loathed privilege in all its forms, particularly in the shape of a slim, successful, rich TV star. Under other circumstances Ally might have sympathized with her.

She seemed to feel that the fact that Ally had a daughter who'd run away the week before her A levels to squat in Divinity Road meant there was at least some justice in the world. The upshot was that no, she was very sorry but there was no way the council could divulge which of their properties were currently being squatted.

Ally checked her watch. It was lunchtime and her other hope, the local Housing Trust, wasn't open till this afternoon. Even though she wasn't hungry she decided to have lunch in a nearby pub just in case she should catch sight of Janey or hear anything useful.

It wasn't easy to blend into the background of the Lancaster Arms for someone who had a famous face but Ally put on her sunglasses, turned up the collar of her jacket and hoped for the best. So far it had worked. Fortunately for her she had competition from the two twenty at Newmarket and most of the regulars were more preoccupied with getting to the betting shop next door than with looking at her.

Ally glanced round. Empties vied with overflowing ashtrays for space on the filthy tables and the floor was knee-deep in crisp packets. Leaning on the bar was a young man in a knitted Rasta hat with three yards of hair tucked inside smoking a joint as he ignored the chaos.

'Calvin! Yo!' shouted the landlord, making him jump. 'Clear them bloody tables up, will you?' In this part of the world obviously being a potman had a meaning of its own.

In a corner Ally noticed a bunch of young people in black leather with jet black hair and nose studs, the now-familiar uniform of the Goth. This lot also had earrings and jeans so ripped they looked like those mops made out of J-cloths. But they might know something useful.

'Excuse me,' she asked hesitantly, 'but do any of you know someone called Adam? Tall, long black hair, always wears leather. He's got a squat in Divinity Road.'

One of the girls looked up antagonistically. Ally counted six rings in her right nostril and another six in her left earlobe. Probably as post-punk girlhood went, she was considered the height of femininity.

'Who wants to know?'

Ally was hopeful. This was better than 'Never heard of him'. 'A friend.'

'I bet you're a bloody spy from the DSS checking up on whether he's claiming.'

'No, she ain't,' leered one of the young men, winking his eyelinered eye at her, 'she's far too well-dressed, aren't you, love? She's probably down here looking for her bit of rough.' He fingered her washed silk skirt knowingly. 'Didn't he ring you back, darling? What a pity. I would have.'

Ally turned and walked out of the pub as quickly as she could, the sound of raucous laughter ringing in her ears.

By the time she got to the Notting Hill Housing Trust it had opened again. She had high hopes of the place, because they were based in Divinity Road itself.

She knew from the moment she walked in they'd be more co-operative. A friendly middle-aged woman in vaguely alternative clothes smiled at her and asked how she could help.

There was one problem: none of their own properties was being squatted. The woman photocopied a map of the street and coloured in all the Trust's houses in red. 'At least you'll know it's none of those.'

Ally looked at the sheet and cheered up. There were about fifty houses left. Surely she could work her way round those.

She took the paper and put it in her shoulder bag. At the door she turned to thank the woman for her help.

'There is one other place you could try. George's Café. George knows what's going on round here before it even happens.'

The atmosphere on The *Matt Boyd Show* was festive, almost like Christmas. Roy had bribed Brendan the barman to open the bar half an hour early and let him have a few bottles of sparkling wine. He was now circulating round the team, who had gathered in Belinda's and Matt's office, pouring it into plastic cups. It went perfectly with Matt's cake selection.

For the first time in months there was a tangible sense of excitement as well as relief in everyone from Belinda down to the newest researcher. They knew they were on to something. Everyone was convinced that today's programme was going to be so brilliant that they refused to believe any rumours about being taken off the air permanently. Television fed off rumours, and hardly any of them were true. In a few hours they'd prove they were still at the top. After the summer break they'd be back in glory.

Matt raised his plastic cup. 'To us. The beginning of a new era for *The Matt Boyd Show*!'

The team cheered.

As Matt put down his cup the phone rang on the programme secretary's desk outside the office.

'It's for you, Matt,' she shouted.

Still smiling Matt leaned forward and shouted an acknowledgement. 'Any idea who it is? One of my greatest fans or just the chairman of Century?'

'Actually it's your daughter Jess.' The girl had just remembered guiltily the message Jess had left earlier. 'She says it's urgent.'

Chapter 31

When Jess heard her father's voice she started to cry with relief. Everything would be all right now.

'Jess. Jessy, darling. What's the matter?' The tenderness in her father's voice only made her cry more. 'What on earth's happened?'

'Oh, Dad,' Jess blurted, 'I didn't think she'd really do it. It was my fault. If I hadn't had a go at her for telling you about Danny Wilde it would never have happened!'

'Jessy, what are you talking about? Who wouldn't have done what?'

'It's Janey, Dad. She's run away.'

'My God! When?'

'Early this morning.' Jess's tone changed subtly from remorseful to proud at being the one with the information. 'Mum's been out looking for her ever since.'

Matt listened, appalled. 'You're sure she hasn't gone to a friend's?'

Jess shook her head. 'We don't think so. We've tried everyone.' Jess felt important and grown up at including herself in this. 'And anyway she took all her clothes and her building society book and everything.'

'Did she have much money in it?' Jess was the saver. Janey always spent everything she had.

'About thirty pounds, Mum thinks.'

Thirty pounds wouldn't last her long.

'Has Mum got any idea where she's gone?'

Jess wondered how her father would take the next bit of information. 'To Adam's, we think. He's got a squat in Notting Hill.'

'Whereabouts in Notting Hill?' Matt's mind raced ahead. He knew the area a little.

'Divinity Road, we think. That's where Mum's searching.'

Matt closed his eyes. He'd seen a documentary about Divinity Road. London's Harlem, the programme had called it. It was a mecca for crack dealers and traffickers in heroin. Janey had chosen the most dangerous place in the city to run away to.

The stark black and white photographs on the government anti-drug posters leapt into Matt's mind. Gaunt, shadowy-eyed young people who'd thrown their lives away because someone talked them into shooting up. Somebody's sons and daughters.

He recalled bitterly how he'd had the minister masterminding the campaign on the show. It had been a failure, said its critics, because teenagers saw images of degradation as glamorous. Young people were drawn to what was bad for them. He hoped to God Janey wasn't.

As he listened, one thought haunted him: would this have happened if he'd still been around?

What the hell was he going to do? It was less than three hours until his Special with Meredith Morgan, the show they were depending on to convince Ritchie Page that he should bring them back after the summer. The Special would go out live and the whole team was counting on him to make it brilliant to assure their future. If he missed it his career would be over, not only at Century but probably anywhere else too. It was unthinkable to risk a show that represented so much to so many people.

And yet. What was worth more? His career in television or Janey? She might be wandering about, lost and disorientated, too proud to come home, sure of only one thing: that she'd been abandoned by anyone who loved her.

Janey wasn't the running away type. This must have cost her all her courage.

Matt looked at his watch. Maybe he didn't have long enough to find Janey, but he had enough time to get to Divinity Road and see for himself. Long enough to show Ally he hadn't abandoned her to worry alone.

He grabbed his car keys. It would only take fifteen minutes to get to Portobello from here.

'Matt?' Belinda had left the office and closed the door behind her. With a sixth sense for danger she'd been trying to listen but hadn't caught much of the conversation. 'Where the fuck are you *going*?' Her voice was sharp with apprehension.

Matt thought about telling her. But he had a pretty good idea what she'd say. 'Let's say it's an emergency. I'll keep in touch.'

The horror on Belinda's face was so comic that despite his worry Matt couldn't help smiling. 'Ah, well,' he said. 'You know what they say. It never rains but it pours.' He began to walk away.

'Matt!' Belinda shouted. 'For God's sake at least take a phone.' But he had already disappeared into the lift.

Back in their office a wave of infectious laughter drifted through the door reminding Belinda how long they'd struggled to create this mood, this sense of enthusiasm. And now they'd finally done it, Matt was risking the whole bloody thing. She watched the animated faces through the glass partition. She didn't feel like going back in and celebrating any more.

As she stood there her thoughts were interrupted by the phone ringing. Angrily she picked it up.

'Is that *The Matt Boyd Show*?' Belinda immediately recognized the voice as Ally's. 'Is Matt there?'

Belinda glanced towards the swing doors, but Matt would be out of the building by now. Suddenly she felt furious. Furious that Ally was taking their slot and still expected Matt to jump when she called. Furious that Matt *did* jump. Standing there, pale with anger, Belinda knew her jealousy was more than simply for the show.

'No, he bloody well isn't,' she snapped. 'As a matter of fact he's just run out of the building.'

Exhausted though she was Ally could hear the venom in Belinda's voice.

'I take it this crisis,' Belinda asked nastily, 'is your doing?'

'Absolutely.' Ally might be tired, but not too tired to feel an answering flash of anger. 'I purposely arranged for our daughter to run away expressly to ruin your show.'

Belinda was momentarily thrown. So that was where Matt had gone. To try and find his daughter. How crazy of him! How did he think he could possibly find a lost kid just like that? Jesus, she'd better get on to presentation and make sure they had an old *Matt Boyd Show* standing by. If Ritchie Page got to hear of this they really were finished.

Belinda could tell Ally was about to put down the phone and couldn't resist one last stab. 'You do realize, I suppose, that we're due to go on air for the biggest programme in Matt's career in less than three hours? Today was supposed to be make or break.' The incredulity rang through Belinda's voice. She couldn't understand how Matt could do it.

'Thanks for pointing it out.' Despite her tiredness and worry Ally's heart lifted and she smiled faintly. 'It could be make or break for our daughter, too.'

As Matt drove slowly along Lancaster Road his sense of unease multiplied. It was a hot afternoon and the area round Divinity Road teemed with street life. Kids kicked a football with no thought of getting out of the way of approaching cars. Leaning out of upstairs windows and lounging against the peeling cast-iron railings people watched him incuriously. If they recognized him they made no sign. From time to time someone ducked down into a basement or alley clearly doing a deal. Matt had read that the pusher carries only a couple of hits of crack, leaving the supply somewhere else and going back to replenish it. When a customer approaches he passes it from his mouth to theirs. Due to some weird aberration in the law the police couldn't search your mouth.

A couple of cops cruised by, trying uselessly to make their presence felt, but Matt sensed even in them a reluctance to get out of the safety of their cars.

He drove up and down Divinity Road twice and then stopped. What should he do if he couldn't find Ally, if she'd got discouraged and given up?

And then with an enormous sense of relief he saw her. She was talking to a young police constable at the far end of the road. Even from this distance he could sense her exhaustion. He accelerated towards them and got out of the car.

'Ally!' he shouted and ran to her.

She turned, white and strained. 'Oh, Matt, thank God you're here!' He held her tightly and all the strength that had kept her going when she was on her own ebbed out of her. She had been knocking on doors, getting either a stony silence or outright hostility, all afternoon.

Matt helped her gently into the car and squatted beside her, the rifts between them forgotten in their concern for Janey.

'Ally, you've got to go home. I'll take over now.' He stared around him at the insalubrious street. 'Have you any idea which number it is?'

'She's not at any of these houses. I've checked.' Ally

handed him the map the Notting Hill Housing Trust had given her. Less than half the numbers were crossed out. Matt felt a shiver of defeat. It would take hours to work his way through the rest. 'Somebody suggested trying George's Café. He knows everything that goes on apparently. Matt?'

'Yes, love?'

'Before I go home do you think I'd better go down to the police station and officially report her as missing?'

Matt squeezed her hand. 'Not yet.' He knew what she must be going through. 'If I can't find her I'll do it later. Go home to Jess.' He touched her face very lightly. 'She needs you too.'

Ally smiled. She knew he was making it easier for her to give up and was grateful. She could hardly walk another step.

'What about your show?'

Matt grinned, a flash of humour lighting up his blue eyes. 'Ah, well, as my mother would say, it's only television.'

George's Café turned out to be a greasy spoon near the corner of Portobello and Westbourne Park Road and George himself an affable Cypriot. It was the sort of place that opened for local workmen while it was still dark and did bacon, egg, sausage, chips and beans all day until the custom dried up. Despite George's origins there wasn't a doner kebab or baklava in sight. At the moment the café was almost deserted.

When Matt walked in George greeted him like an old friend. Obviously having a major TV star choose to patronize his café at four thirty on a Wednesday afternoon seemed the most natural thing in the world to him. 'Matt, how are you? Cup of tea, is it?'

Matt took a cup gratefully, glancing at his watch at the same time. Two hours to go.

'So, Matt,' George said, hoping some of his customers would notice him sitting at a window table with the famous Matt Boyd, 'tell me, what I can do for you?'

At Century Television Ritchie Page was in the middle of a meeting with their lawyer, honing down some of the finer points of the contract they were drawing up to offer Danny Wilde. Jack Saltash had more than lived up to his wily reputation on this one, and every clause had been an agony of brinkmanship. Danny Wilde was going to be a very rich young man. They had got to the end of clause 56(c)(V) when the phone buzzed on Page's desk.

It was his secretary Lorraine. 'I thought you might like to know, Mr Page, that when I was down in the canteen a moment ago I overheard one of the PAs from *The Matt Boyd Show* tell her friend what a flap they're in down there. It's his big show tonight and Matt's left the building. Apparently his daughter's run away from home and he's gone to look for her.'

Page glanced across his desk at the lawyer and smiled. His wife had cooked him a perfect four-minute egg this morning and he'd known it was going to be a good day. The lawyer had overheard everything and was nodding contentedly. 'Well,' he said, 'that would certainly solve a lot of our problems. A clear breach of contract.'

'Yes,' Page grinned, thinking of the 1.6 million pounds Matt's quixotic gesture might save him. He reached behind him for a bottle of twenty-two-year-old single malt he'd been saving for just such an occasion. 'I think we might drink to that.'

George recognized the description of Adam at once. He shared a squat with a bunch of other young people, some students, some musicians. They often came into his café and sometimes brought their guitars. If the café wasn't too busy George let them play and take round a hat afterwards. He liked music.

He nodded his head enthusiastically when Matt mentioned Divinity Road, but when he asked what number George's face turned into a pantomime of dismay. He had no idea.

Matt had to hold on to himself. He'd felt so close. George's description of Adam had been so accurate that he could almost see him sitting at one of the tables in the café. And now another blank. He was no nearer than Ally had been.

Suddenly George jumped up and opened the door behind the counter. 'Ariadne!' he yelled up the stairs. 'My daughter,' he explained. 'She's friendly with one of the musicians.' He screwed up his face. 'A lout, so I tell her not to see him.'

A slim young girl with long dark hair and straight black eyebrows, neat in a summer frock, not looking at all like the kind of girl who'd hang out with friends of Adam's, appeared. She did a double take when she saw Matt.

'Ariadne, Mr Boyd is looking for his daughter. He thinks she's with Adam, the tall boy in leather, your friend's friend. Do you know what number they live at?'

The girl looked wary, as though if she gave her father the information he wanted she might be offering herself up to his paternal Cypriot wrath.

To Matt's intense relief, George understood this. 'I will not be angry if you do. This is an important matter.'

The girl stood for a moment, weighing up the eternal loyalty of children against the encroachment of their parents, and also the prospects of her musician asking her out again. They were pretty negative.

'OK,' She turned to Matt. 'They live at number thirty-eight, next door to the pub. Do you want me to show you?'

Matt half walked, half ran back to Divinity Road. He didn't need Ariadne to show him. He'd been up and down it enough times.

He stopped and looked at the unprepossessing exterior of number thirty-eight. Although it was a brilliantly sunny afternoon some of the curtains were tightly drawn. The ground floor and basement still had some planks nailed across the lower half and the rest had obviously been removed to get access. A motorbike, partly dismantled, took up most of the top step. Loud music blared from one of the upstairs rooms. Disconcertingly out of character, a canary in a cage chirruped on a high window-sill as though they were in the Mediterranean instead of Notting Hill Gate. Everywhere was the pungent smell of spicy Afro-Caribbean food and the faint aroma of rotting rubbish.

As he stood there, Matt realized how nervous he was. His palms were sweating and his breath was coming in fast little bursts that had nothing to do with his exertions. What if after all this she wasn't there? Or if Adam refused to let him in? The fact was, he hadn't thought beyond this moment.

Plucking up more courage than he'd needed in twenty years of live television, Matt forced himself to ring the bell.

There was a long silence, after which nothing happened. A couple of minutes later he rang it again. This time there were distant stirrings then the sound of someone coming down the stairs.

Finally the door opened three inches and a suspicious, long-haired youth peered out. It wasn't Adam. Matt felt a contradictory sense of relief. Maybe it was the wrong house.

The youth watched him beadily. ''Ere, aren't you that bloke from the telly?' He looked round to see if this was some elaborate set-up and that a camera crew would jump out at any moment announcing they were on live television and being beamed into the sitting rooms of millions.

'Yes, I am that bloke from the telly. Does Adam live here?'

The youth sized him up, then shrugged. He turned back into the house and yelled, 'Adam! There's someone here wanting to see you.'

As he stood on the doorstep waiting Matt had to admit to himself that he'd never felt so scared in his life.

Chapter 32

Soon Matt heard the clump of heavy boots on the un-carpeted stairs. Then Adam's face appeared round the door, glaring suspiciously.

'Mr Boyd!' To Matt's surprise his tone was almost respectful. 'Hello.'

'Hello, Adam.' Matt decided a neutral friendliness would be best. 'Is Janey here?'

'Yes, I –' Quite out of character, Adam lost confidence for a moment. 'I . . . I'll go and find her.'

He disappeared into the dark house leaving Matt on the doorstep again. Matt felt conflicting emotions flooding through him. Excitement at the thought of seeing Janey and terror that she'd refuse to come home. He had to remind himself that he couldn't play the Victorian father. It wasn't his authority that was at stake today but her safety and happiness.

The same boots clumped down the stairs. There was no one with Adam. Maybe he'd come to ask Matt in.

'Look . . . Matt . . .' Adam's white Goth's cheeks were tinged with embarrassment. 'I'm afraid she doesn't want to see you. She says she's happy here.' He turned back slowly, but catching sight of the pain in Matt's expression he added lamely, 'I did try to persuade her. But I'm afraid she's absolutely sure.'

Gently he shut the door leaving Matt standing there unsure of what to do.

Furiously Matt ran down the steps. Ungrateful brat! How dare she turn him away? Across the road he saw a shabby launderette. At least it would have a phone and he could call Ally and tell her Janey was safe.

In spite of its scruffy appearance the launderette was spotless inside. The evocative smell of washing took him straight back to childhood when things had been safe and certain. Or had they? What about his mother stifling her dreams as she fed his father's shirts through the mangle?

He flopped down on to a bench for a moment, drinking in the warm clean-smelling air, grateful that there was no one else in the place. He'd made such a mess. He'd misjudged Ally and screwed up his marriage, his daughter had run away and wouldn't speak to him, and today he'd probably banged the final nail in the coffin of his career. Lucky Matt Boyd.

When he heard the door opening behind him he looked up with the absurd idea it was going to be Janey saying she'd changed her mind. Instead a small Asian lady with a red mark in the middle of her forehead and a saree under her blue nylon overall smiled at him and began to tip a bulging carrier bag into one of the machines.

Matt stood up and searched for coins for the phone. Ally answered on the third ring. She had just got home, had a shower and felt better though just as worried.

'It's me. I've found her. She was at number thirty-eight.'

'Matt, that's brilliant!' Relief and pleasure bubbled over in her tone.

'Ally, she refused to see me.' Ally could hear the pain seeping into his voice. 'She wouldn't even let me in.'

'Oh Matt, how awful. But she's safe anyway. At least we don't have to worry about that. Maybe she'll change her mind in a day or two.' She wished she could be with him. 'Matt, where are you? Jess says they've been trailing your show all day. Are you going to make it?'

Matt looked at his watch. He had nearly an hour. 'Yes, it'll be fine. I'll call you later.'

'Matt?'

'Yes?'

'Thanks for looking. I know what it cost you.'

Matt shrugged. 'She's my daughter too and I love her.'

'I know. I know you do.' Her voice sounded somehow soaked in sadness.

As they said goodbye he realized he ought to phone Belinda and reassure her. They'd be shitting themselves at Century by now. But as he picked up the phone the door of number thirty-eight opened and a group of black-clad young people spilled out on the pavement, Adam and Janey among them. They were all laughing. He didn't have to wonder what about.

Then Adam leaned down so that his long hair fell in a dark curtain hiding Janey's face. He was kissing her. They went on, locked in a passionate embrace, for almost a minute while the others cheered.

A stab of anger laced with jealousy ran through Matt so strong that it was almost physically painful.

He watched while another youth came out and slammed the door behind him, then the group started walking, laughing and catcalling, down the street.

Standing in the warm safety of the launderette, an idea occurred to Matt. It was a crazy mad, dangerous idea. And its appeal was so powerful that Matt knew he couldn't possibly resist it. What was it about Adam and the life he could offer that was making Janey turn her back on her parents and everything they'd given her?

He was going to break in and see for himself.

'Roy,' Belinda shouted across the tea bar outside studio three, 'is Meredith Morgan here yet?'

Roy picked up his clipboard and came towards her. 'The lady and her entourage – and I do mean entourage, she's brought her PR man, her own make-up girl *and* her press agent with her – have just arrived in reception. I'm going to meet them now. Meredith needs the full hour in make-up, apparently.'

Belinda sat down in her chair behind the control panel, trying to hide the blind panic she was feeling. They had less than an hour and there hadn't been a word from Matt. The press were here in force. And then there was Meredith herself. Belinda went cold for a moment. It had been extraordinary that a Hollywood legend like her had agreed to come on at all. Meredith Morgan hardly did any talk-shows. She was too rich and too famous and much too eccentric to care about getting any more publicity. She'd only agreed because she liked Matt so much. How the bloody hell was Belinda going to explain to her that she'd come six thousand miles and Matt was nowhere to be found?

Matt crossed the street, noticing that the groups of youths had dispersed from the front steps now that the day was cooling down.

He ran up the steps of number thirty-eight two at a time. He couldn't believe he was doing this, risking his whole reputation on an impulse. He only knew he had to see inside the place Janey wouldn't allow him into, as though it held the secret of winning her back.

Glancing round nervously to make sure no one was looking he put his shoulder to the door and heaved. It didn't give but he could feel the elasticity in the door on its cheap and flimsy lock. This time he ran at it, relatively unobtrusively. It gave a little more. The third time the rotten wood splintered and the door burst open. Willing himself to keep calm even though he'd just committed a criminal act, Matt walked in. He wasn't intending to steal anything, just to look around.

Across the other side of the road a young man loading his guitar into a battered Transit van watched him

463

curiously. He was in the same band as Joe, one of Adam's friends. He got into the van and started it up.

Matt stepped over the threshold. Inside was a dark corridor carpeted with old newspapers leading into a big front room. He looked in. The floorboards were bare but there were scraps of old patterned carpet here and there. Four or five old mattresses, doubled over like futons, some covered with Indian bedspreads, had been pushed against the walls to serve as sofas. The walls were painted with garish coloured murals, clearly added to by anyone who felt like it. Everywhere ashtrays overflowed with suspicious looking dog-ends.

Round the corner, two blocks away, the young man who lived opposite saw the group dancing down the street towards George's Café.

''Ere, Joe!' he yelled at his friend. 'I've just seen some geezer breaking into your house.'

The group stopped and looked at each other.

Joe laughed. 'They can help themselves. There's nothing in my room worth nicking.'

Adam swore. 'Well, there is in mine. It took me years to save up for my guitar and I'm not letting some creep flog it for a tenner just because he wants the next hit.'

He turned back towards Divinity Road.

Janey took his arm anxiously. 'Adam, don't go on your own. You know what it's like round here.'

'Who's coming with me, then?'

No one volunteered. A moment ago Janey had noticed a police car circling the area. As they talked it drove slowly into sight. She flagged it down.

The policeman stopped and opened his window.

'Constable,' Janey said in her best Surrey débutante voice, 'someone's just broken into our house. We think they're in there now.'

The constable thought for a moment, weighing up the risks of trying to apprehend anyone in this area against the thrill of actually catching someone in the act. The clear-up rate round here was abysmal and the young constable was new in the force. He decided it was worth it. He opened his door. 'Hop in.'

'You go to George's with the others.' Adam waved Janey on. 'I'll catch up with you later.'

Matt stood in the hall and listened, frozen. Upstairs he could hear a noise. Someone was in. He turned quickly and made for the door. Suddenly something wrapped itself round his legs. Matt almost laughed out loud. It was a cat.

Smiling to himself at his own fear, Matt walked down the corridor. Beyond the sitting room was a small kitchen. A pile of half-eaten Indian takeaways, still in their foil cartons, stood on top of the draining board. Cooking clearly wasn't one of their hobbies.

Matt went upstairs. He reckoned there would be five or six bedrooms at least in a place like this. He opened the first door off the landing. Essence of unmade bed with a dash of stale sweat hit him. But there was nothing in the room he recognized as Janey's.

As he ran up the next flight of stairs, he asked himself what he was looking for. He didn't really have an answer.

On the top landing there were three more rooms. One of these had to be Adam's. He opened another door, getting used to the familiar staleness of the air. As usual the bed was a tangle of dirty sheets. Piles of clothes were strewn on the floor. By the side of the mattress was an ashtray full of cigarette ends, in the middle were two used condoms. Matt steeled himself. Was this Adam's room?

In the corner next to the grimy window was an open suitcase. A tangle of women's clothes tumbled out of it.

Matt bent down. None of them looked like Janey's. He felt an absurd relief and knew he was being ridiculous. Of course they were sleeping together.

The next room was up a small half-staircase. Holding his breath he opened the door, then stopped transfixed for a moment on the threshold.

This room was quite unlike all the others. It was neat and tidy and bursting with personality. Instead of bare boards it had an ancient carpet on to which some dusty Turkish rugs had been thrown, their colours faded but still visible. Exotic hangings were draped on the walls and twisted into a tent above the bed. On the bedside table a scarf shaded an art nouveau lamp.

By the window an acoustic guitar leaned on a chair. He walked carefully over to it, feeling like an intruder. There was a pad next to the guitar. He picked it up. It was the words of a love song. He didn't recognize the writing but the words leaped out at him. It was about Janey.

As he read it, a gust blew through the open window, knocking some papers to the floor from a table by the window. He bent down to put them back on and noticed that it had been arranged as a makeshift desk. On top was Janey's copy of T.S. Eliot and underneath it a prospectus from Sussex University. Matt stared at it in amazement.

Propped up next to it was a garish card in the 'Love Is' series. A fat little boy held out a heart to a fat little girl. 'Love Is . . . Being There.' Matt opened it, recognizing Janey's writing. 'To Adam,' Janey had written, 'thank you for being there when no one else was.'

Matt put it down, feeling his throat close over painfully with emotion. Tears began to prick at the back of his eyes. It was so trite and ghastly and yet so heartfelt. But Janey was right. Adam had offered her the one thing he and Ally had failed to give her. They had given her love and they had showered her with material possessions. But they hadn't been able to give her the one thing she really wanted: security.

And in some extraordinary and unexpected way, Adam had.

Matt stood holding the card, so absorbed in his thoughts that he didn't notice the footsteps on the stairs.

When the door opened he turned suddenly.

Adam stood there. And looking over his shoulder, his face a comic mask of amazement, was a uniformed policeman.

'Where the fuck *is* he?' shouted Ritchie Page, bursting into the control room with all the force of a nuclear reaction. In fact Page was hugely enjoying himself but he didn't intend to let anyone on the programme guess that. 'We've been trailing this frigging show all day. Hacks from half the tabloids are here to watch it and you tell me Matt's gone off on some bloody wild goose chase looking for his long-lost daughter?'

'I know. I know.' Belinda tried not to give in to her panic. The only way she was going to get through the next hour was if she kept absolutely calm. 'But presentation does have a standby.' She was never going to forgive Matt for this. He was ruining her career as well as his own. There was only three-quarters of an hour to go. As Page stormed out again threatening that if Matt didn't get back they could both clear their desks today, she wondered how much longer she had before she'd have to break the news to Meredith Morgan.

Matt watched the two men speechlessly. He couldn't think of a single good reason why he should be standing here.

Fortunately Adam was quicker off the mark.

'Matt!' he exclaimed walking towards him as though

467

finding Britain's top chat-show host in the middle of his bedroom was exactly what he might have expected.

Adam turned to the baffled young policeman. 'Mr Boyd is my girlfriend's father. We'd asked him to drop round. Janey was supposed to leave a key. She must have forgotten. You know women.'

The police constable, a nineteen-year-old rookie who lived at home with his mother, nodded sagely. He was relieved they hadn't had to tackle a drug-crazed house-breaker.

Finally Matt found his voice. 'I didn't want to spend hours on the pavement so I got a bit carried away. I'll pay for the door, of course.' He reached into his jacket for his wallet.

'Aren't you supposed to be doing your show?' The young policeman looked puzzled. 'I saw it advertised down at the station.'

'Jesus!' Matt looked at his watch in horror. 'We're due on in twenty-five minutes.'

'Tell you what,' said the PC, whose mother was one of Matt's greatest fans. 'Would you like a lift in the jam sandwich? You'll get there a bloody sight quicker.'

Matt grinned. 'I've always wanted to ride in a police car with the siren on.' He held out his hand to Adam. 'Thanks a lot.'

'I'm coming with you. I'll phone Janey from the studio,' insisted Adam, ignoring Matt's outstretched hand and gesturing towards the door. 'I wouldn't miss this for the world.'

Chapter 33

'Fifteen minutes to on air, studio,' the PA warned, not looking up from the shot list she was checking.

Belinda turned round to find Bernie Long standing behind her. Jesus, that was all she needed. 'What the hell are you doing here?' she snapped. 'Come to dance on my grave? Get to the back of the queue.'

For once Bernie looked sympathetic. 'I heard Matt had gone AWOL and wondered if there was any way I could help.'

Belinda looked at the clock on the wall of the control room and ran her fingers through her dark hair. 'Not unless you can do miracles.'

'So when are you going to tell Meredith he's not back yet?' He could see she was holding out until the very last minute and he found himself genuinely admiring her. No one could say she didn't have nerve.

'In five minutes. I've palmed off her agent with some bullshit about Matt not liking to meet his guests, that it spoils the spontaneity. But he's beginning to get suspicious.'

She glanced behind her at the mahogany-coloured gnome who had guided Meredith through the last forty years of her stardom. He didn't look happy.

'And what if Matt doesn't make it?'

'Presentation's standing by with another show. They'll put out one of those apologies that it's beyond our control.'

'How's Page taking it?'

'Pretending to be furious but gleeful underneath.'

'Ten minutes to on air,' reminded the PA.

Belinda sighed and pulled herself up. 'Time I went and broke the news to Meredith.' She shook Bernie's hand. 'It was nice knowing you.'

In his executive suite Ritchie Page grinned as he called Danny Wilde and told him that they had finished drafting the contract and would be biking it to his agent tomorrow morning.

Page zapped on the giant television in the corner of his office with the remote control.

'If you tune into Century now, Dan, you'll witness Matt Boyd missing his own Special and terminating his contract with us in front of nine million witnesses.' Page still couldn't get over this particular piece of good luck.

Things had gone so much better than he could have hoped. The Boyds' marriage was in ruins, their daughter had run away, and now Matt was going to miss his own Special. A few days ago he'd decided that instead of waiting for Matt to resign he'd have to buy him out. Now he wouldn't need to. There was nothing Ritchie Page enjoyed quite as much as saving millions of pounds. Except, perhaps, screwing Matt Boyd.

Jock Wilson, the security guard on duty at the entrance to Century's underground car park, thought the police car screeching towards them must be something to do with one of the cop shows the drama department was making. A real police car would hardly be coming straight towards the barrier at that speed. To his amazement he saw Matt Boyd in the passenger seat and lifted it just in time to avoid a nasty accident.

'Thanks, Jock,' shouted Matt as he bundled out of the car and began running up the steps to the studios.

'Five minutes to on air.' The PA checked her stopwatch, ready to start counting. 'Settle down studio, please.'

Belinda strode on to the studio floor wishing she hadn't asked Meredith Morgan to be in studio for the opening shot. She held her hands up for attention. 'Ladies and gentlemen, and, of course, our very welcome guest, Miss Morgan. I have a short announcement to make . . .'

Belinda was interrupted by a commotion at the back of the studio and Matt skidded on to the floor followed by a tall young man with jet black hair.

'Jesus fucking Christ!' shouted the director. 'He's made it!'

Belinda lassooed a sound recordist. 'Quick. Get him miked up,' she barked. 'Fast!'

'Three minutes to opening titles,' said the PA, her eyes like saucers. She'd never seen anything like this before in fifteen years of TV.

The audience looked at each other bemused. Suddenly there was a long low laugh from Meredith Morgan. 'Well,' she drawled in her sex-for-breakfast tones, 'that was some entrance.'

'Thank you,' Matt kissed her on the cheek as he dashed for his seat. 'I never was any good at being punctual.'

Belinda dashed back to the control room as the theme music began and Matt started reading the witty description of Meredith's film career, her eight marriages and the fact that she'd made millions out of property.

'Oh my God!' Belinda half leaped out of her seat. 'He hasn't got his questions. He can't ad lib for a whole hour.'

'Yes, he can.' Belinda whipped round to find Bernie Long still standing there. 'You're about to see what makes Matt Boyd the best there is.'

Belinda slumped in her seat, realizing there was absolutely nothing she could do. Matt didn't even wear an earpiece. He was on his own.

★

In George's Café Janey was looking worried and wondering if she should phone the police station for news of Adam and the break-in. He should have been here by now. None of the others seemed concerned, they were too busy hooting with laughter at George's favourite soap opera blaring from the TV attached to the wall.

Behind the counter the phone rang and she saw Ariadne pointing her out to George. She almost ran to get it. She had to edge her way past piles of dirty plates waiting to be stacked in the dishwasher. Clearly George didn't encourage customers to use the phone.

'Adam, thank God, I was worried sick.' She'd had visions of him lying in a pool of blood, blasted by some crackhead's bullet. 'What happened? Are you at the police station?'

Adam grinned. 'No actually. I'm at Century's studios.'

Janey couldn't take in what she was hearing. 'What on earth are you doing there?'

'I'm with your father. He's just going on air now.' Janey listened in disbelief. 'You should watch. It's going to be a great show. Look, I've got to go. Why don't you go back to Divinity Road after the programme? Don't worry, it wasn't a burglar after all. I'll explain it all when I get back. Love you.'

Janey heard the receiver click and stood staring at it. What the hell was going on? What was Adam doing at Century? It didn't make sense.

'Look, Miss Boyd,' George shouted enthusiastically. 'It's your dad on the box. And the lady with all the husbands.' He beckoned her across. Matt must have found her earlier, George reflected, but clearly she hadn't gone with him. English men were too soft on their kids. He wouldn't stand for such nonsense from his daughter.

Janey put the phone down and looked up at the wall. She'd been wondering how upset he would be that she'd refused to see him, but clearly it was business as usual.

She flopped down into a chair underneath the television set, where it was almost impossible to see it.

Ally and Jess sat holding hands on the sofa in the sitting room as the familiar music for *The Matt Boyd Show* started. Belinda had made it crystal clear to Ally what it would mean if Matt didn't make it back for the show, and knowing Ritchie Page as she did Ally was a hundred per cent sure Belinda was right.

They held their breath as the titles ended and the camera panned across. When it stopped on Matt they both let out a cheer and Jess jumped off the sofa and started to do a cancan round the room. He'd made it. He might not have been able to persuade Janey to come home, but at least they knew she wasn't wandering the streets and he'd got to the studio in time. Ally watched in amazement. From his cool witty manner there was no way you could guess the pressure he'd been under for the last three hours.

Jess stopped dancing and eyed her father closely for a moment. 'Tell you what, Mum.' She sat down next to her mother again as Matt exchanged thrusts with Meredith Morgan. 'He looks like he's really enjoying himself.'

Up in his office Ritchie Page was still talking to Danny Wilde. He had switched the volume down and swivelled round so that he could put his feet on his desk, his favourite posture for negotiating deals.

Ritchie was in the middle of explaining to Danny why he musn't let his agent bully him on the subject of residuals when Danny began to laugh.

'What's so funny about residuals?'

'Nothing.' Danny continued to laugh disconcertingly. 'But I think you'd better look at your television.'

473

Ritchie Page swivelled back. What he saw made him take his feet off his desk and stand up, his blood pressure rising so fast that he felt light-headed. Matt Boyd had only bloody well made it. He zapped the volume up until laughter drenched his office. The show was going brilliantly.

As it happened Matt could remember the questions he was supposed to ask perfectly well. But he was having far too much fun to stick to them.

'Meredith, you've had a wildly distinguished career. Oscars and recognition. A vast property empire. But your personal life . . . Seven husbands, wasn't it? That sounds like carelessness.'

'Eight,' corrected Meredith Morgan briskly. 'The first was the best of them. I loved that man.'

Matt listened, intrigued. 'Then why did you divorce him?'

Meredith's false-eyelashed eyes twinkled more than the sequins on her Halston gown. 'Because I found him in bed with the chauffeur.'

The audience erupted with delight.

'But I learned one thing from him. Never marry the man you fall in love with. That way you don't mind so much when you have to divorce him. By the way' – she tapped him on the knee as though he was an unruly boy – 'you haven't been doing so well in that department yourself, from what I read.'

Matt pretended to hide his face in his hands as the audience cheered. 'Now, Meredith, I have to ask you this.' Matt leaned forward. In the control room, Belinda noticed that unconsciously everyone else leaned forward too. 'What about the drink problem?'

Belinda closed her eyes. Meredith's agent had banned any mention of drink. What was Matt doing?

474

'Drink problem?' Meredith repeated innocently. 'I don't have a drink problem.' She paused. 'It's the rest of the world that has a drink problem. They can't keep up with me.'

The audience clapped delightedly. 'Seriously, darling, I've given up. No vodka, not even a teeny Martini.'

Matt looked disbelieving.

'Just a bottle of champagne a day and not a drop more.'

Matt threw back his head and laughed. He loved this woman.

'Well, Meredith, some of our audience have come specially here today with a question to ask you.'

'Fire away. I'll tell them everything I tell my analyst.'

'OK, lady in red, third row down.' He pointed, and the sound recordist ran towards her with his boom.

'I wanted to know what Meredith thinks of film actors today. Are they stars like they used to be?' The woman blushed and sat down.

'I love 'em, honey.' Meredith smiled wickedly. 'I only wish I could remember some of their damn names.'

A woman in the front row raised her hand. 'Miss Morgan, I get the impression you don't have too high an opinion of men. Is that right?'

'I don't need to, sweetie, they already have it of themselves.'

Bernie, leaning on the back of Belinda's chair in the control room, laughed out loud. 'I must say, she's on cracking form. How long to go?'

'Five minutes,' said the PA.

Belinda glanced round the control room at all the battle-hardened professionals. They were watching Matt, mesmerized. She realized they had found their magic formula.

And it felt great.

'One more from the audience and then back to Matt,' Belinda informed the floor manager.

Matt scanned the hundred or so people in the audience and chose a sprightly old lady in the second row.

'Miss Morgan, you've had eight husbands and you seem to have enjoyed them all.'

'Not all,' corrected Meredith. 'I married my share of rotters, I can assure you.'

'But,' the old lady went on undaunted, 'you've had no children. Don't you like children?'

'Three minutes to closing credits,' reminded the PA.

For the first time in the show the atmosphere changed. For the next fifteen seconds Meredith sat in silent contemplation. They were the longest Belinda could ever remember.

'What's the matter?' she blurted. 'Say something, Matt!' But before he got the chance, Meredith spoke. 'Well, now, you see that isn't the whole truth. I did once have a baby.'

Behind Belinda in the visitors' gallery Meredith's agent jumped up. Clearly this wasn't on the usual chat-show schedule.

'I was eighteen and it got in the way of my brilliant career. So I gave him away.' There was a gasp from the audience. 'I never saw him again. And then, when I tried again, I found I couldn't have children.' She looked at the old lady in the audience. 'So you could say it was poetic justice, I guess.' There was suddenly no sign of the wisecracking woman of a moment ago. 'But I learned one thing. Success doesn't matter a damn compared to a child.'

Matt sat transfixed. There was no way she could know what had happened to him this afternoon.

The floor manager passed on the signal to Matt that there were two minutes left. He was about to ask Meredith Morgan a last question, then the impact of her words hit him again and he knew what he wanted to do. But did he have the nerve? The image of Ally during the Telethon putting her arms around the mother whose child was sick flashed into his mind. He'd admired her for showing emotion, but had known he could never do it. Well, here was his chance.

Unexpectedly he turned away from Meredith into the lens of the camera.

'Meredith, you don't know how those words speak to me.' Belinda exchanged glances with Bernie and shrugged. She had no idea what was coming next, but there was something about Matt's manner that made her sit up.

'You know, though the viewers don't, that I nearly missed the show today. They would have been told I was ill, but actually I'd gone to look for my daughter.' Matt paused. The audience were completely quiet. 'She ran away from home this morning. And when she wouldn't see me I broke the door down where she was staying.'

At home, Ally's hand flew to her mouth. Matt hadn't told her this.

'My God!' shouted the director to Belinda. 'What shall I do? Pull the plug?'

But Belinda wasn't listening. She was watching Matt with total attention. She'd never seen him show real feeling on the programme before.

'Janey,' he went on. I just wanted to say how sorry I am. If you can't come home that's up to you. But we love you.' Matt's voice was thick with raw emotion now. 'We really do.' He took Meredith's hand. 'Meredith, you couldn't be more right. Children matter more than any career.'

In George's Café Janey was listening intently, craning her head to see the television screen, unable to believe what she was hearing.

477

'There, can't you see how he loves you!' George, tears of fatherly empathy coursing down his face, jumped up and clutched Janey by the shoulders.

Janey sat still for a moment, then shook herself free. 'Yes.' She turned away, grabbing her leather jacket from the back of the chair. 'It was a brilliant publicity stunt, wasn't it? Begging for a reunion with his own daughter? He'll probably want to do it on camera. That way it'll be better for the ratings.' She stood up. 'There was only one little problem. He forgot to tell his millions of fans why I went.' She pushed her way through the tables, tears stinging her eyes. 'Because he walked out and left us.'

In front of the control panel the phones were flashing continually. Belinda knew what it would be. Ritchie Page telling her to cut Matt off. But she wasn't going to. Sitting there she realized for the first time how much Matt loved his daughter and that she herself had been as responsible as anyone in causing Janey's unhappiness. She felt, to her utter amazement, a lump forming in her throat and she had to flick away a tear. Jesus Christ!

Meredith Morgan turned towards Matt. 'After that' – she nodded in the direction of the camera – 'she'd better forgive you.'

Through the far door of the control room Lorraine skidded in, pink and out of breath. 'Mr Page says –' she began before Belinda cut her off.

'Lorraine . . .' Belinda knew she'd pay for this but it felt good all the same. She swivelled slowly round towards her. 'Just fuck off, will you?' She smiled her most disarming smile. 'Or shall I put that more bluntly?'

'Oh Mum,' Jess said, putting her arms round her mother, 'I hope Janey saw that.'

*

As the credits rolled chaos erupted in the studio. The hacks who had been in hospitality burst on to the floor to try and get the story.

Meredith Morgan's press agent, plump and indignant, his head as bald and shiny as a billiard ball, waddled up. 'I'm sorry, honey,' he buzzed angrily, 'they promised not to mention the drink.'

Meredith gave Matt a warm, natural, unstarry smile that took her press agent quite by surprise. 'Screw the drink. I just divulged my darkest secret. And I don't regret it a bit,' she said to Matt. 'I hope your daughter comes back. That was some speech.'

As Matt unhooked himself from his radio mike and slipped into the control room to get away from the pack of journalists, he saw Ritchie Page walking towards him, white-faced and livid.

Seeing the signs of volcanic eruption, Matt pre-empted him. 'It's all right, Page. You don't have to fire me. I'm resigning anyway.'

He looked far more cheerful, Page noted with irritation, than anyone kissing goodbye to 1.6 six million ought to.

'Congratulations, Matt. That was really moving.' Adam stepped from the wings where he'd been watching the show. He grinned. 'Pity we don't have a television.'

Matt suddenly cracked with laughter. All that, and Janey probably wouldn't have even seen it. He put his arm round Adam, still laughing at the absurdity of the situation.

Adam decided he liked Matt. He wasn't how he'd always imagined a TV star would be. 'Never mind.' Adam flicked back his long hair and smiled. 'I'll give her the message anyway.'

Maggy Mann had put on the television while she was changing to go out. She'd intended it as background, since she hated silence at any time, but halfway through she'd abandoned trying to put on yet another layer of make-up and just watched the show. She'd never seen Matt Boyd like this before. Carefree, witty yet with almost an air of danger. And when he'd suddenly launched into the appeal to his daughter she'd wept into her G. and T. Now she was staring at the screen wondering what to do.

When she'd found out that Danny Wilde was negotiating with Century she'd filed it away for later use. Watching Matt's appeal she'd felt an unfamiliar emotion: unselfishness. So unfamiliar was it that it had taken her a while to recognize it. Why *should* Danny Wilde break up Matt's family *and* get his show? The very thought of Danny Wilde made her angry anyway. The rotten sod had dumped her unceremoniously to pursue Ally and now Matt would be out on his ear because of him. Maybe for once she should do the decent thing and tell Ally.

Before she changed her mind she reached for the phone.

Ritchie Page was a happy man. Matt Boyd had resigned without costing him a penny and the next person he'd get out was Belinda Wyeth. He'd never liked her. She'd been as responsible as Matt for humiliating him. How dare she insult his secretary and let Matt get away with that ludicrous broadcast? She should have cut him off. Danny Wilde would be signing in the morning. He could announce it tomorrow when he told the press about Matt's departure.

There had been times when Danny had almost lost his nerve. Page knew that Big City Television had got wind of the negotiations – probably from Danny's own agent; it was always the bloody agents who let it out, playing one TV company against the other to jack up their client's fee – and Big City had tried to bribe Danny to stay. But, sharp lad that he was, he knew where his future lay.

As it happened Ritchie Page was wrong about Danny Wilde. He hadn't yet decided which of the options to go for. In fact, for the last half an hour he'd been lying on his squashy red-lipped sofa trying to make up his mind. Like millions of other people he'd watched Matt Boyd's appeal and come to the conclusion that after tonight Matt would be a very hard act to follow. Plus there was the fact that Big City Television had indeed increased their offer. In fact they had virtually given him *carte blanche* to name his own conditions. And somewhere in his brain, even though he had tried to dismiss it as irrelevant, was the certainty that if he went ahead Ally would think he was a complete shit.

All in all, Danny decided, jumping off the sofa, maybe he'd be better off staying where he was. There was life in Matt Boyd yet.

Striding over to the huge, almost empty fridge, he opened himself a celebratory bottle of Grolsch and drank it down in one. Then he reached for the phone and dialled Ritchie Page's private number.

Feeling wrung out by the events of the day, Matt walked down the steps to the company car park with Adam behind him, completely forgetting his car was still in Notting Hill. Beyond the exit barrier he glimpsed a posse of journalists lying in wait, and cursed. He dodged behind a pillar to think. How the hell was he going to get through that lot?

'Evening, Mr Boyd.'

Matt and Adam looked round to find the young police-man was still there, leaning on his car.

481

Matt was serious for a moment. 'Have you come to arrest me?'

The policeman grinned. 'Not this time, but I could give you a lift.' He jerked his head at the ratpack outside. 'Then you could avoid that lot. If you want to, that is.'

'I want to, all right.' Matt climbed gratefully into the back of the huge white Rover with the red stripe down the side.

'Sorry, Matt,' the policeman said, 'but I'm afraid you'll have to lie on the seat. I'll put a rug over you.'

Adam laughed as he got in next to Matt. 'I always wondered what car rugs were for.'

Turning expertly, the constable drove towards the exit barrier. Jock Wilson pressed the button to raise it. They drove sedately across the pavement and the journalists parted like the Red Sea.

As he lay hidden under the rug Matt smiled, thinking of the shot the photographers were missing. Matt Boyd being driven off in a police car.

'OK, Matt, you can sit up now.'

Matt felt the car rug being lifted off him. He sat up obediently.

'Right then,' said the copper. 'Where is it you want to go to?'

Chapter 34

Ally wandered restlessly about the house, unable to sit still, desperate to know if Janey had seen Matt's appeal.

Jess watched her anxiously. 'You can't just do nothing after that, Mum.' Jess, too, felt the moment called for some kind of action. 'Why don't we try and phone Dad?'

'I don't know where he is.'

Jess shrugged in irritation. Really her mother could be trying at times. 'Try Century. He's probably still there.'

After five minutes of holding on and being transferred, Ally finally got through to *The Matt Boyd Show*'s offices. To her amazement it was Bernie who answered the phone.

'Bernie? Is Matt there?'

'No he isn't, Ally.'

'Does anyone know where he is?' She was damned if she was going to mention Belinda by name.

'Well, I don't want to worry you, but one of the researchers saw him in the underground car park getting into a police car.'

'Oh my God.' Ally turned to Jess, the colour draining from her face. 'They think Matt's been arrested.'

She sat down on the faded tapestry chair that stood by the phone in the hall. Why on earth had Matt gone and confessed to a crime on camera in front of millions of viewers? If the police wanted to prosecute he wouldn't have a chance of being cleared. Then it struck her why he'd done it. He wasn't thinking about the consequences. He'd wanted to explain what his worry about Janey had driven him to. It had been an unselfish act and she couldn't blame him for it.

When the phone rang a few seconds later Ally pounced on it, convinced it would be Matt making the one phone call you were allowed to from a police station.

It took her a few seconds of total confusion to work out that far from being Matt it was, in fact, Maggy Mann.

'Hello, Maggy.' Speaking to her at a time like this seemed almost unreal. 'This is a surprise.'

'Yes.' Maggy's voice was hesitant for once.

'Is it about Matt?'

'No, it isn't.' Maggy sounded surprised. 'Look, you'll probably loathe me for this, but it's about Danny Wilde. We share an agent and it slipped out that he's been negotiating with Ritchie Page to take over from Matt in the autumn.'

'But he can't be.' A wave of horror passed over her. 'He wouldn't do that to Matt.' She didn't add, 'Or me.'

'I'm afraid he is. Ally?'

Ally's mind was racing, unable to take in this new information. 'Yes?'

'He's been negotiating the deal for months now. Ever since Bernie left the show.'

Ally went cold. That meant even before she'd met him. And throughout their whole relationship. For a moment she was tempted to break down. Then she remembered that Matt might be trying to get through. 'Look, Maggy, I've got to go. Thanks for letting me know.'

'Ally, I'm sorry.' And to Ally's amazement she actually sounded it.

'Will this do, Matt?' inquired the young constable as the police car, its siren mercifully silent or every window for miles would be open, drew quietly to a halt outside number thirty-eight Divinity Road. Matt and Adam climbed out. 'By the way, call me Kevin.'

'Thanks a lot, Kevin.' Matt held out a hand.

'Don't mention it. It's been the most exciting day I've had on the force. Tell you what: why don't I hang round for a bit? You never know, you might want a lift home.'

'Won't they miss you at the station?'

Kevin grinned, his freckled features lighting up. 'Nah. I came off duty at six.'

'What about this?' Matt indicated the police car.

'Due in for a service tomorrow. They probably won't have noticed.'

Matt thought about his car parked somewhere, he couldn't remember exactly where, in Powis Gardens he thought. The offer of a lift seemed infinitely preferable to trudging round looking for it. 'OK, then. You're on.'

'Want to try Janey again?' Adam asked Matt. 'See if your impassioned appeal has done the trick? You won't have to break in this time.' He smiled provocatively. 'I've got my key.'

'I thought you didn't have a television,' Matt countered dryly.

'No, well . . . there's one at George's. I'd forgotten.' He put the key in the door, then turned. 'Matt?'

'Yes?' Matt looked at Adam's dark luminous eyes and his pale face and noticed he wasn't cracking jokes any more. He realized how much he'd got to like Adam in their brief acquaintance.

Adam held out his hand unexpectedly. 'Good luck.'

Matt shook it, feeling curiously moved. Then Adam turned back to the door.

Ritchie Page tried to keep calm. He opened his drawer and took out some of the pills he'd been given to control his blood pressure. He couldn't credit it. He couldn't believe that Danny Wilde could have strung him along like that. Now Century would be left without anyone to front their chat-show!

As he poured himself a glass of water to swallow the pills Matt Boyd's face appeared on the TV screen in front of him. He was only on the bloody news! Page zapped the volume up. It was an extract from Matt's appeal. Belinda must have agreed to release it. Why hadn't the cow asked him first? As if he didn't know.

Suddenly the impact of what he'd seen hit him. In losing Matt Boyd they'd kissed goodbye to a fucking hero! Of course there'd be a song and dance about breaking in, but every parent in the country would be rooting for him.

Page became thoughtful for a moment, then he picked up the phone and rang down to the hospitality suite. It sounded like a bloody party there.

'Belinda.' He hoped she had a short memory when it suited her. 'What do you think the chances are of Matt reconsidering?'

'I don't know, Ritchie.' Belinda struggled not to laugh out loud at this turn-around. 'Maybe you'd better ask him. That is,' she added wryly, 'if you can find him. Somebody says he was driven off in a cop car.'

Page closed his eyes. Matt Boyd had only been arrested. It would be everywhere tomorrow.

Belinda put the phone down as the post-show party went on around her. She didn't know whether she believed this stuff about Matt. It sounded highly unlikely, especially as he'd arrived with a tame cop. Knowing Matt, he'd talked his way into a police escort. In fact, though she didn't know for certain, she had a pretty good idea where he'd gone.

Across the other side of the room she caught Bernie's eye and she saw that he understood what she was thinking. That she might have lost Matt.

He came to her side. 'Come on, gel,' he said in the friendliest voice she'd ever heard him use. 'I loved the way you told Page's secretary where to get off. I couldn't have put it better myself. Let me get you a drink.'

Belinda's face chipped gradually into a slow grin.

'All right,' she conceded. 'Provided it's a very large one.'

Adam pushed open the door and walked into the dark hall. Feeling his confidence draining away, Matt stayed on the doorstep tactfully out of sight. Adam stood on the bottom stair and shouted up the stairwell.

Four floors up Matt heard someone running down, then Janey's worried face appeared one flight up, leaning over the banisters.

'Adam, thank God!' Her face cleared and she smiled. 'What on earth were you doing at Century? I've been worried sick about you.'

Matt, hidden by the overhang of the door heard the tenderness and concern in her voice and almost turned around. Maybe he should simply accept that she'd grown out of them and the life they could offer. She was searching for something else here. And perhaps she'd found it.

'Janey, love,' Adam called, 'there's someone to see you.'

Matt stepped out into the hall and looked up.

Without speaking Janey disappeared.

'Don't worry,' Adam said. 'She's probably still upset. Let me talk to her.'

'No. This is ridiculous.' Matt felt dangerously near the edge. 'I'll come back tomorrow and she can talk to me then if she wants to.'

But as he turned away Janey appeared at the bottom of the stairs. She hadn't gone to their bedroom after all. To Adam's surprise she seemed totally unmoved by the sight of her father. Instead she was watching him levelly, almost as though she were weighing up his suitability as a parent. Adam found himself hoping she would be lenient.

'Hello, Dad.' She made no move towards him. 'I saw you asking me to come home on television.' Her tone was neutral, faintly hostile even. 'It was a great performance.'

Matt watched powerlessly. The audience might have been moved, but not his own daughter.

'There's one thing I wanted to know.'

'What's that?'

'Did it do the trick? Will it get you back to the top of the ratings?'

Without answering, Matt walked out of the door and down the street, ignoring Kevin waiting there. Janey had cut him to the quick. If she distrusted him that much then all this was a pathetic charade.

He'd walked halfway down the street before he heard the footsteps clattering behind him. He didn't dare look round.

'Dad, Dad!' He felt Janey's hand clutching his sleeve, stopping him. 'It's just that it's so unlike you to do anything like that.'

'Maybe that was the point, Janey.' He looked at her, still unsure of her reaction. 'Maybe it took losing you to make me realize how stupid I'd been.' He turned away. 'You don't have to believe me.'

Suddenly Janey flopped down on the steps they were passing, put her head in her hands and began to cry. Every sob sounded as though it were being wrenched out of her.

'Don't, Janey.' Matt couldn't bear it. He kneeled next to her, oblivious of the fascinated stares of the passers-by. 'I only want you to be happy. Stay with Adam if you want.'

'Dad?' Janey looked up at him, her face tear-stained. 'If I come home, will you?'

Matt laughed in spite of himself. 'I don't know, darling. It isn't really up to me.'

Janey smiled, lighting up her face under the tramlines of black eyeliner that had run, witchlike, down her face. 'Maybe I'll make it a condition.'

'God almighty.' Matt ruffled her hair, his face filled with love. 'You sound like Ritchie Page.'

Behind them the gentle honk of a horn reminded Matt that their police escort had arrived.

'But I've already told you, Mrs Boyd, no arrest was made on your husband this evening.' The busy desk sergeant spoke down the phone very slowly and patiently. 'I've checked with all the authorities. It just didn't happen.'

Ally sat on the bottom stair in the hall next to the huge vase of lilies with Sox at her feet and listened in disbelief. She felt as though she'd wandered into a Kafka novel. How could Matt have been taken off in a police car and no one know about it? He had one of the most famous faces in Britain.

'Then why was he taken away by a uniformed officer?'

'I think that's highly unlikely.'

'But he was seen by one of the people working on the programme. A journalist.'

'That probably explains it. They always get their facts wrong. Perhaps it was some kind of stunt.'

Janey curled up on the surprisingly comfortable upholstery in the back of the police car and thought about all the suspects who must have sat here sweating. Thank God she wasn't on her way to some horrible police cell, but to her own home. Next to her Adam had dozed off, his long hair curtained across his face and his legs up on the seat. She glanced at her father sitting in the passenger seat. The occasional person in another car looked at him, looked again and gaped.

Janey closed her eyes, and started to fantasize about

the welcome waiting for them at Fairlawns, the front door open, Sox running out and almost knocking her down in doggy ecstasy. Maybe her mother standing on the steps waiting for them. Jess lost in admiration that Janey had been the one to effect her parents' reconciliation. Happy ever after. Or maybe happyish ever afterish.

As they drove south out of London through the leafy suburbs Matt gazed out of the window. It was a beautiful night and everywhere teemed with outdoor life, as though in such perfect weather staying inside would be a sacrilege. Pubs overflowed on to the pavements where young people sprawled, their glasses at their feet, sitting half in the road and ignoring the filthy concrete. In their small front gardens old couples pottered, mowing lawns and trimming edges. Suddenly this glimpse of ordinary life haunted Matt with a sense of something missed, something unknown and quite alien to him, and yet irresistibly wonderful. And he realized that these everyday pleasures, this ordinariness, were things he had always been too driven, too busy to appreciate. And he told himself that if Ally would take him back he would bring these to her, like a gift, and they would share them together.

But would she want him? He'd failed her in so many ways. Grudging her success, hurting and humiliating her by his affair with Belinda. He remembered Jess calling him a selfish shit. Was that ingrained? Being a man might mean you had a certain set of attitudes, but being a husband – surely that was different? There were good husbands and bad husbands. Was he capable of being a better one? He smiled, imagining Jess telling him there was plenty of scope.

Kevin slowed down to let a young woman cross the road. Matt saw why. She was tall and dark and sinuous. She smiled at the policeman lazily, not noticing who was sitting next to him. She reminded Matt faintly of Belinda.

Belinda! What on earth was he going to do about his relationship with her? And he knew that even if Ally didn't want him back it was time they parted. She was young and talented and she had her whole life before her. He admired her energy and her strength but he knew they wouldn't make each other happy. As soon as he could he would have to try and explain.

As they turned down off the main road a couple of miles from Fairlawns, Matt felt as nervous as he had outside Janey's door. What if, like Janey, she wouldn't let him in? She had a perfect right to turn him away.

In the back Janey stirred with a catlike sense that home was near, stretched and sat up. Matt wound down his window. It was so familiar, yet different, new. The scent of cut grass and nightscented stock from their neighbours' gardens, the birds striking up their evening chorus, the faint smell of a barbecue.

And then there it was, the entrance to their drive. Matt realized he was holding his breath. As they turned in he had a sudden nightmare image of Fairlawns, as dark and closed as Manderley, empty of Ally, stonily unforgiving. But there it was, the front door propped open as usual by an antique wooden horse, three-legged because Matt had never mended its fourth, achingly familiar.

In the kitchen it was Jess, attuned to any news of her father, who heard the car first. Without a word she got up and dashed through the hall, Sox at her heels, both of them skidding on the polished wood of the hall.

'Dad!' she screeched and threw herself into his arms almost before he'd got out of the car while Sox jumped up at Janey in a delirium of excitement.

'Janey, thank God!' Ally, following behind, shooed Sox out of the way and stood for a moment, overwhelmed by emotion yet unsure of how Janey would react. Last time she'd seen her there had been so much hate in her. Then she held out her arms and Janey ran into them. For a moment everything faded as she held her beloved daughter and knew from the strength of her embrace that she was forgiven. 'Thank God you're back.'

'Oh, Mum, I'm sorry. I do love you, you know.'

Over Janey's head she caught Matt's gaze on her, alight with a tenderness she hadn't seen for months, and then she took in the significance of the police car.

'Matt! Oh, my God! It was true! You have been arrested.'

Matt exchanged glances with Kevin, then smiled. 'It's a long story.'

Kevin, deciding it was time to effect a discreet departure, got into his car and waved goodbye. Seeing Ally's worried face Matt stepped forward. Ally let go of Janey and Matt put his arm round his wife, leading her into the house. 'I think we'd better talk about this.' He closed the door firmly in the face of an indignant Janey and Jess.

Once inside the house Matt lost his nerve momentarily. He felt almost like a guest. Instead of taking her into the kitchen or sitting room as he'd intended, he sat her down on the stairs and perched next to her, searching for words.

But before he could speak Ally jumped in first. 'Thank God you brought Janey home.' She paused, gazing at the floor. 'I know the risk you took.'

Any thoughts of a carefully prepared speech disintegrated at the gratitude in her voice, which he knew instantly he didn't deserve.

'Ally, my God, I'm the one who should be sorry. It was probably my fault she went. I've let you all down, running off to Belinda. God knows what I was thinking of, hurting you all like that. I suppose in my pathetic male way I was flattered that she wanted me. I was so jealous of your success. It undermined me. Yet I knew I ought to be bigger than that. And then you got involved with Danny and I couldn't bear it . . . yet the way I was behaving I almost pushed you into his arms.'

Ally studied her hands, consumed by guilt and humiliation at the mention of Danny. 'We both made mistakes. Danny wasn't really concerned with me. You were right, Matt. He wanted me because I was your wife. Like he wanted your show.'

Matt heard the pain in her voice and part of him wanted her to believe this about Danny because it strengthened his own case. But he couldn't bear the hurt in her eyes. She obviously thought she'd been made a fool of.

'No. I don't believe that. He wasn't pretending. I saw the way he looked at you. He was in love with you.' For a moment Matt wondered whether he was mad, pleading Danny Wilde's case.

Ally turned to him and he saw that she'd been crying. 'Maggy Mann rang to say he's been negotiating with Ritchie Page to take over your show for months.'

Matt didn't seem surprised. 'That would make sense. But I still think he loved you. Maybe it was too much for him. I don't think he's used to thinking about anyone else.'

Ally held his eyes with hers for a second. 'I'm sorry, Matt. I got so caught up in my success. It was all so new, so exciting. I forgot about what it must be like for you.'

'But why shouldn't you enjoy it? You deserved it. Ally, can you forgive me? Can we try again?'

Ally looked away. Part of her wanted to shout with joy, but she also had a strong streak of realism. She'd been through so much. Fought so hard for her confidence and for her freedom. She wasn't going to throw it away.

'I've changed, Matt. I couldn't go back to standing in your shadow. I need my own life.'

'I know. I wouldn't want you to give up.' She could tell from the certainty in his voice that he'd been thinking about it. 'You're far too talented. You taught me to take risks. I only dared to do what I did tonight because of you.'

Ally turned her face away to hide how moved she felt. There was no doubting the genuineness of his admiration and respect. And she had to admit she'd done some stupid things. She'd gone from doormat to driven career woman in a matter of months. And then there'd been Danny . . .

'Ally' – Matt took her hand, his tone serious – 'whether you want me back or not, I want to say something. You were right to break out. I did take you for granted.' He smiled his familiar crinkly smile. 'But I wouldn't make the same mistake twice.'

Ally smiled back for the first time. 'You wouldn't get the chance.'

Matt looked at her, still uncertain of what she was thinking. Then very slowly he leaned forward until she caught the familiar spicy notes of his cologne and breathed it in. It was so distinctively Matt. Even when he'd gone she'd been able to picture him standing there just by spraying it on her wrist. She smiled again. 'You never did know how much to put on.' And then his lips were on hers, cutting off all further protest.

The phone on the hall table began to ring and Matt looked hopefully round for Janey or Jess but neither of them materialized.

'Yes?' he barked discouragingly into the receiver.

'Hello, Matt, Ritchie Page here.'

'Hello Page,' Matt made a face for Ally's benefit. 'I didn't expect to be hearing from you.'

'No, well . . . Bernie Long thought I might find you at home.' Ally and Matt exchanged glances. Typical of

Bernie to have got there before they did. To Matt's surprise Page sounded faintly embarrassed. 'Look, Matt, I'm calling to ask you to reconsider your resignation. You finally cracked it tonight, Matt. The format we've all been looking for.'

'Thanks.' Matt grinned, thoroughly enjoying Page's unease. 'But I don't want to make any decisions now. Except one. But whatever I decide I'm planning to take a little time off. Discover the ordinary things in life.'

Ally was startled. Matt never took time off.

'Spend more time with your family, Matt?' Page's tone was sarcastic. 'People will say you've been fired.'

'I don't give a stuff what people say.'

Ally signalled to Matt that she wanted to talk to Page before he went. He handed her the phone.

'Hello, Ritchie, I don't want to spoil your day . . .'

'Feel free,' Page muttered gloomily. 'It couldn't get any worse.'

But he was wrong.

'I thought I'd better tell you that I'd like to think about things for a while after my contract's up.'

'Oh, great. Just when you'll be really big. Tell you what, don't be hasty. Take the weekend to make up your mind.'

'I've already thought about it, Ritchie. I've been meaning to tell you for days.'

'Hang on, Ally, why don't you pop in and discuss –' But Ally had put the phone down. 'I see,' muttered Page into the dead phone, 'and we don't need to ask if the happy couple are back together.' He slammed the phone back into its cradle and reached for the single malt. He was going to need the whole bloody bottle.

'Ally, you didn't mean that, did you?' Matt took her hand again. 'You're not really going to give up?'

Ally looked at him levelly. 'I don't want the same thing happening when Jess has her exams.'

'Ally' – Matt's voice was urgent – 'Ally, listen, I've been thinking about going independent. I didn't want to say so to Page until I'd discussed it with you.' Ally was taken aback. He didn't usually talk things like that through with her, more gave her a *fait accompli*. 'If I did I'd be running my own company. Maybe even from home at first. I might earn less but I could make a point of being around more for Janey and Jess.' She looked into his eyes and saw only concern for her. 'Don't give up. You're too talented. Between us we'll manage.'

Slowly she smiled. 'Actually' – to Matt's surprise her voice was low and teasing – 'I'm not thinking of giving up altogether. Just getting away from Ritchie Page.'

'Great!' Matt congratulated her. 'You could come and work with me.'

'Could I now?' Ally's smile widened. 'As a matter of fact, Bernie and I are thinking of setting up together, so you could come and work with *us*.'

'Ouch.' Matt realized how tactless he'd been. He had a lot to learn about the new Ally. 'I suppose I deserved that.' The famous grin surfaced again. 'But then, why not? I like working for a woman.'

Ally pretended to hit him and he caught her wrist, serious for a moment.

'It'll never happen again, you know.'

'I should bloody well hope not.' Ally's tone was astringent.

Slowly Matt bent his head and kissed her again.

Neither of them noticed when Jess opened the front door and closed it again discreetly. 'Keep out of sight,' she hissed. 'The wrinklies are getting it together on the stairs.'

'You've given Page his answer.' Matt held Ally's face

496

in his hands and gazed into the greeny-blue depths of her eyes. She saw that he wasn't entirely confident of himself and was glad. 'But you haven't given me mine.'

'You haven't told me the proposition.'

With great difficulty, since they were still on the stairs, Matt got down on one knee. 'Wilt thou, Allegra, take me, Matthew, to have and to hold, to make tea on alternate weekdays; to clean out the toilet each month with an R in it, to celebrate your success instead of grudging it, and not to blame you for things that are actually my fault.' He took her hand and held it to his cheek. 'Then according to God's holy ordinance I plight thee my troth.'

'I will,' said Ally, ignoring the now audible giggling from outside the front door. There was only one way of knowing if this was a terrible mistake or not.

'I think,' Matt said, sitting beside her once more, 'we should have a second honeymoon where no one under twenty-one is allowed.'

'Good idea,' seconded Ally lifting her lips to his.

'Congratulations!' The door burst open and Janey and Jess appeared with Adam standing a few paces behind. 'Seeing as we're not allowed on the honeymoon,' Janey insisted, grinning from ear to ear, 'can't we go out and celebrate?'

Matt stood up and reached a hand down to Ally. 'I don't see why not.'

'Oh, my God!' Halfway across the hall, Jess clapped her hand across her mouth. 'We can't go out!'

'Why ever not?' Ally asked in alarm.

Jess held open the door of the kitchen. 'Because Dad' – she stood back to reveal the incriminating evidence – 'hasn't remembered to load up the dishwasher!'

BASIC INSTINCT

Richard Osborne

A brutal murder.

A brilliant killer.

A cop who can't resist the danger.

When San Francisco detective Nick Curran begins investigating the mysterious and vicious murder of a rock star, he finds himself in a shadowy world where deceit and seduction often go hand in hand. Nick can't stay away from his number one suspect – stunning and uninhibited Catherine Tramell – a novelist whose shocking fiction mirrors the murder down to the smallest, bloodiest detail.

Entangled in love and murder, Nick is headed for trouble, with only his basic instinct for survival to keep him from making a fatal mistake . . .

⦰ SIGNET

Published or forthcoming

INDECENT PROPOSAL

Jack Engelhard

After too many years looking for answers a man marries the most beautiful woman in the world. With her, he's got most of the things he's ever wanted in life. Except money...

Yet everything changes the night when they meet a handsome – and very rich – stranger. Almost immediately he makes a startling offer: one night alone with the beautiful wife. *In exchange for one million dollars in cash.*

It's an indecent proposal. A pact with the devil. And a test for their love...

What will they do about it? What would *you* do?

SIGNET

Published or forthcoming

SUCH DEVOTED SISTERS

Eileen Goudge

Eve and Dolly are aspiring Hollywood starlets, hungry for fame and success. When one of them betrays the other a tragic chain of events is set in motion that irrevocably changes their lives and the futures of Eve's children, Annie and Laurel.

Forced to leave their home, Annie and her sister run away to New York. There Annie, drawn into the delicious, fragrant world of the chocolate business, determines to become a top chocolatier, while Laurel becomes an artist. Full of unspoken secrets they live for each other – until they fall in love with the same man and the past returns to haunt the future . . .

A MATTER OF FAT

Sherry Ashworth

Eating is sexy, sensual, wonderful, indulgent – how could they resist temptation . . .

At the Heyside branch of Slim-Plicity the women are valiantly struggling with their waistbands while waiting for the spare flesh to melt away. Stella, their mentor, is so proud of them – they are going to be the slimmest group in the north-west, and qualify for the celebration buffet. Meanwhile, in a nearby meeting room, the unabashed members of the Fat Women's Support Group virtuously agree that dieting is a tool of women's oppression used by men and the media to torment the overweight . . .

'In *A Matter of Fat*, Ashworth has retained a wicked sense of humour, while raising some very important questions. Does she have the answers, though? You'll have to read the book if you want to find out!' – *New Woman*

Published or forthcoming

Sherry Ashworth

While her husband Richard is away, Stella embarks on a dazzling new career...

Having ostensibly conquered her own personal problems, Stella Martin – once the high priestess of Slim-Plicity – is now preparing to liberate other people from theirs.

Undergoing therapy with the slip-hipped Roland Temple after the departure of her previous therapist Gill, Stella decides that an absentee husband is no bad thing, and in a positive frame of mind she starts up her own therapy group.

Stella visualized the group; now it has formed with the terminally indecisive Sandra and her 'victim' friend Zoë, with Carol the professional patient and Jim the compulsive liar. Stella is their guru. But who, if not common-sense Sandra, will guide Stella through the storm when she finds out the bitter truth about the people she trusts most in the world: Richard and the delicately vulnerable Roland?

SIGNET

Published or forthcoming

DEFINITIVE I.Q. TEST FOR CATS
and
I.Q. TEST FOR CAT OWNERS

Melissa Miller

A brand new edition of the accurate, entertaining assessment of your cat's brainpower.

When your cat is wearing an expression of mystic beauty, is it contemplating the meaning of life, or just wondering what's for dinner? When it winds itself round your legs does it simply want another saucer of milk? And how suitable an owner are you? Do you toss and turn, disturbing puss's valuable beauty sleep? Are you suitably grateful when your cat drops small, dead rodents at your feet? Is your cat an Einstein of the feline world?

FIND OUT IN THIS IRRESISTIBLE, ORIGINAL CAT I.Q. TEST

Four tests for your cat and four for you so that you can check your mutual compatibility or choose a suitable breed of cat for your way of life. Packed with historical and mythological references, literary quotations and a whole new section of reader's humorous anecdotes, this book is a must for all cat owners, potential cat owners and felines everywhere.

SIGNET

Published or forthcoming

The Stars Burn On

Denise Robertson

On New Year's Day 1980, Jenny and seven friends watch the dawn from a northern hill. On the brink of adulthood, confident of their futures, they vow to meet there again at the end of the decade. Just two weeks later, one of the group is dead. The others, irrevocably affected, go on to pursue careers in the law or media, and make new lives for themselves as husbands, wives and parents. Jenny, who establishes herself as a successful journalist in London, remains their linchpin – and only Jenny knows that the secret that binds them is a lie.

'A saga that'll keep you turning the pages . . . told with perception and humour' – *Prima*

'Her prose has a fine flow, her knowledge of the region is deep and instinctive. Above all, her compassion and great understanding of life show in all she writes' – *Evening Chronicle*, Newcastle upon Tyne

SIGNET

Published or forthcoming

THE BELOVED PEOPLE

Denise Robertson

In the Durham mining village of Belgate, the legacy of World War I has far-reaching consequences for rich and poor, socialist and aristocrat, Jew and gentile alike.

Howard Brenton, heir to the colliery, back from the trenches with a social conscience, but robbed of the confidence to implement it...

Diana, his beautiful, aristocratic wife, afraid of her dour new world and fatally drawn to the jazzy gaiety of twenties London...

Miner **Frank Maguire**, and his bitter wife **Anne**, fired by union fervour as they struggle to survive the slump...

Esther Gulliver, to whom kindly Emmanuel Lansky shows new roads to prosperity beyond the pit...

Linked by place, chance and time, the people of Belgate grapple with the personal and general costs of war, of coal, of childbirth. And in the mid-1930s, face together a new and terrifying crisis in Europe...

'Humour and warmth keep you turning the pages' – *Annabel*